The
Destructionists

Also by Dana Milbank

Homo Politicus
Tears of a Clown
O Is for Obama
Smashmouth

THE DESTRUCTIONISTS

The Twenty-Five-Year Crack-Up
of the Republican Party

Dana Milbank

DOUBLEDAY
New York

All rights reserved. Published in the United States by Doubleday,
a division of Penguin Random House LLC, New York, and distributed in Canada
by Penguin Random House Canada Limited, Toronto.

www.doubleday.com

DOUBLEDAY and the portrayal of an anchor with a dolphin
are registered trademarks of Penguin Random House LLC.

Jacket photographs: (clockwise from upper left)
Ron Adar / Shutterstock; Saul Loeb / AFP; Jeff Siner /
The Charlotte Observer; Nicholas Kamm / AFP; Dave Einsel; Ramin Talaie /
Corbis; all Getty Images
Jacket design by John Fontana

Library of Congress Cataloging-in-Publication Data
Names: Milbank, Dana, author.
Title: The destructionists : the twenty-five-year crack-up of the Republican Party /
by Dana Milbank.
Description: First Edition. | New York : Doubleday, 2022. | Includes index.
Identifiers: LCCN 2022005056 (print) | LCCN 2022005057 (ebook) |
ISBN 9780385548137 (hardcover) | ISBN 9780385548144 (ebook)
Subjects: LCSH: Republican Party (U.S. : 1854–)—History—20th century. |
Republican Party (U.S. : 1854–)—History—21st century. | Political corruption—
United States—History—20th century. | Political corruption—United States—
History—21st century.
Classification: LCC JK2356 .M55 2022 (print) | LCC JK2356 (ebook) |
DDC 324.273409—dc23/eng/20220225
LC record available at https://lccn.loc.gov/2022005056
LC ebook record available at https://lccn.loc.gov/2022005057

MANUFACTURED IN THE UNITED STATES OF AMERICA

3 5 7 9 10 8 6 4 2

First Edition

For my daughter, Paola,
And my stepchildren,
Sadie and Jasper

And they shall rebuild the old ruins.

—ISAIAH 61:4

I wish we had been able to obstruct more.

—MITCH McCONNELL

Contents

The
Destructionists

Introduction

It began where it ended, on the West Front of the United States Capitol.

On January 6, 2021, a mob incited by President Donald Trump smashed barriers, overpowered police, and stormed the steps of the Capitol on the side of the Rotunda facing the Washington Monument across the Mall. The insurrectionists scaled the scaffolding that had been erected on the West Front for President-elect Joe Biden's inauguration en route to sacking the U.S. seat of government for the first time since the War of 1812.

Sent with instructions from Trump to "fight like hell" and a call from Trump lawyer Rudy Giuliani for "trial by combat," the mob halted Congress's certification of Biden's victory, sending lawmakers fleeing for their lives and hiding under desks. At least seven people died in the riot and its aftermath, and more than 140 police were hurt. Some 800 insurrectionists, many with ties to white supremacist or violent extremist groups, faced charges.

The bloody coup attempt shocked the nation. But a sober view of history might have lessened the shock. For the seeds of sedition had been planted earlier—twenty-six years earlier—in that same spot on the West Front of the Capitol.

On September 27, 1994, more than three hundred Republican members of Congress and congressional candidates gathered where the insurrectionists would one day scale the scaffolding. But on this sunny morning, they assembled for a nonviolent transfer of power.

Bob Michel, the unfailingly genial leader of the House Republican minority for the previous fourteen years, had successfully ushered Ronald Reagan's agenda through the House. But he had now been forced into retirement by a rising bomb thrower who threatened to oust Michel as GOP leader if he didn't quit.

Newt Gingrich had almost nothing in common with the man he pushed out. Michel was a portrait of civility and decency, a World War II combat veteran who knew that his political opponents were not his enemies and that politics was the art of compromise. Gingrich, by contrast, rose to prominence by forcing the resignation of a Democratic speaker of the House on what began as mostly false allegations, by smearing another Democratic speaker with personal innuendo, and by routinely thwarting Michel's attempts to negotiate with Democrats. He had avoided service in Vietnam and regarded Democrats as the enemy, impugning their patriotism and otherwise savaging them nightly on the House floor for the benefit of C-SPAN viewers.

"My friends, I'll not be able to be with you when you enter that promised land of having that long-sought-after majority control of the House of Representatives," Michel said that morning to the gathered Republicans, who were within striking distance of a majority for the first time in forty years. "I can only stand with you today and see that vision from afar."

Minutes later, that vision took on a distinctly dystopian hue.

"Newt! Newt! Newt! Newt!" the candidates and lawmakers chanted. They waved miniature American flags. A pudgy fifty-one-year-old with a helmet of gray hair approached the lectern.

"The fact is that America is in trouble," Gingrich declared. "It is impossible to maintain American civilization with 12-year-olds having babies, 15-year-olds killing each other, 17-year-olds dying of AIDS and 18-year-olds getting diplomas they can't even read. This is a crisis of our entire civilization, and within a half mile of this building these conditions happen in our nation's capital, and they happen in every major city, and they happen in West Virginia and they happen in most Indian reservations and across this country." (The areas mentioned were all Democratic strongholds.)

The pejoratives piled up in Gingrich's shouted, finger-wagging harangue: "Collapsing . . . Failed so totally . . . Worried about their jobs . . . Worried about their safety . . . Trust broke down . . . Out of touch . . . Wasteful . . . Dumb . . . Ineffective . . . Out of balance . . . Malaise . . . Drug dealers . . . Pimps . . . Prostitution . . . Crime . . . Barbarism . . . Devastation . . . Human tragedy . . . Chaos and poverty."

"Recognize that if America fails our children will live on a dark and bloody planet," Gingrich told them.

Somewhere in this catalogue of catastrophe, Gingrich signed the "Contract with America," a ten-point legislative agenda proposing a balanced budget amendment, congressional term limits, and other reforms. "We have become in danger of losing our own civilization," Gingrich warned. "Today, on these steps, we offer this contract as a first step towards renewing American civilization."

Americans had seldom heard a politician talk this way, and certainly not a speaker of the House. But that's what Gingrich became after the GOP's landslide victory in the "Republican Revolution" of 1994. The "Contract with America" made little headway—only three relatively minor provisions (paperwork reduction!) became law—but the rise of Gingrich and his shock troops fundamentally altered American government for a generation and counting, and set the United States on a course toward the ruinous politics of today.

The epic government failures of the last quarter century can all be traced back to Gingrich and the savage politics he pioneered: three impeachments; two botched wars and a botched pandemic response; several government shutdowns; a sevenfold increase in the federal debt; a market collapse and the Great Recession; and failure to address crucial matters such as climate change, inequality, and immigration. It's no wonder that there has been a wholesale loss of faith in American democracy.

Today, Americans' confidence in virtually all the pillars of a free society—Congress, the presidency, the Supreme Court, public schools, the media—has declined from where it was in 1994. One of America's two major political parties has embraced the "Big Lie" that the 2020 presidential election was stolen from Trump, and they have convinced two thirds of Republican voters—tens of millions of people—to accept this democracy-killing fiction.

A ferocious, racialized, and sometimes violent partisanship has consumed us. White nationalist and antigovernment violence is spreading, and a significant chunk of the country is living in a parallel universe of "alternative facts" and conspiracy theories.

The CIA's Political Instability Task Force ranks countries from the most autocratic (–10) to the most democratic (+10) to predict the likelihood of civil war. Using the same data series, political scientist Barbara Walter, who served on the CIA task force during the Trump years, calculated that the United States had dropped from +10 before Trump's rise to +5, its lowest since 1801. The United States is now technically an "anocracy"—somewhere between a democracy and an autocracy—after a precipitous decline that puts us at greatly increased risk of civil war. "We are closer to civil war than any of us would like to believe," Walter writes in her 2022 book, *How Civil Wars Start*.

Or maybe the war has already begun. To use one measure, in October 2020, the Department of Homeland Security—*Trump's* Department of Homeland Security—concluded that white supremacist violence was the "most persistent and lethal threat in the homeland." A study by the nonpartisan Center for Strategic and International Studies found that white supremacists and like-minded extremists conducted 67 percent of terrorist plots and attacks in the United States in 2020, compared to 20 percent by anarchist, antifascist, and like-minded extremists. In one such case, members of an antigovernment paramilitary group allegedly plotted to kidnap the Democratic governor of Michigan.

How did we get into this mess? What led us from the moment when Republicans waved miniature flags with Bob Michel on the Capitol steps to the moment, a quarter century later, when Republicans in that same place used flagpoles bearing the American flag to beat police officers and smash windows? This book answers these questions—and in so doing, I hope, provides clues that can eventually help rebuild what we've lost. As I write this, in early 2022, six in ten Republicans say the 2020 election was fraudulent, and 40 percent think political violence can be acceptable, a *Washington Post*–University of Maryland poll just found. A *Post* tally found that at least 163 Republicans who have embraced Trump's election lies are running in 2022 to become senators, governors, or other statewide officials who would have sway over the administration of elections. At least five candidates for the House were at the Capitol during the January 6 insurrection and at least twelve of the top Republican House prospects have accepted the Big Lie. Embrace of Trump's lie has become the primary prerequisite for winning Republican primaries.

Congressional Republican leaders have abandoned any attempt to punish, or even contradict, rank-and-file lawmakers who fantasize publicly about killing elected Democratic officials. Virtually the entire GOP boycotted events commemorating the first anniversary of the January 6 attack on the Capitol, and some elected Republicans have joined the likes of Fox News's Tucker Carlson in suggesting that the insurrection was a false flag operation perpetrated by the FBI.

Republican lawmakers and opinion leaders, amplified by Fox News, have overwhelmingly succeeded in deterring their followers from getting the Covid-19 vaccine by promoting disinformation about imagined dangers of the inoculations. As a result, the Covid death rate in the most pro-Trump decile of America (as measured by counties' vote share for Trump in 2020) is now nearly *six times* the death rate in the most anti-Trump decile. The GOP has become a death cult.

While Republican lawmakers have refused to censure the violent or anti-Semitic words of their peers, those Republicans who dared to vote for a bipartisan infrastructure bill have been branded "traitors." Republican officials have made a pariah of Representative Liz Cheney, a Wyoming Republican and daughter of the former vice president, as punishment for Cheney's rejection of Trump's election lie. Since Trump departed office, Republicans in Congress have been fighting to rewrite the history of the January 6 insurrection as a "normal tourist visit" in which the insurrectionists were the victims and the police were the villains. Republicans killed a bipartisan commission to examine the attack and boycotted a House committee assigned the same task. The Republican National Committee approved a resolution that referred to the insurrection as "legitimate political discourse."

States under Republican control have undertaken dramatic efforts to impose new voting restrictions in ways that disproportionately disenfranchise voters of color. A dozen GOP-controlled states have enacted legislation giving partisan figures more control over the counting and reporting of votes.

Some Republican lawmakers proposed an "America First Caucus" to protect "Anglo-Saxon political traditions" against immigrants who are putting the "unique identity" of the United States at risk. Republican members of Congress have been refusing security sweeps and mask requirements, brandishing guns on Capitol Hill, and adding warnings of "bloodshed" to their continued false claims of election fraud. Two House Republican lawmakers in February participated in a conference tied to white supremacists.

This has real-world impact. After a 73 percent rise in hate crimes against Asian Americans in 2020 (when Trump spoke of the "Kung Flu" and the "China virus"), violence continued with a massacre of mostly Asian Americans at Atlanta-area massage parlors. Ferocious anti-mask activists have become antivaccine activists, leading to threats and actual violence against health care workers, flight attendants, and others. Republicans' focus on the phantom menace of "critical race theory" has provoked threats and violence at school boards across the country, leading the National School Boards Association to plead for help from the FBI. Ten Black people in Buffalo, New York, were killed by a gunman motivated by the racist "Great Replacement" conspiracy theory—a theory promoted by, among others, third-ranking House Republican leader Elise Stefanik, Fox News's Carlson, and Gingrich.

Much has been made of the "polarization" in American politics, and it's true that moderates are a vanishing breed. But the problem isn't polarization. The problem is that one of our two major political parties has ceased good-faith participation in the democratic process. Of course there are instances of violence, disinformation, racism, and corruption among Democrats and the political left, but the scale isn't at all comparable. Only one party fomented a bloody insurrection in the Capitol and even after that voted in large numbers (139 House Republicans, a two-thirds majority) to overturn the will of the voters in the 2020 election. Only one party is embracing violence. Only one party has been promulgating a web of conspiracy theories in place of facts. Only one party is trying to restrict voting and discredit elections. Only one party is stoking animosity toward minorities and immigrants. Only one party is sabotaging the norms and institutions of American government.

Admittedly, I'm partisan—not for Democrats but for democrats. At the moment, they are one and the same. Republicans have become an authoritarian faction fighting democracy. There's a perfectly logical, if deeply cynical, reason for this. Democracy is working against Republicans. In the eight presidential contests since 1988, the GOP candidate has won the popular vote only once, in 2004.

As the United States approaches majority-minority status (the white population, 76 percent of the country in 1990, is now 58 percent and will drop below 50 percent around 2045) Republicans have chosen to become the voice of white people, particularly those without college degrees, who fear the loss of their way of life in a multicultural America. White grievance and white fear drive Republican identity more than any other factor—and drive the tribalism and dysfunction in the U.S. political system.

There are many other contributing factors to the crack-up of the party. Concurrent with the rise of Newt Gingrich was the rise of Rush Limbaugh and conservative talk radio, followed by the rise of Fox News, followed by the advent of social media. Combined, they created a media environment that allows Republican politicians and their voters to seal themselves in an echo chamber of "alternative facts." Globally, south-to-north migration has ignited nationalist movements around the world and given rise to a new era of autocrats. The disappearance of the Greatest Generation, tempered by war, gave rise to a new generation of cultural warriors who came of age during Vietnam; by the end of Biden's current term, the country will have been led by baby boomers for thirty-two years.

But the biggest cause by far is race. The parties re-sorted themselves after the epochal changes of the 1960s, which expanded civil rights, voting rights, and immigration, and the Republican Party made the fateful decision to pursue Richard Nixon's "Southern Strategy" of appealing to white voters alienated by racial progress. In the years that followed, a new generation of Republicans took the politics of racial resentment to a new level and fused it with a new style of partisan warfare and dishonesty. This book describes how a few of these unprincipled leaders—Gingrich, Lee Atwater, Tom DeLay, Karl Rove, Mitch McConnell, Sarah Palin, Rudy Giuliani, and others—repeatedly put short-term self-interest ahead of the national interest. These are the people who broke American democracy.

This book will show that Donald Trump didn't create this noxious environment. He isn't some hideous orange Venus emerging from the shell. Rather, he is a monster the Republicans created over a quarter century. He is a symptom of their illness, not the cause. Whatever else he is, Trump is a brilliant opportunist; he saw the direction the Republican Party was heading in, and the former pro-choice advocate of universal health care reinvented himself to give Republicans what they wanted. Sadly, because Trump is merely a reflection of the sickness in the GOP, the problem won't go away when—if?—he does.

Before the Big Lie about the 2020 election, Republicans fabricated libels about Obamacare "death panels," the false accusation that Saddam Hussein perpetrated 9/11, and an endless stream of conspiracy theories holding that Bill and Hillary Clinton were nothing short of serial killers.

Before the insurrection at the Capitol on January 6, 2021, there was the "Brooks Brothers Riot" at the Miami-Dade elections board in November 2000, and a siege of the Capitol to intimidate lawmakers in March 2010.

A quarter century before Trump Republicans spread rampant disinformation about Covid-19, Newt Gingrich began the crusade against science by abolishing Congress's Office of Technology Assessment.

Before Trump rose to power on a tide of vulgar insults, future Supreme Court justice Brett Kavanaugh penned an obscene, sexually explicit line of questioning for Bill Clinton.

Before the antigovernment MAGA (Make America Great Again) rallies, there were the rage-filled Tea Party town halls of 2010 and the Republican Revolutionaries of 1994, advised by Gingrich to call Democrats "traitors," "sick," and "corrupt."

Before Trump and his aides contorted the Electoral College to justify an attempted coup, Republican lawmakers contorted their constitutional authority to justify impeaching a president for lying about oral sex.

Before the shutdowns of 2018 and 2019 were the Republican-engineered shutdowns of 2013, 1996, and 1995.

Before the sedition of 2021 was the unpatriotic smearing of Senator Max Cleland, who lost three limbs fighting for his country, as an abettor of Osama bin Laden.

Before Republicans endorsed Russian propaganda about Ukraine during Trump's impeachment trial, there was Darrell Issa's false claim that Hillary Clinton ordered the military not to help besieged Americans in Benghazi, Helen Chenoweth's paranoia about the government's black helicopters, and Dan Burton shooting a melon to prove a Clinton aide was murdered.

Before Trump Republicans made common cause with QAnon and the Proud Boys, earlier Republicans cozied up to the antigovernment militia movements of the mid-1990s and 2010s and stood with rancher Cliven Bundy in his armed standoff with the U.S. government.

Before Trump spoke of immigrants as rapists and murderers and told Democratic congresswomen of color to "go back" to other countries, Republicans joined the effort to portray President Barack Obama as an African-born Muslim and embraced the racist pronouncements of Limbaugh, Pat Buchanan, and Steve King.

I aim to show how extensively Republicans and their allied donors, media outlets, and interest groups have been pulling at the threads of democracy and of civil society for the last quarter century—making the current unraveling inevitable.

The Trump phenomenon cannot be understood without its many antecedents explored in these pages: the Vince Foster "murder," Ken Starr's smut, the violence of the militia movement, the lies that started the Iraq War, the use of the "War on Terror" to impugn Democrats' patriotism, the racism of the "Birther" movement, the antigovernment rage of the Tea Party, the lies about the Affordable Care Act, the politicization of the Supreme Court from *Bush v. Gore* to *Citizens United*—and much more. This is a story I have been telling, in one form or other, since I came to Washington in 1995, during the early months of the Republican Revolution. I began as a young congressional correspondent for *The Wall Street*

Journal. I later covered Bill Clinton's presidency, and his impeachment, for *The New Republic.* I covered George W. Bush's presidency as a White House correspondent for *The Washington Post,* and I've been writing a column about political Washington for the last sixteen years. This has provided me a front-row seat for the worst show on earth: the crack-up of the Republican Party, and the resulting crack-up of American democracy.

This book contains four roughly equal sections: the Clinton presidency (defined by the slashing style of Gingrich), the George W. Bush presidency (defined by the dishonesty of Karl Rove), the Obama presidency (during which democratic norms were assaulted from within by Mitch McConnell and without by Sarah Palin), and, finally, the ruin of the (still ongoing) Trump era. Interwoven throughout are the four ways in which Republicans have been hacking away at the foundations of democracy and civil society for a quarter century: their war on truth, their growing exploitation of racism and white supremacy, their sabotage of the institutions and norms of government, and their dehumanizing of opponents and stoking of violence.

In the process, they became the Destructionists: they destroyed truth, they destroyed decency, they destroyed patriotism, they destroyed national unity, they destroyed racial progress, they destroyed domestic stability, and they destroyed the world's oldest democracy.

BACK IN OCTOBER 2015, Mitt Romney, the 2012 Republican presidential nominee, spoke to a group of Georgetown University students about the man who would become the 2016 Republican presidential nominee.

"Donald Trump will not be the nominee," Romney said with confidence, because "when all is said and done, the American people usually do the right thing." He went on: "I know there's some skunks in any endeavor—business, politics—and they get most of the visibility, but there are also some really good people. The American people are a very good people and by and large find people of similar character to elect to the highest office in the land."

Romney read to the students from a cautionary letter John

Adams wrote to the political philosopher John Taylor in 1814. "Remember," the nation's second president wrote, "democracy never lasts long. It soon wastes, exhausts, and murders itself. There never was a democracy yet that did not commit suicide."

This notion, that American democracy would someday murder itself, was very much on the minds of the founders. In his farewell address, George Washington warned of a moment when "cunning, ambitious, and unprincipled men will be enabled to subvert the power of the people and to usurp for themselves the reins of government, destroying afterwards the very engines which have lifted them to unjust dominion."

James Madison, the author of the Constitution, wrote in Federalist 55 that the survival of American democracy would depend on character: "As there is a degree of depravity in mankind . . . so there are other qualities in human nature which justify a certain portion of esteem and confidence. Republican government presupposes the existence of these qualities in a higher degree than any other form."

"We've beaten the odds," Romney told the Georgetown students that day, "in part because we've had, I think, people of real character who have led our country as presidents . . . and the American people have risen to the occasion time and again and have in fact then elected good people."

I was so sure Romney was right that I wrote a column that day saying I would "eat the page on which this column is printed" if Trump won the Republican nomination. And so, in May 2016, I sat down to a meal of newspaper-smoked Wagyu steak, fried fish wrapped in buttermilk-soaked newspaper, grilled newspaper guacamole, ground newspaper dumplings, and grilled newspaper falafel.

I had bet on the wisdom of the American voter, predicting that 2016 "won't be the year American democracy murders itself." I had to eat my words.

Romney soon found himself a pariah in his own party. So did John McCain, the 2008 Republican nominee. And George W. Bush, the 2000 and 2004 nominee. Ronald Reagan, were he alive, would have been likewise excommunicated.

"There is no Republican Party. There's a Trump Party," former

Republican House speaker John Boehner, who retired as Trump seized control of the GOP, said in May 2018. "The Republican Party is kind of taking a nap somewhere."

But Boehner, who was one of Gingrich's lieutenants in 1994, knows better. This isn't a nap. The Republican Party, as we knew it, is dead.

For a quarter century, Republican officials invited Trump's takeover of the party by trafficking in conspiracy theories, welcoming white nationalists, sabotaging the engines of government, and winking at violence. And in the process, they murdered democracy.

CHAPTER 1

Shooting at Melons

At the start of the Civil War, Union troops built Fort Marcy, on a ridge above the Potomac in Northern Virginia, as one of the fortifications ringing Washington to protect the capital from Confederate attack. The Union commander, General George McClellan, named it for his father-in-law and chief of staff, Randolph Marcy. Its earthworks measured up to eighteen feet thick in parts, and it bristled with three howitzers and eighteen field guns, defending the Chain Bridge river crossing below.

In the end, Fort Marcy wound up seeing no major action in the Civil War. But more than a century later, it became the site of the first shot in another conflict: the Republican Party's war on truth.

The afternoon of July 20, 1993, brought the kind of oppressive weather that keeps almost everybody indoors: a high of 96 degrees and near 100 percent humidity. But sometime after the lunch hour, a gray Honda Accord with Arkansas plates, heading westbound on the George Washington Memorial Parkway, pulled off at Fort Marcy, now a national park. A man in his late forties, lanky and nearly six feet five inches tall, emerged from the Honda wearing a white dress shirt, gray dress pants, and black dress shoes. He left his sports jacket and his swan-pattern tie folded on the passenger seat, and he pocketed the car keys.

The man proceeded to walk uphill some eight hundred feet from the parking lot to the walls of the old fort, then continued to the second of two vintage 12-pound howitzers on display. Stopping on the steeply sloping earthworks just below the old cannon, the man pulled from his pants pocket an antique Colt .38 revolver. He put the barrel of the gun in his mouth and, with his right thumb, squeezed the trigger.

Hours later, after the man's body had been discovered by a passerby, U.S. Park Police searching the Honda found, under the suit jacket, the man's White House identification. The deceased was Vince Foster, the deputy White House counsel and personal friend of President Bill Clinton and First Lady Hillary Clinton.

Foster's death was a tragic suicide. Since moving to Washington with the new administration, Foster had been battered in the press, particularly in the editorial pages of *The Wall Street Journal,* for his role in various penny-ante scandals of the first year of the Clinton presidency that ultimately amounted to nothing. Four days before his death, Foster broke down in tears at dinner with his wife and talked of resigning. He also told his sister he was depressed, and she gave him the names of three psychiatrists (the list was found in his wallet), and he tried to reach one of them but got an answering machine. The day before his death, he called his doctor in Little Rock and complained of stress, anorexia, and insomnia, and he received a prescription for an antidepressant.

Investigators deduced that the gun was an eighty-year-old model he had inherited from his father. He transported it in an oven mitt, found in his car's glove compartment. Forensic evidence— gunshot residue on his hands, a mark on his thumb matching the trigger rebound, no indication of struggle—overwhelmingly pointed to suicide. And there was a note—torn into twenty-seven pieces, it was found in his briefcase, which he had left at the office.

"I made mistakes from ignorance, inexperience and over-work," it said. "I did not knowingly violate any law or standard of conduct." He listed various grievances—"The GOP has lied. . . . The public will never believe the innocence of the Clintons and their loyal staff. The WSJ editors lie without consequence"—and ended with this: "I was not meant for the job or the spotlight of public life in Washington. Here ruining people is considered sport."

Alas for Foster, even death offered no relief from that sport. Republicans were about to ruin him—posthumously.

Almost exactly a year after Foster's suicide, Dan Burton, a Republican congressman from Indiana and a close ally of Republican whip Newt Gingrich, stood in the well of the House of Representatives, giving an hour-long special order speech.

His purpose: to make the case that Vince Foster had been murdered. His proof: Burton shot a melon in his backyard.

The precise identity of the gourd Burton shot is a matter of some dispute. It has been identified, variously, as a watermelon, a pumpkin, and a cantaloupe. But this much is clear: Burton had used the fruit as a stand-in for Foster's head—"a head-like thing," he called it—to prove that it's impossible Foster shot himself at Fort Marcy and nobody heard the gunshot.

"We, at my house, with a homicide detective, tried to re-create a head and fired a .38 inch barrel into that, to see if the sound could be heard from 100 yards away," Burton declared on the House floor. "Even though there was an earth mover moving around in the background, making all kinds of racket, you could hear the bullet clearly."

Investigators of Foster's death found the lack of witnesses reporting a gunshot unsurprising: the strip of woods, with infrequent foot traffic, lies between the parkway and another busy road. But Burton took the unheard gunshot as evidence that Foster had been murdered at a different location, rolled up in a carpet, and carried in broad daylight uphill to the fort, with care being taken to hold the six-foot-four-and-a-half-inch corpse upright to keep the blood off his clothing.

"He died under very mysterious circumstances," Burton told the House. "His body was moved. There is no question about it." Burton suggested that the gun was planted in Foster's hand and that the torn note was planted in his briefcase. Burton floated the possibility of a secret entrance to the park, and killers hiding in the trees. He asserted that "there is a connection" between Foster's death and probes of the Clintons' finances. And the scores of federal agents who investigated were trying to "cover up" the facts.

This was, of course, pure madness. The Park Police, investigating with the FBI and the Justice Department, found "no evidence of foul play" and concluded that "the condition of the scene, the medical examiner's findings and the information gathered clearly indicate that Mr. Foster committed suicide."

Independent counsel Robert Fiske, who had been appointed to probe the Clintons' finances, undertook his own investigation of Foster's death, using FBI resources and expert pathologists. He found that "the overwhelming weight of the evidence compels the conclusion . . . that Vincent Foster committed suicide in Fort Marcy Park on July 20, 1993."

The top Republican on the Government Operations Committee, William Clinger, did a third investigation and concluded that "Foster died from a self-inflicted gunshot wound to the mouth while at Fort Marcy Park."

A bipartisan Senate committee undertook a fourth probe and declared that "the evidence overwhelmingly supports the conclusion" that "Foster died in Fort Marcy Park from a self-inflicted gun shot wound."

Clinger, closing his probe, said he hoped his findings would "put to rest any lingering questions regarding the events of July 20, 1993." He lamented: "Perhaps the unexpected death of any high government official will needlessly bring cries of conspiracy from many in our society. That is unfortunate."

There have always been conspiracy theories in politics. For decades after John F. Kennedy's assassination, some still claimed there was a second gunman on the grassy knoll. But with Foster's suicide, something new and different happened. This time, the conspiracy theories were promoted by wealthy interests in the Republican Party and allied right-wing media platforms, and embraced by the highest officials in the Republican Party.

Even after four separate, independent probes reached the same conclusion of suicide, Newt Gingrich, who had become speaker of the House in January 1995, threw the weight of the speakership behind the Vince Foster conspiracy theory.

"There's something that doesn't fit about this whole case and the way it's been handled," Gingrich proclaimed in July 1995. As for Foster's suicide, "I'm not convinced he didn't. I'm just not convinced he did."

"I just don't accept it," he said of the repeated findings of suicide. "I believe there are plausible grounds to wonder what happened and very real grounds to wonder why it was investigated so badly."

So Gingrich stoked the lie, which had already been four times disproven. A few months later, he would name none other than Dan Burton, of murdered melon fame, to replace the retiring Clinger as chairman of the House Operations Committee, which Republicans renamed the House Committee on Oversight and Reform and stocked with new, plenary investigative powers.

Why would the man second in line to the presidency publicly endorse an obvious lie? Well, if you were conspiracy minded, you might have observed that one of the largest contributors to Gingrich's political action committee, GOPAC, was billionaire Richard Mellon Scaife, who funded the "Arkansas Project" solely to dig dirt on the Clintons. A chunk of the hundreds of millions of dollars he spent on conservative causes went to groups promoting conspiracy theories about Foster's death. His *Pittsburgh Tribune-Review*, which he founded in 1992, was a leading promoter of the Foster fiction. He called Foster's death "the Rosetta stone to the Clinton administration." Bill Clinton, Scaife alleged to *George* magazine in 1998, "can order people done away with at his will. . . . God there must be 60 people who have died mysteriously."

Scaife in 1995 hired right-wing journalist Christopher Ruddy, who had touted Foster conspiracy theories for the *New York Post,* to do the same for his *Tribune-Review*. Three years later, the two men would launch Newsmax, a disreputable right-wing website, and Ruddy would go on to become a friend and informal adviser to another born conspiracy theorist: Donald J. Trump.

The new genre of conservative talk radio, which traces its origins to 1988, when provocateur Rush Limbaugh's AM radio show went national, fueled the Foster lies. After a financial newsletter made the fantastic and baseless claim that Foster's corpse had been moved from an apartment in Virginia, Limbaugh upped the ante, telling his nationwide radio audience that the newsletter had reported that "Foster was murdered in an apartment owned by Hillary Clinton."

As *Newsweek* reported at the time, "after Limbaugh's broadcast, stock and bond prices tumbled—the Dow dropped nearly 23 points. . . . Elaine Garzarelli, the highly regarded Lehman Brothers market analyst who predicted the 1987 crash, said that European traders were particularly spooked by the Foster case. 'They were afraid Hillary Clinton was involved in a murder,' she said."

One day in the summer of 1995, two lawyers in the Clinton White House, Chris Lehane and Mark Fabiani, tried to figure out the origins of the constant stream of Vince Foster allegations. Lehane later wrote:

> Online we found early versions of chat rooms, postings and other information showing there was an entire cottage industry devoted to discussing conspiracy theories relating to Foster's death, including numerous online reports of people claiming to have seen him. Those reports would be picked up by so-called news sources that most Americans at the time had never heard of—conservative outlets such as Eagle Publishing's *Human Events* or Richard Mellon Scaife's *Pittsburgh Tribune-Review.* From there, the story would migrate to right-leaning outlets we were familiar with, such as the *New York Post,* the *Washington Times,* and the editorial pages of *The Wall Street Journal*—all before eventually ending up in the mainstream press.

They assembled their findings in a 332-page report—the basis for what Hillary Clinton would famously describe as "this vast right-wing conspiracy that has been conspiring against my husband since the day he announced for president."

The wild theories also captured the imagination of a thirty-year-old lawyer working in the independent counsel's office: Brett Kavanaugh. The future Trump appointee to the Supreme Court had secured a job on the staff of Ken Starr, the fiercely partisan prosecutor who replaced Fiske and made it his office's mission to run a rolling investigation of any allegation made against the Clintons.

"We are currently investigating Vincent Foster's death to determine, among other things, whether he was murdered in violation of federal criminal law," Kavanaugh wrote to his colleagues in a March 24, 1995, memo obtained years later by my *Washington Post* colleague Michael Kranish and shared with me.

Kavanaugh admitted that the absurd claims weren't part of Starr's mandate, but, he argued, "we have received allegations that Mr. Foster's death related to President and Mrs. Clinton's involvement" in the Whitewater financial dealings that Starr was investigating. The "allegations" were that Foster was murdered, or killed himself, because of the Clintons' financial dealings and what he knew about them. Based on such allegations, Starr should launch "a full-fledged investigation of Mr. Foster's death."

Where did these "allegations" come from? Kavanaugh's files showed that he was referring to the conspiracy theories promoted by Ruddy, by right-wing media critic Reed Irvine, and by a British writer who had claimed that the Oklahoma City bombing by right-wing militants was really a botched FBI plot.

Kavanaugh, naturally, knew that the probe he promoted was nonsense. "I am satisfied that Foster was sufficiently discouraged or depressed to commit suicide," he wrote in a June 1995 memo. "I base my conclusion on the fact that Foster was found with a list of three psychiatrists in his wallet, the fact that Foster obtained a prescription on July 19 for an anti-depressant, and the many witness interviews describing his state of mind in the days and weeks preceding his death."

But he would spend the next two years investigating—and thereby legitimizing—all the ludicrous claims: that Foster had an affair with Hillary Clinton; that blond hairs found on Foster's clothing (Hillary's?) were suspicious; that Foster was being blackmailed by Israel's Mossad over a secret Swiss bank account; and that the White House had covered it all up. He kept a prurient "discrepancy list" in his files, with items such as "large semen stain in the decedent's underwear."

In October 1997, after two more years of anguish for Foster's family, Starr would issue a report affirming precisely what the previous four investigations had found about Foster's suicide. Kavanaugh and Starr, like Gingrich and virtually anybody else paying attention, had to have known the truth all along. But they also had to recognize that stringing out another "investigation" for two more years would give those who weren't paying attention the impression that something sinister had happened in the Clinton White House.

A poll done by *Time* and CNN in 1995 found that despite the numerous probes ruling Foster's death a suicide, only 35 percent of adults were convinced that Foster had really killed himself. Republican leaders and allied media figures had discovered that if they embraced a fringe conspiracy theory, they could convince millions to believe a lie. Vince Foster's suicide gave them a prototype.

THE VINCE FOSTER LIE was big and audacious, but it employed the same techniques Gingrich had used to get to Congress in 1978 and then to lead the Republicans to a majority sixteen years later: proclaiming falsehoods with righteous certainty.

Gingrich won election to Congress on a lie. After two unsuccessful tries in 1974 and 1976, he finally succeeded, with a campaign that falsely accused his opponent, Virginia Shapard, of violating campaign finance laws. He also accused his opponent of breaking up her family. "Newt will take his family to Washington and keep them together," one of Gingrich's ads announced. "Virginia will go to Washington and leave her husband and children in the care of a nanny." As it happened, Gingrich was carrying on multiple affairs at the time and divorced his wife two years later.

The "Gingrich approach seems to have gone beyond vigor and into demagoguery and plain lying," *The Atlanta Journal Constitution* editorialized in 1978, after endorsing Gingrich in '74 and '76. "We regret that his campaign strategy has been of such a low order that we cannot consider extending our support this third bid for election." The paper said his imagination "seems to be running away with him."

He gained prominence in Congress based on another deception. C-SPAN began televising House proceedings in 1979 as Gingrich arrived. He quickly realized that because the TV cameras filmed only those who were speaking, the viewers wouldn't know the chamber was otherwise empty. He used this to pose rhetorical challenges to Democrats, accusing them of disloyalty and communist sympathies—and used the silence in the chamber as evidence that they had no response. Gingrich later told *The Washington Post:* "Without C-SPAN, without talk radio shows, without all the alternative media, I don't think we'd have won [control of Congress]."

Gingrich voted for a congressional pay raise, then campaigned against Democrats for supporting it. Gingrich campaigned against Democrats for overdrawing their accounts in the House bank, even though he had made twenty-two overdrafts himself. He proposed a mandate requiring individuals to have health insurance, then later attacked Democrats for proposing the same. He succeeded in killing a comprehensive lobbying reform bill in 1994 by falsely claiming that violators "might go to jail"; it contained no criminal penalties. In an extraordinary moment of projection, Gingrich declared in 1995 that "for Bill Clinton, the truth is transactional."

One of Gingrich's early acts as speaker was to abolish Congress's nonpartisan Office of Technology Assessment in 1995. The office, which had existed since 1972, provided Congress with "competent, unbiased information concerning the physical, biological, economic, social and political effects" of policy options. He saved all of $20 million a year eliminating the office, the first in a long series of moves to purge the federal government of expertise. The facts had become expendable.

Gingrich once remarked that he felt he was "drowning" as speaker because "I couldn't do what I did differently, which is to tell the truth as I understand it. It's not the truth," he readily admitted. "The truth is known by God and the rest of us seek it."

Gingrich's idea of truth was indeed something he did "differently"; it was not the truth but what he thought should be the truth. The "truth as I understand it" (later reformulated during the Trump administration as "alternative facts" or "truth impressions") and the denial that there is objective truth were how Gingrich gave himself permission to lie.

Gingrich's Republican Revolution of 1994 succeeded in part because of more deception. The Christian Coalition, a religious-right group given start-up funds by the Republican National Committee and backed by televangelist and former presidential candidate Pat Robertson, launched a stealth campaign to tag Democrats in key House races with all manner of falsehood: they supported obscene art, or a national school board, or abortion on demand, or "promoting homosexuality to schoolchildren." The tax-exempt nonprofit shipped 20 million "voter guides" to evangelical churches but had them held for distribution until October 30, the *Wall Street Journal*'s Glenn Simpson reported, a week before the election. That left no chance for the accused to set the record straight. "I do guerilla warfare," explained the Christian Coalition's director, Ralph Reed. "I paint my face and travel at night. You don't know it's over until you're in a body bag."

This asymmetric warfare—guerrilla attacks on the facts— gained amplification on conservative talk radio from the likes of Limbaugh, Watergate ex-con G. Gordon Liddy, and young Sean Hannity in Atlanta. By 1995, there were reportedly 1,130 radio stations with talk formats, up from two in 1960. Seventy percent of them were conservative, and Limbaugh alone had 20 million listeners. But also joining the guerrilla fight was a new email newsletter, the Drudge Report, which launched in 1995, and Rupert Murdoch's Fox News, which launched in 1996. The new media created by Limbaugh, Drudge, and Murdoch needed content, and Gingrich recognized that by providing it, he could make these new outlets the house organs of his revolution.

Gingrich's Republicans kept them saturated with wild, often unsubstantiated allegations. Whitewater. Troopergate. Travelgate. Filegate. Furnituregate. The Gennifer Flowers and Paula Jones sex scandals. Fallen Clinton aide Webb Hubbell fathered Chelsea Clinton! Al Gore wore a wire in a presidential debate! Commerce Secretary Ron Brown's death in a plane crash in Croatia was a Clinton-arranged hit! Republicans investigated Brown over personal finances, Clinton's energy secretary and labor secretary over campaign finances, the housing secretary over what he told the FBI, the interior secretary over a casino, and the head of service agency AmeriCorps over conflicts of interest.

Deploying an innuendo-spreading technique that would become commonplace in the GOP, Gingrich in June 1996 told a gathering of hundreds of GOP officials about unfounded reports by the far-right *American Spectator* alleging that the Clinton administration delayed disclosing Brown's April plane crash in Croatia to provide time to shred the commerce secretary's papers. Gingrich's spokesman, Tony Blankley, declared that the baseless claims "are serious allegations if subsequent facts support them" and are "something other news outlets ought to look at."

In the Senate, an ambitious Republican senator from Kentucky, Mitch McConnell, gamely joined in. In 1997, he took over the National Republican Senatorial Committee, and in one of his first fundraising letters he told donors to send money immediately to "help to protect our country from a potentially devastating nuclear attack." He also alleged that the Clinton White House was "sold for ILLEGAL FOREIGN CASH," and that Democrats were "accepting ILLEGAL FOREIGN CASH from the world's strongest remaining Communist regime."

The busiest contributor in the conspiracy caucus was Burton. In 1998, he said of Clinton: "If I could prove 10 percent of what I believe happened, he'd be gone. This guy's a scumbag. That's why I'm after him."

Even beyond Clinton, Burton had a prolific imagination. He proposed mandatory AIDS testing for everybody, and a friend of his said Burton wouldn't eat soup in a restaurant for fear of catching AIDS. He brought his own scissors, comb, and razor to the barber for the same reason. He fought to ban thimerosal from vaccines because he thought it caused autism. He supposed that anti-Apartheid sanctions were a "scorched-earth" policy that would benefit "communists."

Given the gavel of the House Oversight Committee by Gingrich, he tried to prove that illegal foreign contributors bankrolled Clinton and that Clinton had "improper motives" in using his pardon power. He issued hundreds of subpoenas to Clinton officials and even probed whether a fan club dedicated to the Clintons' cat, Socks, was using taxpayer funds.

His most celebrated assault on the truth (since the melon shooting, at least) came when he selectively edited prison tapes of former Clinton official Webb Hubbell, convicted of mail fraud and tax evasion at his law firm, talking to his visiting wife.

The transcript Burton released said: "Editorials are all talking about how all this is designed to keep me and Susan [McDougal, another Clinton friend] quiet. We have to make sure that it's our personal friends that are helping."

Burton omitted five sentences that separated those two sentences that utterly changed their meaning. Hubbell had said that "most of the articles are presupposing that I, my silence is being bought. We know that's not true. You know, we're dead solid broke and getting broker." Burton also left out Hubbell's statement indicating Hillary Clinton had "no idea" about billing irregularities at the law firm, where they both worked.

Even Gingrich said he was "embarrassed" by Burton's "circus." Burton's only feint at contrition was accepting the resignation of an aide, dirt digger David Bossie, who would continue to go after the Clintons as head of Citizens United (a partisan nonprofit that would become the focus of a landmark Supreme Court case) and then as a top campaign adviser to Trump.

BRETT KAVANAUGH WAS DEEP in the fever swamps of conspiracy theory, as he stretched his probe of the Foster suicide for more than two years. He looked at autopsy photos and toured Fort Marcy. Papers released two decades later, when he was nominated to the Supreme Court, showed that he worked closely with cranks. His files included 195 pages of articles by Ruddy, who had alleged that the Foster investigation was "one of the biggest cover ups in American history, that Park Police had changed the location of the body 'by several hundred feet,' and that federal officials were guilty of 'issuing false reports' and 'lying to the press and public.'" Also in Kavanaugh's papers: a Limbaugh transcript titled "Foster Note a Forgery." Kavanaugh, in his papers, mentioned frequent conversations with Ruddy and commended "the Ruddy articles" to a new investigator joining the team.

Kavanaugh reported to colleagues that "we have asked numerous witnesses about Foster's alleged affair with Mrs. Clinton," and he asked sexually explicit questions of a witness. Never mind that the "confidential witness" who birthed many of the conspiracy ideas was not terribly credible; he claimed he pulled off at the park because he needed urgently to urinate, but then wandered hundreds of feet around the heavily wooded fort before doing so.

The Foster probe also introduced Kavanaugh and colleagues to Linda Tripp, a secretary in the counsel's office who would, three months after the Foster probe closed, provide Starr with evidence of White House intern Monica Lewinsky's affair with Clinton. But in this case, she affirmed that Foster had been tired, had called in sick for two days a week before his suicide, had become quiet and removed, and was losing weight.

The Starr probe of Foster lasted three years and cost about $2 million, before confirming, in October 1997, all the previous investigations' findings. "In sum, based on all of the available evidence, which is considerable, the OIC [Office of Independent Counsel] agrees with the conclusion reached by every official entity that has examined the issue: Mr. Foster committed suicide by gunshot in Fort Marcy Park on July 20, 1993." Starr even tracked down the infamous "carpet fibers" found on Foster's clothing. They were from his house.

But the extended Starr probe had only fueled the conspiracy beliefs. Foster's sister, Sheila Foster Anthony, said on the day Starr's findings were released that Starr had allowed people to believe "that the president of the United States somehow had complicity in Vince's death." Twenty years later, Bill Clinton complained bitterly about Kavanaugh "making us put up with three years of Vince Foster nonsense that was a total charade," *The Washington Times* reported.

Once Starr sided with reality, Ruddy simply responded that Starr was involved in the cover-up, too. He started claiming autopsy X-rays had been "destroyed" and that "senior military people" were alleging that Foster had been shot in the back of the head. He wrote in his 1997 book, *The Strange Death of Vincent Foster,* that Foster's "killers" may have been wearing orange vests posing as park volunteers. As Michael Isikoff, who followed the Foster probes for *The Washington Post,* wrote at the time in *Slate:* "Ruddy's book—and the entire movement he has helped create—is utterly preposterous."

But enduring. Limbaugh made Foster's death a recurring theme. He said that people should "start searching Fort Marcy Park" for the body of somebody who crossed Clinton attorney general Janet Reno. He speculated that Senator John Kerry and antiwar activist Cindy Sheehan would likewise be found in Fort Marcy Park for running afoul of the Clintons.

Conservative propagandist Ann Coulter advised that "if you

attack the Clintons publicly, make sure all your friends know that you are not planning suicide." The conspiracy crowd set up a "Clinton Body Count" on the web, alleging Hillary and Bill Clinton are responsible for murdering about ninety people, including Ron Brown, John F. Kennedy Jr., and a former CIA director.

Twenty-five years after Foster's death, a viral Facebook post said: "On this date in 1993, Vince Foster went to Fort Marcy Park and shot himself 3 times in the back of the head to avoid testifying against Hillary Clinton." Starr himself told Fox News's Tucker Carlson in 2018 that the true reason for Foster's suicide "haunts me to this day."

During the Republican National Convention in 2016, the one that nominated Donald Trump for the presidency, Roger Stone, longtime confidant and informal adviser to Trump, revisited the Foster murder conspiracy in a speech at a pro-Trump rally. "They told us that he died in Fort Marcy Park and his body was found 50 yards down a muddy trail," Stone said. "But there was no mud or dirt on his shoes. . . . There was carpet fiber all over his body because they rolled him in a carpet. Hillary Clinton ordered a guy named Sullivan and a guy named Kennedy, her hoodlums, her thugs, [to] move his body."

Congressman Pete Olson, a Texas Republican, claimed that Bill Clinton admitted to Attorney General Loretta Lynch in 2016 that "we killed Vince Foster." And Donald Trump, in an interview with *The Washington Post* in 2016 after he had secured the Republican nomination for president, said claims that Foster was murdered are "very serious" and the circumstances of Foster's death "very fishy." Foster "had intimate knowledge of what was going on," Trump told *the Post*. "He knew everything that was going on, and then all of a sudden he committed suicide. . . . I will say there are people who continue to bring it up because they think it was absolutely a murder."

In response, Foster's sister, Sheila Foster Anthony, who also served in the Clinton administration, wrote an essay in the *Post* pouring out twenty-three years of suffering. She recalled the tragic but unremarkable details of her brother's depression and suicide:

Vince called me at my office in the Justice Department a few days before he died. He told me he was battling depression and knew he needed help. But he was worried that such an admission would adversely affect his top-level security clearance and prevent him from doing his job.

I told him I would try to find a psychiatrist who could help him and protect his privacy. After a few phone calls, I gave him three names. That list was found in his wallet with his body at Fort Marcy Park in McLean, Va. I did not see a suicide coming, yet when I was told that Vince was dead, I knew that he had killed himself. Never for a minute have I doubted that was what happened.

I think Vince felt he was a failure, this brilliant man who had so many talents, had achieved so many honors and was so well-respected by his peers. He must have felt that he couldn't stay in his job at the White House, and he couldn't go back to Little Rock. He was so ill, he couldn't see a way out.

She also recalled all the cruelty done to her family and to the memory of her late brother. "These outrageous suggestions have caused our family untold pain because this issue went on for so long and these reports were so painful to read," she wrote. "For years, our family had to wage a court fight to prevent release of photographs of Vince's dead body. My heartbroken mother was plagued by harassing phone calls from a reporter."

"How wrong. How irresponsible. How cruel," she wrote of Trump's revival of the "murder" lie. "This is scurrilous enough coming from right-wing political operatives who have peddled conspiracy theories about Vince's death for more than two decades. How could this be coming from the presumptive Republican nominee for president?"

How? Because Burton, Gingrich, Starr, Kavanaugh, Ruddy, and Limbaugh had shown him the political power of an endlessly repeated lie.

CHAPTER 2

Personal Destruction

The wording by itself was shocking.

"If Monica Lewinsky says that you inserted a cigar into her vagina while you were in the Oval Office area, would she be lying?"

"If Monica Lewinsky says that on several occasions in the Oval Office area, you used your fingers to stimulate her vagina and bring her to orgasm, would she be lying?"

"If Monica Lewinsky says that you ejaculated into her mouth on two occasions in the Oval Office area, would she be lying?"

"If Monica Lewinsky says that you masturbated into a trash-can in your secretary's office, would she be lying?"

But the wording was just the beginning of the obscenity. The person to whom the questions were addressed was the president of the United States. And the person proposing such questions was a future Supreme Court justice, Brett Kavanaugh.

There never was some halcyon golden age when politicians all got along; as the nineteenth-century saying goes, "politics ain't beanbag." But this was something new: the gratuitous vulgarity, the malice, the fury.

Kavanaugh's contempt for Bill Clinton was palpable in the young lawyer's memo arguing for the invasive questioning. "I am strongly opposed to giving the president any 'break' in the questioning regarding the details of the Lewinsky relationship—unless before his questioning on Monday, he either (i) resigns or (ii) confesses perjury and issues a public apology to you," Kavanaugh wrote in the August 15, 1998, memo to Ken Starr and the other lawyers in the independent counsel's office, on the eve of Clinton's grand jury testimony about the Lewinsky affair. Because Kavanaugh could think of no good defenses for Bill Clinton's "disgusting behavior," he wrote, "the idea of going easy on him at the questioning is thus abhorrent to me. . . .

"[I]t is <u>our</u> job to make this pattern of revolting behavior clear—piece by painful piece," Kavanaugh went on. "I am mindful of the need for respect for the Office of the President. But in my view, given what we know, the interests of the Office of the President would be best served by our gathering the full facts regarding the actions of this president so that the Congress can decide whether the interests of the presidency would be best served by having a new president."

Kavanaugh's line of questioning, with its purpose of driving the president from office because he lied about sex with an intern, was too much even for Starr, who had, by that point, spent almost five years in partisan pursuit of any and all accusations against Clinton, no matter how far-fetched. He spared Clinton the most explicit questioning. But the report he delivered to Congress, and which Congress released to the public, was every bit as pornographic as Kavanaugh desired.

"According to Ms. Lewinsky, she performed oral sex on the President on nine occasions," it reported. "On all nine of those occasions, the President fondled and kissed her bare breasts. He touched her genitals, both through her underwear and directly, bringing her to orgasm on two occasions. On one occasion, the President inserted a cigar into her vagina. On another occasion, she and the President had brief genital-to-genital contact."

Starr was as precise as he was prurient.

"On four occasions, the President also touched her genitalia."

"The President and Ms. Lewinsky also had phone sex on at least 15 occasions."

"When Ms. Lewinsky next took the navy blue Gap dress from her closet to wear it, she noticed stains near one hip and on the chest. FBI Laboratory tests revealed that the stains are the President's semen."

"[T]he caller was a Member of Congress with a nickname. While the President was on the telephone, according to Ms. Lewinsky, 'he unzipped his pants and exposed himself,' and she performed oral sex."

"She also showed him an e-mail describing the effect of chewing Altoid mints before performing oral sex. Ms. Lewinsky was chewing Altoids at the time, but the President replied that he did not have enough time for oral sex. They kissed, and the President rushed off for a State Dinner."

"At one point, the President inserted a cigar into Ms. Lewinsky's vagina, then put the cigar in his mouth and said: 'It tastes good.'"

There was no legal need for Starr to produce 211 pages of taxpayer-funded pornography. Clinton had by then admitted to the Lewinsky affair, and the whole world knew he had previously lied about it in a civil deposition for a different sexual misconduct case. Neither did Starr's report serve to inform the public in any meaningful way; the president's serial philandering had long been known.

Rather, the obvious purpose of Starr's explicit, vulgar report was to humiliate a political opponent—to "own" him, as it would come to be called. The public obscenity produced by Starr and his fellow Republican warriors in the independent counsel's office was stunning, but it fit with a new politics Newt Gingrich's Republican Revolution had brought to Washington: not simply disagreeing with opponents, but demonizing them, dehumanizing them, destroying them.

TRAITORS.
Sick.
Corrupt.
Cheat.
Betray.
Lie.
Steal.
Greed.
Destroy.
Decay.
Failure.

Incompetent.
Bizarre.
Radical.
Selfish.
Shallow.
Hypocrisy.
Shame.
Pathetic.
Abuse of power.
Anti-flag.
Anti-family.
Anti-child.
Anti-jobs.

In the summer of 1990, Newt Gingrich's political action committee mailed a memo to Republican candidates for public office instructing them in the fine art of demonizing Democrats. It contained a list of about sixty-five words and phrases (including all of the above) to be used against Democrats, and another group of favorable words (empowerment, opportunity, hard work) to be used in praise of Republicans.

From Republican candidates across the country, the GOPAC memo said, "we have heard a plaintive plea: 'I wish I could speak like Newt.'" It continued:

> That takes years of practice. But, we believe that you could have a significant impact on your campaign and the way you communicate if we help a little. That is why we have created this list of words and phrases.
>
> This list is prepared so that you might have a directory of words to use in writing literature and mail, in preparing speeches, and in producing electronic media. The words and phrases are powerful. Read them. Memorize as many as possible. And remember that like any tool, these words will not help if they are not used.

This was a new politics of us versus them—literally. The memo ("Language: A Key Mechanism of Control") encouraged Republicans to speak of fellow partisans as "we/us/our" and Democrats as "they/them." Democrats were to be defined by terms such as "machine," "bosses," "criminal rights," "welfare," "red tape," "permissive attitude," and "stagnation," while Republicans alone had "courage," "common sense," "strength," and "truth."

The memo made no mention of policies or specific issues; its only purpose was to teach demonization. In that sense it was a perfect distillation of Gingrich's signature innovation in American politics. He wasn't particularly ideological; he was a Rockefeller Republican in 1968 and a self-described "moderate" when first elected to Congress ten years later; there had been whispers that he supported abortion rights before he found opportunity in being a conservative. His speakership was brief—just four years—and produced little of lasting significance. But Gingrich deserves one dubious distinction: he changed forever the language of politics. He shoved aside the genial cordiality of an earlier generation of leaders and replaced it with the slashing, personal, bitter language we routinely hear from political figures today.

"I think that one of the great problems we have in the Republican Party is that we don't encourage you to be nasty," Gingrich told a group of College Republicans meeting at an Atlanta-area Holiday Inn during his successful run for Congress in 1978. "We encourage you to be neat, obedient, and loyal and faithful and all those Boy Scout words, which would be great around the campfire, but are lousy in politics."

Gingrich, who liked to cite Mao's maxim that "politics is war without blood," went on to compare his profession to fighting in Vietnam (which he did not do): "This is the same business. . . . You're fighting a war. It is a war for power."

The Republican Party, Gingrich said, "does not need another generation of cautious, prudent, careful, bland, irrelevant, quasi-leaders. What we really need are people who are tough, hardworking, energetic, willing to take risks, willing to stand up in a ugh, ugh, in a slug fest and match it out with their opponent."

And he left them with an admonition: "Raise hell. Raise hell all the time."

He practiced what he preached. In his unsuccessful run for Congress in 1974, Gingrich said the incumbent Democrat was a "moral coward" and a "political hack" who "has disgraced every citizen he is supposed to represent" and engaged in "activities that, if not illegal are so clearly on the borderline of conflict of interest." In his unsuccessful 1976 campaign for Congress he went to a local penitentiary and proclaimed that "there are men serving in the House of Representatives who would better serve in this United States prison. . . . [W]e are literally governed by criminals."

Democratic leaders were "thugs" and "crooks," and Democrats were "sick," "corrupt," and "socialists." The Democratic Party represented "total hedonism, total exhibitionism, total bizarreness, total weirdness." The House of Representatives was a "corrupt left-wing machine."

As a backbencher in the 1980s, Gingrich called House Speaker Tip O'Neill a "dictator" and likened his foreign policy to Neville Chamberlain's appeasement of Hitler. Gingrich in 1984 accused Democrats of coddling communist governments by giving them "unlimited sway" and claiming them to be "enlightened." Democrats—he mentioned several by name—"trash America, indict the president and give the benefit of every doubt to Marxist regimes."

O'Neill, furious, responded to Gingrich in his own speech: "You deliberately stood in that well before an empty House and challenged these people and you challenged their Americanism, and it is the lowest thing that I've ever seen in my 32 years in Congress." O'Neill was ruled out of order for calling Gingrich's words "the lowest" (Gingrich's accusation of communist sympathies were not disallowed) and Republicans gave Gingrich a standing ovation. This was Gingrich's breakout moment.

He eventually turned his attention to O'Neill's successor, Jim Wright, whose leadership team Gingrich described in 1989 as "sick. They are destructive of the values we believe in. They are so consumed by their own Mussolini-like ego that their willingness to run over normal human beings and to destroy honest institutions is unending."

Wright was "ruthless, corrupt," afflicted with "megalomania," and the "most dangerous man ever to be speaker" who committed "the most destructive undermining of U.S. foreign policy in our country's history."

The adjectives poured from his lips—"irresponsible," "destructive," "corrupt," "unrepresentative"—accompanied by the occasional noun ("thugs") and verb ("They cheat every day"). He called the 1988 Democratic presidential nominee Michael Dukakis "nuts" and "Daffy Dukakis." He accused Democrats of attempting "chameleon-like actions to destroy our country." The "values of the left," he said in 1989, "cripple human beings, weaken cities, make it difficult for us to in fact survive as a country. . . . The left in America is to blame for most of the current, major diseases which have struck this society." Speaking to journalist John Harwood in 1989, Gingrich expanded on his epithets for Democrats: "Grotesque," "loony," "stupid." He compared Democrats to Woody Allen in 1992, saying the disgraced filmmaker "had non-incest with his non-daughter because they were a non-family." It's a "weird situation," he said "and it fits the Democratic Party platform perfectly." He also blamed Democrats' policies for the "sick" society that led a South Carolina woman to drown her two children. He called Democrats "the enemy of normal Americans" and Bill and Hillary Clinton "left-wing elitists" and "counterculture McGoverniks."

And those with whom he differed were, invariably, corrupt. "You live today with the most corrupt congressional leadership we have seen in the United States in the 20th century," he told the Conservative Political Action Conference in 1992.

Though Democrats received most of his abuse, Gingrich at times lost control of his vitriol and it landed on Republicans. The Reagan administration had "failed" and was in "danger of becoming another Jimmy Carter." Reagan's policies toward the Soviet Union were "pathetic" and "incompetent." The Republican leader of the Senate, Bob Dole, was the "tax collector for the welfare state." White House chief of staff James Baker made a "declaration of war on the Republican Party," which spread "dismay and despair among your own troops."

Gingrich, who never served in uniform, often used military terms—"troops," "commando," "enemy," "war"—to describe politics. In a 1988 speech, he called for "war" on the left. "This war has to be fought with a scale and a duration and a savagery that is only true of civil wars," he said. A Gingrich adviser likened

Gingrich and his allies to the Vietcong, a "revolutionary guerilla movement."

By contrast, Bob Michel, the House Republican leader, had known real combat. He was wounded by machine-gun fire in the Battle of the Bulge. As House minority leader for most of Gingrich's time in Congress, Michel knew his opponents were not his enemy, and he treated them like colleagues. He didn't like what he saw in Gingrich and his fellow bomb throwers. "I have given them some fatherly advice," Michel once said of Gingrich and his gang. "Be gentlemanly, and once you've made your point, get on with the business of governing."

But Gingrich, who had informed Michel that he would oust him as leader if Michel didn't retire after 1994, hadn't come to govern. He had come to fight. The news media "love fights," Gingrich said, explaining his technique. "When you give them confrontations, you get attention. When you get attention, you can educate."

Or, you can destroy.

The election of 1994 ended the domination of Congress by Michel's generation of World War II veterans. Baby boomers became an outright majority of the House in 1998 and in the Senate soon after, replacing shared experience in war with opposing experience in culture war. Gingrich lieutenant Dick Armey claimed that "all the problems began in the sixties."

Gingrich's invective was infectious. Armey, in one of his first acts as majority leader under Gingrich after the Republican takeover in 1994, referred to a prominent gay Democrat in Congress, Barney Frank of Massachusetts, as "Barney Fag." Armey later claimed it was a mispronunciation. Replied Frank: "I turned to my own expert, my mother, who reports that in 59 years of marriage, no one ever introduced her as Elsie Fag."

Frank's skepticism was warranted. Five years later, when humorist Dave Barry asked Armey if he really was Dick Armey, Armey replied: "Yes, I am Dick Armey. And if there is a dick army, Barney Frank would want to join up."

Spreading similarly vulgar attacks far and wide was Rush Limbaugh, who by the end of 1994 was on 659 radio stations, and a few hundred imitators had started local conservative talk shows. Limbaugh referred to then-thirteen-year-old Chelsea Clinton as the "White House dog." Limbaugh, who spoke of "femiNazis," joked to his listeners that he was on an elevator with Hillary Clinton, who tore off her clothes and begged, "Rush, make a woman out of me." So Limbaugh tore off his own clothes, threw them at Clinton, and said, "Fold those." Limbaugh would later talk of the "Clinton Library massage parlor" and Hillary Clinton's "testicle lockbox."

A month after they won control of the House in 1994, newly elected Republicans attended a dinner honoring Limbaugh in Baltimore, where they made him an honorary member of their class, and gave him a "Majority Makers" pin and a plaque announcing "Rush was right." Gingrich, as speaker, became a regular guest on talk radio shows. Gingrich and Armey set up a communications system to be in regular contact with the conservative talk radio hosts, and they would send Republican talking points to the hosts via "blast fax."

The medium would change, from fax to Fox, and from talk radio to the web and social media. The purveyors of hate-filled attacks would also change, from Gingrich to Palin to Trump. But this was the beginning of the Republican Party's separation from conservatism and, indeed, from any ideology. Gingrich defined Republicans by their visceral, tribal hatred of their political opponents—and that stuck.

The journalist Michael Kelly, writing in *The New York Times Magazine* in 1994, marveled at the animosity directed at Clinton. "What threatens this president seems to be much larger than mere partisanship," he wrote. "There is a level of mistrust and even dislike of him that is almost visceral in its intensity. In Washington, where power is generally treated with genuflecting reverence, it is no longer surprising to hear the president spoken of with open and dismissive contempt. . . . President Clinton is routinely depicted in the most unflattering terms: a liar, a fraud, a chronically indecisive man who cannot be trusted to stand for anything—or with anyone."

Clinton decried the "politics of personal destruction," and Gingrich found he couldn't control the vile sentiments he had provoked in the electorate. When he shared a stage with Clinton in New Hampshire in June 1995 conservatives savaged him for being too civil toward the president. Gingrich himself was trapped by the savagery he had stoked.

Years later, as Trump conquered the Republican Party in early 2016, Limbaugh explained in similar terms the phenomenon that had gripped the party. "There are a lot of people in this country who are conservative," he said. "But that's not the glue that unites them all. If it were, if conservatism—this is the big shock—if conservatism were the glue, the belief and understanding of deep but commonly understood conservative principles, if that's what defined people as conservative and was the glue that made the conservative movement a big movement, then Trump would have no chance." He went on: "The point is that if conservatism were this widely understood, deeply held belief system that united conservatives and united people as conservatives, then outsiders like Trump wouldn't stand a prayer of getting support from people. Yet he is."

So what united Republicans, if not conservatism? "The thing that's in front of everybody's face and it's apparently so hard to believe, it's this united, virulent opposition to the left and the Democrat Party and Barack Obama," Limbaugh answered. "And I, for the life of me, don't know what's so hard to understand about that."

Of course he understood it. He helped create it.

FIVE YEARS BEFORE THE GOP takeover of the House, Gingrich drafted a speech for a private GOPAC event outlining his plans for an electoral "realignment" that would give Republicans long-term political dominance. In the speech, which Glenn Simpson and Larry Sabato detailed in their 1996 book *Dirty Little Secrets,* Gingrich listed the components of realigning elections in history. Number three on his list: "Delegitimizing the Opposition."

But for Gingrich, it wouldn't do merely to delegitimize the opposition; because Democrats had been in control of the House for decades, they were synonymous with the institution. Therefore, he set out to delegitimize Congress itself.

At this, he succeeded handsomely. In 1977, the year before

Gingrich was elected to Congress, Gallup found that 40 percent of Americans had "a great deal" or "quite a lot" of confidence in Congress. After fifteen years of Gingrich's relentless attacks on the "corrupt" Congress, only 18 percent had a "great deal" or "quite a lot" of confidence in the institution during the Republican Revolution of 1994—a drop of more than half. Gingrich was self-righteous in taking credit for the destruction. "Before I came here the Democrats and Republicans played golf, and the Democrats came off the course and beat [their] brains out," he said. "Now Republicans feel it is legitimate for them to do the same."

The biggest triumph in Gingrich's long quest to delegitimize the House—and the event that propelled him from the back benches to the party leadership—was his takedown of a Democratic speaker of the House, Jim Wright.

Soon after Wright became speaker in 1987, succeeding O'Neill, Gingrich began leaking to the press speculative (and, it turns out, incorrect) allegations about Wright, and, when news articles resulted, he would circulate those as evidence that his allegations were correct. He filed charges with the House Ethics Committee suggesting that Wright had used his official powers to enrich himself in oil markets, had used a sweetheart book deal to launder campaign funds, and used his staff for his private business.

Gingrich and his allies worked up a media feeding frenzy, Republicans saw potential political advantage, and ultimately Wright was forced by political pressure to resign, the first time in history a speaker was ousted because of scandal. As Julian Zelizer observed in his book about the Gingrich-Wright episode, *Burning Down the House,* many of Gingrich's original allegations proved false. Yet Wright resigned, even though "the Ethics Committee had not yet proven that Wright had broken any House rules or that he had engaged in any kind of extraordinary wrongdoing that went beyond the ethically gray behavior citizens often saw from legislators, including Gingrich himself. The blockbuster allegations were not proving to be true. But Gingrich had moved at such a fast and furious pace that his efforts paid off."

Wright, in his resignation speech in 1989, decried "this period of mindless cannibalism." His fellow Texas Democrat Jack Brooks declared: "There is an evil wind blowing in the Halls of Congress today that is reminiscent of the Spanish Inquisition. It is replacing comity and compassion with hatred and malice."

The Republican leader, Michel, was on the side of comity. He had long been uncomfortable with Gingrich's "pyrotechnics," and he publicly warned Gingrich, after Gingrich became House Republican whip as a reward for the Wright takedown, that he'd have "to be much more responsible than he was as a junior member of Congress." That didn't happen, of course. When Michel, pushed out by Gingrich, announced his retirement in 1993, he lamented those who were "trashing the institution."

Gingrich kept on trashing. As soon as Wright was out, he began spreading slander against the next Democratic speaker, Tom Foley. The Republican National Committee, run by the like-minded Lee Atwater, released a memo declaring, "Tom Foley: Out of the Liberal Closet." It compared Foley to Barney Frank. Gingrich took the baseless insinuation of homosexuality a step further. One of his aides, Karen Van Brocklin, encouraged reporters to look into Foley's personal life. Another aide told a *New York Daily News* columnist, "We hear it's little boys."

Vice President Al Gore, in the days before Gingrich's 1994 election triumph, offered this prescient remark: "The Republicans are determined to wreck Congress in order to control it—and then to wreck a presidency in order to recapture it."

The great irony in Gingrich's sanctimony is that he was guilty of the sort of corruption he accused others of. As a congressional candidate, he accepted speaking fees and personal funds from campaign contributors to write a book that was never published. Later, right after Republicans took control of Congress in 1994, Gingrich accepted a $4.5 million book deal from a publishing house owned by Rupert Murdoch, who had stakes in several matters before Congress.

As the head of GOPAC, Gingrich skirted election laws by accepting funds nominally intended to help Republicans in state legislatures—and therefore not subject to federal campaign spending limits—but then using the funds to attack congressional Democrats and to promote himself.

Later, in 1997, Gingrich became the first speaker ever to be punished for violating the chamber's ethics rules. The House reprimanded Gingrich, 394–28, and he paid a $300,000 fine, for using funds from a nonprofit for "a partisan, political goal"—and for misleading the Ethics Committee.

Gingrich, without a trace of self-awareness, reportedly sobbed with self-pity over his personal ethics imbroglio ("no one knows what my wife and kids have gone through"), and produced a non-apology apology after his reprimand: "To the degree I was too brash, too self confident or too pushy I apologize."

ON MAY 27, 1997, THE United States Supreme Court issued one of the dumbest decisions in its history. A unanimous court ruled against President Bill Clinton and allowed the continuation of a civil lawsuit alleging that Clinton sexually harassed a state employee, Paula Jones, when he was governor of Arkansas in 1991.

"As we have already noted, in the more than 200-year history of the Republic, only three sitting Presidents have been subjected to suits for their private actions," Justice John Paul Stevens wrote for the court. "If the past is any indicator, it seems unlikely that a deluge of such litigation will ever engulf the Presidency. As for the case at hand, if properly managed by the District Court, it appears to us highly unlikely to occupy any substantial amount of petitioner's time."

The opinion didn't age well. Within eight months, the civil litigation against Clinton hadn't merely occupied a "substantial amount of petitioner's time." It had destroyed his presidency.

Either the justices were naïve, or they simply hadn't been paying attention to the new politics of personal destruction. Contrary to Stevens's reasoning, the past wasn't any indicator, and the "200-year history of the Republic" had been fundamentally altered by the brutal, slashing attacks Gingrich, Starr, and their ilk had popularized.

Clinton's infidelity and sexual predation had been a prominent feature of his image for some time. His 1992 campaign had nearly been derailed by Gennifer Flowers's allegations to a tabloid that she had a twelve-year affair with Clinton. In 1993, two Arkansas troopers had peddled stories of more Clinton sexual misconduct as governor. In 1994, Jones filed her sexual harassment case and eventually received funding and support from conservative interests. But Clinton easily won reelection; the voters didn't seem to care about his appalling behavior.

Then, in 1998, Clinton's foes tried a different tack: they set a perjury trap for him that would turn his attempts to conceal his sexual affairs into a legal liability.

Starr had until then come up empty in his four-year quest to undo Clinton. "Starr's investigators, having reached a dry well in searching for provable financial wrongdoing by the first couple, had now turned their attention to Clinton's attempts to cover up his extracurricular love life," Peter Baker, then of *The Washington Post,* wrote in his book *The Breach.*

On January 8, Starr's luck changed. His office received a tip from Paula Jones's legal team about a Clinton affair with a young woman. Starr soon learned that the person alleging the affair was Linda Tripp, a disaffected holdover in the Clinton administration who had helped Starr's office on various other attempts to probe Clinton. Starr's investigators quickly wired up Tripp so she could record the private confessions of Clinton's love interest, White House intern Monica Lewinsky, whom Tripp had befriended. Starr gave Tripp immunity but, curiously, left her free to talk with Paula Jones's lawyers—which she did.

Tripp told the Jones lawyers all about the Lewinsky affair, the evening before they were to depose Clinton for six hours. They ambushed him with questions about Lewinsky in hopes that he would lie to conceal the affair. The perjury trap had been set—and it worked.

"Have you ever had sexual relations with Monica Lewinsky?" they asked.

"I have never had sexual relations with Monica Lewinsky," Clinton replied. "I've never had an affair with her."

That lie under oath, teed up by Starr, would form the basis of his campaign to get Clinton impeached.

Starr's lawyers, in order to force Lewinsky's cooperation, threatened the twenty-four-year-old with twenty-seven years in prison for falsely denying the affair in an affidavit. They tried to get her to agree to an immunity deal without her lawyer present, and even discouraged her from calling her mother. Starr hauled Lewinsky's mother before a grand jury for two hours. He forced Secret Service agents to violate their professional standards and divulge Clinton's personal secrets.

Among the questions his lawyers asked Lewinsky in a deposition: "And did he bring you to orgasm?"

"Back to the touching of your breasts for a minute, was that then through clothing or actually directly onto your skin?"

"On that occasion, did you perform oral sex on the President?"

"Who unzipped his pants?"

Starr's report to Congress revealed every excruciating, humiliating detail of Clinton's affair. And House Republicans promptly released it to the public. Gingrich, with typical vitriol, called Clinton's behavior the "most systematic, deliberate obstruction of justice, cover up and effort to avoid the truth we have ever seen in American history. . . . I will never again, as long as I am speaker, make a speech without commenting on this topic."

Gingrich's lieutenant, Republican Whip Tom DeLay, took charge of the Republicans' effort to oust Clinton, which DeLay dubbed "The Campaign." The former pest exterminator from Texas, nicknamed "The Hammer," established an impeachment "war room," distributed anti-Clinton talking points to Republican colleagues, and gave multiple talk radio interviews daily to whip up enthusiasm for impeachment. DeLay declared that Clinton had "no shame, no integrity, no dignity," and said that if he "has cheated on his wife, he will cheat on the American people."

When Gingrich, Judiciary Committee chairman Henry Hyde, or Appropriations Committee chairman Bob Livingston and other Republicans wavered on impeachment and suggested censuring Clinton instead, DeLay mobilized pressure from outside conservative groups to force his colleagues to forswear anything short of impeachment. "Silence sends the message that censure is acceptable," DeLay said, calling the censure resolution "a Democratic cop-out." His chief of staff told *The Washington Post:* "Resignation is what's best for the country."

The National Republican Campaign Committee, the campaign entity run by House Republican leaders, ran ads before the

1998 midterm elections showing Clinton wagging his finger and denying the Lewinsky affair. "Should we reward not telling the truth?"

The public was fairly disgusted by what they perceived as the Republican obsession with Clinton's sex life. Though polls showed Americans had a dim view of him personally, more than 60 percent approved of his work as president throughout 1998—rising to 73 percent in the Gallup poll after impeachment. Democrats picked up five House seats in the midterms, the first time this happened in the sixth year of a presidency since 1822—and the only time, it turned out, Republicans were punished by voters for their new politics of dehumanizing opponents.

The politically unpopular impeachment campaign, and the lost seats, led Republicans to oust Gingrich as speaker in a hail of recriminations. Gingrich, telling fellow Republicans he would resign, decried the "hateful" colleagues who criticized him. "I am willing to lead, but I won't allow cannibalism," he said, also advising colleagues that "we need to purge the poisons from the system."

Gingrich probably didn't realize at the time that he had echoed, near verbatim, Jim Wright's "mindless cannibalism" complaint when Gingrich had ousted him as speaker. But the poisons that Gingrich had injected into the political ecosystem would not be purged. They would grow more and more toxic.

Once released, Gingrich's poisons were indiscriminate in their victims. Several Republicans succumbed because their righteousness about Clinton's sex life made their own sex lives, and their hypocrisy, relevant.

Livingston, the Republicans' choice to succeed Gingrich as speaker, resigned before he could assume the office. *Hustler* publisher Larry Flynt, mobilized by the attacks on Clinton's adultery, had said four women had alleged affairs with Livingston, who acknowledged that he had "strayed from my marriage."

The man who got the speakership instead, Denny Hastert, would years later be given a fifteen-month prison sentence related to his attempts to hide his sexual abuse of high school wrestlers when he was their coach.

Congresswoman Helen Chenoweth of Idaho, days after she

ran ads demanding Clinton resign over the Lewinsky affair, was forced to admit to a long-term affair with a married man. News of old extramarital affairs by Hyde and Burton became public. In years to come, an affair with a staffer would force the resignation of Mark Souder of Indiana, Mark Sanford of South Carolina would get national attention for his affair with an Argentine mistress while claiming he was hiking the Appalachian Trail, and John Ensign of Nevada would resign after word got out that his parents paid the family of his ex-mistress $96,000.

And then there was Gingrich. In 1983, he pushed for the House to expel two members for having affairs with House pages, saying "a free country must have honest leaders if it is to remain free," and "people are looking for a guidepost as to how they should live."

But his righteousness was selective. "The important thing you have to understand about Newt Gingrich is that he is amoral," L. H. Carter, one of Gingrich's closest friends and advisers before an estrangement, told *The Nation*'s David Osborne back in 1984. "There isn't any right or wrong, there isn't any conservative or liberal. There's only what will work best for Newt Gingrich."

Gingrich had multiple affairs before divorcing his first wife, Jackie, in 1980. He went to her hospital room when she was recovering from cancer surgery and pulled out a legal pad to discuss divorce details, Jackie has alleged. He then married Marianne in 1981—and cheated on her, too. During the impeachment proceedings against Clinton, the fifty-five-year-old Gingrich was carrying on an affair with Callista Bisek, a House staffer twenty-three years his junior.

Marianne Gingrich alleged that her husband, in May 1999, told her about his affair with Bisek and presented Marianne with the choice of having an open marriage or a divorce. Days later, the former speaker gave a family values talk in Pennsylvania called "The Demise of American Culture." In it, he spoke of decency and civility, denounced the "secular assault on the core values of this country," and called for "traditional values" in Hollywood.

He divorced Marianne later that year—and Callista Bisek became Callista Gingrich the next year. "How could he ask me for a divorce on Monday and within 48 hours give a speech on family values and talk about how people treat people?" Marianne Gingrich later said in an interview with *The Washington Post*.

Once a private citizen, and (briefly) as a presidential candidate, Gingrich would go on slashing and trashing, with out-of-control language, for decades:

The Democrats' "secular-socialist machine represents as great a threat to America as Nazi Germany or the Soviet Union once did."

"There is a gay and secular fascism in this country that wants to impose its will on the rest of us" and is "prepared to use violence."

Barack Obama's agenda "would mean the end of America as it has been for the last 400 years."

"The destructive, vicious, negative nature of much of the news media makes it harder to govern this country, harder to attract decent people to run for public office."

Ah, so it was the media that made the country ungovernable with its "destructive, vicious, negative nature"? Self-awareness is not among Gingrich's attributes.

During the 1990s, Republican pollster Frank Luntz advised Gingrich on his use of language, and he has been credited with the "speak like Newt" memo GOPAC put out in 1990 ("traitors," "sick," "corrupt"). But during Trump's 2016 campaign, in which Trump embraced the slashing rhetoric Gingrich pioneered, Luntz disavowed authorship of the memo that started it all. "It's the most destructive political memo written in modern politics," Luntz told *Mother Jones*'s David Corn. "All it did was teach hate and division. . . . It's a precursor of what's going on today." After suffering a stroke in 2020, Luntz said that he no longer considered himself a Republican.

But it's too late for regrets. The whole Republican Party now speaks like Newt.

CHAPTER 3

A Dysfunctional Family

The Sperling Breakfast had been a Washington institution for three decades. Once a week or so, Godfrey Sperling, an octogenarian correspondent for *The Christian Science Monitor,* assembled a dozen éminences grises of political journalism in a gilded meeting room at the Sheraton Carlton hotel, a Beaux Arts beauty at 16th and K Streets Northwest. Over plates of scrambled eggs, sausages, bacon, potatoes, and roasted tomatoes, the journalists sat around a massive oval table and pushed their microcassette recorders toward the center of the table, where Sperling sat beside the day's newsmaker—a cabinet member, legislator, White House official, or the like—who had agreed to an hour-long discussion, informal but on the record. There were no TV cameras: just a lot of cholesterol and old men.

On November 15, 1995, the day's newsmaker was Speaker Newt Gingrich, always a big draw but particularly on this day. The federal government had shut down the day before. Some 800,000 federal workers were furloughed. The national parks and Smithsonian museums closed their gates. The government stopped processing applications for Social Security and other benefits. The American public was angry.

Maybe it was the clubby atmosphere of the Sperling Breakfast. Maybe Gingrich thought he was among friends. Whatever the cause, he decided to confide in the reporters that he was the one to blame for the shutdown. What's more, he said, he forced the shutdown because he was angry that President Bill Clinton ignored him while the two flew aboard Air Force One to and from the funeral for slain Israeli prime minister Yitzhak Rabin—and that Gingrich was then asked to deplane using the rear stairs.

"This is petty. I'm going to say up front it's petty, but I think it's human," Gingrich began. "When you land at Andrews [Air Force Base] and you've been on the plane for 25 hours and nobody has talked to you and they ask you to get off by the back ramp," he continued, "you just wonder, where is their sense of manners? Where is their sense of courtesy? Was it just a sign of utter incompetence or lack of consideration, or was it a deliberate strategy of insult?"

The speaker continued to describe his narcissistic injury. He and Senate Republican Leader Bob Dole "got on that airplane expecting to spend several hours talking about the budget and how do we avoid the shutdown," Gingrich said. "Every president we had ever flown with had us up front. Every president we had ever flown with had talked to us at length."

Gingrich suggested the snub was a major, once-in-a-century insult, such as when Republican presidential candidate Charles Evans Hughes failed to pay a courtesy call on the California governor in 1916, likely costing Hughes the presidency. "The President walked by twice and thanked us while standing there for being on the trip," Gingrich whined. Chief of staff Leon "Panetta came back at four o'clock in the morning as the plane was approaching Andrews and said maybe we can work something out. That was it. The conversation with Panetta was three minutes out of a 25-hour trip."

Then there was the worst part of the epic complaint. Gingrich said he was so insulted that it caused him to add two poison-pill provisions to a bill to keep the government open—thereby leaving Clinton with little choice but to veto it. "I think, by the way, that is part of why you ended up with us sending down a tougher continuing resolution," he said.

Gingrich shut the government down because he perceived a personal snub? Gingrich himself would later note that his press secretary, Tony Blankley, turned "positively white with horror" upon hearing his boss's complaint at the breakfast.

The next morning, the cover of the *New York Daily News*

captured the absurdity. "CRY BABY," proclaimed the banner, accompanied by a full-page cartoon of Gingrich as a rotund toddler, in diapers, crying, clutching a bottle, and stomping his foot. "Newt's Tantrum," the headline said. "He closed down the government because Clinton made him sit at back of plane."

Lars-Erik Nelson's article ran inside:

> Here was Newt Gingrich, leader of the Republican Revolution and defender of civilization on this planet, forced to sit for 25 hours in the back of Air Force One, waiting for President Clinton to stop by and negotiate a budget deal. But Clinton never came back. So Gingrich, in his rage, drafted two resolutions that forced Clinton to bring the federal government to a grinding halt. . . . Clinton, who seemed to be genuinely grieving over Rabin's death, stayed up front in a cabin with former Presidents Jimmy Carter and George Bush on both the outward-bound and return trips. Then, when the plane landed at Andrews Air Force base outside Washington, Gingrich and Senate Majority Leader Bob Dole were asked to deplane by— gasp!—the rear door.

Rubbing it in, the White House released a photo showing Clinton, Dole, and Gingrich chatting aboard Air Force One.

The Republicans, after Gingrich's PR debacle, had no choice but to fold. Polls had turned decisively against them. Dole took over negotiations and, within three days, had reached a deal to reopen the government for thirty days while leaders held more talks. Gingrich told his House colleagues that he was benching himself. He had "thrown one too many interceptions," he said.

The shutdown disaster captures the essence of Gingrich's brief and woeful tenure as speaker. There was nobody better at attacking, destroying, and undermining those in power. But he had no skills in building coalitions, legislating, and governing. In truth, even a brilliant manager would have had difficulty leading the fractious House that Newt built. The slash-and-burn politics he brought to the Capitol made it ungovernable, and the zealots he brought into the Republican Party had no wish to govern. It has been that way ever since.

IN ST. PAUL'S CATHEDRAL IN London, the tomb of the great architect Christopher Wren bears a Latin inscription: *Si Monumentum Requiris, Circumspice.* If you seek his monument, look around you. Now it can be said similarly of Newt Gingrich. Everywhere we look today in the American political scene we see dysfunction. The architect of our dysfunction was Gingrich. Let's measure the wreckage by the numbers.

From 1973 to 1992, each two-year Congress passed an average of 703 bills that were enacted into law. Then Clinton was elected, and Gingrich, the de facto head of the opposition, began an attempt to thwart the president at every turn. The number of laws enacted during the 1993–94 Congress plunged to 473. The 1995–96 Congress, Gingrich's first as speaker, dropped further, to 337 (and only 88 during the first year, the fewest in six decades). The 1997–98 Congress, Gingrich's last: 404 laws. The "Do-Nothing Congress" of 1947–48, by contrast, passed 908 laws.

Congress's ability to function never returned. Over the decade ending in 2020, each two-year Congress has seen an average of just 339 laws enacted—less than half the productivity that prevailed before Gingrich. Since the modern budgeting practice was created in 1974, Congress had managed to pass a budget every year—until Gingrich. In 1998, Republicans couldn't agree on a budget, a new failure of government that would be repeated ten times in the years that followed.

Other measures, compiled by Tom Mann of the Brookings Institution and Norm Ornstein of the American Enterprise Institute, tell the rest of the story. In 1994, before Gingrich's takeover, all thirteen of the fiscal year 1995 appropriations bills had been enacted by the start of the new fiscal year. The next year, Gingrich's first as speaker, not a single appropriations bill had been enacted before fiscal year 1996. Instead, thirteen temporary "continuing resolutions" had been enacted—essentially putting government spending on autopilot. This was the beginning of government by continuing resolution, or CR. There were six in 1999, seven in 2000, twenty-one in 2001, eight in 2002.

In the House, the work of committees, the heart of the legislative process for centuries, became almost meaningless under Gingrich. In the late 1970s, the House held more than 7,000 committee and subcommittee meetings in each two-year Congress. There continued to be more than 5,000 in each Congress through 1992. In Gingrich's first two years, the number of committee and subcommittee meetings plunged to 3,796—and has never again risen above 4,000 since. In the 2017–18 Congress, there were all of 1,841 meetings—a quarter of the historic standard.

Or, consider the frequency of party-line votes. The numbers fluctuated, but from 1953 into the early 1990s, such votes averaged 40 to 50 percent of the total. In Gingrich's first year as speaker, party-unity votes soared to 73.2 percent, the highest since record-keeping started in 1953. The 1995 high has since been eclipsed by 2011 (75.8 percent), 2015 (75.1), and 2016 (73.4). Gingrich made party-line votes standard.

One more measure: presidential legislative victories. Richard Nixon's position prevailed 72.7 percent of the time in the (Democratic-controlled) House. Gerald Ford won 51.0 percent, Ronald Reagan 46.5, and George H. W. Bush 40.6 percent, all under Democratic Houses. But once Republicans took over the House in the 1994 elections, Bill Clinton's win percentage dropped from 87.2 percent in his first two years to 26.3 percent in 1995— the lowest level, again, since recordkeeping began in 1953. Two decades later, Barack Obama was dealt a new record for presidential defeats by the GOP-controlled House. He prevailed just 13.0 percent of the time in 2016.

None of this happened by accident. When Gingrich took over, he encouraged the seventy-four Republican freshmen not to move their families to Washington. He imposed what was essentially a Tuesday-to-Thursday workweek for the House. In the 1960s, 1970s, and 1980s, a typical Congress spent about 300 days in session. In Gingrich's second and final Congress, 1997–98, days in session dropped to 252, the fewest since 1958. The shortened workweek, and more lawmakers commuting home to families, loosened the glue that had held lawmakers together before: the dinners with spouses and the card games that built across-the-aisle friendships and alliances.

Gingrich also decimated congressional staff, which provided

legislative expertise. The overall level of House staff was 10,873 in 1993. In Gingrich's first term as speaker, that dropped to 9,913— and kept shrinking, to 8,501 in 2012. Congressional support staff at the General Accounting Office, Congressional Budget Office, and Congressional Research Service, likewise, fell from 6,166 in 1993 to 4,458 at the end of Gingrich's speakership—and it, too, continued falling, to 4,075 in 2012. The practical effect of this loss of expertise meant that industry lobbyists wound up writing legislation.

Gingrich upended the seniority system on committees, putting loyalists in chairmanships instead and choosing committee members himself. He made Republican members of the Appropriations Committee sign loyalty pledges. He created a "Speaker's Advisory Group," stocked with loyalists, that circumvented the committees and took charge of shaping legislation.

Even before taking the speaker's gavel, Gingrich maintained lockstep unity in opposition to Clinton's economic plan in 1993 (it passed by two votes). Republicans doomed Hillary Clinton's attempt at health care legislation ("Hillarycare"), in part by alleging the fiction that, under her proposal, doctors could go to jail if they received funds from patients outside a government plan. In this, they got assists from the Christian Coalition and from the health care industry, which flooded the airwaves with "Harry and Louise" ads showing a couple lamenting government takeover of health care ("they choose, we lose"). To deny Clinton any victories before the 1994 election, Gingrich, Rush Limbaugh, and the Christian Coalition successfully persuaded Republicans even to block bills that had overwhelming bipartisan support, including a ban on gifts from lobbyists and tougher financial disclosure requirements for lobbyists.

This had been Gingrich's modus operandi from his early days in Congress. In 1982 he had tried to get conservatives to shut down the government by blocking appropriations bills, saying "we want to force a crisis." In 1985, he led a walkout on the House floor over objections to Democrats seating a lawmaker from Indiana whose election was disputed (Gingrich compared the Democrats' action to the Holocaust). After some time, Gingrich's authorized biographer Craig Shirley wrote, Republicans "fully embraced Gingrich's idea of guerilla warfare, introducing resolutions, forcing paper ballots rather than electronic voting, denouncing the Democrats from the well in the most acerbic terms allowed." Gingrich's "Conservative Opportunity Society" met every Wednesday to plot mayhem. As historian Julian Zelizer recounted, Republican Leader Bob Michel was wary of Gingrich's "parliamentary pyrotechnics," but Gingrich told Michel: "If you teach them how to be aggressive and confrontational, you will increase their abilities to fight Democrats on the floor."

TOWARD THE END OF his first year as speaker (and a couple of weeks before he would complain about his treatment aboard Air Force One) Gingrich took the unusual step of appearing as a witness before the House Oversight Committee. His opening statement rambled on for twenty-five minutes. His topic: indigestion.

"Three antacids, Pepcid AC, Tagamet and Zantac, spend $300 million a year" on advertising, he said. "So on the concept of what you should put in your stomach if you need an antacid, we spend $300 million a year."

By contrast, he continued, "in 1992 a major political party spent $110 million. That is, the Democrats or the Republicans nationally, in the general election of '92, spent one-third what we spend on antacid." And spending on congressional elections was $600 million—"the equivalent of two antacid campaigns," the dyspeptic speaker declaimed. "And yet we're told politics is too expensive."

The post-Watergate campaign finance reforms had already broken down by then, as parties exploited a loophole allowing them to raise "soft money" from wealthy donors without limit. Yet Gingrich argued that the solution was not to limit spending by campaigns or parties or to ban political action committees, but to spend *more* on campaigns. "One of the greatest myths in modern politics is that campaigns are too expensive," he testified. "The political process, in fact, is not overfunded, but underfunded."

With Republican leaders opposing restrictions (even those proposed by Republican reformers such as Chris Shays in the House and John McCain in the Senate), the floodgates opened in the late 1990s, and the political system was bathed in unlimited funds.

In the 1992 presidential cycle, Republicans raised $398 million through their national party committees, of which $50 million was largely unrestricted soft money. In the 1996 cycle, they raised $752 million, of which $221 million was soft money. In 2000, they raised $892 million, of which $364 million was soft money. Democrats, though less well funded, increased fundraising by similar proportions.

Gingrich also sought to use taxpayer money to his party's advantage. In 1996, Gingrich issued a memo to the chairmen of House Appropriations subcommittees, telling them to draft spending bills based on this consideration: "Are there any Republican members who could be severely hurt by the bill or need a specific district item in the bill?" Congressional "earmarks" for members' pet projects nearly doubled under Gingrich, from $7.8 billion in 1994 to $14.5 billion in 1997.

The Republican National Committee chairman, Haley Barbour, used the Republican takeover of the House to make a new push to raise soft money. Such contributions to Republicans doubled in the first six months of 1995. At the same time, Tom DeLay, the Republican whip, formed, with conservative activist Grover Norquist, the "K Street Project" to remake the lobbying industry to Republicans' benefit.

Norquist kept track on a public website of the partisan leaning of trade association lobbyists so that industry groups were pressured to hire Republicans. As journalist Matthew Continetti recounted in his book *The K Street Gang,* DeLay made a list of political contributions from the four hundred largest corporate PACs and then called in the directors of the PACs to discuss their contributions to both parties. Another House GOP leader, Bill Paxon, kept up pressure on individual lobbyists to contribute to Republicans.

Lobbyists who hired, or funded, Democrats got the cold shoulder. Friendly lobbyists were invited into DeLay's office to write a major antiregulatory bill. As *The Washington Post*'s Michael Weisskopf and David Maraniss wrote at the time: "As the measure progressed, the roles of legislator and lobbyist blurred. DeLay and his assistants guided industry supporters in an ad hoc group whose name, Project Relief, sounded more like a Third World humanitarian aid effort than a corporate alliance with a half-million-dollar communications budget. On key amendments, the coalition provided the draftsman. And once the bill and the debate moved to the House floor, lobbyists hovered nearby, tapping out talking points on a laptop for delivery to Republican floor leaders." The bill that passed the House called for a thirteen-month moratorium on regulations. And while they were shaping the bill, the various corporate interests were estimated to have contributed some $30 million to DeLay's "Project Relief."

This became a prototype for the pay-to-play system that has allowed wealthy donors and corporate interests to dominate the political system for the last quarter century. Gingrich was brazen about his intentions. On the eve of the Republican victory in 1994, he sent a memo to major contributors to his political action committee, GOPAC: "Will you help me draft the Republican legislative agenda for the 104th Congress?"

HE HAD RAISED A new generation of Republican lawmakers to believe that compromise was a crime. He had embittered Democrats with years of caustic attacks on their integrity and their patriotism. And he had effectively turned over legislating to corporate representatives. Is it any wonder Gingrich couldn't run the place?

House Republicans began with a flurry of activity, passing all but one of the ten provisions in the "Contract with America." The shift of attention to Congress led a plaintive Bill Clinton to protest in April that "the president is relevant." But most of the "Contract" provisions died in the Senate.

Next, Gingrich turned his attention to forcing major cuts in federal spending. From the beginning, he made clear that he sought a fight on the federal budget for the new fiscal year beginning October 1, 1995. "The budget fight for me," he said in August, "is the equivalent of Gettysburg in the Civil War."

What he didn't know was he was about to reenact the role of General George Pickett.

Republicans had vowed to eliminate some three hundred federal programs and to abolish the Departments of Education, Energy, and Commerce. Republicans demanded that Clinton agree to a seven-year plan to create a balanced budget, to cut Medicare by $270 billion and overall spending by $1.2 trillion, and to provide a tax cut. Clinton, relying on rosier economic forecasts, countered with a $128 billion cut to Medicare and a $750 billion overall cut.

Then, Gingrich found himself stuck. His no-compromise caucus wouldn't accept anything but total capitulation from Clinton. The Republican caucus insisted on sending Majority Leader Dick Armey (who has been credited with the aphorism "bipartisanship is another name for date rape") to chaperone Gingrich to negotiations so he didn't give too much away. And Clinton, rather than capitulate, ran television ads accusing the Republicans of trying to take health care away from old people. In phone conversations, Gingrich confided to Clinton that he was feeling pressure from his caucus not to negotiate a deal.

The talks got more tense as the new fiscal year began and funds began drying up. Gingrich complained bitterly to Clinton about the Medicare ads. "You have a chickenshit operation here, Mr. President," Gingrich said, according to Bob Woodward's account in his 1996 book, *The Choice*. "You've been calling me an extremist," he shouted at Gore.

Retorted Gore: "At least we didn't accuse you of drowning those little children in South Carolina"—a reference to Gingrich blaming Democrats for the mother who killed her two kids.

Years later, Dick Gephardt, who as House Democratic leader participated in the White House talks, described the talks to journalist Major Garrett: "Clinton was disagreeing with Newt about what to do. Newt looked at him and said, 'You know, the problem here is you've got a gun to my head. It's called the veto. But what you don't understand is that I've got a gun to your head and I'm going to use it. I'm going to shut the government down.'"

Gingrich did as promised. Clinton asked for a "clean" temporary spending bill while negotiations continued; instead, Gingrich sent one that increased Medicare premiums. The government shut down, and remained shut until Gingrich's "cry baby" moment forced Republicans to reopen government for thirty days—only to have another shutdown when that expired.

"Gingrich became a captive of his own rhetoric and his own

revolution," the historian Steven M. Gillon wrote in his 2008 book, *The Pact.* "He understood the difference between public posturing and private negotiating, but most of his young followers did not. His rhetoric limited his negotiating room and prevented him from making a deal with the president."

The zealots Gingrich brought to Washington, who actually believed Gingrich's wild, callous pronouncements, wouldn't be governed. "Gingrich had proven that he could lead a rebellion," Gillon wrote, "but did he possess the skill and political dexterity to manage a coalition?" The answer was obvious. During the shutdown talks, Dole would often ask Gingrich, "What's our endgame?" Gingrich had none.

As shutdown talks resumed in December, Gingrich could find no way to defuse the crisis he created. Even as polls showed Republicans losing the standoff, Armey wrote to House Republicans that "we are in the middle of one of the defining battles of our nation's history." Appropriations Committee chairman Bob Livingston, on the House floor, proclaimed: "We will never, never, never give in. . . . We will stay here till Doomsday." Gingrich, though privately arguing for Republicans to compromise, publicly declared that "we are prepared to stay the course for as long as it takes."

Two weeks into the second shutdown, Gingrich and Armey were in Dole's office, speaking by phone with Clinton. A petty but irate Armey was complaining bitterly to Clinton about an unflattering photo of him released by the White House when, according to an account Armey later told to Garrett, Gingrich said, "Give me the damn phone."

Then, shouting at the president of the United States, the speaker announced: "You are a goddamn lying son of a bitch!"

Dole told Gingrich he had never heard a lawmaker speak that way to a president. Gingrich replied: "We've never had a president of the United States like this."

Dole, like Michel, was a World War II veteran. He knew political opponents weren't his enemies—and he had no use for Gingrich's scorched-earth tactics. He went to the Senate floor the next day and announced: "We need to end this impasse. It's gotten to the point where it's a little ridiculous as far as this senator is concerned." He said the Senate would pass "whatever it takes" to end the shutdown.

The government soon reopened. Dole had realized that the shutdown had become "a test of manhood" for House Republicans, he said later in his account to Garrett for his 2005 book, *The Enduring Revolution.* "It was Armey and Newt who were holding the fort and were going to shut down the government for as long as it took. I kept saying, 'There's got to be some other way we can address this. You just don't cut people off at the knees.' . . . It demonstrated to me that they didn't know anything about politics when it came to people. That hurt us a lot."

THE TWENTY-ONE-DAY December-through-January shutdown was, at the time, the longest in U.S. history (shutdowns didn't happen until the 1980s, and before 1996 the longest had been three days). But the record wouldn't stand. If there was an event that presaged the breakdown of self-governance in America, the shutdowns of 1995–96 were it.

The old guard of the Republican Party made known its disdain for the saboteurs. Senator Alan Simpson of Wyoming, who denounced the "bug-eyed zealots" of the class of 1994, announced his retirement. At the same time Dole decided to abandon Gingrich and reopen the government, he also backed away from supporting an unrealistic constitutional amendment banning abortion. "I think it's time for adult leadership," he declared—and was branded a defector.

Dole, during his doomed challenge to Clinton in the 1996 presidential election, quit the Senate. It was just as well: the saboteurs were now in charge.

Gingrich, chastened by his shutdown debacle, tried to make deals with Clinton, reaching a welfare reform deal in 1996 and a sweeping Balanced Budget Act in 1997, passed by a coalition of Democrats and Republican moderates. That, and a booming economy, put the federal budget into surplus for four years. "I made a very conscious decision that it was better for America and better for the Republican Party to prove that we could govern,"

Gingrich told *The Washington Post* after the 1997 budget deal. "We decided that four years of incremental achievement in our direction are superior to four years of obstruction while we scream about values."

But the success was short-lived. Gingrich could not control his own caucus. The hardliners were angry over the shutdown surrender, but also because they made no progress shutting down cabinet agencies, slashing entitlement programs, and amending the Constitution to ban flag burning and to impose term limits, balanced budgets, and school prayer. Some demanded Gingrich step down.

Steve Chabot of Ohio said Gingrich was "fumbling the ball badly." Mark Neumann of Wisconsin called Gingrich's deal making "an exercise in futility." Mark Souder of Indiana accused Gingrich of "deceit." Steve Largent of Oklahoma said Gingrich "cave[d] in." Paul Weyrich, an influential conservative activist, said Gingrich "turned" against the Class of '94. The hardliners removed some of Gingrich's powers and restored authority to the committees. Against Gingrich's wishes, they insisted on adding partisan provisions to an emergency disaster-relief bill—and were forced to surrender again to Clinton.

In July, DeLay secretly plotted with about fifteen Republican hardliners—most from the Class of '94—to attempt a coup against Gingrich. It might have worked, but Armey, upon learning that he was not chosen to replace Gingrich as speaker, tipped off Gingrich—and the coup plot dissolved in recriminations. Said Mark Foley of Florida: "It's like a circular firing squad." Peter King of New York called Gingrich "roadkill on the highway of American politics" and said his caucus was "really becoming the gang that just couldn't shoot straight."

Even Gingrich described his House Republicans as a "dysfunctional family" and admitted a "sense of failure on my part." Things only worsened after the coup attempt. In 1998, Gingrich let his hardliners draft a budget for fiscal year 1999 with new spending cuts and tax cuts, but Senate Republicans rejected it. The failure was the beginning of a new era, still with us, in which government funding became a patchwork of omnibus spending packages and continuing resolutions.

Gingrich was finally done in by Clinton's impeachment and

the Republicans' loss in the 1998 midterm elections. Livingston, once a Gingrich loyalist, said he would run against Gingrich for speaker. "Revolutionizing takes some talents, many talents," Livingston said. "Day-to-day governing takes others." Gingrich surrendered. According to Peter Baker's 2000 account, Gingrich told his chief of staff: "I'm just not going to be able to govern this place with the situation the way it is."

It was a belated realization. Gingrich was never going to be able to govern the place. Nobody could. He had built a Republican majority full of people whose goal was to throw sand in the gears of government, to "reduce it to the size where I can drag it into the bathroom and drown it in the bathtub," as Gingrich ally Norquist put it.

Why did Gingrich ever think he could persuade the saboteurs to do the hard work of governing? Why did he think these attack dogs wouldn't bite him?

In 1999, for a *New York Times Magazine* piece, I spoke to the disillusioned revolutionaries who brought Gingrich to power in 1994. Tom Coburn of Oklahoma, who participated in the coup attempt, lamented that some had "become addicted to the morphine of power" and "the intensity for change is not there anymore." Coburn, known as "Dr. No," won election to the Senate in 2004, part of a group of former House members who taught the Senate the uncompromising ways they learned in Gingrich's House.

Others became disenchanted with the bomb throwing. "I'm a chastened revolutionary," Joe Scarborough of Florida, another anti-Gingrich coup plotter, told me. "The revolution that got us here is over. Now it's time for us to decide whether we want to govern effectively or move into the minority, and I choose to govern."

Governing didn't last. Scarborough quit Congress two years later and became a successful TV host on MSNBC. He later became a strident critic of the Republican Party under Donald Trump.

But the Class of '94 had started it; Trump was the consequence of the Republican Revolution. Gingrich's revolutionaries would be succeeded by ever more zealous waves—the Tea Party Republicans, the MAGA Republicans—with ever more hostility to the government they were supposed to be running. The destruction began with Newt.

CHAPTER 4

Black Helicopters

Watergate convict G. Gordon Liddy, who parlayed his infamy into a gig as a national talk radio host, was not a fan of the U.S. Bureau of Alcohol, Tobacco and Firearms, the agency that botched the raid on the Branch Davidian cult's compound in Waco, Texas. Seventy-six people, including children, died in the bungled operation on April 19, 1993.

So Liddy offered his listeners a thoughtful plan for dealing with ATF agents: "Kill the sons of bitches." Specifically: "If the Bureau of Alcohol, Tobacco and Firearms comes to disarm you and they are bearing arms, resist them with arms. Go for a head shot; they're going to be wearing bulletproof vests," he said on the air on August 26, 1994. He elaborated: "You don't aim at that ATF patch because he's got a bullet-proof vest underneath. You need a big target. . . . Kill the sons of bitches."

The Nixon dirty tricks specialist, who took rifle practice on targets he named "Bill" and "Hillary," later said he had given his listeners bad advice when he told them how to kill an ATF agent. "You shoot twice to the body, center of mass, and if that does not work, then shoot to the groin area," he revised. "They cannot move their hips fast enough and you'll probably get a femoral artery."

Others on conservative talk radio offered similar calls to violence. In Colorado Springs, Chuck Baker warned "patriots" to resist Bill Clinton's alleged plan to confiscate guns and surrender to a "New World Order" global government. He called for an "armed revolution" and a "cleansing" of the government, and he said armed militias were on "our side" against the U.S. government. One of Baker's listeners, Francisco Duran, tried to kill Clinton by firing more than two dozen bullets at the White House.

And there was Bob Mohan on air in Phoenix, who said gun control advocate Sarah Brady, wife of James Brady, the Reagan aide severely wounded in the 1981 assassination attempt on Reagan, "ought to be put down. A humane shot at a veterinarian's would be an easy way to do it."

This is the sort of thing Americans were hearing from conservative talk radio, and even from Republican elected officials, in the spring of 1995.

Newt Gingrich, the new House speaker, had for years been riling the right with apocalyptic warnings. Democrats supported "a culture of violence which is destructive of this civilization," he announced. Under Democratic policies "we would truly have tyranny everywhere, and we in America could experience the joys of Soviet-style brutality and murdering of women and children." Bill Clinton was the "enemy of normal Americans," and he "despises the values of the American people." Democrats, who would "stop at nothing," encouraged incest and child murder, caused an "acceptance of brutality" and promoted "multicultural nihilistic hedonism" in their "bureaucratic tyranny of America."

A Gingrich ally, Robert "B-1 Bob" Dornan, had declared on the House floor that Clinton gave "aid and comfort to the enemy." In the Senate, Jesse Helms warned against presidential travel to his home state of North Carolina: "Mr. Clinton better watch out if he comes down here. He'd better have a bodyguard."

Newly elected representative Helen Chenoweth issued a press release on February 15, 1995, accusing the federal government of violating the Idaho constitution by sending "armed agency officials and helicopters" to enforce wildlife regulations. She warned the U.S. Fish and Wildlife Service that if such activity didn't stop, "I will be your worst nightmare for at least the next two years." In fact, Fish and Wildlife didn't even have helicopters; Chenoweth was echoing the militia groups' conspiracy theory in which "black helicopters" were bringing the New World Order to power. Chenoweth had been featured in a video sold by the Militia of

Montana in which she warned that "we are facing an unlawful government."

Another lawmaker, Steve Stockman of Texas, wrote to Attorney General Janet Reno in March 1995, saying that "reliable sources" told him that the government was about to launch "a paramilitary style attack against Americans who pose no risk to others," and he was concerned that it could be "an ill-considered, poorly planned, but bloody fiasco like Waco." Four other members of Congress and three senators also wrote to Reno seeking answers to militias' claims that law enforcement agencies were undergoing training and "militarization" in apparent preparation for an attack on citizens.

And the king of conservative talk radio told his millions of listeners that their rights were under "attack" and that bloodshed was imminent. "The second violent American revolution is just about—I got my fingers about a fourth of an inch apart—is just about that far away," Rush Limbaugh warned on air on February 22. "Because these people are sick and tired of a bunch of bureaucrats in Washington driving into town and telling them what they can and can't do."

This was the political atmosphere in America on April 19, 1995. On that day, the second anniversary of the Waco tragedy, Timothy McVeigh, a violent white nationalist outraged by the ATF raid in Waco, pulled a Ryder rental truck up to the Alfred P. Murrah Federal Building in Oklahoma City. Inside the building was, among other things, a field office of the ATF. Inside the truck were nearly five thousand pounds of explosives, which detonated, killing 168 people, including children as young as four months old who were in a daycare center in the building.

Later, before he was executed for the murders, McVeigh explained his purpose was "to put a check on government abuse of power," to stop a "federal juggernaut running amok." He was particularly angered by the federal assault weapons ban, a favorite target of Republican lawmakers and conservative talk show hosts, and he had believed the militia-generated conspiracy, legitimized by Stockman and other Republican members of Congress, that there were planned "Waco-style raids scheduled for spring 1995, to confiscate firearms."

The logic had clear echoes of the apocalyptic pronouncements coming out of Gingrich's mouth; McVeigh's "abuse of power" formulation had been one of the attack phrases Gingrich specifically recommended Republicans use.

Three days after the bombing, Gingrich paid an early morning visit to the destroyed Murrah building, after which a reporter asked him if his attacks on government and bureaucrats may have "helped create a climate" for the bombing. Gingrich shot back: "That's grotesque! I think that's grotesque and offensive."

Two weeks later, Gingrich had a whole hour with Tim Russert on *Meet the Press* to expand on his thoughts about the bombing to a nationwide audience. Incredibly, he defended the armed, antigovernment militia groups. He pledged to hold fresh hearings to probe the Waco raid, which he said was "clearly mishandled." And he vowed to take a new stab at repealing the assault weapons ban.

He was, in effect, reading the militias' talking points.

"Well, I think that people are allowed in a free country to get together for a lot of reasons, and I don't think you should condemn any group as a group," he said when Russert asked about the antigovernment militias. "There is, across the West, a genuine sense of fear of the federal government. And this is not an extremist position in much of the West." His lecture in defense of violent extremism went on at length. "I do think we have to understand that there is in rural America a genuine—and particularly in the West—a genuine fear of the federal government and of Washington, D.C., as a place that doesn't understand their way of life and doesn't understand their values."

Here was the third-highest figure in the U.S. government, given a chance to dispel the paranoia and rage that had just resulted in the largest domestic terrorist attack on American soil. Instead, he validated the paranoia. Thus began a new era in which leaders of the Republican Party would court the support of violent white nationalists.

ANTIGOVERNMENT VIOLENCE HAS BEEN part of the United States since 1794, when western Pennsylvania settlers opposed to an excise tax on whiskey destroyed the home of a tax inspector.

And white supremacy has stained America since the first slave ship arrived in 1619. There have been countless incarnations over the years: the Ku Klux Klan, the Posse Comitatus, the Silver Shirt Legion, the Christian Front, the Minutemen, the Christian Patriot-Defense League, the White Patriot Party, the Aryan Nations.

There was always some overlap between the racial hate groups and the antigovernment groups, but they began to converge in the 1980s. As the University of Chicago historian Kathleen Belew notes, the white power movement became "openly anti-state for the first time in the 20th century." They were disillusioned that Ronald Reagan, who came to office saying "government is not the solution to our problems; government is the problem," did not deliver on his antigovernment rhetoric.

The modern militia movement came together in the early 1990s in reaction to several events that angered the white supremacists and antigovernment extremists: the spring 1992 Los Angeles race riots following the acquittal of police officers in the Rodney King beating; the August 1992 deadly standoff in Ruby Ridge, Idaho, between government agents and armed white separatist Randy Weaver; the election of Clinton, the first Democratic president in twelve years; the 1993 ratification of the North American Free Trade Agreement; the 1993 siege of the heavily armed Branch Davidians in Waco; and the passage of a federal assault weapons ban in 1994.

The militias and related extremists were loosely united by their fear of their guns being confiscated by the government, their belief in conspiracy theories such as the United Nations–led New World Order taking away American sovereignty, and their fear that white American men were losing their ground. The first two, of course, were pure paranoia, essentially just an update of the John Birch Society's Cold War conspiracy theories in which communists were the ones threatening American sovereignty. But the last part had an element of truth: white dominance of the United States was fading.

The United States hadn't been a true democracy until the passage of the Civil Rights Act of 1964 and the Voting Rights Act of 1965. Reaction to Black voting rights gradually drove white southerners, who once pulled the lever for segregationist Democrats, to the Republican Party. The parties, over thirty years, realigned along racial lines. Also in 1965, the Immigration and Nationality Act ended immigration preferences for Western Europe and put all would-be immigrants on equal footing. The proportion of foreign-born Americans gradually tripled, as immigrants arrived from Asia, Africa, and Central America. By the early 1990s, demographers spoke of the United States becoming a majority-minority nation in the middle of the twenty-first century.

The rising racial resentment of a multicultural America, combined with the paranoia about a world government disarming U.S. citizens, fueled the 1990s "Patriot" movement of paramilitaries full of "sovereign citizens." As the Southern Poverty Law Center, the Anti-Defamation League, and other monitors of extremist groups have documented, these groups organized at gun shows and through shortwave radio, newsletters, and the nascent internet. They adopted names such as the Michigan Militia and the Montana Freemen. And they prepared to fight the government.

The militia movement had much in common with its white power, conspiracy-minded forerunners. But it had an advantage over its predecessors: its themes were validated and parroted by some of the most senior Republican officials in the country.

THE REPUBLICAN ATTEMPT TO win over whites hostile to civil rights had been under way since Richard Nixon's Southern Strategy. Ronald Reagan took it up a notch with his derision of the "welfare queen." George H. W. Bush's campaign manager, Lee Atwater, went yet further with his 1988 vow to "make Willie Horton" into the "running mate" of Democratic presidential nominee Mike Dukakis. That was followed by a pro-Bush independent ad tying Dukakis to Horton, a Black murderer who went on a rape-and-stabbing spree while on a prison furlough during Dukakis's time as Massachusetts governor. Later came a Jesse Helms ad against his Black opponent in the North Carolina Senate race showing white hands crumpling up a rejection letter and the narration: "You needed that job, and you were the best qualified, but they had to give it to a minority, because of a racial quota."

Gingrich was well versed in this tradition. In his successful run for Congress in 1978, his campaign distributed a flyer showing a photo of his opponent, Virginia Shapard, alongside the best-known Black politician in Georgia, state senator and civil rights activist Julian Bond. "If you like welfare cheaters, you'll love Virginia Shapard," it said. "In 1976, Virginia Shapard voted to table a bill to cut down on welfare cheaters. People like Mrs. Shapard, who was a welfare worker for five years, and Julian Bond fought together to kill the bill."

Shapard, a white Democrat, responded: "You understand the racial slur implications embodied in a flyer like this. It's just going out in the white community. That sort of campaigning is unconscionable." But it worked. To emphasize the point, Gingrich's TV ads said Shapard was "soft on welfare cheaters." One of Gingrich's campaign officials later told *The Washington Post*'s Dan Balz and Dale Russakoff: "We went after every rural southern prejudice we could think of."

Gingrich's first act as a newly elected congressman, even before he was sworn in, was to call for the expulsion from the House of Charles Diggs of Detroit, the first Black person elected to Congress from Michigan and a founder of the Congressional Black Caucus. Diggs had been convicted of diverting $6,000 from his congressional payroll for personal use, and he would later do prison time, but his constituents returned him to Congress with 79 percent of the vote.

House Republican leaders privately told Gingrich his action would reinforce an image that the party was racist, the historian Julian Zelizer recounted. White lawmakers had gotten much less severe punishments than expulsion for similar violations. But Gingrich proceeded, saying he felt "morally repulsed" to serve with Diggs.

Gingrich claimed to be racially progressive (he favored a Martin Luther King Jr. federal holiday), but he was proficient in racist dog whistles: railing against the "corrupt, liberal welfare state," drafting a Republican Party platform in Georgia warning that "America is in danger of decaying into a jungle of violent crimes," saying that because of civil rights leader Jesse Jackson "it's going to be a Dukakis-Jackson administration no matter who the vice presidential nominee is." He argued for branding Democrats with the words "welfare" and "criminal rights." He claimed that "it is in the interest of the Republican Party . . . to invent new Black leaders, so to speak—people who have a belief in discipline, hard work and patriotism." He decried "multicultural nihilistic hedonism." He fought civil rights groups in trying to add a new category, "multi-racial," to the census.

When Gingrich's Republicans won the House in 1994, it was in large part because, for the first time since Reconstruction, Democrats had lost their southern majority in Congress.

The Republicans' increasingly overt racial politics went well beyond Gingrich. Republican senators called Lani Guinier, Clinton's nominee to run the Justice Department's civil rights division, the "quota queen." She never got confirmed. Republicans blocked another nominee to the same post, Bill Lann Lee, in 1997. As *The Washington Post*'s David Nakamura put it: "the Clinton years established a playbook for a decades-long strategy of opposition to Democratic nominees for the nation's top civil rights post."

Limbaugh, over his long career on the radio, told a Black caller to "take that bone out of your nose and call me back," and said the National Basketball Association should be renamed the "Thug Basketball Association" and the teams renamed "gangs." He said that a National Football League game was like "a game between the Bloods and the Crips," and he said a Black player only received praise because commentators were "very desirous that a Black quarterback do well." He attempted to "translate" the Chinese president on air: "Ching cha. Ching chang cho chow. Cha Chow. Ching Cho. Chi ba ba ba." He said Latino migrants were mounting an "invasion" and belittled Native American genocide: "Only 4 million left? They all have casinos, what's to complain about?"

Limbaugh frequently mirrored white nationalist talking points when discussing Latino immigrants, whom he described as lazy and dependent on the government. He called migrants at America's southern border an "invasion." And white people? "If any race of people should not have guilt about slavery, it's Caucasians." During Barack Obama's run for the presidency, Limbaugh popularized the tune "Barack, the Magic Negro."

Limbaugh's naked racism would soon be emulated by Obama's successor in the presidency, as would Limbaugh's preposterous denial: "I'm the absolute furthest thing from a racist."

But, long before then, it had been echoed by many Republican officeholders in the 1990s.

Ron Paul, the congressman and future Republican presidential candidate, published racist newsletters. Representative Bob Barr of Georgia, Senator Trent Lott of Mississippi, and Republican National Committee Chairman Haley Barbour, also of Mississippi, all addressed the Council of Conservative Citizens, a white supremacist group that grew out of the earlier White Citizens' Councils.

Then there was former Nixon aide Pat Buchanan, who made serious runs for the Republican presidential nomination in 1992 and 1996. Buchanan, demanding to know "who speaks for the Euro-Americans who founded the U.S.A.," wanted affirmative action for "European-Americans" and thought there were too few "non-Jewish whites" in the Ivy League. He called Hitler "an individual of great courage" and said the "so-called 'Holocaust Survivor Syndrome' involves group fantasies of martyrdom and heroics."

Flyers distributed during the 1996 campaign, allegedly by Buchanan backers, pointed out the Korean ethnicity of the wife of Buchanan rival Phil Gramm: "Many conservatives will not vote for him in the primary due to his interracial marriage. He divorced a white wife to marry an Asiatic." Buchanan proposed a border fence to stop a migrant "invasion" and vowed to "take America back" and "put America first"—themes that would win the presidency two decades later.

Buchanan had a big following (he beat Dole in the 1996 New Hampshire primary). But in the 1990s, there was still enough of a moral core in the Republican Party to cast out such hatred. Dole's campaign denied Buchanan a prime-time speaking role at the Republican convention (his "culture war" speech at the 1992 convention divided Republicans). Senator Al D'Amato of New York denounced Buchanan as a "philosophical ayatollah." Even Gingrich called Buchanan "an extremist who is closer to David Duke than he is to the normal mainstream conservative." Buchanan, blocked from the GOP convention in August 1996, accurately predicted that the Republican Party would eventually transform itself into a "Buchanan party"—following his brand of protectionism and isolationism (and, though he didn't say it, racism).

There was also, at the time, enough of a moral core in the Republican Party to pose some resistance to those advocating violence. After Liddy made his on-air recommendation to dispatch federal ATF agents with a "head shot," D'Amato, who was then head of the National Republican Senatorial Committee, strongly denounced the remarks on a different radio show and dropped Liddy as speaker at an upcoming NRSC gala. Liddy, saving face, told his listeners that he received a "private message" from D'Amato saying he disinvited Liddy reluctantly. "If it will help the cause for me not to speak, I'm happy not to speak," Liddy claimed.

But elsewhere, the line was blurring between the white nationalists who wanted to destroy the government and Republican lawmakers who had been elected to defend it. As Buchanan surged in New Hampshire in 1996, a Washington watchdog group called the Center for Public Integrity issued a report documenting that one of Buchanan's campaign co-chairmen, former Virginia legislator Larry Pratt, had participated in meetings organized by militia leaders and neo-Nazis, including prominent figures in the Ku Klux Klan, Aryan Nations, and Christian Identity.

Pratt stepped down, but a defiant Buchanan said he "would urge the gun owners of New Hampshire and America to stand with Larry Pratt and stand with me." Pratt also ran Gun Owners of America, an extremist alternative to the National Rifle Association. Pratt had argued that the United States should "return to reliance on an armed people," and had asserted that "the government behaves as a beast." In one of his meetings with the white supremacists, Pratt reportedly attacked the post–Civil War Fourteenth Amendment, which guaranteed citizenship to all those born or naturalized in the United States.

Buchanan wasn't the only politician with ties to Pratt. His Gun Owners of America had contributed to more than sixty congressional candidates, among them Representative Roscoe Bartlett of Maryland, who had said people with Asian and Indian surnames do not "represent the normal American."

One lawmaker, Steve Stockman, owed his seat in Congress to the Gun Owners of America's campaign assistance and largesse. Moments after the Oklahoma City bombing, Stockman's office received a suspicious bulletin about the blast via fax from somebody connected with the Michigan militia. Just after the bombing, Stockman wrote an article for *Guns & Ammo* magazine saying the Clinton administration staged the Waco raid, in which federal agents "executed" the Branch Davidians, "to prove the need for a ban on so-called 'assault weapons.' "

Helen Chenoweth, of black helicopter fame, had also been funded by Pratt's group, and she reportedly benefited from a thousand volunteers from the U.S. Militia Association helping on her 1994 campaign. (Several others in the House and Senate also benefited from militia money in their campaigns.) After the Oklahoma City terrorist attack, she proposed that Congress "begin to look at the public policies that may be pushing people too far." At a time, just before the Oklahoma City bombing, when threats and even firebombs were being launched at the Bureau of Land Management, the Fish and Wildlife Service, and the Forest Service in Nevada and Idaho, Chenoweth introduced legislation in the House requiring federal agents to receive written permission from local sheriffs before making arrests, holding searches, or carrying guns.

She previously said the Ruby Ridge confrontation explained "why some people live in fear of their own government," and, before the Oklahoma City bombing, she had introduced white supremacist Randy Weaver's lawyer at a town hall meeting. Even after the massacre at the Murrah building, she said she wasn't "opposed to the concept of a militia, because I think people ought to be able to protect themselves."

Chenoweth was eccentric in other matters, too (she claimed Idaho salmon weren't endangered because she could buy canned salmon in the grocery store, she pushed for hunting at Yellowstone National Park, and she claimed the Nazis didn't invade Switzerland because the Swiss owned guns), but her pro-militia views were the most disturbing. "We have democracy when the government is afraid of the people," she said.

And what did the speaker of the House do about such a dangerous person? He put her on a congressional task force on Second Amendment rights. Gingrich called her antigovernment views "a signal. That's telling you something about her constituents, and not just extremists."

Congressman Joe Scarborough of Florida, the future TV host, maintained that while the Oklahoma City bombing "is something we abhor," the militias "consist of groups of people who are not interested in violence." Likewise, New Mexico's Republican governor, Gary Johnson, met with militia leaders after the Oklahoma City bombing and called them "responsible, reasonable, lawful" people. Senator Larry Craig, an Idaho Republican, proposed to disarm forest rangers. Congresswoman Barbara Vucanovich, a Nevada Republican, said federal agents should be prepared for violent resistance: "This is Nevada—people are armed." Dozens of counties in the West passed ordinances asserting that they were the true owners of federal lands. The National Governors Association called off a conference after militia groups spread word that it was actually going to be a Constitutional Convention aimed at repealing the Second Amendment.

Five days after the massacre in Oklahoma City, Clinton gave a speech in Minneapolis to a group of community college representatives, in which he tried to place the precarious moment in history. "We hear so many loud and angry voices in America today whose sole goal seems to be to try to keep some people as paranoid as possible and the rest of us all torn up and upset with each other. They spread hate. They leave the impression that, by their very words, that violence is acceptable," he said.

> Well, people like that who want to share our freedoms must know that their bitter words can have consequences, and that freedom has endured in this country for more than two centuries because it was coupled with an enormous sense of responsibility on the part of the American people. If we are to have freedom to speak, freedom to assemble, and yes, the freedom to bear arms, we must have responsibility as well. And to those of us who do not agree with the purveyors of hatred and division, with the promoters of paranoia, I remind you that we have freedom of speech, too, and we have responsibilities, too,

and some of us have not discharged our responsibilities. It is time we all stood up and spoke against that kind of reckless speech and behavior.

But the promoters of paranoia and the purveyors of hatred were just getting started. Limbaugh, though not mentioned by Clinton, responded by saying it was "outright slander" to blame him. Decades before the Republican National Committee would formally label a violent insurrection "legitimate political discourse," Limbaugh said: "I believe the people who have been . . . calling those people involved in legitimate political dialogue 'extremists,' are in fact promoters of paranoia and purveyors of hate and divisiveness." In years to come, Limbaugh would rewrite the history of the Murrah building bombing. "President Clinton's ties to the domestic terrorism of Oklahoma City are tangible," he claimed.

Republican officeholders, likewise, attacked Clinton for his call to speak out against the promoters of paranoia. Senator Don Nickles of Oklahoma called Clinton's appeal to decency "inappropriate" and tying the bombing to antigovernment rhetoric "more than a stretch of the imagination." Liddy defended the militia members as "fine people," "hard-working people," and "for the most part religious people." And Dole, the Republican standard-bearer, declined to get involved. The day after Clinton's plea, Dole told reporters: "You don't make politics out of people's misery."

This was an ominous turn for the Grand Old Party.

When Senator Joe McCarthy, Republican of Wisconsin, terrified the country with his communist paranoia and lists, seven Republican senators rose almost from the start to oppose him. They issued a "Declaration of Conscience," and Margaret Chase Smith of Maine famously told the Senate: "I don't want to see the Republican Party ride to victory on the Four Horsemen of Calumny: Fear, Ignorance, Bigotry and Smear." After too long—three years—half of Senate Republicans joined in censuring McCarthy.

Robert Welch's John Birch Society attracted a broad following a decade later with his ravings about secret communist control of the government and fluoridation as a communist plot. But figures such as Barry Goldwater, the party's 1964 presidential nominee, called Welch's views "far removed from reality and common sense" and at odds with "most members" of the group. "We cannot allow the emblem of irresponsibility to attach to the conservative banner," he wrote in William F. Buckley's *National Review,* which led the fight against what Buckley called the "paranoid and unpatriotic drivel" of Welch's society.

Ronald Reagan, running for governor of California in 1965, said of the John Birch Society: "I am not a member. I have no intention of becoming a member. I am not going to solicit their support." Senate Republican leader Everett Dirksen joined in, saying "we emphatically reject that sort of thing and . . . they are not a part of the Republican Party. They never have been—and in my judgment they never will be." Concurred Gerald Ford, then the House Republican leader: "There is no place for that organization in the Republican Party."

But this time was different. This time, Republican leaders could not find the political courage or the moral conviction to distance themselves from the militia movement. In fact, some joined in the antigovernment sentiments: DeLay, the House Republican whip, referred to federal agents as "jackbooted thugs." And so the violent white nationalists and the antigovernment extremists were able to graft themselves to mainstream conservatism. They had found a comfortable home in the Republican Party—and there they would remain.

CHAPTER 5

Swift Boating

In the traumatic few months after the terrorist attacks of September 11, 2001, Americans came together in what Franklin Delano Roosevelt once called the "warm courage of national unity." In the capital, many stuck magnetic flags on their car trunks and wore flags on their lapel pins. President George W. Bush, addressing a joint session of Congress soon after the attacks, gave bear hugs on the House floor to Tom Daschle and Dick Gephardt, the Democratic leaders, respectively, of the Senate and the House. Approval of Bush soared to 90 percent nationally after his unforgettable moment, bullhorn in hand, atop the rubble of New York's World Trade Center.

"We can't hear you!" one of the rescue workers called out.

"I can hear you!" Bush replied. "The rest of the world hears you. And the people who knocked these buildings down will hear all of us soon."

"USA!" the workers at Ground Zero chanted. "USA!"

As the United States waged war against the Taliban and al Qaeda, there were no Democrats and Republicans, liberals and conservatives, journalists and public officials. There were only Americans. In his January 2002 State of the Union address, lawmakers cheered when Bush said that "as we act to win the war . . . we must act first and foremost not as Republicans, not as Democrats, but as Americans." At a California town hall meeting in January, Bush declared: "It's time to take the spirit of unity that has been prevalent when it comes to fighting the war and bring it to Washington, D.C."

The overwhelming sense of national purpose in those days after the 9/11 attacks had the potential to transform Washington, to heal the political animosity and dysfunction that had been building over the previous decade. But Karl Rove had other ideas.

Bush's longtime political consultant, who had become Bush's top strategist in the White House, decided that Bush should turn national security into a political weapon against Democrats.

Rove flew down to Austin for the Republican National Committee's winter meeting on January 18, 2002, and there Rove announced his plan. "Americans trust the Republicans to do a better job of keeping our communities and our families safe," he told the party leaders. "We can also go to the country on this issue, because they trust the Republican Party to do a better job of protecting and strengthening America's military might and thereby protecting America." Rove advised the Republicans to "be proud of the record of our party" in keeping Americans safe from attack.

"Shameful," Gephardt responded.

Democratic National Committee chairman Terry McAuliffe called Rove's remarks "despicable."

But Rove prevailed in politicizing the War on Terror.

By mid-May 2002, Bush had keynoted more than two dozen fundraisers for Republican candidates. The White House had approved the sale to Republican donors of a photo of Bush aboard Air Force One on 9/11, and senior officials gave private briefings to big contributors.

In June, a White House intern accidentally dropped a computer diskette in Lafayette Park, across Pennsylvania Avenue from the White House. On the disk, which eventually found its way into Democratic hands, was a PowerPoint presentation by Rove and White House political director Ken Mehlman. The No. 1 suggestion in the bullet points listed under the header "Republican Strategy": "Focus on War and Economy."

Focus on war. Matthew Dowd, who handled public opinion data for the Bush campaign, said the war issue "would put the

Republicans on a very good footing." Faced with a choice between rallying the country against a common enemy or politicizing the war for partisan benefit, the Bush White House chose party over country.

In early September 2002, Vice President Dick Cheney, on the stump for Republicans in Des Moines, Iowa, in advance of the November midterm elections, said: "It's absolutely essential that eight weeks from today, on Nov. 2nd, we make the right choice. Because if we make the wrong choice, then the danger is that we'll get hit again, that we'll be hit in a way that will be devastating."

Vote Republican or die.

Also that month, Cheney spoke in Kansas in support of a Republican congressional candidate, Adam Taff, saying that electing the Republican was "vital" for "winning the war on terror" and "defending our homeland." *The Topeka Capital-Journal* got the message. Its website's headline: "Cheney Talks About Iraq at Congressional Fund-Raiser/ Electing Taff Would Aid War Effort."

And Bush himself, as he barnstormed the country campaigning for Republicans, tiptoed up to the precipice of calling Democrats disloyal—and then finally went over the edge.

On September 25, 2002, just over a year after the 9/11 attacks, I wrote about it in an article that appeared on the front page of *The Washington Post* under the headline, "In President's Speeches, Iraq Dominates, Economy Fades."

> As he seeks to boost Republican candidates in the midterm elections, President Bush is increasing his emphasis on terrorism and national security, shedding his previous determination to demonstrate his concern about the flagging economy.
>
> Four times in the past two days, Bush has suggested that Democrats do not care about national security, saying on Monday that the Democratic-controlled Senate is "not interested in the security of the American people." His remarks, intensifying a theme he introduced last month, were quickly seconded and disseminated by House Majority Whip Tom DeLay (R-Tex.).

Tom Daschle, after reading the article, erupted on the Senate floor that morning. He said that he had all along been reluctant to conclude that the White House was politicizing the war. "I can't bring myself to believe that it is. I can't believe any president or any administration would politicize the war. But then I read in the paper this morning, now even the president—the president—is quoted in *The Washington Post* this morning as saying that the Democratic-controlled Senate is 'not interested in the security of the American people.'"

The normally soft-spoken Senate majority leader was fairly shouting. "Not interested in the security of the American people?" he continued.

> You tell Senator Inouye he is not interested in the security of the American people. You tell those who fought in Vietnam and in World War II they are not interested in the security of the American people. That is outrageous—outrageous! The president ought to apologize to Senator Inouye and every veteran who has fought in every war who is a Democrat in the Senate. He ought to apologize to the American people. That is wrong. We ought not politicize this war. We ought not politicize the rhetoric about war and life and death. I was in Normandy just last year. I have been in national cemeteries all over this country. And I have never seen anything but stars—the Star of David and crosses on those markers. I have never seen "Republican" and "Democrat." This has to end.

The Senate president pro tempore, West Virginia Democrat Robert Byrd, rose to echo Daschle. "What about Max Cleland? Is he interested in the security of the American people?" Byrd demanded. "I am disgusted by the tenor of the war debate that has seemingly overtaken this capital city."

Daniel Inouye, of Hawaii, lost an arm in World War II. Cleland, of Georgia, lost both legs and an arm to a grenade in Vietnam. "It grieves me," Inouye said, "when my president makes statements that would divide this nation."

The White House, caught off guard by the fury of the response, argued that my article had taken Bush out of context, that his "not interested in the security of the American people" remark referred to a dispute over homeland security, not the war. This only further agitated Daschle, who returned to the Senate floor to speak again in the afternoon.

"As I understand it, the administration has stated that if I had understood the context in which the president made those remarks—the remarks that Senate Democrats are not concerned about national security—that I probably would not have been so critical," he said. "What context is there that legitimizes an accusation of that kind? I don't care whether you are talking about homeland security, I don't think you can talk about Iraq, you can't talk about war, you can't talk about any context that justifies a political comment like that. This is politicization, pure and simple. I meant it this morning and I mean it now. I don't know what may have motivated those in the White House to make the decision to politicize this debate, but it has to stop."

It didn't stop—and Daschle, of course, never got his apology—because the vile tactic was working for Republicans. As the election approached, Bush shifted away from talking about his efforts to boost the struggling economy in favor of a campaign message dominated by terrorism and his march toward war in Iraq. The effect: a Gallup poll in late September found that, by 49 percent to 41 percent, voters were more concerned about Iraq than the state of the economy when deciding how to cast their ballots—a 16-point shift toward Iraq in just three weeks.

Rove was right: squandering national unity and politicizing war would win Bush seats; Republicans regained the Senate and added to their House majority. But in winning seats, the party lost its soul. Putting party before country would become routine.

In the past, figures in both parties had fallen short of the famous 1947 admonition by Arthur Vandenberg, the Republican chairman of the Senate Foreign Relations Committee, that "we must stop partisan politics at the water's edge." Claims that opponents were soft on communism were a staple of the Cold War. But Bush and his allies took the politicization of war to a whole new level, with ugly and corrosive results. Opponents weren't just wrong; they were disloyal to their country. It wasn't enough to criticize opponents' policies or even their personal character; Bush, who advertised himself as a "uniter, not a divider," was instead impugning his opponents' patriotism.

Over time, people representing Bush or with ties to his campaigns accused a Vietnam War hero of being mentally unstable because of his time as a prisoner of war, portrayed a decorated Vietnam War veteran as a war criminal, and portrayed a triple amputee from the Vietnam War as an enabler of Osama bin Laden and Saddam Hussein.

Rove got his start during the Watergate era as a specialist in dirty tricks—landing himself in the pages of *The Washington Post* at the ripe old age of twenty-two. "Republican National Committee Chairman George Bush has reopened an investigation into allegations that a paid official of the GOP taught political espionage and 'dirty tricks' during weekend seminars for College Republicans during 1971 and 1972," the *Post* reported on August 10, 1973. "Bush said he will urge a GOP investigating committee to 'get to the bottom' of the charges against Karl C. Rove, 22, who was executive director of the College Republicans National Committee." Rove, it turned out, had "organized 15 regional conferences, attended by 300 members of the College Republicans," on "campaign espionage and disruption."

Rove and a colleague regaled the young Republicans with tales of dumpster diving in opponents' trash and disrupting Democrats' campaigns. In one such instance, Rove used a false name to pose as a supporter of a Democratic candidate for state treasurer in Illinois. He gained access to the candidate's headquarters, stole stationery, then used it to fake invitations to a party at the Democrat's offices. He distributed the invitation to hippies and street drunks, at a rock concert and soup kitchens. "Free beer, free food, girls and a good time for nothing," it said.

Rove evaded punishment for the dirty tricks seminars with the help of Lee Atwater (later of Willie Horton infamy), who had helped Rove become chairman of the College Republicans. George H. W. Bush hired Rove as his special assistant at the RNC, which led Rove to his future client, George W. Bush.

The dirty tricks continued, as Texas journalists James Moore and Wayne Slater detailed at length in their Rove biography, *Bush's Brain:*

In 1982, working for a gubernatorial candidate, Rove pushed suggestions that the Democratic opponent got into a wreck as a drunk driver.

In 1986, working for the same gubernatorial candidate, Rove appeared to have bugged his own office—and then announced the "discovery" on the day of the first debate, a month before the election. Rove, claiming the Democrat in the race had obtained secret information, called in a private security company that "found" a listening device, and Rove claimed "the only ones who could have benefited from this detailed, sensitive information would have been the political opposition." But it turned out the information was publicly available. The battery indicated the bug had been placed the same day it was "found," and Rove's caper followed closely the script of a movie that had just come out, *Power,* in which Richard Gere's character is a political consultant who finds a bug in his phone.

In 1990, in the agriculture commissioner's race, the Democratic incumbent was served with subpoenas the day he had planned for his reelection announcement. Rove had spoken of a possible "indictment" before the matter became public, and he had assisted the FBI agent involved in the case. The Democratic commissioner was never charged (though two aides were convicted).

Curiously, the same FBI agent also kept a probe open for two years into the Democratic Texas land commissioner (no illegal activity was found) and on the eve of an election requested campaign contribution reports for the Texas agriculture commissioner and state comptroller, both Democrats. Later, in a Texas State Senate hearing, Rove was asked: "Do you know why agent Rampton conducted a criminal investigation of Garry Mauro at the time you were involved in the campaign, pulled the finance records of Bob Bullock at the time you were involved in that campaign, pulled the campaign records of Jim Hightower at the time you were involved in that campaign?"

Rove had no idea, naturally.

But he would go on to end the political career of the state

railroad commissioner, another Democrat, over her false claim that she graduated from college. Then, when Bush ran against incumbent Democratic governor Ann Richards in 1994, a whisper campaign broke out that Richards was promoting gay lifestyles. A regional chairman for Bush criticized Richards for "appointing avowed homosexual activists" to state jobs and predicted religious voters would reject her because homosexuality was not something to "encourage" or to "reward." Bush, who obliquely invoked the issue by referring to Richards appointees "who have had agendas that may have been personal in nature," said the gay-bashing chairman spoke for himself but was a man "of great integrity."

With Bush in the governor's mansion, it was time for Rove to take the whispers and smears to the national stage. Bush vowed to run a "positive" presidential campaign—he would rally the "armies of compassion" and "change one heart, one soul, one conscience at a time"—but beneath the surface, the tone was rather different. Retired Admiral James Stockdale, Ross Perot's 1992 running mate, disclosed in November 1999 that he got a call from a friend "close to the George W. Bush campaign soliciting comments on Mr. McCain's 'weaknesses.'" As such, Stockdale said he was "not surprised by reports that Senator John McCain's political enemies have been spreading rumors that his famous temper is a sign of a broader 'instability' caused by his imprisonment in Vietnam."

Bush campaign surrogates in the Senate had also encouraged the unstable McCain slander, and Republican candidates Steve Forbes and Gary Bauer joined the McCain campaign in blaming Bush for the attacks. McCain was pressured to release detailed medical records proving his fitness. Wayne Slater wrote in *The Dallas Morning News* that the episode was similar to Rove's many dirty tricks of the past. The day the article came out, Rove physically confronted Slater, poking him in the chest, and, as journalist Carl Cannon and others reported in their Rove biography, *Boy Genius,* told Slater: "You broke the rules!" Many took that as an acknowledgment that Rove was behind the McCain smear.

Things got markedly worse after McCain beat Bush in the New Hampshire primary. The campaign moved to South Carolina, and Bush shed his "compassionate conservatism." To appeal to the far right, Bush scheduled a visit to Bob Jones University, which banned interracial dating and called Catholicism a "cult." (Rove later said he "came down on the side of going" to Bob Jones.) Bush also sided with those who wanted to keep the Confederate flag flying over the state capitol. One Bob Jones professor, Richard Hand, widely shared an email with "fellow South Carolinians" claiming that McCain had "chosen to sire children without marriage." Voters received mysterious calls suggesting McCain had "fathered an illegitimate black child." (The "black" child was McCain's daughter, adopted from a Bangladesh orphanage.) Other callers told voters McCain's wife, Cindy, was a drug addict. (She had conquered a painkiller addiction years earlier.) In Spartanburg, South Carolina, McCain heard from a distraught mother who said her fourteen-year-old son got a phone call saying "Senator McCain is a cheat and a liar and a fraud."

At a rally in Sumter, South Carolina, Bush shared the stage with J. Thomas Burch Jr., from an obscure Vietnam veterans group, as Burch told the crowd that McCain "has never, ever sponsored or cosponsored a piece of veterans legislation that means anything to Vietnam or Gulf War veterans." Burch said McCain "had the power to help the veterans. But he came home, forgot us." Other veterans demanded Bush condemn this slander of a war hero. Bush's response? Burch was "entitled to his own opinion."

Such sleaze carried Bush to victory in South Carolina and essentially gave him the nomination. A real estate developer in New York must have been taking notes, for Donald Trump would revisit the anti-McCain calumny, and embellish it further, fifteen years later.

It shouldn't be a surprise that similar whisper campaigns and legal shenanigans followed Rove to the Bush White House. Rove made the decision to inject gay rights into the 2004 race as a cultural wedge issue by pushing for Bush to campaign on his support for a constitutional amendment banning gay marriage. Mailings and robocalls claimed, falsely, that John Kerry favored gay marriage—at the time a politically unpopular position. (Cheney, who has a lesbian daughter, disagreed with Bush's decision to inject the issue into the 2004 campaign and blamed Rove.) Rove also was accused, in an affidavit by a Republican lawyer, of contacting the

Justice Department in 2002 about probing Alabama's Democratic governor, Don Siegelman. The affidavit said the purpose was to get Siegelman to withdraw his challenge to contested election results in which he was narrowly defeated. (After a prosecution tainted with allegations of partisanship, Siegelman was eventually convicted of bribery years later.)

Rove, it should surprise no one, denied wrongdoing in all matters.

The presence of a dirty trickster at the highest level of the White House gave critical mass to the stockpile of political animus that, with the exception of the weeks after 9/11, had been steadily building since the Gingrich era.

In the House in 2003, after Democrats on the Ways and Means Committee staged a walkout because the Republicans had rewritten a pension bill in the middle of the night, the Republican chairman of the committee, Bill Thomas, called the Capitol Police to evict the Democratic lawmakers, by force if necessary, from a nearby library where they were meeting. He later admitted to "poor judgment" in sending police to break up the meeting.

On the Senate floor in 2004, Cheney, who as vice president was also the president of the Senate, encountered Senator Patrick Leahy and berated the Vermont Democrat for alleging the oil-services business Cheney had run, Halliburton, was war profiteering. Leahy reminded Cheney that the vice president had called Leahy a bad Catholic for opposing a Bush nominee who was Catholic. "Fuck yourself," Cheney said to Leahy.

Racial politics, too, were getting ever uglier. Trent Lott of Mississippi lost his position as Senate Republican leader in late 2002 after saying his state was "proud" to have supported Strom Thurmond's segregationist presidential bid in 1948. "And if the rest of the country had followed our lead, we wouldn't have had all these problems over all these years, either," he said.

In Georgia, Republican Sonny Perdue scored an upset victory over Democratic governor Roy Barnes because of his promise to allow Georgians to restore the Confederate battle flag to the state flag. Barnes had demoted the Confederate emblem, which had been added to Georgia's flag in 1956 in defiance of court-ordered school desegregation. The flag issue proved decisive in the 2002 election, aided by Bush-hosted rallies and a get-out-the-vote push among rural white men led by Republican state chairman Ralph Reed, late of the Christian Coalition. At Perdue's victory cele-bration, where somebody displayed the Confederate version of the Georgia flag, the governor-elect had the audacity to quote Martin Luther King Jr.: "Free at last, free at last. Thank God Almighty, free at last."

But Rove's singular contribution, and that of the Bush presi-dency generally, was the routine portrayal of political opponents as traitors. John Ashcroft, appointed attorney general after losing to an opponent who died before Election Day, said of Democrats who disagreed with some of the increased law enforcement powers in the Patriot Act: "Your tactics only aid terrorists. . . . They give ammunition to America's enemies and pause to America's friends." In response to Leahy's quibbles with parts of the Patriot Act, White House officials privately called him "Osama bin Leahy," the jour-nalist Peter Baker reported. Congressman Tom Davis of Virginia, who ran the National Republican Campaign Committee, accused Daschle of "giving aid and comfort to our enemies."

DeLay, the House majority whip, accused Democrats of "con-stantly throwing up hurdles to keep us from doing what we have to do to protect the American people" and said Democrats "don't want to protect the American people." Instead, "they will do any-thing, spend all the time and resources they can, to avoid con-fronting evil."

When Scott Ritter, a former Marine who later served as a United Nations arms inspector in Iraq, said that the administra-tion's claims about Iraq's weapons were false, Republicans called him "the Jane Fonda of Iraq" and asked what he would call his exercise videos. Dan Bartlett, the White House communications director, said Democrats' attempts to learn what warnings Bush received before the 9/11 attacks were doing "exactly what our opponents, our enemies, want us to do."

In the summer of 2002, Democrats looked to be in a strong position for the midterm elections; the economy was slumping, the stock market had taken a beating, and corporate malfeasance was in the news. But when reporters in August asked Jim Jordan, who directed the Democratic Senatorial Campaign Committee, how the war might affect the election, he answered: "You mean when General Rove calls in the air strikes in October?"

He wasn't far off the mark. The White House began to beat the Iraq war drums after Labor Day. Andy Card, the White House chief of staff, explained to Elisabeth Bumiller of *The New York Times* that "from a marketing point of view, you don't introduce new products in August." Meanwhile, *Time* magazine reported at the time, Rove was telling friends: "Let me put it this way: If you want to see Baghdad, you'd better visit soon." Rove, though his portfolio didn't include national security, had been photographed with the president in meetings about Iraq.

Karen Hughes, another top Bush adviser, said that because of 9/11 Bush shouldn't be on the campaign trail in 2002, but Rove opposed her—and prevailed. White House spokesman Scott McClellan later wrote: "Soon the president began campaigning openly again for Republican congressional candidates, including against incumbent Democratic members of Congress, touting his and GOP leaders' management of the war. As governor, [in contrast,] he'd maintained good relations with friendly legislators by refusing to campaign against them, even if they were members of the opposing party."

Bush demanded the Democratic-controlled Senate hold a vote before the midterm elections authorizing him to use force in Iraq. Daschle told the *Los Angeles Times* he asked Bush to delay the vote until after the election to "depoliticize" the matter—as Bush's father did before the Gulf War of 1991. But the younger Bush "looked at Cheney and he looked at me, and there was a half-smile on his face," Daschle recounted. "And he said: 'We just have to do this now.'"

Bush publicly warned Democrats not to wait for a United Nations resolution before authorizing an attack on Iraq. "If I were running for office, I'm not sure how I'd explain to the American people—say, vote for me, and, oh, by the way, on a matter of national security, I think I'm going to wait for somebody else to act," he said.

Tom Davis, the head of the House Republicans' campaign committee, put it bluntly: "People are going to want to know, before the elections, where their representatives stand."

Republican candidates eagerly joined in, portraying Democrats as terrorists' allies. In Georgia, Saxby Chambliss, trying to unseat Democrat Cleland in the Senate, accused Cleland of "breaking his oath to protect and defend the Constitution" because of his position on Iraq weapons inspections.

Next, Chambliss ran a television ad that opened with images of Osama bin Laden and Saddam Hussein, then immediately switched to similar, grainy photos of Cleland. "Since July, Max Cleland has voted against the president's vital homeland security efforts 11 times," the ad announced. In reality, Cleland had introduced legislation creating a Department of Homeland Security over Bush's objections—and he voted against various Republican efforts to gut the department.

The ad was obscene, aimed at a man who lost three limbs in Vietnam by a man who avoided the war with five deferments. But they worked. Cleland accurately blamed "Bush-led, Karl Rove–inspired Republican politics" for his defeat. He felt that his opponents "took away my service" in Vietnam. "Another grenade had blown up in my face—this time on the political battlefield rather than the military battlefield. But it felt the same way," Cleland wrote in his memoir, *Heart of a Patriot: How I Found the Courage to Survive Vietnam, Walter Reed and Karl Rove*. "When I lost my Senate seat, I lost my way of coping with life after Vietnam. . . . The afternoon of Thanksgiving 2002, I started crying, and I was to keep crying off and on for the next two and a half years as the worst depression of my life swallowed me whole."

Rove liked the ad that doomed Cleland. "I thought it was effective because it was factual," he later wrote.

Rove enjoyed the smear so much that the next year, even though it wasn't an election year, the Bush-controlled Republican National Committee ran an ad against the Democrats, just for the heck of it, claiming that "some are now attacking the president for attacking the terrorists."

The Bush campaign used a similar script in 2004. They picked New York for the convention to highlight 9/11, and former New York mayor Rudy Giuliani gave a speech that mentioned "terror," "terrorist," or "terrorism" forty-four times and suggested that Democratic nominee John Kerry didn't see terrorism "for the evil that it is." Zell Miller, a disaffected Democrat from Georgia who was retiring from the Senate, told the convention that Democratic leaders are "motivated more by partisan politics than by national security" and believe that "America is the problem."

Worse was a TV ad by a Republican-backed group with the voices of men claiming to have served in Vietnam with Kerry, who had volunteered to operate a swift boat in the Navy and earned three Purple Hearts, a Silver Star, and a Bronze Star. The men in the ad took turns denouncing Kerry's service:

> John Kerry has not been honest about what happened in Vietnam. He is lying about his record. I know John Kerry is lying about his first Purple Heart because I treated him for that injury. John Kerry lied to get his Bronze Star. I know. I was there. I saw what happened. His account of what happened and what actually happened are the difference between night and day. John Kerry has not been honest. And he lacks the capacity to lead. When the chips were down, you could not count on John Kerry. John Kerry is no war hero. He betrayed all his shipmates. He lied before the Senate. John Kerry betrayed the men and women he served with in Vietnam. He dishonored his country—he most certainly did.

It was yet another new low: Republicans, whose own nominee avoided Vietnam by serving in the Texas Air National Guard, took Kerry's honorable military service and turned it into crimes and betrayal. Similar ads followed, with more false allegations, in battleground states. Another one, about Kerry's later antiwar efforts, charged: "John Kerry gave the enemy for free what I and many of my comrades in the North Vietnam prison camps took torture to avoid saying." The claims about Kerry's service were contradicted by official military records and by many other men who served with Kerry. It turned out some of those making the allegations weren't in a position to know, and others had obvious political motivations. But it didn't matter. The smear worked. Polls showed voters found the attacks credible, and Kerry's support dropped among veterans.

Following the now familiar pattern, the Bush campaign denied involvement, but Bush refused to disavow the scurrilous charges made by the "Swift Boat Veterans for Truth." It was revealed that the chief counsel to Bush's campaign was also legal adviser to the Swift Boat Veterans. A member of the Bush campaign's veterans steering committee appeared in one of the Swift Boat Veterans' ads. Seven of the ten initial funders of the group were Bush campaign contributors. And the primary funder of the group, Texas homebuilder Bob Perry, was a major donor to Bush's gubernatorial and presidential campaigns and, Rove acknowledged, "a good friend of mine."

In his Bush biography, *Dead Certain,* Robert Draper reported that "the Bush campaign had been notified at least a day beforehand that the ads would be broadcast and made no efforts to intervene." Rove, while as usual denying any involvement, later said of the slanderous campaign: "It damaged Kerry's campaign because it was true." He added: "The Swifties did a damn good job."

Risking life and limb for country was no longer a measure of patriotism. Representative Jack Murtha, a Pennsylvania Democrat with a strong pro-military record in Congress, had earned a Bronze Star, two Purple Hearts, and the Vietnam Cross of Gallantry during his time as a Marine in Vietnam. But when he proposed a pullout from Iraq because of the flawed war policy, Jean Schmidt, a Republican freshman from Ohio, went to the House floor and said she'd been asked by a Marine colonel "to send Congressman Murtha a message: that cowards cut and run, Marines never do." The White House said Murtha would "surrender to the terrorists." DeLay said "the national Democrat Party declared its surrender in the war on terror." Representative Michael Burgess of Texas said the Democrats were "giving aid and comfort to our enemies."

Grumbled Murtha: "I like guys who got five deferments and never been there, and send people to war, and then don't like to hear suggestions about what needs to be done."

The "chicken hawks" kept squawking. Bush said Democrats "embolden an enemy" and said that "defeatists" on the left were not a "loyal opposition." House Speaker Dennis Hastert said "the Democratic Party sides with those who wish to surrender." John Thune, in his successful bid to unseat Daschle in 2004, said the

Senate Democratic leader's "words embolden the enemy." Rove accused Dick Durbin of Illinois, the No. 2 Democrat in the Senate, of "putting our troops in greater danger" with his words. "No more needs to be said about the motives of liberals," Rove said.

A Republican National Committee ad in 2006 showed the words of Osama bin Laden ("what is yet to come will be even greater") over the ticking of a timer and a globe being incinerated by nuclear bombs. Its conclusion: "What is yet to come will be even greater. These Are the Stakes. Vote November 7th." John Boehner, the House majority leader, said he wondered if Democrats "are more interested in protecting the terrorists than protecting the American people." Congresswoman Marsha Blackburn of Tennessee demanded of House Democratic leader Nancy Pelosi: "Where do your loyalties lie?" The Republican National Committee chairman, Mike Duncan, said "Democrats are hoping our troops fail in the War on Terror in the craven desire that it will boost their party's electoral fortunes." Republican Senator Kay Bailey Hutchison of Texas said a Democratic plan would "put a bullet right in the hearts of our troops."

On and on it went: Democrats were trying to hurt the troops, giving aid and comfort to the enemy, and choosing terrorists over Americans. The Republicans had declared that their domestic political opponents were traitors to the United States. And in doing so, they had dismantled another norm of American democracy—and decency.

CHAPTER 6

Culture of Deception

On a clear May afternoon in 2003 over the Pacific Ocean, a U.S. Navy S-3B Viking jet, built for antisubmarine warfare, performed two fly-bys above the USS *Abraham Lincoln,* then made a tailhook landing at 150 mph on the aircraft carrier's deck, catching the last of four cables. Its fuselage read "Navy One" and, under the cockpit window, "George W. Bush, Commander in Chief."

President Bush emerged from the cockpit, in olive flight suit and combat boots, his helmet tucked under his left arm. He strode across the deck, exchanging salutes and handshakes and posing for photos with the sailors. His ejection harness, hugging him tightly between the legs, gave him the bowlegged swagger of a top gun.

"Major combat operations in Iraq have ended," Bush announced that day. "In the battle of Iraq, the United States and our allies have prevailed." Above him, from the carrier's tower, flew a huge banner announcing, "Mission Accomplished."

The event was a fraud wrapped in a deception tied up with a lie.

The Bush administration took the nation to war based on a lie that it sold to the American public: that Saddam Hussein was responsible for the 9/11 attacks. It built the case for war on a deliberate deception: that Iraq was on the verge of acquiring nuclear weapons. And then, after six weeks, Bush declared victory in a war that would go on for years and claim the lives of thousands of American troops.

Bush received underwater survival training in the White House swimming pool to prepare for his stunt (he wisely left the landing itself to the professionals). He did the jet landing even though, it turned out, the aircraft carrier was within easy helicopter range of San Diego. And he staged his "Mission Accomplished" moment even though he had been warned—accurately—that the invasion of Iraq could lead to a long and deadly insurgency.

"My belief is we will, in fact, be greeted as liberators," Vice President Dick Cheney proclaimed on NBC's *Meet the Press* just days before the invasion. He knew the intelligence didn't support such claims.

"While some policy makers were eager to say that we would be greeted as liberators, what they failed to mention is that the intelligence community told them that such a greeting would last for only a limited period," George Tenet, then CIA director, wrote in his account of the period, *At the Center of the Storm*. "Unless we quickly provided a secure and stable environment on the ground, the situation could rapidly deteriorate."

And that's exactly what happened.

During the Clinton years, Republicans learned through the Foster suicide and other "scandals" to weaponize disinformation, keeping the Democratic administration constantly off-balance with an unending stream of baseless allegations. Now, in the Bush years, Republicans opened a dangerous new front in their assault on truth. The Bush administration used disinformation to justify the single most consequential action a government can undertake: waging war on another country.

There had always been some measure of deception in the national security sphere. Dwight Eisenhower misled the public about the U-2 spy plane shot down by the Soviet Union. John F. Kennedy tried to hide U.S. involvement in the Bay of Pigs fiasco. Lyndon Johnson exaggerated North Vietnam's hostile actions in the Gulf of Tonkin.

For that matter, there had always been deception in politics generally. Richard Nixon lied about Watergate. Bill Clinton lied about sex. Democrats and Republicans alike routinely lied about opponents' records, and their own. It was, of course, routine for public officials to exaggerate and take things out of context to score a point.

But here we had something new: an administration systematically and repeatedly exaggerating, misstating, and outright inventing the facts in order to launch a war that would cost some five thousand American lives, perhaps half a million Iraqi lives, $800 billion—and the credibility and prestige of the United States. Americans' trust in their government has never recovered.

ON OCTOBER 22, 2002, I had the bad luck to be in the White House traveling press corps on a campaign trip President Bush took to Downingtown, Pennsylvania. That morning, an article I wrote ran on the front page of *The Washington Post* under the headline, "For Bush, Facts Are Malleable." The subhead said Bush was "embroidering key assertions."

Top officials in the White House erupted. White House press secretary Ari Fleischer, spotting me near the entrance to the gymnasium where Bush was speaking, stalked over to me, worked himself to well within my personal space—and, as I recall it, started screaming.

This is beneath the Post! *We demand a retraction! We're calling your editors! Every single thing you wrote has been refuted!*

When he finally finished the harangue, I had to wipe the spittle off my face.

Not long after that, the *Post*'s national political editor, Maralee Schwartz, got a call from the White House. It was Karl Rove, requesting that I be removed from the White House beat. She respectfully declined. An anonymous "senior administration official," meanwhile, called ABC News's popular tip sheet, "The Note," and "made some remarks about Milbank himself," ABC reported: "On Milbank, the official took the unusual step of saying: 'This was a story that was cooked and ready to go before any due diligence of the facts,' by a reporter who 'is more interested in style than substance.'"

Apparently, I had hit a nerve. ABC called the article "one of the most sweeping 'the emperor has no clothes' pieces anyone has written for a mainstream media property during the Bush presidency," and the Bush White House would not tolerate anybody pointing out its naked mendacity—particularly when it came to the case it was building for war in Iraq.

The piece reported that Bush told the nation that Iraq had a growing fleet of unmanned aircraft that could be used "for missions targeting the United States." But further examination revealed that the aircraft in question lacked the range to reach the United States.

Bush, the article noted, cited a report by the International Atomic Energy Agency saying the Iraqis were "six months away from developing a weapon." In fact, the IAEA report Bush mentioned said Iraq had been six to twenty-four months away from nuclear capability—before the 1991 Gulf War.

Bush spoke of a "very senior al Qaeda leader who received medical treatment in Baghdad this year." But, the article reported, Bush failed to note that U.S. intelligence said the figure was no longer in Iraq and there had been no hard evidence Iraq's government knew he was there.

Bush, the piece continued, had also claimed that in 1998 "information from a high-ranking Iraqi nuclear engineer who had defected revealed that . . . Saddam Hussein had ordered his nuclear program to continue." But Bush neglected to mention that the defector retired in 1991.

And Bush had alleged that "Iraq could decide on any given day to provide a biological or chemical weapon to a terrorist group or individual terrorists." But the article pointed to congressional testimony from the CIA saying it expected Iraq would take such an "extreme step" only if it were provoked by a U.S. attack.

In retrospect, the only thing wrong with the article was that I hadn't known the half of it. The president, the vice president, and other top officials were deliberately cooking the books to build a case for war in Iraq.

Much of the underlying intelligence, particularly about weapons of mass destruction, was wrong in the first place, and some of the claims by Bush, Vice President Cheney, and others may have been unintentional falsehoods. But even when Bush and aides were warned that what they were alleging was wrong, they continued to repeat the same untruths. Those weren't just misstatements;

those were lies. They repeatedly lied about Saddam Hussein's 9/11 involvement, about Iraq's nuclear threat, and about the progress of the war itself.

Scott McClellan, then the deputy White House press secretary and later Fleischer's successor, acknowledged in a 2008 book, *What Happened,* that Bush and his aides were "shading the truth," in making the case for war:

> trying to make the WMD threat and the Iraqi connection to terrorism appear just a little more certain, a little less questionable, than they were; quietly ignoring or disregarding some of the crucial caveats in the intelligence and minimizing evidence that pointed in the opposite direction; using innuendo and implication to encourage Americans to believe as fact some things that were unclear and possibly false (such as the idea that Saddam had an active nuclear weapons program) and other things that were overplayed or completely wrong (such as implying Saddam might have an operational relationship with al Qaeda).

McClellan explained the cynical rationale:

> The White House knew the national media would cover its arguments for war even if the underlying evidence was a little shaky. Questions might be raised, but the administration had the biggest platform, especially when something as dramatic and controversial as war was at stake. And the public is generally inclined to believe what the White House says, or at least give it the benefit of the doubt until the watchdog media proves it is unreliable.

McClellan blamed the media for being too credulous—a fair point. But even when we blew the whistle on the deception, it didn't matter: those who occupied the bully pulpit simply drowned us out with repeated lies.

Two days before the war began, on March 18, 2003, Walter Pincus, the *Post*'s venerable intelligence reporter, and I wrote: "As the Bush administration prepares to attack Iraq this week, it is doing so on the basis of a number of allegations against Iraqi President Saddam Hussein that have been challenged—and in some cases disproved—by the United Nations, European governments and even U.S. intelligence reports." We debunked the claims one by one: that Iraq had ties to 9/11, that it was aggressively producing biological and chemical weapons, that it had sought to buy uranium and had bought aluminum tubes to make nuclear weapons, and that it had illegal long-range missiles.

But the truth never had a chance.

Eventually, the world would learn that Bush's case for war was rubbish. Iraq had no biological, chemical, or nuclear weapons, and it wasn't actively pursuing them. But by then, it was too late.

EVEN BEFORE THE WAR, Bush tended to have a casual relationship with the facts. He went around claiming that 300,000 jobs were "on hold" because Congress hadn't passed terrorism insurance legislation—but the figure turned out to be something the White House "extrapolated," or made up. He frequently complained that a union was blocking customs workers from wearing radiation detectors—months after the union had dropped its objection. He claimed that his tax cut would disappear after ten years because of a "quirk in the rules"—but it was actually a deliberate budgeting decision made by proponents of the tax cut. He boasted about making "the biggest increase in education spending in a long, long time"—when in fact the increase was smaller than the previous year. Bush said "no one could have imagined" al Qaeda flying hijacked planes into buildings. Perhaps not. But Bush had been cautioned before 9/11, in a memo titled "Bin Ladin Determined to Strike in U.S.," that since 1998 the FBI had seen "patterns of suspicious activity in this country consistent with preparations for hijackings."

TREASURY SECRETARY PAUL O'NEILL, fired by Bush at the end of 2002, told journalist Ron Suskind that Bush was "like a blind man in a room full of deaf people," committed to predetermined outcomes, impervious to contrary facts. Bush's lack of intellectual curiosity had the effect of elevating the role of two men in the administration, Cheney and Rove—master prevaricators both.

Cheney was the sort of guy who would say "I have no financial interest in Halliburton of any kind and haven't had now for over three years"—when during the time he referenced he received $2 million from Halliburton in deferred compensation. His respect for the public's right to know was best illustrated by his decision to wait a day before disclosing that he had shot his friend in the face and chest in a hunting accident (the man eventually suffered a heart attack from the birdshot)—and then to make the disclosure to a small, local newspaper, in defiance of White House colleagues.

But Rove was the "grand manipulator," as McClellan put it: "Having a brilliant political strategist and grand manipulator of sources of public approval like Rove working in the White House isn't necessarily a problem in itself. It's a problem, however, when political strategy takes over excessively, and governance becomes merely a subset of campaigning. And when the strategist is someone with the skills, personality, and reach of Karl Rove, it's all too easy for that to happen."

Rove wasn't the first political strategist to have a taxpayer-funded job in the White House, but he outdid his predecessors in the audacity of his mendacity. "Ultimately," Rove biographers James Moore and Wayne Slater concluded in *The Architect*, "Karl Rove, we think, will be a man who's remembered for figuring out how to game the American political system. Under Rove, the politics of deception has become a conventional political tool." Rove's ads created "an alternative reality," they wrote. "He is American politics' most talented, prolific and successful dissembler."

In Rove's telling, Bush didn't lie about the Iraq threat. "Absolutely not," he wrote in his 2010 memoir, typically immodestly titled *Courage and Consequence*. The president who condoned waterboarding "never authorized torture" in Rove's alternate reality. "He did just the opposite." Though Bush consistently favored oil and gas producers, Rove asserts that Bush was "aggressive" against climate change. In the reality-based community, Bush turned a budget surplus into a record deficit and nearly doubled the national debt. In Rove's version, spending was "far below average" under Bush. In reality, Bush's term ended in economic collapse and the Great Recession. Rove preferred to view it as Bush presiding over "the longest period of economic growth since President Reagan."

WAR IS PEACE. Freedom is slavery. Ignorance is strength. And Democrats are brain damaged. Years later, after Hillary Clinton suffered a concussion in 2012 because she fainted while fighting a stomach virus and hit her head, Rove floated a conspiracy theory. "Thirty days in the hospital?" he asked. "And when she reappears, she's wearing glasses that are only for people who have traumatic brain injury? We need to know what's up with that."

In reality, Clinton spent four days in the hospital, and the glasses were of the sort commonly used to reduce double vision after a concussion. But "reality" didn't matter.

THE EVENING AFTER THE 9/11 attacks, Richard Clarke, the counterterrorism coordinator on the National Security Council, found President Bush wandering around the White House Situation Room. As Clarke described the encounter in his book, *Against All Enemies,* Bush closed the door and addressed Clarke and a few others.

> "Look," he told us, "I know you have a lot to do and all . . . but I want you, as soon as you can, to go back over everything, everything. See if Saddam did this. See if he's linked in any way . . ."
>
> I was once again taken aback, incredulous, and it showed. "But, Mr. President, al Qaeda did this."
>
> "I know, I know, but . . . see if Saddam was involved. Just look. I want to know any shred . . ."
>
> "Absolutely, we will look . . . again." I was trying to be more respectful, more responsive. "But, you know, we have looked

several times for state sponsorship of al Qaeda and not found any real linkages to Iraq. Iran plays a little, as does Pakistan, and Saudi Arabia, Yemen."

"Look into Iraq, Saddam," the President said testily and left us.

The CIA immediately identified al Qaeda as the culprit. But earlier that day, Clarke had "realized with almost a sharp physical pain" that Defense Secretary Donald Rumsfeld and his deputy, Paul Wolfowitz, "were going to try to take advantage of this national tragedy to promote their agenda about Iraq." They had wanted to oust Saddam Hussein since the Gulf War, a decade earlier, when President George H. W. Bush declined to pursue that goal.

George Tenet, the CIA director, found Richard Perle, head of the Pentagon's Defense Policy Board, leaving the West Wing on September 12, 2001. "Perle turned to me and said, 'Iraq has to pay a price for what happened yesterday. They bear responsibility,'" Tenet wrote.

Never mind that the CIA found "absolutely no linkage between Saddam and 9/11." The defense undersecretary for policy, Doug Feith, like Perle and Wolfowitz a hawkish neocon, reportedly told a senior military officer on September 12, 2001, that "the campaign should immediately lead to Baghdad."

And so began a campaign to sell a lie.

In late 2001, Cheney went on NBC's *Meet the Press* and declared that it was "pretty well confirmed" that 9/11 mastermind Mohamed Atta, one of the hijackers, met with a senior Iraqi intelligence official. But the supposed meeting, in Prague in 2000, was not pretty well confirmed. Indeed, investigators had no evidence of Atta leaving the country then, and phone records placed Atta in Florida during the time of the supposed meeting.

As time went on, Cheney said evidence of a link between Iraq and al Qaeda was "overwhelming," proclaiming himself "very confident there was an established relationship there," and he asserted that the relationship "stretched back through most of the decade of the '90s" and that Saddam Hussein "had long established ties with al Qaeda." (Perle, too, called evidence of a relationship "overwhelming.") In a return trip to *Meet the Press*, Cheney proclaimed: "If we're successful in Iraq . . . then we will have struck a major blow right at the heart of the base, if you will, the geographic base of the terrorists who had us under assault now for many years, but most especially on 9/11."

Bush, while not directly implicating Iraq in 9/11, began suggesting a link in almost every speech on Iraq. "There's no question that Saddam Hussein had al Qaeda ties," he said at one point. In his "Mission Accomplished" speech, Bush linked Iraq to the September 11, 2001, attacks: "The battle of Iraq is one victory in a war on terror that began on September the 11th, 2001."

Moments later, Bush added: "We've removed an ally of al Qaeda. . . . We have not forgotten the victims of September the 11th—the last phone calls, the cold murder of children, the searches in the rubble. With those attacks, the terrorists and their supporters declared war on the United States. And war is what they got."

The bipartisan September 11 commission, which had access to all relevant intelligence, concluded in 2004 that there had been contacts between Iraq and al Qaeda but no cooperation and no "collaborative relationship." It said it found "no credible evidence that Iraq and al Qaeda cooperated on attacks against the United States."

But by then, Americans had already been deceived by the lie. Two years after the 9/11 attacks, a *Washington Post* poll found that 69 percent of Americans thought it likely, if not certain, that Saddam Hussein had a role in the attacks.

"Seventy percent of the American people think Iraq attacked the Pentagon and the World Trade Center," National Security Council counterterrorism official Rand Beers, who quit five days before the Iraq War began, complained to Clarke. "You wanna know why? Because that's what the administration wants them to think!" Democrats, too, were furious. The 2000 presidential nominee, Al Gore, accused the Bush administration of a "systematic effort to manipulate facts in service to a totalistic ideology."

And it worked.

IN LATE AUGUST 2002, the beginning of what the White House chief of staff had referred to as the "marketing" of the Iraq War, Cheney gave a speech to the Veterans of Foreign Wars convention.

"The case of Saddam Hussein, a sworn enemy of our country, requires a candid appraisal of the facts," he told them. And what "facts" were these? "The Iraqi regime has in fact been very busy enhancing its capabilities in the field of chemical and biological agents," Cheney said. What's more, "we now know that Saddam has resumed his efforts to acquire nuclear weapons. . . . Many of us are convinced that Saddam will acquire nuclear weapons fairly soon."

"Simply stated," the vice president concluded, "there is no doubt that Saddam Hussein now has weapons of mass destruction. There is no doubt he is amassing them to use against our friends, against our allies, and against us."

In fact. We now know. There is no doubt. But everything he said was wrong—and, in the case of Cheney's nuclear claims, completely at odds with U.S. intelligence. Tenet later said he was "surprised" by the Cheney speech, because the "intelligence community's belief was that, left unchecked, Iraq would probably not acquire nuclear weapons until near the end of the decade." Cheney certainly knew that—but he claimed otherwise. "Policy makers have a right to their own opinions," Tenet judged, "but not their own set of facts."

The Bush administration, however, retired that aphorism. It invented its own facts and then convinced the American public that the fabrications were real. In March 2002, Cheney said on CNN that Saddam Hussein "is actively pursuing nuclear weapons at this time." In September, Bush warned that Hussein "poses a much graver threat than anybody could have possibly imagined." In October, Bush, addressing the nation, said without qualification that Iraq "possesses and produces chemical and biological weapons. It is seeking nuclear weapons." Iraq, he continued, "has attempted to purchase high-strength aluminum tubes and other equipment needed . . . to enrich uranium for nuclear weapons. If the Iraqi regime is able to produce, buy, or steal an amount of highly enriched uranium a little larger than a single softball, it could have a nuclear weapon in less than a year."

And this: "We cannot wait for the final proof, the smoking gun that could come in the form of a mushroom cloud."

January 2003 brought Bush's State of the Union address, and a fresh, sixteen-word allegation: "The British Government has learned that Saddam Hussein recently sought significant quantities of uranium from Africa."

In March 2003, Bush had "no doubt that the Iraq regime continues to possess and conceal some of the most lethal weapons ever devised." At one point Cheney eliminated all qualifiers and said that Iraq has "in fact reconstituted nuclear weapons."

Almost all of this was contradicted by U.S. and foreign intelligence. The head of the International Atomic Energy Agency reported that "there is no indication of resumed nuclear activities." ("Wrong," Cheney retorted.) The IAEA also said the aluminum tubes were for conventional weapons and likely couldn't be used to produce nuclear material.

The IAEA also said the allegations about Iraq buying uranium in the African country of Niger were based on forged documents. The CIA raised significant doubts about the claim, too, and insisted the White House remove references to it in earlier Bush speeches. But though the national security adviser, her deputy, and the chief White House speechwriter had all been warned that the allegation was suspect, they included it in Bush's State of the Union address anyway. When Tenet later furnished Andy Card, the White House staff chief, with the CIA memos to White House officials objecting to the Niger allegation, "Andy shook his head and simply said, 'I haven't been told the truth,'" Tenet recounted.

Neither had America, nor the world, been told the truth. Bush required Colin Powell, the secretary of state and revered former general, to put his credibility behind the cause by making a February 2003 presentation to the United Nations. "My colleagues, every statement I make today is backed up by sources, solid sources," he declared in that pivotal speech. "These are not assertions. What we're giving you are facts and conclusions based on solid intelligence." In reality, it was mostly wrong. One bogus assertion, about mobile bioweapons labs, was the fabrication of an Iraqi defector codenamed "Curveball" that CIA analysts considered unreliable. Tenet later claimed the CIA got most of the "garbage" out of Powell's presentation—but much unrefuted refuse remained.

Without question, the intelligence community overstated the case against Iraq (though Tenet said his claim that the case against Iraq was a "slam dunk," attributed to him in a Bob Woodward book, was "intentionally misused" against him). But the administration went well beyond what the intelligence showed. After O'Neill, who had been part of Bush's war cabinet, was fired as treasury secretary, he told *Time* magazine: "I never saw anything that I would characterize as evidence of weapons of mass destruction. . . . To me there is real evidence and everything else. And I never saw anything in the intelligence that I would characterize as real evidence." O'Neill told his biographer Ron Suskind that he "expected to find a bigger market for the truth, but [that] didn't turn out to be right." O'Neill, a veteran of the Nixon and Ford administrations, concluded that "politics, as it's now played, is not about being right. It's about doing whatever's necessary to win."

In lieu of real evidence, Bush officials badgered intelligence officials until they heard what they wanted to hear. Cheney, frequently escorted by his old congressional classmate Newt Gingrich, made regular trips to Langley to meet with (read: intimidate) CIA analysts. Wolfowitz, Feith, and Cheney chief of staff Scooter Libby were also frequent meddlers.

Paul Pillar, the CIA's national intelligence officer for the Near East at the time, wrote in a 2006 article in *Foreign Affairs* that he and others felt pressure not to contradict Bush administration claims. "This poisonous atmosphere reinforced the disinclination within the intelligence community to challenge the consensus view about Iraqi WMD programs," he wrote. The agency's top analyst, Jami Miscik, complained to Tenet that the Bush officials "never seemed satisfied" with the answers they got. Tenet marveled at Bush officials' "willingness to blindly accept information that confirmed preconceived notions." When told by the CIA that North Korea and Iran represented potentially greater threats than Iraq, Feith called this "persnickety."

And woe to those who called out the Bush fallacies.

After Joe Wilson, a career diplomat, wrote a *New York Times* op-ed in 2003 debunking Bush's claim about Iraq seeking uranium in Niger—Wilson had investigated the claim for the CIA—Bush officials punished Wilson by publicly unmasking his wife, Valerie Plame, an undercover CIA operative. That ended her career as a clandestine officer, and two years later she left the CIA. The CIA reported this potential crime, the Justice Department named a special prosecutor, and a four-year investigation ensued. Suspicions quickly focused on Cheney aide Libby and—who else?—Karl Rove, the in-house dirty trickster.

Libby ultimately was convicted of perjury and obstruction of justice. Rove, who had participated in outing Plame to two journalists, narrowly escaped indictment after an extended campaign of public dissembling and after changing his testimony when prosecutors uncovered his role in the unmasking. Bush had promised to fire anybody involved, but he kept Rove (and commuted Libby's sentence). McClellan, who had vouched for both men, was bitter.

"The top White House officials who knew the truth—including Rove, Libby, and possibly Vice President Cheney—allowed me, even encouraged me, to repeat a lie," he said. "During 2003 and 2004, the White House chose not to be open and forthright on the Plame scandal but rather to buy time and sometimes even stonewall. . . . In retrospect it was all too characteristic of an administration that, too often, chose in defining moments to employ obfuscation and secrecy rather than honesty and candor."

Rove, after destroying McClellan's integrity as White House press secretary, called him to say "I'm sorry for what you're going through"—as if it were an illness. "It's clear to me Karl was only concerned about protecting himself from possible legal action and preventing his many critics from bringing him down."

Wilson never got his wish to see "Karl Rove frog-marched out of the White House in handcuffs," and even jurors were surprised. After Libby's conviction, juror Denis Collins told reporters that jurors had a "tremendous amount of sympathy" for the man they convicted. "It was said a number of times, 'What are we doing with this guy here? Where's Rove?'" The juror said it seemed as if Libby were "the fall guy."

THEY DECEIVED AMERICANS ABOUT Iraq being involved in 9/11. They deceived Americans about the WMD. And then they deceived Americans about the war itself.

Before the war, Perle predicted that "support for Saddam . . . will collapse after the first whiff of gunpowder." Rumsfeld had said he didn't know whether "the use of force in Iraq today would last five days, or five weeks or five months, but it certainly isn't going to last any longer than that." And privately, Cheney had assured Dick Armey, the skeptical House majority leader, that "it'll be like American troops going through Paris," Peter Baker reported. (Armey, a Texas Republican, later complained: "I deserved better than to have been bullshitted by Dick Cheney.")

The deception continued. When usual allies wouldn't join the war in Iraq, the administration created a forty-six-member "coalition of the willing" to give the false impression of broad international cooperation in the war. Six members of the coalition—including Palau and the Marshall Islands—didn't even have a military. (At the *Post,* our weekly happy hour became known as the "coalition of the swilling.") The Bush administration and Republican lawmakers mocked European allies France and Germany (a tactic that would later be revived by the Trump administration) for opposing the war. Rumsfeld derided them as "old Europe." Republican lawmakers required House cafeterias to rename "French fries" "freedom fries."

And while Bush was proclaiming "Mission Accomplished," his administration was working to hide the sight of flag-draped caskets returning from Iraq in the belly of transport planes. "There will be no arrival ceremonies for, or media coverage of, deceased military personnel returning to or departing from Ramstein airbase or Dover base, to include interim stops," the Pentagon decreed in a March 2003 directive—and then enforced with vigor. Later, Arlington National Cemetery tried to prevent media coverage of funerals for the Iraq war dead, even after families of the fallen granted permission for coverage. When I wrote contemporaneously about the restrictions, the Army fired the whistleblower.

Meanwhile, the Bush administration kept up the happy talk

about the war, detached from reality. Iraq had "turned a corner," Cheney announced. The insurgency is in its "last throes." "The campaign mentality at times led the president and his chief advisers to spin, hide, shade, and exaggerate the truth, obscuring nuances and ignoring the caveats that should have accompanied their arguments," McClellan wrote. "Rather than choosing to be forthright and candid, they chose to sell the war, and in so doing they did a disservice to the American people and to our democracy."

It fueled a "culture of deception," he wrote in 2008. "Selling war through a political marketing campaign rather than openly and forthrightly discussing the possible need for war with the American people is fraught with danger."

The danger was all the greater because of the newly powerful Fox News, which joined conservative talk radio as the destination of choice for conservatives. The four-year-old cable news network's viewership soared after Bush's election (the Bush White House, in turn, tuned TVs on Air Force One to Fox and showered the network with exclusive interviews), and it carried the administration's war sales pitch uncritically. Academic researchers found in 2003 that consumers of Fox News were far more likely than viewers of other networks to believe the falsehoods that there was collaboration between Saddam Hussein and al Qaeda, that weapons of mass destruction had been found in Iraq, and that world opinion supported the U.S. invasion.

As ominous as the Bush administration's misleading of the public was the new willingness among other Republicans to defend the deception. During the 1970s Watergate investigation, Senator Howard Baker of Tennessee, the Republican on the Watergate committee, asked these immortal words of the Republican president: "What did the president know, and when did he know it?" But there were no longer any Howard Bakers in the GOP of the Bush era. Instead, there was Senator John Cornyn, a Texas Republican.

"The latest accusation by some in the Democratic leadership, that the administration has manipulated intelligence and has exaggerated the threat, is nothing more than an effort to use the war in Iraq for political gain. That is shameful," Cornyn thundered on the Senate floor in 2005 in one of many such speeches. "It devalues the sacrifice our men and women are making on the battlefield every day. It places at risk everything that Americans have sacrificed on behalf of the cause of liberty here and abroad."

Like other Republicans, Cornyn pointed to the findings of the Bush-appointed Robb-Silberman Commission that the Iraq intelligence provided to the Bush administration was "dead wrong." Cornyn said the findings "do not support the charges of manipulation." As Cornyn surely knew, that was because the commission was forbidden by Bush from investigating that. "We were not authorized to investigate how policymakers used the intelligence assessments they received from the Intelligence Community," the commission's report said.

The Senate Intelligence Committee was so authorized, and in 2008 it found that top Bush administration officials' claims about Iraq and al Qaeda, about the post-invasion environment in Iraq, and about weapons of mass destruction, were "not substantiated" or were "contradicted" by the intelligence, or did not reflect the intelligence agencies' uncertainty.

Two Republican senators on the committee joined Democrats in endorsing those findings, but four others denounced the bipartisan findings as "political gamesmanship" and a "partisan exercise."

Bush had proven that, through sheer repetition of falsehoods, you could fool enough of the people enough of the time to start a war based on a fictional premise. And he had proven that the pull of partisanship had become so strong that Republican lawmakers would defend the president rather than defend the truth—even on a matter as consequential as war. Republicans had scored another win in the war on truth.

It was a key lesson for an unscrupulous aspirant to the presidency who, ironically, saw the deception for what it was: "Bush got us into this horrible war with lies, by lying, by saying they had weapons of mass destruction, by saying all sorts of things that turned out not to be true," Donald Trump told CNN's Wolf Blitzer in 2008. For once, Trump spoke the truth.

CHAPTER 7

A Heckuva Job

Things were tense the morning of November 22, 2000, on the eighteenth floor of the Stephen P. Clark Government Center in downtown Miami. The night before, the Florida Supreme Court had given counties a tight deadline for completing a manual recount of ballots in the disputed presidential election between Al Gore and George W. Bush. The Miami-Dade elections board concluded it was impossible to complete a full hand recount in time, so they voted to review only the 10,750 ballots that the machines had skipped, and they moved the counting operation to the nineteenth floor to escape the commotion of reporters and onlookers in the elections office.

The Bush campaign, clinging to a precarious lead in the recount, didn't like this one bit. And so Bush aides stepped in to stop the recount—by fomenting a riot.

Karl Rove's political operation had spent millions of dollars flying in Republican operatives from around the country and putting them up in hotels. Now a group of these operatives, many of them young men in shirtsleeves and ties, crowded into the elections office. A call went out on Radio Mambí, a pro-Bush Cuban American outlet, to converge on the elections office to protest. Brad Blakeman, the Bush campaign's lead advance guy, coordinated the effort. Also lending a hand: Roger Stone, a Trump adviser at this time.

At the elections office, Republican operatives led chants with bullhorns:

"Let us in!"

"We want Bush!"

"Stop the count!"

"Stop the fraud!"

"Cheaters!"

"Denounce the recount!"

"Shut it down!"

Things turned ugly when protesters spied the county Democratic chairman with a ballot in his pocket. It was clearly marked as a sample "training" ballot for recount observers, but that didn't matter. Protesters shouted "Arrest him!" and "This guy's got a ballot!" The mob cornered him and started pushing him and jumping on him, requiring police to escort him to safety. Another Democratic county official said he was punched twice and kicked in the back.

The mob turned its rage on the three-person elections board. "Bring the three stooges out here," they yelled. And the board, intimidated by the melee, gave the Bush mob what it really wanted: they voted to stop the recount. The supervisor of elections said the protesters' complaints of unfairness "weighed heavy on our minds."

The "Brooks Brothers Riot," as it would come to be called because of the hooligans' attire, was a triumph of mob rule over the democratic process—and an ominous precedent for election violence on a grand scale two decades later.

In the end, it probably didn't matter that they succeeded in shutting down the Miami-Dade recount, because the fix was in at a much higher level. Three weeks later, the U.S. Supreme Court's conservative majority, in a brazenly partisan ruling, put an end to all recounts and effectively declared Bush the winner. The 5–4 *Bush v. Gore* decision was so flimsy—a strained application of the Fourteenth Amendment's Equal Protection Clause—that the majority felt the need to add a disclaimer to its ruling so that it wouldn't be cited as a precedent for future cases: "Our consideration is limited to the present circumstances."

For twenty years after the decision, the infamous case was cited only once by the High Court justices (in a Clarence Thomas dissent) until Justice Brett Kavanaugh revived it in deciding to restrict mail-in ballots in the 2020 election. (Kavanaugh, like Justice Amy Coney Barrett and Chief Justice John Roberts, all helped Bush during the Florida recount.) Evan Thomas, in his 2019 biography of Justice Sandra Day O'Connor, reported that Justice Antonin Scalia, who joined the *Bush v. Gore* majority opinion, privately called its reasoning, "as we say in Brooklyn, a piece of shit."

Unofficial recounts later conducted by the media concluded that Bush probably would have won Florida anyway if the official recounts had proceeded. In a broader sense, though, postelection reviews also left little doubt that tens of thousands of Floridians had supported Gore but were prevented from casting a vote.

The U.S. Commission on Civil Rights concluded that Florida officials, led by the president's brother, Governor Jeb Bush, were "grossly derelict" in conducting the election. The commission concluded that "countless" eligible voters "were wrongfully purged from the voter registration rolls, turned away from the polls, and by various other means prevented from exercising the franchise." It found that Black voters, heavily pro-Gore, were "nearly ten times more likely than white voters to have their ballots rejected in Florida." The "notorious, state-sponsored, erroneous purging procedures significantly contributed to the dilution of the African American vote," it found.

It's not a stretch to say that Gore, who won the popular vote nationwide, would have become president if Jeb Bush's Florida hadn't blocked so many Black voters from casting their ballots.

The 2000 election was over, but the Republicans had learned from Florida an insidious, antidemocratic lesson: with the Supreme Court in its corner, and with the ability to suppress the opposition's vote in GOP-run states, Republicans didn't necessarily need a majority to win. All they had to do was howl about election fraud.

The Brooks Brothers rioters shouted about fraud. Also during the 2000 recount, Karl Rove and Bush campaign chairman Don Evans, in a news conference, falsely alleged Republican ballots hadn't been counted in Iowa. Rove tried to tie Gore's campaign chairman, Bill Daley, to past ballot fraud in Chicago. Republicans alleged fraud in Missouri, where Republican senator John Ashcroft lost to an opponent who had died three weeks earlier in a plane crash. Bush appointed Ashcroft attorney general, and Ashcroft, a longtime Rove client, used the post to launch a crackdown on fictitious voter fraud.

"Votes have been bought, voters intimidated and ballot boxes stuffed," Ashcroft said. "The polling process has been disrupted or not completed. Voters have been duped into signing absentee ballots believing they were applications for public relief. And the residents of cemeteries have infamously shown up at the polls on Election Day."

There was, and is, no such widespread fraud in U.S. elections. But Republicans, in order to justify more restrictions on voting, had planted a seed in their supporters' minds by telling them elections were rigged. That seed, in years to come, would sprout an invasive weed of authoritarianism.

The ends-justify-means thinking didn't stop when the Bush campaign set up shop in the White House. Bush's "iron triangle" of campaign advisers—Rove, campaign manager Joe Allbaugh, and communications director Karen Hughes—were among many Bush political aides to take taxpayer-funded jobs in the White House. Once in power, those advisers concluded that it would be politically advantageous to Bush to govern as a hard-charging partisan rather than to follow his promise to be "a uniter, not a divider." They set about dismantling many of the guardrails that had kept government on course for decades—because it was expedient for Bush.

They mounted a political campaign to intimidate Republican lawmakers into suspending the usual checks and balances. In the name of national security, they circumvented both U.S. and international law to justify torture of detainees and eavesdropping on Americans without a court's permission. They installed Bush cronies in crucial jobs, placing loyalty above expertise. And they used the levers of the federal government to disqualify Democratic voters in future elections.

By the time they had finished, many of democracy's safeguards had been hollowed out—leaving the political system vulnerable to more audacious assaults in the future.

———

JUST TWO MONTHS INTO Bush's first term, Matthew Dowd, Bush's campaign polling coordinator, presented Rove with a revolutionary concept: that the age-old strategy of appealing to the political center no longer made sense. Dowd compared the 2000 election results with results going back to 1976 and found that the number of "swing" voters, those of moderate leanings who can be persuaded to switch sides, had shrunk from 22 percent to 7 percent. Most of the so-called independents were in fact reliably Democratic or Republican. There was, Dowd concluded, no "gettable middle." In Robert Draper's account, *Dead Certain*, Dowd told Rove: "It's about *motivation* rather than *persuasion*. We maximize the number of Republicans on election day, and we win."

Most expected Bush, after his razor-thin victory, to attempt bipartisan governance. But Dowd's, and Rove's, new thinking called for an entirely different governing strategy: forget about building consensus, and instead keep doing what the party's core supporters, the "base," wants. With a few exceptions (Bush's education bill was crafted with Teddy Kennedy), the "compassionate conservative" agenda was gone, and so was any thought of working with Democrats.

Bush, who campaigned on a promise to take climate change seriously, pulled out of the Kyoto climate accords and abandoned the International Criminal Court. He tried to ram a $1.6 trillion tax cut through the Senate with only a single Democratic vote—then accepted a slightly smaller cut after two moderate Republicans defected.

John DiIulio, an academic brought in by Bush to shepherd his "compassion" agenda, quit the White House in disappointment. "There is a virtual absence as yet of any policy accomplishments that might, to a fair-minded nonpartisan, count as the flesh on the bones of so-called compassionate conservatism," he wrote in an email to journalist Ron Suskind in October 2002.

DiIulio, apparently an *Andy Griffith Show* fan, blamed the "Mayberry Machiavellis—staff, senior and junior, who consistently talked and acted as if the height of political sophistication consisted in reducing every issue to its simplest, black-and-white terms for public consumption, then steering legislative initiatives or policy proposals as far right as possible. These folks have their predecessors in previous administrations (left and right, Democrat and Republican), but, in the Bush administration, they were particularly unfettered."

The Mayberry Machiavellis lived in fear of Rove, "maybe the single most powerful person in the modern, post-Hoover era ever to occupy a political adviser post near the Oval Office." As such, "Little happens on any issue without Karl's okay."

When *Esquire* published the email, White House press secretary Ari Fleischer erupted over the "groundless and baseless" charges—and a spooked DiIulio promptly apologized for his "groundless and baseless" claims.

But it was all true. Fleischer's deputy, McClellan, later wrote that "no political operative before Rove arguably had so much influence within a White House. As senior adviser overseeing political affairs and strategy, Rove controlled an inordinately influential power center in the White House. . . . Rove's role was political manipulation, plain and simple, which explains the machinations within the White House and their consequences."

Rove, known as the "architect" of Bush's political rise, made sure the apparatus of government worked to enhance Bush's political advantage. Federal grants went disproportionately to targeted states and congressional districts. Cabinet officials scheduled pre-election travel to targeted areas. Federal agencies offered campaign-style briefings about Bush's accomplishments. And the White House worked relentlessly to keep Republican lawmakers in line. After Senator Jim Jeffords, a Vermont Republican, opposed Bush's tax cut, incessant White House slights and threats to cut his pet programs finally drove him to quit the GOP, temporarily throwing control to the Democrats. "Tolerance of dissent is the hallmark of a mature party, and it is well past time for the Republican Party to grow up," Senator John McCain, Bush's former opponent in the Republican primaries, said of the Jeffords episode.

Republicans in Congress, taking their cues from the White House, reached new pinnacles of partisanship. In the House, Speaker Denny Hastert created what came to be known as the "Hastert Rule," under which he would only allow legislation to come to a vote on the House floor if it had the support of a majority of Republicans. That sharply curtailed the potential for compromise and essentially gave hard-right lawmakers a veto over legislation in the House. Republicans, who once complained about the Democratic majority's heavy-handedness in running the chamber, now outdid their predecessors. The number of "closed" rules—that is, bills taken to the floor with little or no possibility of amendment—increased from 19 percent in the two years before Republicans took control to 49 percent in 2003–2004, political scientists Norman Ornstein and Thomas Mann found. Republican leaders would sometimes hold votes open for hours as they strong-armed wayward members to toe the party line.

In the Senate, Bush was enjoying a high level of success in getting his judges confirmed; in 2003, according to Ornstein and Mann, there were only 39 vacancies in the judiciary of 859 total judgeships. But Majority Leader Bill Frist, a close Bush ally, wanted more. When Democrats blocked some of Bush's nominees to appellate courts, he threatened to trigger the "nuclear option"—abolishing the longtime standard that nominees would not get a vote unless sixty of the one hundred senators agreed to it. A bipartisan group of senators temporarily defused the crisis Frist had caused, but his willingness to go nuclear set a precedent for both parties to invoke the nuclear option in the future, gradually eroding the filibuster, the Senate's tradition of unlimited debate, and other rules designed to encourage consensus.

The increasingly lockstep partisanship was worsened by outside groups that worked to purge lawmakers who strayed from hard-right positions. It had begun years earlier when antitax activist Grover Norquist devised a "no tax pledge" in which lawmakers vowed not to raise taxes. Those who went back on their word (most famously George H. W. Bush) got pummeled by the party's base.

Next, in 1999, came the Club for Growth, which by 2002 had become the largest source of campaign funds for Republicans other than the party itself. Supported financially by hardline conservatives such as House Majority Leader Tom DeLay (who in 2002 gave the group $50,000 from his political action committee), it used this money to defeat moderate Republicans in primaries.

In 2004, the Club had a list of twenty-one congressional "RINOs"—Republicans in Name Only—it wanted to oust, and to replace with Republicans who passed an ideological purity test administered by the Club's "chief inquisitor." Among its victims over time were longtime Republican senators Dick Lugar of Indiana and Robert Bennett of Utah (defeated in primary contests), Arlen Specter of Pennsylvania (quit the GOP when the Club for Growth backed a primary challenger), and Florida governor Charlie Crist (quit the GOP when the Club backed a challenger in his Senate primary). Several other veteran Republican moderates decided to retire before they were shown the door.

The conservative Heritage Foundation, eager to join the purity police, formed "Heritage Action for America" and vowed to oust Republican members of Congress who didn't vote the hard-right position on its "scored" votes.

Conservative talk radio and Fox News provided the soundtrack for the purging of the ideologically impure. In the 1990s, Rush Limbaugh counseled conservatives not to oppose Republican moderates such as Mitt Romney (who ran against Ted Kennedy for the Senate in 1994) because their election, Limbaugh said, would be a "step in the right direction." But "this détente started to break down as the 2000s progressed," University of Pennsylvania historian Brian Rosenwald wrote. By 2005, Limbaugh was calling out Republican lawmakers who opposed Bush policies, declaring that a "moderate is just a liberal disguise."

Fox's Sean Hannity, on his radio show, denounced McCain and Senators Chuck Hagel of Nebraska and Lindsey Graham of South Carolina as RINOs. As conservative hosts and outlets proliferated, they competed for audiences by becoming ever more intolerant of those who strayed from conservative orthodoxy.

This was no way to run a country. The Rove-dominated White House governed by catering to the Republican base. Republicans in Congress, terrified of being purged for any heresy, allowed no daylight between themselves and the White House. The usual checks on presidential power broke down. And the Bush administration, free of congressional oversight, showed its hubris.

Bush abandoned the Republicans' traditional concern about fiscal restraint, quickly squandering the budget surplus he inherited with a series of tax cuts and spending increases. "Reagan proved deficits don't matter," Vice President Dick Cheney famously said when Treasury Secretary Paul O'Neill warned that the government was moving toward a fiscal crisis. In the forty years before Bush took office, the average annual increase in inflation-adjusted discretionary spending was 1.7 percent, the libertarian Cato Institute calculated in 2004; the increases in Bush's first three years were 10.3 percent, 9.7 percent, and 8.3 percent.

Bush also abandoned any serious attempt to crack down on corporate misbehavior, exemplified by the collapse of energy company Enron in 2001 in a massive accounting fraud. Then–Federal Reserve chairman Alan Greenspan warned that "there has been too much gaming of the system" and "there has been a corrupting of the system of capitalism," Suskind reported. But Greenspan and O'Neill were shut down in their attempts to implement corporate reform by Bush's top economic adviser, Larry Lindsey, who told them "there's always the option of doing nothing." That option, which Bush repeatedly took, would lead to ruin years later in the financial collapse of 2008.

Repeatedly, the administration exempted itself from the usual checks and balances. It refused to disclose to Congress which corporate executives met with Cheney's energy task force. It drafted a series of "torture memos" justifying "enhanced interrogation techniques" such as waterboarding, which had been illegal. It set up "black-site" prisons and the Guantánamo Bay detention facility exempt from the U.S. court system and asserted the right to wiretap U.S. citizens without court warrants. In one dramatic episode, White House officials Andy Card and Alberto Gonzales in March 2004 went to the hospital room of Attorney General Ashcroft, incapacitated by gallbladder problems, to get him to sign off on the surveillance of U.S. citizens in ways Justice Department lawyers called illegal.

With the Republican Senate disinclined to use its advice-and-consent power to check the administration, Bush stocked his administration with loyalists of dubious qualifications. To run the Federal Emergency Management Agency he tapped Michael Brown, who had been a commissioner of the International Arabian Horse Association but had precious little experience in emergency management. When Hurricane Katrina devastated New Orleans in 2005, displacing 1.3 million, and leaving 1,800 dead and many more without food or water, Brown seemed bizarrely unaware of events as his agency bungled the rescue and relief efforts. Yet Bush famously told his hapless aide: "Brownie, you're doing a heckuva job."

Weeks later, Bush nominated his woefully unqualified White House counsel, Harriet Miers, to the Supreme Court. She had experience running the Texas Lottery Commission under Bush, but she didn't know much about the law (she reportedly didn't know basic legal terms such as "reasonable suspicion" and "probable cause"), she had had her law license suspended for unpaid dues, and the Senate Judiciary Committee returned her legal questionnaire for a redo because her original answers ranged from "incomplete to insulting." She withdrew in humiliating fashion.

Republicans took what Bush called a "thumping" in the 2006 midterm elections. But the president's chief political strategist took the long view. Rove, affectionately nicknamed "Turd Blossom" by Bush after a flower that grows in cow manure, would use his high government position to disable Democrats in future elections—including by ending the careers of federal prosecutors who didn't do the Republican Party's political bidding.

In Arkansas, for example, the Bush administration fired the U.S. attorney in order to appoint Tim Griffin, a Republican operative who had been a Rove aide in the White House. In Missouri, Rove approved a deal removing the U.S. attorney, Todd Graves, because Senator Kit Bond, a Missouri Republican, had a dispute with Graves's brother. Rove also had a hand in firing the U.S. attorney in Nevada because Rove wanted him to make immigration more of an issue. Most famously, Rove pushed vigorously for the removal of the U.S. attorney in New Mexico, David Iglesias, because he hadn't pressed voter fraud cases and other accusations against Democrats by New Mexico Republicans. Rove prevailed in ousting Iglesias, even overcoming objections from Bush's attorney general, Gonzales.

Rove also hatched an elaborate scheme with DeLay, the House majority leader, to redraw congressional maps in Texas so that seven Democratic members of Congress, their constituencies diluted, would lose their seats.

First, DeLay had to get Republicans elected to a majority in the Texas legislature—and to do that, he had to figure out how to funnel corporate money donated by groups seeking favorable treatment by DeLay in Congress to state candidates. Inconveniently, a one-hundred-year-old Texas law prohibited corporations from giving money directly or indirectly to candidates.

So DeLay arranged for groups seeking influence in Congress to donate to a Texas state political action committee he set up that was run by a Rove friend. The nursing home industry, an Indian tribe, energy interests, tobacco and liquor companies, railroad and retail corporations, and others contributed some $190,000. DeLay's Texas PAC then donated the corporate contributions to the Republican National Committee, which, using a different account, immediately sent an identical sum of money to Republican state candidates in Texas chosen by DeLay.

The funds proved to be effective, and enough of DeLay's candidates won to take control of the Texas state legislature. DeLay then got the governor (another old Rove client, Rick Perry) to declare a special session—and then another, and another—to force through a new congressional map designed to dilute the Democratic vote.

It was an extraordinary breach of trust. For decades, both parties had agreed nationwide to conduct redistricting only after the decennial census, to avoid getting mired in constant political warfare. But DeLay didn't care about political norms. He wanted immediate power. He also convinced Texas's skeptical lieutenant governor, David Dewhurst, to suspend the legislative rules requiring a two-thirds vote in the Senate, thereby allowing the new map to pass on a simple party-line vote.

From Washington, Rove worked the phones in support of the maneuver. When Texas senator Bill Ratliff, a moderate Republican, resisted part of the redistricting plan, Rove called to tell him the matter "could be important to the president." Ratliff relented.

State Democrats, infuriated, tried to thwart the plan by denying the legislature a quorum. Several House Democrats left the state in May 2003, hoping to run out the clock on the special session.

DeLay wouldn't have it. His staff called the Justice Department to see if the FBI would arrest the fleeing Democratic legislators. His staff also called the Federal Aviation Administration with the tail number of a plane carrying some of the Democrats in hopes that federal authorities could track it down.

Thus did DeLay enlist the federal government in an attempt to hunt down and lock up his political opponents. The FAA's "air interdiction" center in California, and thirteen FAA officials, spent forty minutes searching for the plane and calling regional airports and flight control centers. The Republican House speaker in Texas issued an order that the missing Democrats be arrested, and the Texas Department of Public Safety joined, illegally, in the attempt to round up Democratic lawmakers. One public safety officer enlisted help from the FBI, claiming falsely that there was a warrant out for their arrest. (The Texas DPS then destroyed records of the incident.)

DeLay, meeting with Bush and Rove at the White House after the new map was enacted, said he received congratulations from the two men. Six Democratic members of Congress lost their seats (a seventh targeted lawmaker survived).

Republicans, to their delight, realized they had found a way to keep themselves in the majority even if the voters favored the Democrats. Because of Texas and similar gerrymandering in other states, and because of heavy concentration of Democratic voters in urban areas, the deck was stacked against the Democrats so much that they had to win the popular vote by 7 percentage points in order to win a majority in the House. It would take a near landslide for Democrats just to break even. As one Republican staffer put it after the Texas redistricting, the move "should assure that Republicans keep the House no matter the national mood."

The situation was even worse in the Senate, because Republican-dominated rural states are overrepresented. (California, for example, has 68 times the population of Wyoming but the same number of senators.) Because of population patterns, about one fifth of the U.S. population controls more than half of the Senate.

DeLay, in 2004, started celebrating his voter-resistant Republican majority, now well insulated from the will of the people.

"Two-thousand four," he said, "is the year we start thinking like a permanent majority." And when you think you're a permanent majority, you don't much think about how you treat the minority.

During the redrawing of the Texas map, DeLay went to a fundraising dinner for his political action committee at Ruth's Chris Steak House in downtown Washington. The place, housed in a federal building, had a strict no-smoking policy, but DeLay decided to light a cigar anyway. Told by the maître d' that the federal government prohibited smoking there, DeLay replied: "I am the federal government." (A DeLay spokesman later claimed he said, "I'm with the federal government.")

DeLay paid a heavy price for his Texas shenanigans. He was indicted in state court for money laundering in 2005 (for funneling the corporate contributions to Texas candidates through the RNC) and sentenced to three years in prison. He quit the House and, in his post-congressional career, wore a leopard-trim vest on *Dancing with the Stars*. Years later, a state appellate court threw out the jury verdict in a party-line vote: two elected Republican judges against one elected Democratic judge. They accepted that DeLay had done what he was accused of, but they declared that the laundering of corporate contributions through the RNC was perfectly legal. He hadn't served a day of his sentence.

At the Justice Department, career lawyers unanimously decided that the new Texas map discriminated against Black and Latino voters. But, *The New York Times* later reported, the career lawyers were overruled by a Bush political appointee who had helped the Bush campaign in the Florida recount. One of the career officials in that department said the political interference was "more explicit, pronounced and consciously done" than in previous administrations.

A splintered Supreme Court in 2006 tossed out one of the districts for violating the Voting Rights Act, but a conservative majority of justices declared that it was perfectly fine for a state legislature to redraw maps for "the sole purpose of achieving a Republican congressional majority."

With the High Court showing willingness in the Texas case (and in an Arizona case) to bless Republican rewriting of election law for partisan advantage, Republican-controlled states went on a voter suppression spree. Georgia and Indiana enacted laws requiring voter identification, which minority voters were less likely to have. Ohio, Wisconsin, Michigan, and Nevada sought to purge tens of thousands of voters from the rolls, mostly in minority communities. In Michigan, one Republican state legislator spoke the unspoken part: "If we do not suppress the Detroit vote, we're going to have a tough time in this election."

Republicans came up with ever more creative plans to make voting more difficult in minority precincts: closed polling places, limited hours, opposition to early voting, robocalls with false voting information, and aggressive challenges to individual voters' eligibility. They continued to chip away at voting rights until the Supreme Court in 2013 invalidated a large part of the Voting Rights Act of 1965—sharply curtailing the federal government's ability to remedy the disenfranchisement of racial minorities.

More and more states under Republican control joined the voter suppression party: Alabama, Kansas, Mississippi, Pennsylvania, South Carolina, Tennessee, Texas, Virginia. Invariably, they claimed they were combating voter fraud. Wisconsin's Republican governor, Scott Walker, once claimed that in his state Republicans "probably have to win with at least 53 percent of the vote to account for fraud."

That was pure fiction, just as it was when the Brooks Brothers rioters shouted about voter fraud in Florida. But Republicans were no longer going to let truth get in the way of their quest for power.

CHAPTER 8

Bridges to Nowhere

The modest bungalow at 53 Baltimore Avenue stands two blocks from the boardwalk and across the street from the Iguana Grill (try the fish tacos!) in Rehoboth Beach, Delaware, a seaside town favored by Washington's summer vacation set. Beachgoers toting their boogie boards past this unmarked abode in the early 2000s would have had no idea that it stood at the fulcrum of a massive criminal enterprise of, by, and for the people at the highest levels of the Republican Party.

The beach house was world headquarters of the American International Center, which billed itself as "a premier international think tank," founded "under the high powered directorship of David A. Grosh and Brian J. Mann," dedicated to "bringing great minds together from all over the globe," using "21st century technology and decades of experience" and seeking "to expand the parameters of international discourse in an effort to leverage the combined power of world intellect."

In reality, the entire operation was a sham. The "high powered" Grosh was a lifeguard—the 1997 Rehoboth Beach Lifeguard of the Year, in fact—and Mann was a yoga instructor. Both were boyhood pals of Michael Scanlon, a former top aide to House Majority Leader Tom DeLay. Scanlon, with his business partner, Republican superlobbyist Jack Abramoff, traded on their influence with DeLay, and with Karl Rove, to build a sprawling criminal enterprise.

Scanlon and Abramoff defrauded Indian tribes to the tune

of tens of millions of dollars, receiving illegal funds from dodgy entities, then using the phony think tank to disguise the funds as something else.

Abramoff used AIC to pay Ralph Reed, the former director of the Christian Coalition, for his lobbying and public relations work for Indian casinos. Once called "The Right Hand of God" by *Time* magazine, Reed went into business as a political consultant, and he built his business by manipulating evangelical Christians to get them unwittingly to protect his gambling clients (he mobilized Christians to oppose gambling projects that competed with his own gambling clients' interests). Reed didn't want his Christian followers to know that he was being paid with gambling money—so millions of dollars of tribal payments to Reed went through AIC. Another pass-through for Reed's casino money was Grover Norquist's Americans for Tax Reform, the leading force for antitax purity in the GOP; Reed, Norquist, and Abramoff had known each other since their days together in the College Republicans.

Abramoff was also tight with Rove, whom Abramoff lobbied to get a White House meeting with President Bush for the prime minister of Malaysia, Mahathir Mohamad, an outspoken anti-Semite who jailed his political opponents. Rather than register as a foreign agent, as the law requires when you lobby for foreign countries, Abramoff funneled $1.2 million from the Malaysian government through AIC. Abramoff reportedly lobbied Rove, "my friend from the College Republicans past," at least four times to get the meeting. It helped that Rove hired Abramoff's assistant, Susan Ralston, as his own top assistant.

In the end, more than twenty people were convicted in the scandal, which encompassed cruise ships, a feud with a slain billionaire, fake wire transfers, bribes, skyboxes, a kickback scheme called "gimme five," and lavish golfing trips to Scotland. Among those brought down were the Bush administration's chief procurement officer, the chairman of the House administration committee, the deputy secretary of the interior, and a platoon of Republican congressional aides. Abramoff and Scanlon both went to prison. The scandal pushed DeLay, already indicted in the separate money-laundering case in Texas, to resign from the House.

The ideological Republicans of the 1994 revolution had turned into a pay-to-play racket. "The Republicans let the lobbyists go wild, and before you knew it, the lobbyists became a problem for Republicans," the conservative journalist Matthew Continetti wrote in his 2006 book, *The K Street Gang.* "Tom DeLay created Jack Abramoff, and like Frankenstein's monster, Abramoff in turn destroyed DeLay."

A full decade before Donald Trump seized the Republican presidential nomination, Continetti warned: "As Republicans grow more comfortable in power, their standards will drop, whatever restraint they still possess will vanish, and their ranks will swell with more opportunists and con artists." He was remarkably prescient.

In their quest for power, Republicans of the Bush era weakened the institutions of democracy. They obliterated restrictions on campaign spending and shoved aside the norms that had informally constrained public officials' behavior. They replaced those restraints and norms with an anything-goes approach to politics that invited corruption and lawlessness. The Abramoff scandal was the most extreme abuse, but it wouldn't have been possible if Republican leaders hadn't invited corruption with a system that sold government to the highest bidder.

SINCE THE WATERGATE ERA, a system of public financing had dominated presidential elections. Gerald Ford, Jimmy Carter, Ronald Reagan, George H. W. Bush, and Bill Clinton all used the taxpayer-funded system, designed to prevent the presidency from being bought and sold. In exchange for public financing, they agreed to spending limits, to keep the playing field somewhat level.

But in the 2000 election, George W. Bush shattered this safeguard. He knew he could raise so much more money than his Republican primary rivals that he declined to receive the public matching funds, allowing him to blow through the spending limits. It was the death knell for public financing, which officially died eight years later when Barack Obama opted out of the system in the general election.

This was just one of many failures of restraints trying to

limit the corrupting influence of money in politics. Since 1996, overall inflation has been 70 percent. But independent expenditures in political campaigns—those not done by the candidates themselves—have increased 16,000 percent over that same time.

Republicans and Democrats alike contributed to the breakdown. It was illegal for corporations to spend money on federal elections, but both parties found ways around that technicality. In the 2000 cycle, they raised a combined half-billion dollars in soft money from corporations, unions, and wealthy individuals. Bill Clinton demonstrated the transactional nature of such contributions when he invited large soft money donors for overnight stays in the Lincoln Bedroom at the White House.

Republican senator John McCain and Democratic senator Russ Feingold, after a multiyear struggle, got Congress to ban soft money. But their opponents, led by Senator Mitch McConnell (who became Senate Republican whip in 2003 and Republican leader in 2007), found ways to keep the corporate funds flowing.

First came "issue" groups, such as the Swift Boat Veterans for Truth effort that mortally wounded John Kerry's presidential campaign in 2004. Billionaires and corporations could fund such groups (often called "527s" because of their category in the tax code), tilting elections without giving to either candidate or party—when in reality such groups routinely coordinated (illegally) with both.

McConnell sued to have the McCain-Feingold law invalidated, but the Supreme Court upheld most of its provisions. The big-money forces persisted, however, and won rulings in 2007, 2008, and 2009 that chipped away at the law. Finally, in the 2010 *Citizens United* case, the court's conservative majority, with a nod to the legal doctrine of corporate personhood, obliterated any meaningful limit on corporate and billionaire spending on politics. (McConnell filed an amicus curiae brief on the winning side, and the head of Citizens United, David Bossie, had been an investigator for Congressman Dan Burton, of Vince Foster fame.) Thus was born the era of the "super PACs"—political groups that use nonprofit status to conceal the identity of their donors, whose undisclosed contributions are called "dark money." A year later, Republican presidential candidate Mitt Romney said it best: "Corporations are people, my friend."

THERE HAVE ALWAYS BEEN crooks in politics, as in all lines of work.

There was, for example, Congressman William Jefferson, a Louisiana Democrat who, in 2006, was filmed taking $100,000 in cash in a leather briefcase full of $100 bills. The FBI later found $90,000 of that cold cash in his freezer, concealed "inside various frozen food containers." He hadn't realized that it was an FBI informant who had offered him a stake in a Nigerian company in exchange for his political influence. "Dollar Bill," as he came to be known, referred to his ill-gotten gains as "African art." He spent five years in prison.

Then there was Congressman Randy "Duke" Cunningham, a California Republican, who actually wrote up a bribe menu to help a defense contractor buy him off. For a $16 million federal defense contract, Cunningham required a $140,000 yacht. In the early 2000s, the defense contractor bought the congressman not just the yacht but a Rolls-Royce and a Louis Phillipe commode. The bribes added up to at least $2.4 million. Cunningham spent seven years in prison.

But the Republicans' great innovation of the George W. Bush era was to make corruption systematic, and generally legal. It was a new incarnation of old-fashioned, pay-to-play politics: to get what you want from the Republican-led government, you have to give your money to Republican lobbyists, Republican lawmakers, and the Republican Party. They made corruption into a science.

It began, as mentioned earlier, with DeLay and Gingrich's K Street Project, in which friendly lobbyists (those who make political contributions to Republicans) got to write legislation, and lobbyists who hired (or contributed to) Democrats saw their pet projects killed. "We're just following the old adage of punish your enemies and reward your friends," DeLay said in 1995. "We don't like to deal with people who are trying to kill the Revolution. We know who they are. The word is out."

But the coercion got more overt as Republicans cemented their hold on power. In late 1998, Gingrich's office warned the Electronic Industries Alliance, a trade lobby, not to go ahead with its plans to hire as its new president David McCurdy, a former Democratic congressman. Republican leaders wanted the group to hire retiring Republican congressman Bill Paxon instead.

When the EIA hired McCurdy anyway, Republicans exacted retribution. They instructed Republican members and staff not to meet with representatives of the EIA. They even postponed votes on two intellectual property treaties that had no significant opposition—admitting that they were doing so to send the EIA a message.

"To hire a Democrat to represent this group before a current Republican majority and what is certain to be a larger majority is not a shrewd business decision," Michael Scanlon, the DeLay aide who would soon become Jack Abramoff's business partner, told *The New York Times*.

The House Ethics Committee sent DeLay a private letter rebuking him and issued a memo to all House members saying they "are prohibited from taking or withholding any official action on the basis of the partisan affiliation or the campaign contributions or support of the involved individuals." A not-quite-contrite DeLay said he had been "a little over-passionate in my desire to get things done."

But things only got more corrupt, er, "passionate," with Bush's election, giving Republicans unified control of government, and with DeLay's rise to House majority leader in 2003.

That year, Michael Oxley, an Ohio Republican and chairman of the House Financial Services Committee, was preparing with his committee to launch a probe of the mutual fund industry's pricing. But then a committee staffer reportedly told the trade lobby, the Investment Company Institute, that the committee would pull its punches in the investigation under one condition: if the ICI fired its chief lobbyist, Julie Domenick—a Democrat.

In 2004, Hollywood lobbyists were seeking more than $1 billion in tax credits for the film industry. The credits were included in a massive tax bill approved by the Senate, but then the Motion Picture Association of America hired Dan Glickman, a former

Democratic member of Congress, as its chief. Congressional Republicans retaliated by removing the $1 billion in credits from the tax bill.

Grover Norquist, who declared in 2002 that "everyone on K Street [the informal name for the lobbying industry] should be a Republican," circulated lists of lobbyists grouped by party affiliation and political contributions. Rick Santorum, the No. 3 Senate Republican, hosted twice-monthly sessions for lobbyists in the Capitol that he called "K Street meetings." One of the lobbyists' guest speakers: Karl Rove. In response to such activities, the Senate Ethics Committee warned that the lobbyist list "suggests a motive to grant special access, or deny access."

That was exactly the motive, and it worked. American Enterprise Institute scholar Norm Ornstein told *Salon* in 2005 that the K Street Project had essentially secured all entry-level lobbying positions for Republicans, and they were expected to make the maximum contributions to Republican candidates.

Some two dozen DeLay aides cashed in and became lobbyists, for energy, finance, tobacco, pharmaceuticals, and other industries. Corporate lobbyists showered cash on DeLay at parties, golf tournaments, and even a rock concert. In one famous episode DeLay flew dozens of lobbyists to Las Vegas for golf and a hot tub party hosted by his daughter and campaign manager, Dani Ferro.

The majority leader earned several more rebukes from the House Ethics Committee. The bipartisan panel found that he created "an appearance of impropriety" by attending a June 2002 golf fundraiser with lobbyists from Westar Energy after the company gave $25,000 to one of his political action committees. One of the Westar attendees said that DeLay asked the lobbyists to tell him of "any interest we had" in the energy bill. Westar was seeking changes to an energy bill, and its executives concluded that they had to pay $56,500 to "get a seat at the table" because DeLay's "agreement is necessary" to getting the provision they sought.

The Ethics Committee also issued a "public admonishment" of DeLay for telling Republican congressman Nick Smith that Smith had to vote DeLay's way on a Medicare prescription drug bill in order for DeLay to support Smith's bid to have his son succeed him in Congress. In one letter to DeLay, the Ethics Committee members unanimously told him: "In view of the number of instances to date in which the committee has found it necessary to comment on conduct in which you have engaged, it is clearly necessary for you to temper your future actions to assure that you are in full compliance at all times with the applicable House rules and standards of conduct."

But House Speaker Denny Hastert had other ideas. He pushed out the Republican chairman of the Ethics Committee, Joel Hefley of Colorado, who presided over the DeLay rebukes, and installed instead Doc Hastings of Washington, a leadership loyalist. Hastert also ousted two other Republicans from the committee and replaced them with lawmakers who had donated to a legal fund supporting DeLay. The message to Republicans was clear: the old rules don't apply to us.

The moral rot was becoming increasingly evident. In September 2006, Republican congressman Mark Foley of Florida resigned after he was confronted with sexually explicit online messages he sent to teenaged boys working as congressional pages. He allegedly inquired about the size of pages' penises, requested a photograph of one page's erect penis, visited the pages' dorm, and requested oral sex.

Could it be any more appalling? Why, yes it could. Consider that Foley had led the House caucus on missing and exploited children. And consider that the White House initially tried to dismiss the matter as "naughty emails." And the aforementioned Hastert, along with other House Republican leaders, had been warned repeatedly about Foley's misconduct with underage pages—and they did nothing. Republican congressman Jim Kolbe of Arizona said he notified House leaders of the problem as early as 2000. A House Ethics Committee probe called Hastert and others "willfully ignorant" in their refusal to react to the years of warnings about Foley.

A decade later, Hastert himself would be disgraced for sexually abusing boys. A federal judge in 2015 called Hastert, a former high school wrestling coach, a "serial child molester" in sentencing him for financial crimes related to hush money paid to his victims (the statute of limitations had expired for the sex crimes).

———

"I HATE TO ASK you for your help with something so silly," Jack Abramoff wrote to a rabbi friend in late 2000,

> but I've been nominated for membership in the Cosmos Club, which is a very distinguished club in Washington, DC, comprised of Nobel Prize winners, etc. Problem for me is that most prospective members have received awards and I have received none. I was wondering if you thought it possible that I could put that I have received an award from Toward Tradition with a sufficiently academic title, perhaps something like Scholar of Talmudic Studies? Indeed, it would be even better if it were possible that I received these in years past, if you know what I mean. Anyway, I think you see what I am trying to finagle here!

The rabbi, conservative radio host Daniel Lapin, who ran the advocacy group Toward Tradition, consented to the fraud. "Mazel tov," he replied, "the Cosmos Club is a big deal." He later wrote: "I just need to know what needs to be produced . . . letters? plaques?"

Abramoff's needs were simple. "Probably just a few clever titles of awards, dates and that's it. As long as you are the person to verify them (or we can have someone else verify one and you the other), we should be set. Do you have any creative titles, or should I dip into my bag of tricks?"

Abramoff's bag of tricks was bottomless. I know. I got a peek inside.

Covering the first term of the Bush White House in 2001, I sought him out as a source because of his close ties to Rove and to DeLay. He proved to have solid information about happenings in the White House and gave me anonymous tips. We became frequent lunch partners, first at downtown steakhouses (where he made special arrangements to have kosher food served) and then at his own restaurants, Signatures and Stacks. He invited me to a Passover seder one year. After his fall, he wrote in a memoir that, on the day he was fired by his law firm over the growing scandal, "I sent out emails to friends, letting them know I was leaving Greenberg [Traurig] and how they could reach me." I received that email.

I didn't know about the Cosmos Club hijinks, the bilking of Indian tribes, or the lifeguard in Rehoboth Beach, but I did have one clue: he had claimed to have found a species of swine in Asia that chews its cud, thus giving him the ability to serve kosher bacon and ham. (It turned out the Indonesian babirusa, even if arguably kosher, was an endangered species and unavailable to be cured and fried.) After the kosher pig story, I should have smelled a rat.

Abramoff's attitude was of a piece with the grab-what-you-can ethos of the Bush years. On Capitol Hill, Alaska Republicans Don Young and Ted Stevens used their positions as chairmen, respectively, of the House and Senate Appropriations Committees to devote $223 million to the famed "Bridge to Nowhere," a structure linking the remote village of Ketchikan to the island of Gravina, population fifty.

When opponents tried in 2005 to stop the Bridge to Nowhere, Stevens threatened to resign, saying, "I will be taken out of here on a stretcher."

The White House by then had already weathered the Enron scandal. The politically connected energy trading company had collapsed in the final days of 2001, revealing an astonishing fraud. The insolvent company had made itself look prosperous with fake holdings, off-the-books accounting, and phony entities devised to hide debts from regulators and investors. The fraudulent company reached deep into the Bush administration: its disgraced chairman had been a key figure in developing Bush's energy policy; Bush's top economic adviser and three other high-level administration officials had been paid consultants to Enron; thirty-five administration officials held Enron stock (including Rove, whose holdings were in the six figures); several officials had received Enron campaign contributions; Bush's Army secretary was an Enron executive; and the Republican National Committee chairman was an Enron lobbyist.

Also advising Enron: Ralph Reed, the former Christian Coalition leader and Abramoff ally, who had been recommended to Enron by Rove. Reed, while serving as a Bush campaign adviser in

2000, wrote to Enron executives that, for a $380,000 fee, he would influence his "good friends" in Washington to support electricity deregulation. In an October 2000 memo to Enron executives that made its way into the pages of *The Washington Post,* Reed wrote: "In public policy, it matters less who has the best arguments and more who gets heard—and by whom."

Reed was a crucial figure in the perversion of the religious right into an entity more "right" than "religious" and the most reliable part of the Republican Party's base. "In 1996, after Bill Clinton defeated Bob Dole, Margaret Tutwiler, a Republican strategist, declared that in order for Republicans to win, 'We're going to have to take on [board] the religious nuts,'" the late David Kuo, a former official in George W. Bush's White House, wrote in 2006 in *The New York Times.*

They took them aboard—and the "religious nuts" swamped the ship. Kuo quoted various religious conservative leaders lamenting Christianity's turn from "charity, compassion and love" toward "partisan politics," from "a commitment to Jesus and his kingdom" to a movement "more identified by a political agenda."

Reed, when he left the Christian Coalition and started a political consulting business, wrote to his friend Abramoff: "Hey, now that I'm done with the electoral politics, I need to start humping in corporate accounts! I'm counting on you to help me with some contacts."

Abramoff had plenty of business for Reed. He and Scanlon hired Reed to, as Scanlon put it, "bring out the wackos"—Christian conservatives—to fight against casino projects that threatened other casinos run by Abramoff's clients. The Christians thought they were opposing gambling, but in reality they had been manipulated into helping one gambling entity prevail over another.

Abramoff's emails, released by Senate investigators, showed him telling Reed he needed "serious swat from Karl" Rove to help a tribal client, and asking Reed to "ping Karl" on getting help for his Northern Mariana Islands clients who were trying to protect their sweatshops. Reed obliged. When Abramoff mentioned to Reed a plan to get a tribe to fund a golf junket to Scotland in 2002 (funneled through an Abramoff foundation) Reed replied: "OK but we need to discuss. It is an election year."

Abramoff, in his post-prison memoir, wrote of Reed helping him block an internet gambling bill that threatened tribal casinos. "While Ralph didn't want his co-religionists to know he was accepting funds from an Indian tribe with a casino, he threw himself into these efforts," Abramoff wrote, later adding: "Ralph would run his political career aground by denying, first, that he took money from the tribes, and then asserting that the money he took had no nexus to gaming. Both assertions were ridiculous."

Matthew Continetti reported on a 2001 fax from Reed asking his old boss, televangelist Pat Robertson, to tape a message "helping the pro-family forces" fight a casino. Robertson agreed, "almost certainly" unaware that Reed was helping another tribe's casino operation.

In the end Reed's firm pocketed roughly $5 million in indirect payments from Indian casino operators. In one email, Abramoff complained to Scanlon about all the money Reed had spent: "He is a bad version of us!"

Abramoff's tribal work also required the perversion of the fiscal conservatives who formed the other part of the Republican base. In order to get Republicans in Congress to drop plans for a 30 percent tax on Indian tribal gambling revenues, Abramoff got Grover Norquist, founder and head of Americans for Tax Reform, to declare that the policy would violate his no-new-taxes pledge—a suicidal move for a Republican. Norquist also helped Abramoff land a spot on Bush's transition team after the 2000 election.

Abramoff rewarded Norquist. Microsoft hired Norquist "at my suggestion," Abramoff boasted. Abramoff also directed tribal funds Norquist's way.

In May 1999, for example, Norquist asked Abramoff: "What is the status of the Choctaw stuff. I have a $75K hole in my budget from last year. Ouch." Later that year the Choctaw paid Norquist's group $325,000; Norquist served as a pass-through to Reed but kept a fee for his own group.

Reed and Norquist, two lions of the conservative movement, avoided legal trouble in the Abramoff scandal, which focused on the "gimme five" kickback scheme. In that, Abramoff got tribes to hire a grassroots mobilization firm set up by Scanlon, who dramatically overcharged the tribes and secretly split $66 million in proceeds with Abramoff.

Abramoff pleaded guilty in 2006 to conspiracy, fraud, and tax evasion charges related to the tribes. (In a bizarre twist, he pleaded guilty the next day to wire-fraud-related charges in the purchase of a gambling boat fleet in Florida with Dial-a-Mattress executive Adam Kidan. The man they bought the business from was later killed in a mob-style hit.)

Abramoff's lobbying exploits were only possible because of his well-advertised relationships with DeLay and Rove—the House majority leader and the president's chief strategist.

Over the years, Abramoff arranged for trips for DeLay to the South Pacific, Moscow, London, Scotland, and South Korea. On one such trip, DeLay helpfully called Abramoff "one of my closest and dearest friends."

Abramoff became one of Bush's "Pioneers," raising more than $100,000 for his campaign. Abramoff and his team scored nearly two hundred meetings with administration officials during the first ten months of the Bush administration lobbying for the Northern Mariana Islands alone. "Rove would help Abramoff get richer, but only if the lobbyist reciprocated by moving Majority Leader Tom DeLay and other Republicans on Capitol Hill on issues the White House cared about," journalists James Moore and Wayne Slater wrote. "Rove knew the best way to influence DeLay was through their mutual friend—lobbyist Jack Abramoff."

Khaled Saffuri, a business associate of Abramoff's who had introduced the lobbyist to the Malaysian ambassador, was sitting in Abramoff's office when Rove called to tell Abramoff that Bush would host the prime minister. Abramoff "said a few words, he hung up the phone and said, 'Call the ambassador. We've got the invitation,'" Saffuri said in the 2010 documentary *Casino Jack and the United States of Money*. And they did. The meeting with Bush happened in May 2002.

That meeting, it turned out, helped bring about Abramoff's downfall. The Malaysian government's payments were part of the funds passed through AIC—Abramoff and Scanlon's lifeguard-run shell company—to Abramoff's law firm, Greenberg Traurig. AIC figured prominently in a bombshell report about Abramoff and Scanlon's shenanigans by Sue Schmidt on the front page, above the fold, of *The Washington Post* in February 2004: "A powerful Washington lobbyist and a former aide to House Majority Leader Tom DeLay (R-Tex.) persuaded four newly wealthy Indian gaming tribes to pay their firms more than $45 million over the past three years for lobbying and public affairs work, a sum that rivals spending to influence public policy by some of the nation's biggest corporate interests."

In time, it would come out that Abramoff and Scanlon privately mocked the tribes that made them rich, calling them "f'ing troglodytes," "morons," "plain stupid," "f-ing SagChips," "losers," "stupidest idiots," and "mofos." They mocked one tribal leader's "mullet" hairdo, which he couldn't cut because "then he wouldn't look like an Indian." In one of their more grotesque abuses, Abramoff and Scanlon, with Reed's assistance, successfully pushed Texas to shut down a casino operated by the Tigua tribe of El Paso, Texas—an effort financed by the Louisiana Coushatta tribe. Abramoff and Scanlon then got the Tigua tribe to pay them millions of dollars in an unsuccessful attempt to reopen the very same casino.

After it had all come crashing down, Abramoff recounted what he'd been part of: how Microsoft executives sent the Republican National Committee $100,000 after DeLay warned them he wouldn't help companies that didn't contribute; how a Russian oligarch tried to give DeLay $1 million during a round of golf and then, to skirt the U.S. ban on foreign political contributions, sent $1 million to a DeLay-connected advocacy group; and how Abramoff advised a tribal client to send campaign contributions to lawmakers who voted to support its gambling interests.

"What I did not consider then, and never considered until I was sitting in prison, was that contributions from parties with an interest in legislation are really nothing but bribes," he wrote. "The early, grateful contributions by the tribes soon led to contributions designed to create gratitude on the part of the member. . . . Golf, elaborate meals, tickets to sporting events—any favor a representative or staff needed, we were there to provide."

Several Abramoff pals survived the scandal intact and unrepentant. Karl Rove built the American Crossroads super PAC and the Crossroads GPS dark money group. Ralph Reed founded another religious advocacy group, the Faith and Freedom Coalition, that went on to embrace Donald Trump. Grover Norquist continued fighting for the election of small-government conservatives, who once in office expanded the size of the government at a record-setting clip.

Abramoff, after serving his prison sentence and working in a pizza shop, pleaded guilty in 2020 to another set of lobbying crimes, violating a law that Congress updated in 2007—in response to Abramoff's previous offenses.

Abramoff, in his post-prison memoir, offered a telling, if inadvertent, commentary on the conservative movement he exploited. "I believe that the reason our efforts enjoyed so much success," he wrote, "was that our activities were based in the belief system and rhetoric of the conservative movement."

In a perverse way, that was true. For the belief system of the conservative movement, and of the GOP, changed utterly during the George W. Bush years. Devotion to limited government went out the window, replaced by the imperative of holding power at any cost. Bush inherited a federal budget in surplus when he became president and left with a deficit of $1.16 trillion. Annual noninterest spending increases under Bush averaged 5.6 percent—the most since Lyndon B. Johnson's 5.7 percent during the creation of Medicare, the War on Poverty, and other Great Society programs—and the federal debt doubled under Bush, an increase of $5.85 trillion. Meantime, spending on presidential and congressional elections, which had been $2.05 billion in 1996, more than tripled to $6.27 billion in 2008 (en route to total campaign spending of $14.40 billion in 2020). Spending on lobbying doubled from $1.56 billion in 2000 to $3.3 billion in 2008—and that was just the officially reported amount.

Within the GOP, power had triumphed over principle—hastening the surrender of the American political system to the corrupting influence of money.

CHAPTER 9

A Deep-Seated Hatred
of White People

On March 7, 1965, in Selma, Alabama, police beat and gassed John Lewis and the civil rights marchers he led to the Edmund Pettus Bridge, leaving young Lewis with a fractured skull.

Almost exactly forty-five years later, on March 20, 2010, Lewis, who had become a member of Congress from Georgia, was walking from his Washington office to the House floor when he met the racist heirs of Jim Clark and Bull Connor.

Thousands of demonstrators with the Tea Party movement, a conservative backlash against Obama born in 2009 and 2010, had descended on Washington to protest the Affordable Care Act— Obamacare—as President Barack Obama's signal achievement moved toward final passage. A clump of them formed a gauntlet around Lewis and Representative André Carson, an Indiana Democrat and, like Lewis, Black.

"Nig-ger!" came a chant. "Nig-ger!" Fifteen times.

Another Black Democrat, Representative Emanuel Cleaver of Missouri, was walking to the House chamber when one of the Tea Party demonstrators spat on him. Capitol Police led all three men to safety from the mob.

"I heard people saying things today that I have not heard since March 15, 1960, when I was marching to try to get off the back of the bus," Jim Clyburn, the House majority whip and a Black Democrat from South Carolina, said after escaping from the mob.

"It was like going into the time machine," Carson said.

Lewis, then seventy, felt as if he, too, had been forced to

remember the past. "I've faced this before," he said. "It reminded me of the sixties. It was a lot of downright hate."

Messrs. Clyburn, Carson, and Lewis were right about the time warp. The Republicans' Southern Strategy had reached its ultimate destination. The realignment of the parties along racial lines that began with the Voting Rights Act and Civil Rights Act of the 1960s was now complete. Political party had become a proxy for race and racial attitudes.

Now the election of Obama, broadly seen as the triumph of a multiracial United States, triggered a racist backlash of the sort many Americans thought had been consigned to the dustbin of history. And, disgracefully, elected Republicans allied themselves with the sort of white nationalists who harassed John Lewis and his colleagues that day. They joined in a campaign of "othering" Obama, not just opposing his policies but demonizing him as un-American and anti-American.

The demonstrators that day, egged on by Republican lawmakers from the House balcony, carried signs of the sort seen at Tea Party rallies across the country for months:

"Congress = Slave Owner; Taxpayer = Niggar [sic]."

"Barack Hussein Obama: Where were you really born?"

"A Village in Kenya Is Missing Its Idiot: Deport Obama!"

"We don't want socialism, you arrogant Kenyan!"

"Obama's plan: White slavery."

"Impeach the Muslim Marxist."

"Obamanomics: Monkey see, monkey spend."

"Imam Obama Wants to Ban Pork: Don't Let Him Steal Your Meat."

"Obama bin Lyin'."

"I want my country back."

They portrayed Obama as a witch doctor in headdress, Obama in whiteface as the Joker in *Batman,* Obama in turban, Obama in Hitler mustache, Obama in tribal garb with bone in nose, Obama as "undocumented worker."

While a few Republicans recoiled at the overt racism, others excused it. "I got cussed" too, GOP representative Louie Gohmert of Texas said of Lewis and the other Black Democrats, but "I didn't come running to the media and whining and crying."

Sixteen months earlier, there had been hopeful talk of a "post-racial" America, as the voters elected the first Black president by a resounding margin. "If there is anyone out there who still doubts that America is a place where all things are possible, who still wonders if the dream of our founders is alive in our time, who still questions the power of our democracy, tonight is your answer," President-elect Obama said in his victory speech in Chicago's Grant Park, before tens of thousands. "It's been a long time coming, but tonight, because of what we did on this date in this election at this defining moment, change has come to America."

But it wasn't the change he had envisioned on that hopeful night.

Just six months after Obama's inauguration, Fox News star Glenn Beck told the network's viewers that Obama "has exposed himself as a guy, over and over and over again, who has a deep-seated hatred for white people or the white culture."

Newt Gingrich told the conservative *National Review* in 2010 that Obama's behavior, "so outside our comprehension," can best be interpreted "only if you understand Kenyan, anti-colonial behavior."

In a breathtaking breach of protocol, and of civility, Representative Joe Wilson, a South Carolina Republican, shouted "You lie!" at Obama as the president addressed a joint session of Congress in September 2009. His Republican colleague Geoff Davis (the Kentucky congressman, not the homophonous president of the Confederacy) had previously referred to Obama as "boy."

"I think an overwhelming portion of the intensely demonstrated animosity toward President Barack Obama is based on the fact that he is a Black man, that he's African American," former president Jimmy Carter said after the Wilson outburst. "I think it's bubbled up to the surface because of a belief among many white people, not just in the South but around the country, that African Americans are not qualified to lead this great country."

CARTER WAS RIGHT. Resurgent white nationalists did indeed think a Black man unqualified to lead. But it was worse than that:

a number of Republican politicians, and their media allies, encouraged the belief that Obama was *literally* unqualified—because he was foreign-born.

The Birther movement was an attempt to insinuate that Obama was something other than a "natural born citizen"—African? Indonesian? Also a secret Muslim?—and therefore constitutionally ineligible to be president. The idea was racist to the core, an attempt to portray Obama as something other than American, other than Christian.

It was bonkers. Obama was born in Hawaii in 1961 to a mother who was a U.S. citizen. Contemporaneous birth announcements had been published in Hawaiian newspapers. In the summer of 2008, the Obama campaign released an official "certification of live birth" from the state's Department of Health. He had hardly known his deceased, Kenyan father. Other than four years in Indonesia during elementary school—his (white) mother had married an Indonesian man—Obama spent his life in the United States.

But one man, a prominent real estate investor in New York, decided that portraying the first Black president as something other than American was his ticket to political stardom. "I want him to show his birth certificate," Donald Trump declared on ABC's *The View* on March 23, 2011, as the 2012 presidential campaign began.

Trump, flirting with a presidential run that didn't happen, took his case to Fox News. On Fox News's *Fox & Friends* on March 28, he pronounced himself "really concerned" that Obama wasn't born in America and opined that newspaper birth announcements could have been faked.

Two days later, he said on Fox News's *The O'Reilly Factor* that Obama "doesn't have a birth certificate," or that "maybe it says he is a Muslim." Trump warned: "If he wasn't born in this country, it's one of the great scams of all time."

On and on Trump went, saying he had sent investigators to Hawaii ("they cannot believe what they're finding") and that "the birth certificate is missing."

Trump's crusade finally pressured Obama to release a more extensive "long-form" birth certificate from Hawaii, on April 27,

2011. Trump didn't even blink. "Word is . . . he was a terrible student," Trump said. "I don't know why he doesn't release his records."

The first whispers that Obama was secretly a Muslim began when Obama ran for the Senate in 2004, authored by a failed Illinois politician named Andy Martin, who had a history of filing lawsuits and making anti-Semitic comments ("crooked, slimy Jew who has a history of lying and thieving common to members of his race"). The bogus allegation got picked up by fringe outlets such as FreeRepublic.com, and by right-wing conspiracy theorists such as Jerome Corsi as well as a couple of Hillary Clinton supporters (though not her campaign) during the 2008 primaries.

At a gathering of right-wing conspiracy theorists at a Capitol Hill coffee shop in May 2008, organized by Cliff Kincaid, a conservative antimedia fixture, I listened as the assembled asserted that Obama was mentored by a member of the Soviet Communist Party, that he launched his Illinois State Senate campaign in the home of a terrorist, that as a state senator he was a member of a socialist front group, that he would have trouble getting a government security clearance, and that there was reason to doubt his "loyalty to the United States."

But the insanity went mainstream in October 2008 when Sean Hannity hosted Martin on his Fox News show *Hannity's America*. As Jim Rutenberg of *The New York Times* noted at the time, the documentary-style show was seen by three million people and included the accusation that Obama trained "for a radical overthrow of the government." Martin also portrayed Obama as a protégé of former Weather Underground radical Bill Ayers; in reality, the two had a passing acquaintance.

The Birther talk grew from there, with allegations that Obama trained in a madrassa in Indonesia, and with efforts to hold him responsible for incendiary statements by his Chicago pastor, Jeremiah Wright.

Radio and TV hosts G. Gordon Liddy and Lou Dobbs ran with variations of the Birther libel. Rush Limbaugh proposed in 2009 that Obama was "more African in his roots than he is American."

Representative Mike Coffman, a Colorado Republican, said

he didn't know "whether Barack Obama was born in the United States. . . . But I do know this: that, in his heart, he's not an American."

Sarah Palin, after her unsuccessful vice presidential bid in 2008, declared Obama's birth certificate in 2009 to be "fair game" and a "fair question," saying "the public rightfully is still making it an issue."

Republicans in various state legislatures introduced "Birther Bills," requiring presidential candidates to furnish proof of citizenship that is satisfactory to state authorities.

After Republicans took over the House in 2010, they performed a show reading of the Constitution on the House floor, leaving out such things as the three-fifths compromise. When they got to the requirement that a president be a "natural born citizen," a Birther in the gallery screamed: "Except Obama! Except Obama! Help us, Jesus!"

By July 2012, a poll by the nonpartisan Pew Forum on Religion and Public Life found that 17 percent of registered voters thought Obama was a Muslim, including 30 percent of Republicans and 34 percent of conservatives.

To his credit, the 2012 Republican presidential nominee, Mitt Romney, disavowed the Birther slander. "I believe the president was born in the United States," he said. But Romney still appeared with the biggest Birther of them all, Trump, to accept his endorsement.

Fox News had repeatedly elevated Trump and his Birther claims, and he got high marks from the Fox News crowd for his efforts. "It empowers Trump," Bill O'Reilly concluded in 2011.

And so Trump kept going. "Let's take a closer look at that birth certificate," Trump tweeted in 2012, more than a year after Obama released his long-form birth certificate. "@BarackObama was described in 2003 as being 'born in Kenya.'"

Trump followed that with several declarations that the birth certificate "is a fraud" and even suggested murder. "How amazing, the State Health Director who verified copies of Obama's 'birth certificate' died in plane crash today. All others lived," he tweeted. He claimed Israeli scientists had determined the birth certificate to be fake. He urged Republicans to "take the offensive" on the issue. He pleaded with hackers to "hack Obama's college records (destroyed?) and check 'place of birth.' "

After Joe Arpaio, a racist Arizona sheriff, released a report by his "Cold Case Posse" claiming that Obama's long-form birth certificate was "a computer-generated forgery"—and so was his draft registration card!—Trump tweeted: "Congratulations to @ RealSheriffJoe on his successful Cold Case Posse investigation which claims @BarackObama 'birth certificate' is fake."

Trump, with Arpaio's support, would later ride the Birther lie all the way to the White House. During his 2016 campaign, he wasn't merely declaring Obama a Muslim. He was calling him "the founder of ISIS." When *The Washington Post*'s Robert Costa asked Trump whether he accepted that Obama was born in Hawaii, Trump replied: "I'll answer that question at the right time. I just don't want to answer it yet."

When Costa pointed out that Trump's adviser, Kellyanne Conway, had said Trump accepted Obama's U.S. birth, Trump replied: "She's allowed to speak what she thinks."

Finally, Trump later admitted that Obama was American-born—and his campaign claimed that Trump should be thanked because he brought "this ugly incident to its conclusion by successfully compelling President Obama to release his birth certificate."

As for Trump being the primary driver of "this ugly incident," the candidate claimed that "the birther movement was started by Hillary Clinton in 2008." How better to dispense with one slander than to replace it with another?

WITH ROMNEY'S LOSS TO Obama in 2012, the Republican Party had lost the popular vote in five of the last six presidential elections. And demographics pointed to greater trouble ahead. In 2008 and 2012, Obama had won a combined 80 percent of Black, Hispanic, Asian, and other minority voters. They made up 37 percent of the population in 2012, but were forecast to become a majority by mid-century. They were a smaller share of the electorate (28 percent in 2012) but would eventually constitute a majority of voters, too.

Republican National Committee chairman Reince Priebus decided to do something. He commissioned a "Growth and Opportunity Project" to plot a path forward for the party. Run by party elders from the George W. Bush and Jeb Bush orbits, it became known as the 2012 Republican "autopsy."

Surprisingly, there was no sugarcoating. "Public perception of the Party is at record lows. Young voters are increasingly rolling their eyes at what the Party represents, and many minorities wrongly think that Republicans do not like them or want them in the country," they wrote. "Unless the RNC gets serious about tackling this problem, we will lose future elections; the data demonstrates this."

Its recommendations were similarly bold. "We must embrace and champion comprehensive immigration reform," it said plainly, cautioning: "If Hispanic Americans hear that the GOP doesn't want them in the United States, they won't pay attention to our next sentence."

It also said the party "must embark on a year-round effort to engage with African American voters," and "campaign among Hispanic, black, Asian, and gay Americans and demonstrate we care about them, too."

It argued that Republicans should "blow the whistle at corporate malfeasance and attack corporate welfare," and "speak out when CEOs receive tens of millions of dollars in retirement packages but middle-class workers have not had a meaningful raise in years."

And it counseled more accommodation on gay rights and other social issues, concluding that Republicans "need to make sure young people do not see the Party as totally intolerant of alternative points of view." The autopsy warned that "if our Party is not welcoming and inclusive, young people and increasingly other voters will continue to tune us out . . . just because someone disagrees with us on 20 percent of the issues, that does not mean we cannot come together on the rest of the issues where we do agree."

All good advice—and all summarily ignored.

In the Democratic Senate, a bipartisan "Gang of Eight" senators agreed on comprehensive immigration reform that balanced a path to citizenship for illegal immigrants with dramatic investments in border security. It sailed through the Senate, 68–32, in June 2013.

But in the Republican House, conservatives branded the legislation "amnesty" and blocked it from even being considered. After a year of trying to move his caucus, House Speaker John Boehner mocked the conservatives in 2014. "Here's the attitude," he said at a luncheon in Ohio. "Ohhhh. Don't make me do this. Ohhhh. This is too hard." He said it in a whiny voice.

Boehner was forced to apologize to conservatives. Comprehensive immigration reform never saw the light of day in the House.

The next year, Trump kicked off his presidential campaign by calling Mexican immigrants murderers and rapists—the beginning of a constant stream of racist invective directed at Latinos, Blacks, Muslims, and Asian Americans.

To the extent there was a strategy behind the rage, it was that if Trump could stoke enough fear to generate massive turnout among older white voters, that alone could be enough to win the presidency. RNC chairman Reince Priebus, the very man who commissioned the party's introspective report, would become Trump's chief of staff. One of the authors of the report, Sally Bradshaw, would quit the party, calling Trump a "bigot."

The autopsy was dead and buried.

ABANDONING THE AUTOPSY'S RECOMMENDATIONS meant that the Republican Party had to turn out white voters in extraordinary numbers. It also meant suppressing the turnout of non-white voters. With this, the conservative majority on the Supreme Court was there to help.

The Voting Rights Act of 1965 was a triumph. As the Brennan Center for Justice notes, in the decade after the law's passage, the disparity between white and Black voter registration rates dropped from nearly 30 percentage points to just 8 percentage points. This happened largely because of the law's Section 4, which required southern states with a history of voting rights abuses to "preclear" changes to election rules with the Justice Department.

It was such an unquestioned success that Congress reauthorized it many times without controversy. The last time, in 2006, not a single Senate Republican voted against it, only thirty-three House Republicans opposed it, and George W. Bush signed it into law.

But in 2013, the Supreme Court gutted the Voting Rights Act in a 5–4 decision. Chief Justice John Roberts, writing for the conservative majority in *Shelby County v. Holder,* decreed that Section 4 was outdated—even though Congress had said otherwise. "Our country has changed," he wrote, arguing that the law doesn't reflect "current conditions." Roberts, ignoring that significant racial disparities still existed in voting, essentially argued that the law was no longer needed because it had worked too well. Justice Ruth Bader Ginsburg, in her dissent, said that's "like throwing away your umbrella in a rainstorm because you are not getting wet."

She was right. Within hours of the decision, Texas and North Carolina, newly unshackled, introduced new laws that were later found in court to be discriminatory. Mississippi and Alabama implemented restrictive laws already on the books that had previously been blocked by the Justice Department. The Brennan Center found that southern states previously covered by the law purged voters from the rolls at significantly higher rates than other states, causing an additional two million voters to be disenfranchised.

In Congress, Democrats tried to restore the Voting Rights Act, but Republicans suddenly opposed the act they had long supported. A year after the *Shelby* decision, not a single Senate Republican had agreed to co-sponsor legislation restoring the voting protections, and only ten House Republicans signed on. They knew that their only remaining path to victory was to get white people to vote—and non-white people not to vote.

GEORGE W. BUSH, AFTER the 9/11 attacks, frequently spoke up to protect Muslim Americans. "Islam is peace," he would say, and "the enemy of America is not our many Muslim friends." He pushed, unsuccessfully, for comprehensive immigration reform, including a path to citizenship for illegal immigrants. John McCain, in his 2008 campaign, admirably spoke up when a supporter at one of his events called Obama an "Arab." McCain, taking back the microphone, and enduring boos from his own supporters, said: "No, ma'am. He's a decent, family-man, citizen, that I just happen to have disagreements with on fundamental issues."

But with Obama's rise, the hatred could not be contained. Just before the election, a life-size effigy of Obama was found hanging from a tree at the University of Kentucky. Speakers at rallies for McCain and his vice presidential nominee, Sarah Palin, condemned "Barack Hussein Obama," with emphasis on the Hussein to imply that he was Muslim. At a Palin rally, when the candidate tried to connect Obama to radical Ayers, I heard a person in the crowd shout out: "Kill him!" McCain supporters sometimes shouted "terrorist!" when Obama's name was invoked.

Palin was particularly dedicated to "othering" Obama, saying "this is not a man who sees America like you and I see America," someone who's "palling around with terrorists who would target their own country." She later directed Obama to cease his "shuck-and-jive shtick" and referred to racial justice demonstrators as "dogs."

The Tea Party (ostensibly standing for "Taxed Enough Already" but in reality an all-purpose anti-Obama movement) picked up the theme when it was formed months into Obama's presidency. The movement drew some of the same support that libertarian gadfly Ron Paul did in his 2008 and 2012 runs for the Republican presidential nomination. The Texas congressman received—and didn't disavow—endorsements from white supremacist and militia groups, and his "revolution" drew a young and rowdy antigovernment crowd.

Former Republican congressman Tom Tancredo lit up a Tea Party event when he said that "People who could not even spell the word 'vote,' or say it in English, put a committed socialist ideologue in the White House. His name is Barack Hussein Obama."

Mark Williams, leader of Tea Party Express, one of the new movement's organizations, called slavery "a great gig," identified Obama as an "Indonesian Muslim turned welfare thug," and wrote a fictional letter to Abraham Lincoln from "the Coloreds" telling him "we don't cotton to that whole emancipation thing." (The umbrella Tea Party coalition ousted him.)

The founder and president of TeaParty.org, another group,

criticized Obama for spending time with "his homies in the Chicago hood," where he would "bump and grind," while also "shooting hoops, smoking cigarettes and goofing-off with his homies."

Fox News and talk radio amplified the racism. Glenn Beck informed his viewers and listeners that Obama was "moving all of us quickly into slavery" and that he was under the influence of "radical Black nationalism" and "Marxist Black liberation theology." Beck declared that "you are worth more as a minority" than a white person.

"You don't take the name Barack to identify with America," Beck said of Obama's given name at birth. "You take the name Barack to identify with what? Your heritage? The heritage, maybe, of your father in Kenya, who is a radical." Beck further deduced that "everything that is getting pushed through Congress" had been "driven by President Obama's thinking on one idea: reparations."

Limbaugh, for his part, played a song on air called "Barack the Magic Negro." Later, he suggested that Obama was willfully exposing Americans to Ebola from Africa because of a belief that the nation "deserves" an Ebola outbreak as punishment for slavery.

Bigots were emboldened. At the Missouri State Fair, a rodeo clown with an Obama mask appeared. In Texas, the (successful) Republican gubernatorial candidate Greg Abbott invited Ted Nugent to campaign with him even after the rocker called Obama a "subhuman mongrel" and "gangster." At a rally in Nevada opposing federal control of public land, an internet preacher affiliated with the Oath Keepers, a right-wing antigovernment group, called Obama a "half-breed." In Wolfeboro, New Hampshire, an elected member of the three-person police commission called Obama a "nigger" in a public place, then told town officials "I believe I did use the N-word. . . . For this I do not apologize—he meets and exceeds my criteria for such."

The National Association for the Advancement of Colored People released a report concluding: "Tea Party organizations have given platforms to anti-Semites, racists, and bigots. Further, hard-core white nationalists have been attracted to these protests, looking for potential recruits and hoping to push these protesters towards a more self-conscious and ideological white supremacy."

Though the movement first described itself as an antitax rebellion, the study examined the six most influential Tea Party organizations and found that all but one of them had embraced the Birther allegations. It found Tea Party groups overlapping with militia leaders and anti-immigration and anti-Muslim activists. "The Tea Party movement has unleashed a still inchoate political movement who are in their numerical majority, angry middle-class white people who believe their country, their nation, has been taken from them," it said.

That "inchoate political movement" would, a few years later, become choate under Trump.

Republican leaders lost the nerve to push back against the encroaching white nationalism. In 2012, presidential nominee Romney, unlike McCain, didn't counter a woman at his event in Euclid, Ohio, when she said Obama "should be tried for treason." Another Republican presidential candidate, Rick Santorum, declined to correct a woman who called Obama an "avowed Muslim."

When Eric Holder, Obama's (Black) attorney general said, rather mildly, that "for some there's a racial animus" in the vehemence of their attacks on the president, the conservative intelligentsia took offense. At *National Review*, Hans A. von Spakovsky said Holder was "disconnected from reality." Writer Noah Rothman opined at HotAir.com: "Those for who [sic] racism is a religion—ubiquitous and unfalsifiable—nod in agreement at Holder's self-aggrandizement. All others roll their eyes."

They didn't—or didn't want to—see the white nationalism rising in reaction to Obama. And it wasn't directed only at Obama. After Obama nominated Sonia Sotomayor to the Supreme Court, Republicans took issue with her 2001 statement that "I would hope that a wise Latina woman with the richness of her experiences would more often than not reach a better conclusion than a white male who hasn't lived that life." Newt Gingrich called her a "Latina woman racist."

At the Republican National Convention in 2012, a pair of attendees threw nuts at a Black camerawoman for CNN, telling her, "this is how we feed the animals." At a Palin event, one of her supporters shouted a racial epithet at a Black network soundman and said, "Sit down, boy." Nevada rancher Cliven Bundy, whose antigovernment rebellion got support from Fox's Hannity and a pair of Republican senators, wondered aloud about whether "Negro" people were "better off as slaves." Tea Partier Chris McDaniel, mounting a Republican primary challenge to Senator Thad Cochran in Mississippi, was pressured to pull out as keynote speaker of an event promoting a seller of "White pride" merchandise. Representative Ted Yoho, a Florida Republican, and Senator Rand Paul, a Kentucky Republican, both raised doubts about the constitutionality of the Civil Rights Act (both walked back their statements after outcries).

Representative Steve King, an Iowa Republican and leader of the fight in the House against comprehensive immigration reform, kept pushing the bounds of bigotry. Explaining why he opposed legalization for "Dreamers" (those brought illegally to the United States as children), King said: "For every one who's a valedictorian, there's another 100 out there that weigh 130 pounds and they've got calves the size of cantaloupes because they're hauling 75 pounds of marijuana across the desert."

In 2015 he invited to Washington a Dutch extremist who called the Koran a "fascist book" and Islam "the ideology of a retarded culture." In 2016, he opposed multiculturalism and "cultural suicide by demographic transformation."

Eventually, a few years later, King's claim that civilization has survived because of rape and incest, and his overt embrace of white nationalism, led his Republican colleagues to strip him of his committee assignments and his constituents to boot him out of office in a primary. But first, he became an inspiration to Trump. When Trump visited Iowa in October 2014, to tease a presidential run, he did a fundraiser for King. For president, "I want to see someone who is going to make our country great again, which is basically the same thing as Steve." Trump said King had "really the right views on almost everything," so much so that "we don't have to compare notes."

Likewise, Trump formed an alliance with Joe Arpaio, the racist sheriff in Maricopa County, Arizona, in the Phoenix area. Arpaio was famous not just for his Birther activities but for his open-air jail, Tent City (he called it a "concentration camp"), where he humiliated Latinos by making them wear pink underwear, perform public parades, endure extreme heat, subsist on two meals a day, and, for women, go without feminine hygiene products. Yet he was still an "honored guest" at the 2012 Republican convention.

Arpaio was one of the first public officials to endorse Trump, in January 2016. Later, Trump repaid the favor. Arpaio was sentenced to prison for contempt of court because he refused for eighteen months to comply with a judge's order that he cease targeting Latino drivers for traffic stops. Trump pardoned him.

And, of course, there was Sarah Palin. She spoke out in support of keeping "Redskins" as the name of the Washington football team, saying "there's no intent to offend." Her reaction to the Syrian civil war? "Let Allah sort it out." In 2013, the *Duck Dynasty* TV star was suspended for saying that "pre-entitlement, pre-welfare" in the segregated South, Blacks "were godly, they were happy, no one was singing the blues." (He also likened gay relationships to bestiality.) Palin rushed to his defense: "Those 'intolerants' hatin' and taking on the *Duck Dynasty* patriarch for voicing his personal opinion are taking on all of us."

But all was well and good with racial relations—because America had elected a Black president. Senate Majority Leader Mitch McConnell went so far as to use that as an argument against reparations. "I don't think reparations for something that happened 150 years ago for whom none us currently living are responsible is a good idea," explained McConnell, the great-great-grandson of slave owners. "We've tried to deal with our original sin of slavery by fighting a civil war, by passing landmark civil-rights legislation. We elected an African-American president."

This had been a consistent theme for the Senate Republican leader. Back in 1993, he joined Strom Thurmond and Jesse Helms in defending the Confederate flag on the Senate floor.

The chamber had been about to extend patent protection to the United Daughters of the Confederacy for their emblem, which included the Confederate flag. Carol Moseley Braun, an Illinois Democrat and the lone Black senator, gave an impassioned speech on the floor denouncing the action. "The issue is whether or not Americans such as myself who believe in the promise of this country," she said, "will have to suffer the indignity of being reminded time and time again that at one point in this country's history we were human chattel."

Her speech electrified the Senate. Twenty-seven senators changed their votes and abandoned the Confederate flag. Howell Heflin, an Alabama Democrat who descended from a signer of Alabama's secession, said with tears in his eyes that though "I revere my family," he couldn't "put the stamp of approval on a symbolism that is offensive to a large segment of America."

But McConnell could. "My roots, like the senior senator from Alabama, run deep in the South," he said, but unlike Heflin he would vote to protect the Confederate emblem "out of respect for my forefathers who did what they thought was appropriate for their region of the country during this most difficult time." He stuck with Thurmond and Helms, "out of reverence for my ancestors, whose roots run deep in the Southern part of our country."

In another display of his ancestral reverence, McConnell, around the same time, posed for a photograph in front of an enormous Confederate battle flag at a meeting of the Sons of Confederate Veterans.

OBAMA, SOON AFTER RELEASING his long-form birth certificate, delivered a lacerating send-up of Trump at the annual White House Correspondents Association dinner in 2011, with Trump in the audience.

"Now, I know that he's taken some flak lately, but no one is happier, no one is prouder to put this birth certificate matter to rest than the Donald," Obama said. "And that's because he can finally get back to focusing on the issues that matter—like, did we fake the moon landing? What really happened in Roswell? And where are Biggie and Tupac?" The crowd howled. Trump glowered.

It wasn't over. "But all kidding aside, obviously, we all know about your credentials and breadth of experience," Obama said, to more laughter. "For example—no, seriously, just recently, in an episode of *Celebrity Apprentice,* at the steakhouse, the men's cooking team did not impress the judges from Omaha Steaks. And there was a lot of blame to go around. But you, Mr. Trump, recognized that the real problem was a lack of leadership. And so ultimately, you didn't blame Lil Jon or Meatloaf. You fired Gary Busey. And these are the kind of decisions that would keep me up at night. Well handled, sir. Well handled." They were rolling in the aisles. Trump was frozen in place.

"Say what you will about Mr. Trump," Obama continued. "He certainly would bring some change to the White House." The screens in the room all flashed an image of the "Trump White House Resort and Casino." More than a thousand people in the room were in fits of laughter, and stealing glances at the humiliated Birther in black tie. What they saw that night was a grimacing, teeth-clenched portrait of rage.

Trump would spend the next five years plotting revenge, but he had already found his strategy. The Republican Party, by stoking the racial backlash against Obama, had by then turned itself into the party of white grievance. All that was left for Trump to do was to light a match.

CHAPTER 10

Death Panels

Sarah Palin was in need of a second act.

Nine months earlier, she had lost her bid for the vice presidency as John McCain's running mate. Two weeks earlier, she had stepped down as governor of Alaska. Her memoir, *Going Rogue,* wouldn't hit the shelves for three more months. She was a private citizen seeking a way to remain in the spotlight—and, on August 7, 2009, she found it.

"As more Americans delve into the disturbing details of the nationalized health care plan that the current administration is rushing through Congress, our collective jaw is dropping, and we're saying not just no, but hell no!" she wrote in a Facebook post. She claimed that, under the Democrats' plan, government "will simply refuse to pay the cost" of health care.

"And who will suffer the most when they ration care? The sick, the elderly, and the disabled, of course. The America I know and love is not one in which my parents or my baby with Down Syndrome will have to stand in front of Obama's 'death panel' so his bureaucrats can decide, based on a subjective judgment of their 'level of productivity in society,' whether they are worthy of health care. Such a system is downright evil."

It was a preposterous lie. There was nothing in any version of the legislation that proposed the creation of any entity to ration care. There was a proposal to allow Medicare to pay for doctor appointments to discuss living wills and end-of-life choices such as hospice—but these were optional and had nothing to do with rationing, or denying, medical care to anyone.

Crazy claims about euthanasia and eugenics in Obamacare had been bouncing around among right-wing crackpots for months. But Palin's invention of the "death panels" lie marked a new front in the Republicans' long-running war on truth.

The party's most recent vice presidential nominee had decided to base her opposition to President Obama's signature legislation not on the many principled objections conservatives had to the plan but on a lie. And the party rallied around Palin's lie.

"She's dead right," Rush Limbaugh announced on the radio.

Virginia Foxx, a Republican congresswoman from North Carolina, said Obamacare would put "seniors in a position of being put to death by their government."

Even veteran senator Chuck Grassley, an Iowa Republican who surely knew otherwise, proclaimed that "we should not have a government program that determines you're going to pull the plug on Grandma."

House Republican leader John Boehner threw his lot in with the death panel lie, too. "This provision may start us down a treacherous path toward government-encouraged euthanasia if enacted into law," he warned.

In lawmakers' town hall gatherings across the country, the death panel fabrication became topic A. Newt Gingrich, a pioneer in the party's assault on the facts, chimed in: "You are asking us to trust turning power over to the government, when there are clearly people in America who believe in establishing euthanasia."

The AARP, which supported the counseling sessions, called out the lie. PolitiFact branded Palin's claim a "pants on fire" falsehood and later made it the "Lie of the Year." Media outlets debunked the nonsense claim again and again. It made no difference.

Obama at first didn't dignify the absurd allegation with a response. By September, he found himself trying to refute a "cynical and irresponsible" claim "made not just by radio and cable talk show hosts, but prominent politicians, that we plan to set up panels of bureaucrats with the power to kill off senior citizens. . . . It is a lie, plain and simple."

But Palin understood something Obama didn't. Since the days

of the Vince Foster "murder," the Republican base had been fed such a steady diet of lies by their leaders, faithfully echoed by the commentariat of Fox News and talk radio, that truth had little meaning. Republicans rebranded corrective "fact checks" as partisan hits.

"We're not going to let our campaign be dictated by fact-checkers," Mitt Romney's presidential campaign pollster, Neil Newhouse, said at a breakfast panel. And they didn't. Republicans went with what worked—even if it was pure fiction.

In the weeks after Palin launched the death panel falsehood, polls found about 30 percent of Americans believed death panels were in the health care legislation. Democrats removed the optional counseling provision from the bill.

But Republican leaders kept going with the death panel fantasy, even after the law's passage. They moved on to claim that another provision, the Independent Payment Advisory Board, would serve as a death panel, rationing care. Never mind that the law explicitly forbade rationing, and the board had no authority over anybody's care. In 2011, Boehner, joined by Senate Republican leader Mitch McConnell, wrote a letter to Obama refusing to submit appointees to the board—because of "the denied care that seniors would experience."

Six years after Palin's death panel invention, a *Vox* poll found that 26 percent of Republicans *still* believed there were death panels in the law. Is it any wonder?

Republican leaders' assault on the truth began with relatively minor lies, such as the Foster conspiracy. It advanced into justifying the Iraq War with lies. By the time of the Birther and death panel canards during the Obama years, lies had become the currency of the realm. The disinformation was no longer coming from the fringes and working its way to the tongues of Republican leaders. The crazy and the mainstream were merging as Republican leaders embraced the lunatic fringe. And GOP officials themselves were now inventing whatever lunacy they thought might bring down the president and his signature initiative. The truth had nothing to do with it.

IN 2009, THE BUREAU of Alcohol, Tobacco and Firearms began Operation Fast and Furious, a scheme that allowed two thousand guns to be sold illegally in the Phoenix area in order to track the buyers and sellers, who were thought to have ties to Mexican drug cartels. But the tracking of the guns went awry—and one of the missing guns was apparently used to kill a U.S. Border Patrol agent in December 2010.

Though similar to an operation undertaken during the Bush administration, Fast and Furious was a serious screwup for ATF. But Republicans saw it as a scandal that led straight to the Oval Office. They had no evidence to support the incendiary charge, but that didn't matter.

Representative Trey Gowdy, a South Carolina Republican, alleged that he had "proof" that Obama himself was "part of" the program. Representative John Mica, a Florida Republican, accused Attorney General Eric Holder of personally "creating a situation in which an agent of the United States was murdered."

Darrell Issa, a California Republican and chairman of the House Oversight Committee, accused Holder and colleagues of "lying" and "covering up a crime." Issa proclaimed that the operation "went all the way to the White House," that it was approved "at the highest levels of the Obama appointees," and that Justice Department officials had "blood on their hands." When the Justice Department refused to turn over all the documents Issa sought, House Republicans used "emergency" procedures to hold Holder in contempt of Congress—the first such action taken against a sitting attorney general in American history.

But after essentially accusing the attorney general of being an accessory to murder, Republicans still could produce no evidence to support the wild claims. The Justice Department's inspector general issued an extensive report that harshly criticized ATF but concluded there was "no evidence" that Holder, much less Obama, had even known about Operation Fast and Furious before the killing of the border agent. Issa issued his own report with Grassley, but the two also failed to find evidence of involvement by Holder or Obama.

After a long court struggle, the Justice Department released sixty-four thousand pages of documents about the operation. There was nothing to implicate Holder or the White House, but there was this email from Holder to colleagues: "Issa and his idiot cronies never gave a damn about this when all that was happening was that thousands of Mexicans were being killed with guns from our country. All they want to do—in reality—is cripple ATF and suck up to the gun lobby. Politics at its worst."

Issa ran the same play over and over: he made wild, unfounded accusations, which were duly amplified by Fox News and talk radio, and when the accusations were proven false, they simply moved on to the next wild, baseless allegations. Issa launched a dozen or so probes, invariably promising that a scandal would lead to the Oval Office—and just as routinely finding that the "scandals" amounted to low-level mistakes or misbehavior.

He announced that he had discovered "Obama's Watergate"— the White House floating an administration job for a Democratic congressman to keep him out of a Senate primary. But then he found out that George W. Bush's administration had done similarly. In 2010, Issa told Limbaugh that Obama "has been one of the most corrupt presidents in modern times." (He later acknowledged that Obama wasn't "personally corrupt.") After the failure of a government-aided solar energy company, Solyndra, Issa declared that "the president and his cronies are picking winners and losers," perhaps "because there were large contributions given to them." His probe found no cronyism and no involvement at all by Obama.

When complaints surfaced that the IRS had singled out certain Tea Party groups for extra scrutiny of their tax-exempt status, Issa asserted that it was "the targeting of the president's political enemies, effectively, and lies about it." He called the White House press secretary a "paid liar" for suggesting the trouble was limited to the IRS's Cincinnati office. "This is a problem that was coordinated in all likelihood right out of Washington headquarters, and we're getting to proving it," Issa said on CNN.

Getting to proving it? That was his strategy: begin with the verdict, then conduct the investigation.

Fox News jumped on the nonstory. On its airwaves, House Appropriations Committee Chairman Hal Rogers, a Kentucky Republican, said the IRS was shutting down groups on "the enemies list out of the White House," a list "that rivals that of another president some time ago."

The Republican-controlled House held IRS official Lois Lerner, who oversaw the targeting, in contempt of Congress— just as Republicans had done to Holder—because she took the Fifth Amendment. Issa breezily declared that Lerner "acted on" Obama's wishes and that the "nefarious conduct . . . went much higher than Lois Lerner."

But something funny happened as Issa was "getting to proving it."

The Treasury Department's inspector general (like the Justice Department's inspector general independent from the agency's control) found no evidence that anybody from the White House, or any political appointee anywhere, was involved. Worse, the I.G.'s office reported that Issa had directed it "to narrowly focus on Tea Party organizations" and therefore other groups targeted by the IRS were "outside the scope of our audit." It turned out that the IRS also gave extra scrutiny to groups using descriptions such as "progressive," "green energy," "medical marijuana," and "health care legislation."

So much for a White House enemies list. Even Republican Dave Camp of Michigan, the House Ways and Means Committee chairman, eventually acknowledged that it was the work of "a career employee in the IRS."

These were but skirmishes against truth compared to the battle of Benghazi. On September 11, 2012, armed militants attacked the U.S. consulate in Benghazi, Libya, killing the visiting U.S. ambassador and three other Americans. It was a tragedy, and it raised serious questions: Why hadn't the State Department heeded the ambassador's previous requests for added security? Could anything more have been done to repel the attack and save the four American lives?

But congressional Republicans had a different plan: they would blame Hillary Clinton for the killings. They claimed she personally rejected the ambassador's requests for added security and then lied about it.

Clinton testified to Congress that "the security cables did not come to my attention." But House Republicans issued a report trumpeting that they had found a State Department cable rejecting the request from the ambassador for reinforcements. "The cable response to Tripoli bears Secretary Clinton's signature," it concluded, calling the message a "cable from Clinton."

Fox News ran with it. Host Brian Kilmeade said the finding "sharply contradicts her sworn testimony." Issa told Fox that Clinton "said she did not participate in this, and yet only a few months before the attack, she outright denied security in her signature in a cable."

What Fox and Issa didn't tell the viewers was that, under long-time State Department protocols, the secretary of state's "signature" is on every cable that leaves Washington—even though the secretary has knowledge of only a tiny fraction of them. The State Department's Accountability Review Board affirmed that security decisions were made at lower levels.

No matter; Issa moved on to another fiction. He alleged that Clinton had issued a "stand down order" to the military, preventing help from being sent to Benghazi during the attack. "Why there was [sic] not one order given to turn on one Department of Defense asset?" he asked at a fundraising dinner. "I have my suspicions, which is Secretary Clinton told Leon [Panetta] to stand down, and we all heard about the stand-down order for two military personnel. That order is undeniable."

Undeniable? Republicans on the House Armed Services Committee concluded that "there was no 'stand down' order issued to U.S. military personnel in Tripoli who sought to join the fight in Benghazi." The Senate Intelligence Committee issued a bipartisan report finding of the supposed "stand down" orders: "the committee has not found any of these allegations to be substantiated."

The facts didn't matter. As the liberal group Media Matters calculated at the time, Fox News's evening programs did almost 1,100 segments on Benghazi in the twenty months after the attack. Many referred to the fanciful stand down order. " 'Who gave the stand-down order' became the catch-phrase that kept on giving," former Fox News host Alisyn Camerota said on the podcast *Fiasco*. Though it had become clear there was no stand down order, "it never went away at Fox. It was too valuable to get rid of."

Some five hundred other Fox segments were about the Obama

administration's claim in the early hours of the attack that it had begun as a protest; this turned out to be false. Grilled by lawmakers repeatedly about the erroneous "talking points," Clinton responded testily: "With all due respect, the fact is we had four dead Americans. Was it because of a protest or was it because of guys out for a walk one night who decided that they'd go kill some Americans? What difference at this point does it make? It is our job to figure out what happened and do everything we can to prevent it from ever happening again."

But when Fox News covered the exchange, which it did endlessly, it typically cut off the quote after "What difference . . . does it make?"—which made Clinton sound cavalier about the dead Americans. For added effect, Fox frequently brought on the mother of one of the Benghazi fallen, who said of Clinton: "She's got her child. I don't have mine because of her."

Such shenanigans were typical, said Camerota, who switched to CNN. "We did train the audience to become outraged," she said. "Often the scripts would say, 'you'll be outraged, right after the commercial.' We told people, stick around for the outrage, we told them they would be outraged, we told them afterward we're sure they're outraged, and, lo and behold, they became outraged."

Romney took a turn operating the outrage machine. At a presidential debate, he alleged that "it took the president 14 days before he called the attack in Benghazi an act of terror." In reality, Obama had said in the Rose Garden the day after the attack that "no acts of terror will ever shake the resolve of this great nation."

Five separate committees of the Republican-controlled House probed Benghazi but failed to find wrongdoing by Clinton (a conclusion also reached by two bipartisan Senate investigations). So Boehner tried again, creating a select committee to revisit Benghazi anew. The National Republican Congressional Committee attempted to raise political contributions with the committee, asking donors to "fight liberals" and become "Benghazi watchdogs" like chairman Trey Gowdy. "House Republicans will make sure that no one will get away from Gowdy and the select committee," the solicitation promised.

The select committee, after two years and $7 million, eventually issued an eight-hundred-page report in which it, too, found no wrongdoing by Clinton and no evidence that anything more could have been done during the attack to save the four American lives. But no amount of evidence could penetrate the fact-free ecosystem Republicans, with Fox News, had created.

Gowdy, asked whether his findings supported the allegations on bumper stickers and T-shirts across the land claiming "Clinton lied, people died," replied: "You don't see that T-shirt on me, and you've never seen that bumper sticker on any of my vehicles." Gowdy said he would be "shocked" if people concluded the report was about her.

But two of the six Republicans on the committee dissented from their own majority. Jim Jordan of Ohio and Mike Pompeo of Kansas (a future secretary of state in the Trump administration) proclaimed Clinton's actions during the Benghazi attacks "morally reprehensible" and said relatives of the slain had "every right to be disgusted" with the presumptive Democratic presidential nominee.

A day later, the Citizens' Commission on Benghazi, which had pressured Boehner to appoint Gowdy's committee, denounced Gowdy. They suggested new conspiracies: that congressional Republicans were trying to help Clinton, and that they approved "black operations" to run weapons from Benghazi to Islamic State terrorists.

Representative Frank Wolf, a Virginia Republican, attended an event hosted by the influential Heritage Foundation where he lent credence to the idea that the CIA was secretly arming al Qaeda in Benghazi and the Obama administration was funding al Qaeda. Senator Rand Paul, a Kentucky Republican, proposed that the Obama administration was covering up a secret effort in Benghazi to send arms into Syria—"although I have no evidence."

There were no limits. First some claimed that Clinton faked the flu and a concussion in December 2012 to avoid testifying about Benghazi. Then, some claimed she faked a blood clot related to the concussion—"just a scam so that we didn't talk about" Benghazi, Fox's Glenn Beck speculated. Finally, Karl Rove supposed that she had suffered a "serious brain injury" and therefore might be unfit to serve as president.

Amid all the lies, there was one accidental truth. California

Republican Kevin McCarthy, the House majority leader, admitted to Fox's Sean Hannity in 2015 that the real purpose of the Benghazi obsession was to hurt Clinton: "Everybody thought Hillary Clinton was unbeatable, right? But we put together a Benghazi special committee, a select committee. What are her numbers today? Her numbers are dropping."

The inadvertent truth-telling cost McCarthy the House speakership in 2015. But he was right. Though the select committee, like all its predecessors, found Benghazi to be a dry hole, its endless document requests led to the accidental discovery that Clinton had kept a private email server while secretary of state.

Clinton's emails, and the question of whether she mishandled classified materials, would become a central focus of the 2016 campaign and, arguably, cost her the presidency. All because of the Benghazi scandal that wasn't.

THE PROLIFERATING FABRICATIONS WOULD have been comical if so many in the Fox News crowd hadn't accepted them as true. Representative Michele Bachmann, a Minnesota Republican, warned that "young people will be put into mandatory service" by the Obama administration in "what I would call re-education camps." Fox News regular Andrew Napolitano suggested that the administration might have faked the killing of Osama bin Laden, "pulling a fast one to save Obama's lousy presidency." Rush Limbaugh even endorsed a conspiracy theory holding that Obama didn't really attend his daughter's soccer game one Saturday but rather went on a "secret getaway."

In a class by himself was Beck. The Fox News host, on his TV and radio shows, floated the notion that the Federal Emergency Management Agency was operating concentration camps, that Obama advisers wanted to sterilize people through additives to drinking water, that the Obama White House was functioning like the Gestapo and SS with a script taken from Mein Kampf, and that Democrats sought a United Nations takeover of the world. He drew a "Tree of Revolution" on his chalkboard tying Obama to Che Guevara and the Weather Underground, among others.

Increasingly, this lunatic fringe came to control the leaders of the Republican Party. Boehner, in his 2021 memoir, *On the House*, recalled dealing with Bachmann, "a folk hero of the freak show set" who operated in a growing "circle of crazy" (she feared a "One World currency" would replace the dollar). When he refused her demand to be put on the Ways and Means Committee, she threatened: "Well, then I'll just have to go talk to Sean Hannity and everybody at Fox, and Rush Limbaugh, Mark Levin and everybody else on the radio."

Boehner wrote of the "dangerous nonsense" of calling Obama a secret Muslim and the "truly nutty business" of his birth certificate. "To me, the change seemed to happen around 2010 or 2011, when Mark Levin first made a sharp turn to the right," Boehner wrote. "Rush and Sean Hannity . . . were afraid Levin was going to cut into their audience share, so they lurched far to the right too." With all three of the powerful broadcasters in "Looneyville" spouting "crazy nonsense," Boehner appealed to his friend Roger Ailes, the head of Fox News—but he, too, "got swept into the conspiracies and the paranoia and became an almost unrecognizable figure."

Boehner recalled pleading with Ailes to "put a leash on some of the crazies he was putting on the air" because it was impairing the speaker's ability to "accomplish anything conservative." Ailes replied with rants about Benghazi and imagined plots against him by liberal billionaire George Soros, the Clintons, and Obama. "I thought I could get him to control the crazies, and instead I found myself talking to the president of the club," Boehner recounted.

As Boehner watched, Fox News and conservative talk radio "went from real commentary pushing ideals to just pissing people off and making money off the anger." This made governing impossible. Of Obama, Boehner wrote sympathetically: "How do you find common cause with people who think you are a secret Kenyan Muslim traitor to America?"

Tragically, Republican leaders chose to follow the crazies rather than lead them. Romney, as the Republican presidential nominee, joined the Obama-hates-America crowd by saying Obama's first response to Benghazi was "to sympathize with those who waged the attacks."

Romney fired off other wild claims, saying Obama was "ending Medicare as we know it," that "we're only inches away from no longer being a free economy," and that, because of Obama, "Jeep, now owned by the Italians, is thinking of moving all production to China." None of it was true—but none of that mattered. Among those who echoed Romney's bogus claim about Jeeps? Donald Trump, who tweeted: "Chrysler wants to send all Jeep manufacturing to China—and will!"

A senior Chrysler executive replied on Twitter: "You are full of shit!" He added: "I apologize for my language, but lies are just that, lies."

The Atlantic's James Fallows worried about a "post-truth politics." In *Mother Jones,* David Corn wondered: "In politics, does reality matter?" The 2016 election would provide the unsettling answer.

THE OBAMACARE INSANITY CONTINUED after Sarah Palin's death panel lie—and after the law's enactment. Obamacare would give free health care to illegal immigrants! (The law requiring hospital emergency rooms to treat all, including illegal immigrants, predated Obamacare.) "There will be no insurance industry left in three years," Senator Tom Coburn, an Oklahoma Republican and physician, predicted in 2010, claiming the law would "Sovietize the American health care system." (The health insurance industry grew from $726 billion to $1.15 trillion over the next decade.) Rand Paul claimed "you will go to jail" if you don't buy health insurance under Obamacare, and opponents ran similar ads. (The law expressly forbid criminal prosecution for violating the "individual mandate" to have health coverage.) On the year anniversary of the law's passage, Senator Ron Johnson, Republican of Wisconsin, claimed his daughter, born with a heart defect, would have been denied care by a death panel.

Romney's vice presidential pick, Paul Ryan, on Fox News, said Obamacare "funneled out" $716 billion from Medicare. (His own proposals called for similar reductions in the rate of spending increases of Medicare.) Senator Orrin Hatch, Republican of Utah, predicted a government-run, single-payer health care system within the "first year or two" of a second Obama term. (Didn't happen.) Texas representative Louie Gohmert issued a bizarre warning to Supreme Court justices that General Electric would have access to their health care records under Obamacare, and he alleged that Americans would "die early" under the law. Steve King said Obamacare's requirement that insurers cover birth control would "prevent" the birth of a generation and leave America a "dying civilization." Issa held a hearing on the birth control coverage requirement; on his all-male panel he refused to seat Democrats' witness, Georgetown student Sandra Fluke. (Limbaugh helpfully called Fluke a "slut" on the air.)

And don't forget the Nazis! Senator Ted Cruz, the Texas Republican, likened Obamacare to Neville Chamberlain's appeasement of Hitler. Maine governor Paul LePage said the IRS was "the new Gestapo" under Obamacare. Sheryl Nuxoll, a Republican state senator in Idaho, said health insurance companies were setting up a system that was "much like the Jews boarding the trains to concentration camps." Stacey Campfield, a Republican state senator in Tennessee, said that Democrats boasting about Obamacare sign-ups "is like Germans bragging about the number of mandatory sign ups for 'train rides' for Jews in the 40s."

Once you've unhitched yourself from the truth wagon, there's no limit to the places you can visit. Obamacare, in Republicans' telling, was "as destructive to personal and individual liberty as the Fugitive Slave Act of 1850" (New Hampshire state representative Bill O'Brien), "a racist tax" (Representative Ted Yoho of Texas), the "end of prosperity in America" (Glenn Beck), "the most dangerous piece of legislation ever passed" (Representative John Fleming of Louisiana), America's "final death knell" (former senator Rick Santorum of Pennsylvania), and something from which "we will never recover" (Steve King) that "literally kills women, kills children, kills senior citizens" (Michele Bachmann) and means "you're going to die sooner" (Tom Coburn).

Lawmakers, right-wing media, and their hangers-on claimed that members of Congress would be exempt from the law, that it rations care like in Britain, that Muslims were exempt, that as part of this "government takeover" the IRS would keep a database of Americans' intimate medical records, that the elderly would be ineligible for cancer treatment, that the law placed a sales tax on real estate transactions, that it was the largest tax increase "in the history of the world," that it would allow forced home inspections by the government, that it would tax sporting goods, and that it would require microchips to be implanted in all Americans. False, false, false, false, false, false, false, false, false, false, false.

It was a fact-free free-for-all, and because the credibility of the source no longer mattered, anybody could play.

Consider one Betsy McCaughey, a former lieutenant governor of New York. On September 15, 2013, she penned an op-ed in the *New York Post* under the headline "Obamacare Will Question Your Sex Life." She wrote:

" 'Are you sexually active? If so, with one partner, multiple partners or same-sex partners?'

"Be ready to answer those questions and more the next time you go to the doctor, whether it's the dermatologist or the cardiologist and no matter if the questions are unrelated to why you're seeking medical help. And you can thank the Obama health law."

She alleged that the law incentivized doctors to put such information in electronic health records and punished them if they didn't. In reality, it was an entirely different law that created incentives for doctors to shift to electronic records. Even then, the records had nothing to do with questions about sex. It was a thorough fabrication. But it was good enough for Rupert Murdoch's media empire.

McCaughey had built a career on such lies. A quarter century earlier, she helped derail the Clinton administration's attempt at health care reform with a similar fiction. In 1994, when she was affiliated with a conservative think tank, she wrote an article for *The New Republic* making the false claim that, under "Hillary-Care," it would be illegal to get medical care outside the government program. "The law will prevent you from going outside the system to buy basic health coverage you think is better," she wrote. "The doctor can be paid only by the plan, not by you."

This spawned the phony claim, echoing through conservative talk radio, that doctors would be jailed for going outside the government system. Writing in *Newsweek,* George Will suggested that people would be imprisoned for fifteen years for bribing doctors to perform care the government didn't think necessary. Never mind that the proposed legislation said, prominently: "Nothing in this Act shall be construed as prohibiting the following: (1) An individual from purchasing any health care services."

McCaughey, propelled by her doctors-in-prison invention, was elected lieutenant governor of New York that year. The doomed HillaryCare never even came to a vote.

McCaughey reprised her routine with Obama's economic stimulus legislation after the 2008 collapse. In February 2009, she wrote an article, this time for Bloomberg News, alleging that Obama's stimulus plan would create a "new bureaucracy" that would "monitor treatments to make sure your doctor is doing what the federal government deems appropriate and cost effective." This meant "enforcing uniformity," she claimed.

There was just one wee problem with the argument. This "new" bureaucracy to which she referred, the National Coordinator of Health Information Technology, was formed by George W. Bush's administration, and it had nothing to do with restricting treatments doctors could use. A provision in the stimulus bill set up a council to assist in studying the effectiveness of treatments, but with a specific requirement that it not "be construed as mandates or clinical guidelines for payment, coverage or treatment."

But the facts, once again, didn't matter. As *Washington Monthly* chronicled at the time, Limbaugh picked up the claim that the government would "monitor treatments." Matt Drudge's Drudge Report promoted McCaughey's claim prominently. Fox News's Megyn Kelly said it sounded "dangerously like socialized medicine," and Fox's Bill Hemmer reported that there were "new rules guiding decisions your doctor can make about your health care." Beck, for his part, summarized McCaughey's fanciful claim: "Sometimes for the common good, you just have to say, 'Hey, Grandpa, you've had a good life.' " *The Wall Street Journal*'s editorial page picked up the fiction, too.

So it should have surprised nobody that, a few months later, McCaughey hatched yet another lie designed to bring down Obamacare. On July 16, on a radio show hosted by former Republican senator Fred Thompson, she claimed that Congress would "absolutely require that every five years people in Medicare have a required counseling session that will tell them how to end their life sooner." The sessions would, specifically, teach the aged how to "decline nutrition" and thereby "cut your life short."

This became the basis, three weeks later, of Palin's death panel libel and the endless talk of "granny killing" and "death care" that followed.

The moment was ripe for such a claim. Opponents of the nascent health care proposals had already compared them, in the pages of the conservative *Washington Times* and *American Spectator*, to the eugenics practiced by Nazi Germany. *The Washington Times* invoked Hitler's program to exterminate "useless eaters," or babies born with disabilities, and warned of growing "trivialization of abortion, acceptance of euthanasia and the normalization of physician assisted suicide." In the *Spectator*, George Neumayr argued that "Obama's America will pay parents to contracept or kill" children and that "euthanasia is another shovel-ready job for Pelosi to assign to the states."

In eras past, such nonsense would have ended there, on the ideological fringes. But this time Republicans had Palin and others at the top of the party perfectly happy to embrace lies, no matter how far-fetched, to serve their purposes. In the years to come, death panels would be revived repeatedly in the dozens of unsuccessful attempts to repeal a law that never had such panels in the first place. And, seven years after McCaughey inspired the death panel episode, the GOP's presidential nominee, Trump, released a list of key advisers. Prominent on the list: Betsy McCaughey.

CHAPTER 11

Don't Retreat—Reload

On March 23, 2010, the day after the House passed Obamacare, Sarah Palin sounded a call to arms—literally.

"Commonsense Conservatives & lovers of America," she tweeted. "'Don't Retreat, Instead—RELOAD!' Pls see my Facebook page."

Those visiting her Facebook page found a U.S. map with twenty congressional districts held by Democrats, each marked with rifle crosshairs. She named the twenty Democrats and wrote: "We'll aim for these races and many others. This is just the first salvo . . ."

Her thinking was in line with what Sharron Angle, the Republican Senate candidate in Nevada who would face off against Senate Democratic Leader Harry Reid in 2010, had said when she floated the idea of taking up arms. "If this Congress keeps going the way it is, people are really looking toward those Second Amendment remedies and saying my goodness what can we do to turn this country around?" she said on a conservative radio show. "I'll tell you the first thing we need to do is take Harry Reid out."

She argued that the "Founding Fathers . . . put that Second Amendment in there for a good reason and that was for the people to protect themselves against a tyrannical government. And in fact Thomas Jefferson said it's good for a country to have a revolution every 20 years." That was not "in fact" so, but the endorsement of possible violence was unmistakable.

And Michael Steele, chairman of the Republican National

Committee, went on Fox News the same day Palin sounded her call to arms. "Let's start getting Nancy [Pelosi] ready for the firing line this November," he proposed.

People heard them, loud and clear. In the days of the House debate and immediately after, violence erupted.

A Tea Party activist, suggesting people "drop by" the home of Representative Tom Perriello, a Virginia Democrat, posted Perriello's brother's Charlottesville address online thinking it was the congressman's—and somebody did indeed "drop by" and cut a gas line.

Bricks shattered the windows and doors of Democratic Party offices in Wichita, Kansas, Cincinnati, Ohio, and Rochester, New York, apparently in response to the call by an Alabama militia leader, Mike Vanderboegh, who posted a message telling "Sons of Liberty" that "if you wish to send a message that Pelosi and her party cannot fail to hear, break their windows. Break them NOW."

Representative Louise Slaughter, a New York Democrat, was treated to a phone threat mentioning a sniper attack and a brick thrown through the window of her district office.

Representative Bart Stupak, a Michigan Democrat, received a faxed drawing of a noose and a voicemail promising: "You're dead. We know where you live. We'll get you."

Jim Clyburn of South Carolina, the No. 3 Democrat in the House and a senior member of the Congressional Black Caucus, also received a fax with a noose drawing, as well as threats called to his home phone.

Democratic representatives Harry Mitchell of Arizona, Betsy Markey of Colorado, and Steve Driehaus of Ohio received threats of violence, too, and demonstrators besieged Driehaus's home after foes published his home address online.

Representative Anthony Weiner of New York received a letter containing white powder and a threatening letter. Tea Party demonstrators brought a coffin to the office and home of Democratic representative Russ Carnahan of Missouri.

At least ten House Democrats, in addition to Democratic leaders, had to be assigned protection details. The Senate sergeant-at-arms warned senators to "remain vigilant."

And, in Tucson, Arizona, somebody shattered the glass door to the office of Democratic Representative Gabrielle Giffords, possibly with a pellet gun.

Just days earlier, House Republican Leader John Boehner had inflamed passions in the House chamber—and far beyond—with his furious cry against Obamacare: "Hell no you can't!" Others in the House shouted charges of "baby killer" and "tyranny." Days earlier, Boehner told *National Review* that if his fellow Ohioan Driehaus voted for Obamacare, "he may be a dead man"—politically speaking, of course.

Now Boehner made a halfhearted attempt to calm the violence—while validating the rage. "I know many Americans are angry over this health-care bill, and that Washington Democrats just aren't listening," he said on Fox News. "But, as I've said, violence and threats are unacceptable."

It was a weak effort, and one of the targets, Perriello, said so. "No, the answer is, we want those people to go to jail who are committing a crime," he told *The New York Times*. "I think people have to realize what it means to say in a democracy that 'I will kill your children if you don't vote a certain way,'" Perriello said. "What's at stake here is the sanctity of our democracy."

Slaughter, of New York, went further, accusing Republicans of "fanning the flames with coded rhetoric."

But the No. 2 House Republican, Eric Cantor, declared the matter "reprehensible"—not the attacks and threats against Democrats, but the "reckless" complaints by Democrats such as Slaughter about the violence being visited on them. Such statements "only inflame these situations to dangerous levels." Cantor justified his blame-the-victim statement by pointing out that somebody had fired a shot at his district office—but it turned out that it was a stray bullet shot into the air; Cantor's office hadn't been targeted.

In Tucson, staffers to Gabby Giffords were shaken, not just by having the office door shattered but by a flood of threatening calls and emails. An Arizona Tea Party leader, Trent Humphries, proclaimed that "Giffords is toast." Even before the Obamacare vote, a suspicious package had been delivered to the Giffords office, and at a "Congress on Your Corner" event at a Tucson supermarket, protesters shouted Giffords down over the health care bill and somebody dropped a gun, which slid across the ground toward Giffords.

Staffers began to fear for their safety, but Giffords, in an interview with MSNBC's Chuck Todd and Savannah Guthrie after the shattering of her office door, said she wasn't afraid. "Our democracy is a beacon to the world because we effect change at the ballot box and not because of these outbursts of violence," she said, urging both sides to come together and calm the passions. "Look, we can't stand for this. The rhetoric, and firing people up. . . . We're on Sarah Palin's targeted list. The thing is, the way she has it depicted is with the crosshairs of a gunsight over our district. And when people do that, they've got to realize there are consequences to that action."

But Palin pressed on, heedless of the consequences. At a gathering of the Southern Republican Leadership Conference in New Orleans in April, she won hearty applause repeating her new mantra: "Don't retreat—reload!"

In Arizona, Giffords's Republican opponent, Jesse Kelly, hosted an event in June that he promoted with a photo of himself in military garb holding an automatic weapon. "Get on Target for Victory in November," it said. "Help remove Gabrielle Giffords from office. Shoot a fully automatic M16 with Jesse Kelly."

Giffords squeaked to a victory in November, but she had grown discouraged. On January 7, 2011, she wrote a despairing email to her husband and a friend. "My poor state!" it said. "The nut jobs have stolen it away from the good people of Arizona."

Three days after her swearing in to a third term, Giffords scheduled another Congress on Your Corner event outside a Tucson Safeway. Her staff had encouraged her to skip it, but Giffords wouldn't hear of it. She made a robocall to her constituents cheerfully telling them where and when to show up: "This is Congresswoman Gabrielle Giffords and I hope to meet you in person this Saturday." When Saturday morning came, she tweeted: "Please stop by to let me know what is on your mind."

When she arrived, there were more than a dozen people already lined up to talk with her, including a nine-year-old girl, Christina-Taylor Green, who had been elected to her school's student council and wanted to learn more about government. "Thanks so much for coming," she told the crowd with a smile.

Near the front of the line, she encountered twenty-two-year-old Jared Loughner, with a shaved head and a crazed look in his eyes. He raised a Glock 19 9mm semiautomatic handgun and, from two feet away, fired a bullet through Giffords's head.

The gunman continued firing, hitting twenty people in all and killing six of them, including Gabe Zimmerman, a thirty-year-old Giffords staffer, three retirees—and young Christina-Taylor Green, shot in the chest. Also slain was federal judge John Roll, who died heroically shielding Giffords aide Ron Barber. Barber was hit in the cheek and thigh, permanently injuring his leg.

Finally the gunman stopped to reload, and bystanders (including one who had been shot in the head) hit him over the head with a folding chair, wrestled ammunition from him, and knocked him to the ground.

At 2 p.m., National Public Radio erroneously reported that Giffords was dead, and CNN, Fox News, and MSNBC repeated the error. Her husband, NASA astronaut Mark Kelly, broke down in grief when the false report reached him as he rushed home to Arizona on a friend's jet. (He recounted this and other details in a memoir he later wrote with Giffords.)

Giffords—miraculously—survived the assassin's bullet. But her life would never be the same. She had been a rising star, and chatter had already begun about a run for higher office. Instead, her brain injury left her with limited use of the right side of her body and aphasia, which makes speech extremely difficult.

The Giffords tragedy has a personal element for me. My wife was her pollster, and I've had the privilege of observing Gabby's heroic struggle to regain her ability to speak. I've shared in her joy as her husband (who also hired my wife as his pollster) won election to the Senate—the place where everybody thought Gabby would wind up.

There's no evidence that Palin's violent rhetoric, or anybody else's, provoked the massacre in Tucson; the killer was obviously deranged, as his political views suggested (he seemed to believe government used grammar to exert mind control). But when the

New York Post asked Giffords's father if his daughter had any enemies, he responded: "Yeah, the whole Tea Party."

Palin unquestionably deserves blame for one thing: she refused to tone down her rhetoric even after the Tucson massacre. In the days after the shooting, many cited Palin's violent rhetoric and her crosshairs image over Giffords's district. Palin called this "a blood libel that serves only to incite . . . hatred and violence"—a bizarre invocation of the anti-Semitic "blood libel" alleging that Jews consumed the blood of Christian children.

Six months later, she was back to her violent talk. "Now is not the time to retreat," she told Fox News's Sean Hannity, "it's the time to reload." Eleven months after that, she told a gathering of conservatives in Las Vegas: "Don't retreat—reload and re-fight."

Palin and others like her had introduced a new relationship between the Republican Party and political violence. With the rise of the Tea Party, elected officials in the Republican Party chose to fan the antigovernment rage. They tried to ride the tiger, harnessing the energy of the anti-Obama rebellion. In the end, the antigovernment rage wound up consuming the Republicans and turning the GOP into an antigovernment party with an often violent audience.

By historical standards, twenty-first-century political violence hasn't been particularly lethal. The Equal Justice Initiative has documented 4,384 lynchings by white supremacists between 1877 and 1950. Some 750,000 died in the Civil War. There was Black nationalist, revolutionary leftist, and Puerto Rican nationalist violence in the 1960s and 1970s, and, later, jihadist terrorism.

What made this moment different was that, on the airwaves and online, right-wing personalities recklessly fed their audiences paranoid conspiracy theories about the Obama administration that made them fear for their country, and their lives. With Republican leaders also validating those fears, it became a recipe for rage and, inevitably, violence.

The militia movement of the 1990s, which faded after the Oklahoma City bombing, and was quiet during the Bush presidency, came roaring back. In the first year of Obama's presidency, the number of antigovernment "Patriot" groups rose to 512 from 149 the year before, the Southern Poverty Law Center reported, with the number of paramilitary groups tripling. By the end of 2012, such Patriot groups had grown to 1,360, SPLC reported.

Then, in 2013 and 2014, something interesting happened: the number of violent groups began to decline. But this wasn't good news. They had migrated to online organizations such as Stormfront. And, the SPLC reported: "The highly successful infiltration into the political mainstream of many radical-right ideas about Muslims, immigrants, black people and others have stolen much of the fire of the extremists, as more prominent figures co-opt these parts of their program. . . . [A] wide variety of hard-right ideas, racial resentments and demonizing conspiracy theories have deeply penetrated the political mainstream, infecting politicians and pundits alike."

New racist, antigovernment groups sprang up, such as the Oath Keepers (March 2009) and the Three Percenters (late 2008). Registered users of Stormfront murdered close to one hundred people over a five-year period, SPLC found.

Authorities found plots to kill U.S. government officials and attack federal property and mosques. Domestic terrorists went on a spree of lone-wolf attacks on Muslims, police, and government sites. Conspiracy theorists went wild, and not just with the Birther, death panel, and Nazi eugenics lies. Obama planned to impose martial law and socialism and to declare himself president for life. Oklahoma City and 9/11 were false flag operations—inside jobs. The Federal Reserve was facilitating world government and FEMA was building concentration camps. The feds planned door-to-door gun confiscation.

Facing the rise of both the Tea Party and the Patriot groups—and increasing overlap between them—Republican officeholders faced a choice: get on board, or get run over. Senator Lindsey Graham, a Republican of South Carolina who voted to confirm Obama nominee Sonia Sotomayor to the Supreme Court, held a town hall meeting in December 2009, at which he was called a "traitor" in a "pact with the devil."

Responded Graham: "We're not going to be the party of angry white guys." But Graham got the message, and became an angry white guy himself.

Joe Wilson, Republican of South Carolina, debuted the angry-white-guy routine with his infamous "You lie!" shout at Obama on the House floor in September 2009. Boehner tried to persuade Wilson to apologize on the House floor, but Wilson, who said he apologized privately, refused. Boehner excused the Wilson outburst by saying, "Americans are frustrated, they're angry, and, most importantly, they're scared to death."

Now why would that be?

FreedomWorks, a group started by former House Majority Leader Dick Armey, a Texas Republican, tightly affiliated itself with the Tea Party. Representative Tom Price, a Georgia Republican, celebrated the Tea Partiers at one rally by invoking Samuel Adams: "It doesn't take a majority to prevail, but an irate and tireless minority keen on setting brush fires of freedom in the minds of men. Thank you so much for setting those brush fires."

Armey himself told the Tea Party faithful their lives were in danger: "Patrick Henry said, 'Give me liberty or give me death.' Well, Barack Obama is trying to make good on that."

The rage of the Tea Party crowd was palpable as they shouted down lawmakers at town hall meetings and carried posters with menacing messages: threats to stop Obamacare with "a Browning"—a gun; an image of an assault rifle with the message "Come and Take It"; and, everywhere, Thomas Jefferson's saying: "The Tree of Liberty must be refreshed from time to time with the blood of patriots and tyrants." At one rally across the Potomac River from Washington in Virginia, a group of armed demonstrators, carrying AK-47s and pistols, observed the fifteenth anniversary of the Oklahoma City bombing. They were led by Mike Vanderboegh, the man who had called for bricks to be thrown through windows of Democratic Party offices. He told his armed followers that Democrats "are pushing this country toward civil war and they should stop before somebody gets hurt." He suggested they might have reached the point where they would be "absolved from any further obedience" to the government.

Cravenly, Republicans opened the doors to the Capitol and welcomed such sentiments—and the people voicing them.

On the weekend in March 2010 when the House neared final passage of Obamacare, Tea Party demonstrators besieged the Capitol. The mob got to within fifty feet of the Capitol, and

Democrats worried aloud about the possibility of violence. Police struggled to hold back the crowd. But many Republican lawmakers chose to whip the protesters into a frenzy. GOP officials—including the head of the House Republicans' 2010 campaign committee—went out onto the balcony, waved handwritten signs, and led the crowd in chants of "Kill the bill." A few waved the yellow "Don't Tread on Me" flag appropriated by the Tea Party movement. Inside the chamber, they howled out of control: "Baby killer!" "Say no to totalitarianism!"

"That's kind of fun," Representative Mary Fallin of Oklahoma said cheerfully after riling the crowd with a sign saying "NO" in red letters.

Representative Barney Frank of Massachusetts, an openly gay Democrat who had been called "faggot" and "homo" by the mob, accurately observed that some Republicans "think they are benefitting from this rancor."

One hundred days before the 2010 midterm elections, a few dozen Republican members of Congress, led by Michele Bachmann of Minnesota, formed the House Tea Party Caucus, which invited Tea Party leaders to the Capitol and paraded them in front of the TV cameras. It was, in effect, a merger: the activists allowed themselves to be co-opted by the Republican Party, and Republican officeholders allowed themselves to become the faces of the Tea Party movement. Republican lawmakers shared the stage while the activists accused the Democrats of "21st-century Marxism" and "socialist policies." The Tea Partiers endorsed Republican House candidates, and the lawmakers pledged to "take this country back." At another House Tea Party Caucus meeting, Supreme Court justice Antonin Scalia was the guest speaker.

Bachmann, who like Palin was testing the waters for a 2012 presidential run, called Obama and the Democrats "anti-American," accused Obama of running a "gangster government," and suggested that people be "armed and dangerous" as they fought climate change legislation. She voiced "grave doubt" about the nation's survival and said it "is my firm belief that America is under greater attack now" than ever before. (She also called John Quincy Adams a "Founding Father," claimed the American Revolution began in Concord, New Hampshire, instead of Concord, Massachusetts, and alleged that the founders "worked tire-lessly until slavery was no more.") Bachmann endorsed an event at which Tea Party leaders denounced Boehner and Paul Ryan, top Republican on the House Budget Committee, and threatened to mount primary challenges to Republican incumbents. "I hear you and I agree," Bachmann said.

Boehner, in his memoir, came to realize that Bachmann "had the power now" because she was "a conservative media darling." Wrote Boehner: "[S]he had me where it hurt."

Republican leaders therefore accelerated their capitulation to the Tea Party and their co-opting of its message. "There really is no difference between what Republicans believe in and what the Tea Party activists believe in," Boehner told conservative radio host Mike Gallagher in 2010. Later, when Boehner (reluctantly) embraced the Tea Party strategy of forcing a government shut-down, he asserted: "There's no daylight between the Tea Party and me." (There was no daylight between the Tea Party and most Republicans: the American Conservative Union found that 86 per-cent of House Republicans voted the conservative line at least 80 percent of the time in 2009.)

RNC chairman Michael Steele invited Tea Party leaders to the National Republican Club for a private meeting. "Guess what? I'm a Tea Partier," Steele announced. "I'm a town-haller, I'm a grass-roots-er." Another time, he told Fox News's Greta Van Susteren: "If I weren't chair of the RNC, I'd be out there in the Tea Party movement."

In a Delaware Republican Senate primary, Tea Party darling Christine O'Donnell beat the favorite, Representative Mike Cas-tle. Her campaign ran aground over her previous admission that she "dabbled into witchcraft" and "had a midnight picnic on a satanic altar." (She tried to salvage her campaign with an ad saying "I'm not a witch.") But Senator John Cornyn of Texas, chairman of the National Republican Senatorial Committee, still sent her a party check for $42,000. (Karl Rove, after correctly declaring in a Fox News interview that O'Donnell was unelectable, heard complaints from Palin and then returned to Fox to say she's "not out of the game.")

After Tea Party favorite Rand Paul (the libertarian gadfly Ron

Paul's son) won the Republican Senate primary in Kentucky over the candidate preferred by Senate Republican leader (and fellow Kentuckian) Mitch McConnell, McConnell got with the program. He started using Tea Party terms such as "government takeover" and made his famous declaration that "the single most important thing we want to achieve is for President Obama to be a one-term president."

Ryan, Cantor, and Kevin McCarthy of California clambered aboard the Tea Party train by publishing a book celebrating "angry citizens confronting often dazed and defensive members of Congress" and accusing Obama of trying to "take us past the tipping point" toward a socialist state. (Sometimes the members of Congress *were* the angry citizens: Representative Michael Grimm, a New York Republican, threatened on the night of an Obama State of the Union address to throw a reporter off a balcony, saying, "I'll break you in half. Like a boy.")

McCarthy, who became majority whip in 2011, tried to rally his caucus by screening for members a clip from the 2010 film *The Town,* in which Ben Affleck's bank robber character tells the Jeremy Renner character: "I need your help. I can't tell you what it is, you can never ask me about it later, and we're gonna hurt some people." Renner replies: "Whose car we takin'?" McCarthy's clip ended before the shooting and beatings that followed.

Cantor, a conservative hardliner who became majority leader in 2011, was ideologically in sync with the Tea Party. But, as an observant Jew, he was also uneasy with the move toward bigotry the party was taking. Later, in 2013, he urged colleagues to "stop the revival stuff" with the Tea Party, and he tried to nudge the party toward an inclusive immigration position; for his troubles, he lost a 2014 primary in a spectacular upset by a far-right unknown, Dave Brat.

Two decades earlier, Republican Senate leader Bob Dole had the power to coerce extremists in his caucus into striking deals with President Clinton on matters such as the budget and welfare reform. But with the Tea Party's rise, no congressional leader had such clout. The leaders became followers.

In October 2010, Mike Pence of Indiana, the No. 3 House Republican, told radio host Hugh Hewitt: "Look, there will be no compromise on stopping runaway spending, deficits and debt. There will be no compromise on repealing Obamacare. There will be no compromise on stopping Democrats from growing government and raising taxes. And if I haven't been clear enough yet, let me say again: no compromise."

Boehner, who failed in several attempts to cajole his colleagues toward sanity, eventually sided with the hardliners in 2011 on repealing Obamacare. "This is not a time for compromise," he told Sean Hannity. "We're going to do everything—and I mean everything—we can do to kill it."

When it was reported in October 2010 that Republican senator Bob Corker of Tennessee had told donors that "crazier Republicans" would be blocked by leaders from repealing Obamacare, both McConnell and Corker rushed out statements pledging their devotion to repeal.

Around the country, ambitious, establishment Republicans, seeing which way the winds were blowing, reinvented themselves as Tea Partiers. One such figure, Ted Cruz of Texas, was a Princeton- and Harvard-trained debater and a Chamber of Commerce type (I met him when he worked for George W. Bush's campaign), but he won a Senate seat in 2012 as an uncompromising bomb thrower. Other elites—a Yale Law grad in Alaska, a Princeton grad in Colorado—remade themselves as Tea Party Senate candidates.

Multimillionaires and billionaires with corporate backgrounds recast themselves as Tea Party candidates for statewide races in Connecticut, Wisconsin, Michigan, New York, Florida, and California. Fox's Glenn Beck helped the plutocrats masquerade as populists, telling his followers: "If you have a dollar, please go to . . . the U.S. Chamber of Commerce and donate today." The response crashed the Chamber's servers. In addition to Armey's FreedomWorks (run by former Chamber of Commerce employee Matt Kibbe), GOP consultant Sal Russo created the Tea Party Express, designed to boost his consulting firm's profits. The billionaire Koch brothers, Republican mega-donors, funded another Tea Party group, Americans for Prosperity.

The Republican Party's co-opting of the Tea Party inevitably meant the mainstreaming of fringe ideas, many of them antigovernment. Republican-run states took up legislation to nullify federal laws, including health care reform, gun and food-safety laws, and the Endangered Species Act. They took up measures promoting citizen militias, restricting the FBI's operations in their states, and requesting an end to membership in the United Nations. Various county sheriffs vowed not to enforce federal gun or tax laws.

After figures such as Bachmann and Beck warned that the Census could bring about "slavery" and "internment camps," so many Republican voters refused to comply with the count that other Republican officials scrambled to counter the "blatant misinformation." When Fox News helped spread the fantasy that Muslims planned to enact Sharia law in the United States, Republican-run states rushed to ban Sharia law and Republicans put an anti-Sharia plank in their 2012 platform banning "foreign sources of law." The platform also called for studying a return to the gold standard, auditing the Federal Reserve, constitutionally banning tax increases, and building a border wall.

Todd Akin, the 2012 Republican Senate nominee in Missouri, opined that rape victims rarely get pregnant, because "if it's a legitimate rape, the female body has ways to try to shut that whole thing down." He opposed abortion even in cases of rape—and this became part of the official GOP platform, too. The platform also had an anti-abortion "salute" to states such as Virginia, where Republican governor Bob McDonnell had sought to force women to undergo invasive and unnecessary "transvaginal ultrasounds" before being allowed to have an abortion.

Leading Republicans attacked the Federal Reserve and its chairman, Ben Bernanke, for the aggressive intervention the central bank took to stabilize and grow the economy. Texas governor Rick Perry called Bernanke's behavior "almost treasonous" and said the chairman would face an "ugly" greeting in Texas. Newt Gingrich called him "dangerous and power-centered." Rand Paul and others called for abolishing the Fed.

As the Obama administration progressed through a second term, so did the antigovernment broadsides. In 2012, the House voted overwhelmingly to extend the charter of the Export-Import Bank, with only ninety-three Republicans opposed. Three years later, the right-wing Republican Study Committee, representing 170 House conservatives, opposed renewal because they suddenly saw the bank as an example of big-government overreach—and the bank, a lifeline for U.S. small businesses, was mothballed for five months.

In 2015, Republican presidential candidates Mike Huckabee and Rick Santorum signed pledges not to "respect an unjust law that directly conflicts with Higher Law." Huckabee, attacking the "imperial" Supreme Court, said the justices "cannot overturn the laws of nature or of nature's God," and he entertained the idea of using federal troops to block people from getting abortions. Perry said Texas wouldn't comply with a federal prison-rape law (its standards were too stringent), Paul called for "civil resistance" over a church-state conflict in Houston, and McConnell encouraged states not to comply with an Obama administration environmental rule.

A county clerk in Kentucky, Kim Davis, defied the Supreme Court by refusing to issue marriage certificates to gay couples. She claimed she operated "under God's authority." She was backed in her defiance by Matt Bevin, the GOP gubernatorial candidate, and by Cruz, who decried "judicial tyranny" when a federal judge ordered Davis jailed for contempt of court.

GOP presidential aspirants Bobby Jindal (the Louisiana governor), Paul, and Wisconsin governor Scott Walker also supported Davis in her defiance. Senator Marco Rubio of Florida said broadly that "God's rules always win." Various judges and clerks across the country decided to engage in similar rebellions against the Supreme Court's authority, and Davis's husband threatened violence against any gay marriage proponents who "come knocking on my door."

Jeb Bush, the former Florida governor, was one of the few willing to state the obvious: that Davis "is sworn to uphold the law." Such notions had become anachronistic in the GOP, as Bush learned when his presidential bid collapsed.

Prominent Republican officials also embraced the lawbreaking of Nevada rancher Cliven Bundy, who had for years refused to pay cattle grazing fees for the use of federal land. He defied a federal court order, affirmed by an appellate court, requiring him to remove the cattle. When the U.S. Bureau of Land Management came in to impound the livestock in April 2014, the Bundys began an armed standoff with federal agents. Hundreds of militia members from across the country came to the ranch to support the Bundys in their standoff.

Bundy made clear his contempt for the federal government, telling the *Los Angeles Times* "I abide by almost zero federal laws," while his wife, Carol, explained their approach: "I've got a shotgun. It's loaded and I know how to use it. We're ready to do what we have to do."

Key Republicans, sworn to protect the Constitution, instead protected Bundy. Senator Dean Heller of Nevada called the Bundys "patriots" and said he told the Bureau of Land Management very clearly that "law-abiding Nevadans must not be penalized by an overreaching BLM." Nevada's Republican governor, Brian Sandoval, objected to the treatment of Bundy's armed supporters, saying, "No cow justifies the atmosphere of intimidation which currently exists nor the limitation of constitutional rights that are sacred to all Nevadans."

Rand Paul said the Bundys raised "a legitimate constitutional question." Cruz blamed the Obama administration for putting liberty "under assault" and "using the jackboot of authoritarianism." Perry blamed the federal government for "putting citizens in the position of having to feel like they have to use force to deal with their own government." Herman Cain, a 2012 presidential candidate, said he had "sympathy" for Cliven Bundy. Texas attorney general (and future governor) Greg Abbott declared himself "deeply concerned" about the BLM's actions. And Michele Fiore, a Nevada state assemblywoman who joined the rebellion at the Bundy ranch, said "the way this was handled was really suspicious."

Later, these Bundy defenders were embarrassed when it came out that Cliven Bundy wondered whether "Negro" people were "better off as slaves, picking cotton." But they shouldn't have been surprised: the Patriot militia movement and the white supremacist movement are inseparable.

To avoid carnage, the federal government called off the Bundy cattle roundup and told federal workers to stay away. The militia movement exulted in its victory and the support it received from Republican officials—and then it tried for another win against the United States.

In January 2016, Ammon and Ryan Bundy, two of Cliven's sons, led an armed takeover of the Malheur National Wildlife Refuge in Oregon in support of nearby ranchers. The ranchers, father-son pair Dwight and Steven Hammond, after years of land disputes with the federal government, had been convicted of arson in 2012 for setting a fire that spread to federal land; authorities said the pair were trying to hide evidence of a slaughtered deer herd.

The Bundy-led standoff lasted forty-one days, ending with police shooting dead one of those occupying the federal land. In 2018, President Donald Trump would pardon the two ranchers whose arson prompted the armed rebellion against federal authority.

Certainly, no side has owned political violence in American history. Even in the recent era, a deranged man who supported Senator Bernie Sanders, the independent socialist from Vermont, fired at Republican members of Congress as they practiced on a baseball field, nearly killing Representative Steve Scalise of Louisiana; he recovered and now serves as the No. 2 GOP House leader.

But the new threat of violence from the right during this time was unique, because of the rage and fear stoked by GOP officials and amplified on the airwaves and the web.

Conservative blogger Andrew Breitbart, a former Matt Drudge acolyte and self-described "cultural warrior," started Breitbart News online in 2007 with a view that he is "at war" with the "evil" left. "Let's weaponize this," he liked to say, and "I war with these people," and "I'm going to go start taking out more media people—um, metaphorically."

Future Fox News host Tucker Carlson, who had been a country-club Republican and writer for the temperate *Weekly Standard,* decided to radicalize and in 2010 started *The Daily Caller,* in a vein similar to Breitbart.

Alex Jones, a conspiracy monger, had a radio show and a website, *InfoWars,* dedicated to the wildest claims about imminent martial law, globalists, and the New World Order, FEMA concentration camps, and claiming everything from 9/11 to the gun massacre of children at Sandy Hook in Connecticut were false-flag operations by the government.

Rush Limbaugh kept his massive audience riled. After Bill Clinton gave a speech warning about the return of "hatred" on the airwaves similar to that preceding the Oklahoma City bombing, Limbaugh said it was the Obama "regime" that "set the stage for violence." Clinton "gave the kooks out there an excuse to be violent," he announced. "He just offered them an opportunity to be violent."

Fox News's Bill O'Reilly fantasized about violence—against me. In November 2010, reacting to a critical column I'd written, he made "a joke" by asking: "Does sharia law say we can behead Dana Milbank?" Responding to a viewer's complaint about it the next night, O'Reilly was unmoved. "If Dana Milbank did in Iran what he does in Washington, he'd be hummus," he said. The next night, he put up a photo of my editor, Fred Hiatt, criticized him for not taking action against me, and said: "Fred, have a nice weekend, buddy." He concluded that he and another Fox host "should go and beat [me] up."

But none stoked violence as often as Beck. "We are not going to play defense at all!" he bellowed two days after the Giffords shooting—in defense of Palin. "Offense!"

Beck routinely likened Obama to Hitler and called him "dangerous," promoting the nonsense that Obama was creating a "civilian national security force" and concentration camps for dissidents. Drawing nonexistent links on his blackboard between various figures on the left, he fomented rage: "The clock is ticking . . . The war is just beginning . . . Shoot me in the head . . . Be prepared to take rocks to the head . . . There is a coup going on . . . Grab a torch . . . Drive a stake through the heart of the bloodsuckers . . . They are taking you to a place to be slaughtered."

After Beck, with his blackboard of paranoia, railed repeatedly on Fox against the little-known Tides Foundation, police in Oakland, California, pulled over a man driving erratically—and the man, in body armor, fired at them with a 9mm handgun, a shotgun, and a .308-caliber rifle with armor-piercing bullets. Two officers were shot. The assailant told investigators he wanted to "start a revolution" by "killing people of importance at the Tides Foundation." His mother said he was upset about what he'd seen on TV news.

Beck wasn't to blame for this violent act any more than Palin was for the Giffords shooting. But for Beck, this wasn't a one-time thing. Another man, charged with killing three cops in Pittsburgh, had posted a video to a neo-Nazi website of Beck warning about FEMA concentration camps.

White nationalist violence exploded in 2015, with a massacre at a Black church in Charleston, and numerous other attacks on police, government officials, Muslims, Jews, and even children. The Anti-Defamation League calculated that "domestic extremist killers" killed more people in 2015 than in any year since 1995—the year of the Oklahoma City bombing. The number of hate groups and violent Patriot groups resumed its climb, the Southern Poverty Law Center found. Beck, Palin, Bachmann, Cruz, and others had instigated fury—and Republican leaders did nothing to calm the tensions.

CHAPTER 12

Wacko Birds and RINOs

Supreme Court Justice Antonin Scalia took a chartered flight to Cibolo Creek Ranch in West Texas on February 12, 2016, for a weekend of hunting. He spent the day bagging blue quail with Houston businessman John Poindexter, the ranch's owner, then attended a private party Friday evening before retiring early to his 1,080-square-foot El Presidente Lakeside Suite with whirlpool, wet bar, and 600-thread-count sheets.

Saturday morning, Scalia didn't come to breakfast. When he still hadn't appeared by late morning, Poindexter knocked on the door of Scalia's suite and, receiving no reply, went inside. There he found the seventy-nine-year-old justice in his pajamas, in bed, looking peaceful—and dead.

It took until early Sunday morning to transport the body from the remote ranch to El Paso, and until late Sunday afternoon for word to get out, via a tweet by the *San Antonio Express-News*. The implications were immediately obvious: Scalia was part of the five-to-four conservative majority on the High Court, and President Barack Obama had eleven months left in office to install a successor. But the initial reactions were appropriately respectful.

Senator Bernie Sanders, competing for the Democratic presidential nomination, called Scalia "brilliant" and offered his prayers.

Harry Reid, the Senate Democratic leader, wrote: "Justice Scalia was a brilliant man. We had many differences, but he was a dedicated public servant."

"Sad news indeed," tweeted Democratic senator Chuck Schumer of New York. "While we disagreed on many issues, Justice Scalia was a brilliant man & a great son of Queens w/ a genuine joy for life."

And then there was Mitch McConnell.

One hour and fifty-eight minutes after the news of Scalia's death broke, the Senate Republican leader issued a Sunday-evening statement of condolence ending with this: "The American people should have a voice in the selection of their next Supreme Court Justice. Therefore, this vacancy should not be filled until we have a new president."

McConnell's declaration hit like a thunderclap. He had lacked the decency to allow the country even a moment to absorb Scalia's death before injecting politics. Worse, he had blithely shattered the norms and practices of the constitutional advice-and-consent clause that had guided the United States since its founding. And he had delivered yet another message to Republican voters that Obama, then in the eighth year of his presidency, was not a legitimate president.

McConnell's indecency even caught some fellow Republicans by surprise. Upon learning of Scalia's death, Senate Judiciary Committee chairman Chuck Grassley, an Iowa Republican, told *The Des Moines Register* that "I wouldn't make any prognostication on anything about the future."

But forty minutes after McConnell's bombshell, Grassley quickly got in line. He revised his statement to say Americans "will elect a new president to select the next Supreme Court justice" and that "it's been standard practice over the last nearly 80 years that Supreme Court nominees are not confirmed during a presidential election year."

This was categorically false, and Grassley later had to correct it. Justice Anthony Kennedy was confirmed in 1988, a presidential election year. Over time, the Senate had confirmed seventeen Supreme Court nominees during election years and rejected two. Now McConnell was proposing to break the record for the longest vacancy on the Supreme Court since the nine-member court was created in 1869. And that delay, of 391 days in 1969, was because the Senate rejected two of President Richard Nixon's nominees—not because it refused to consider any.

In saying "the American people should have a voice" in the selection, McConnell was denying the American people their voice: they had chosen Obama as president in 2012 and a Republican Senate majority in 2014. The majority had the right to reject Obama's nominee, but instead it refused even to consider *any* Obama nominee. No hearings. Not even courtesy meetings.

Senator Thom Tillis, a North Carolina Republican, said two days after McConnell's pronouncement that if Republicans block a nominee "sight unseen, we fall into the trap of being obstructionists." Yet that's exactly what they did.

The deterioration of the High Court's credibility that had begun with the *Bush v. Gore* decision, and continued with the evisceration of campaign finance laws and the Voting Rights Act, was now complete: the highest court in the land had become another political branch of government—and Republicans in the Senate would go to any length to keep it in GOP hands. "Now, this will be a test, one more test, of whether or not norms, rules, basic fair play can function at all in Washington these days," Obama said two days after McConnell drew his line in the sand. It had already become clear that Republicans would fail the test.

Republicans like to say the politicization of the Supreme Court began with the "Borking" of Ronald Reagan nominee Robert Bork in 1987. And it's true that the left mounted a ferocious campaign to defeat Bork, who had a rather extreme record of opposing the Civil Rights Act and gender equality and thought it legal to ban birth control, even for married couples. But at least Democrats, honoring their advice-and-consent responsibilities, gave Bork the courtesy of hearings and a vote; it took only one hundred days between his nomination and his rejection, by a bipartisan vote of 58–42. And, after Reagan's next nominee, Douglas Ginsburg, withdrew over marijuana use, Kennedy sailed to unanimous confirmation.

The comparisons to the Bork fight (and to the ugly confirmation of Clarence Thomas in 1991) are also illustrative in a broader sense. There was a case to be made during the Reagan years, and to a lesser extent during the Clinton years, and to an even lesser extent during the George W. Bush years, that both parties could be blamed for the deteriorating civility and rising dysfunction of politics. But in the Obama years and beyond, such "whataboutism" no longer applied. One of the two major parties in American politics had gone off the rails—shattering norms and routinely sabotaging government and democracy itself for partisan advantage. The result was planned dysfunction and an erosion of democratic institutions that left American democracy vulnerable to populist demagoguery and creeping authoritarianism.

"The Republican Party has become an insurgent outlier— ideologically extreme; contemptuous of the inherited social and economic policy regime; scornful of compromise; unpersuaded by conventional understanding of facts, evidence, and science; and dismissive of the legitimacy of its political opposition," Norman Ornstein of the conservative American Enterprise Institute and Thomas Mann of the center-left Brookings Institution wrote in their 2012 book, *It's Even Worse Than It Looks.*

In 2016, the pair added: "One of our two major political parties has become so radicalized that at critical times and on critical occasions it will not or cannot engage constructively in the governing process anticipated by our constitutional charter. It is as if one of the many paranoid fringe movements in American political history has successfully infected a major political party."

Since Obama's inauguration, the pair argued, Republicans "pursued a strategy of unified opposition to every Obama policy and initiative, including those they had recently supported, such as investment in infrastructure, health care reform and climate change. They also worked with their counterparts in cable television and talk radio to demonize every victory and to delegitimize the president."

The impact was obvious. When the modern budgeting process began in the 1970s, Congress routinely passed annual budget resolutions outlining government spending. In the 2000s, Congress failed to enact a budget resolution in three years. Then, in the 2010s, Congress failed to enact a budget resolution in seven of the ten years—and none for a five-year period beginning in 2011, when the Tea Party wave arrived in Congress. Likewise, Congress routinely passed the dozen annual appropriations bills that specifically detailed spending—but did so only once in the decade beginning with fiscal year 2011, the Tea Party's debut. In five of the ten years beginning with fiscal year 2011, the breakdown was total: not a single appropriations bill passed both chambers. Instead, government has mostly operated on autopilot, under a series of omnibus bills and continuing resolutions.

The Senate's confirmation process for executive branch nominees, meanwhile, slowed to a crawl. The average confirmation, which took fifty-six days during the Reagan administration, took double that during the Obama administration (and beyond), the Partnership for Public Service calculated. The number of times cloture was invoked in the Senate—a rough approximation of filibuster use—averaged 10.6 per each two-year Congress in the 1980s. In the 2010s the average was 143 per two-year Congress—nearly fourteen times greater.

Not surprisingly, Americans lost confidence in their government. In 1964, trust by Americans in their government was 77 percent, the modern high, as tabulated by the Pew Research Center. It has declined steadily since (with occasional blips such as after the 9/11 attacks) to a low of 10 percent in 2011 and has remained below 26 percent since.

Though many factors have caused the dysfunction, the greatest contributor has been the new Republican politics of hostage taking—holding up the normal functioning of government until a demand is met—which accelerated after Obama's election and became routine with the Tea Party's arrival in Congress.

Even before Obama was elected, the hostage takers gave a taste of things to come when they refused to support the $700 billion financial rescue plan following the September 2008 market crash. President Bush, whose administration negotiated the package, pleaded for Republican support, as did the Republican presidential nominee, John McCain, and House GOP leader Boehner. But only a third of Republicans—sixty-five House members—voted for the package, causing it to fail in the House despite broad Democratic support. Markets plunged 7 percent further. "You can't break their arms," a defeated Boehner said after the vote.

The House reversed itself a few days later, but the markets

didn't. "Too many Republicans in Congress cared more about what Sean Hannity thought than the secretary of the Treasury or the Speaker of the House or the president of the United States," Boehner wrote in his memoir, *On the House*. "They were ready to destroy the economy for decades rather than come up with any realistic alternatives—just as long as it looked as if they were standing up to the 'establishment.' . . . Some of the more reasonable members were panicked. But the nuts were even more emboldened. They were proud to send this bill to its death, and they didn't give a shit if the economy collapsed."

The nuts were egged on by outside pressure groups "in the name of conservative purity," Boehner wrote, though "[i]t wasn't about any so-called principles—it was about chaos. But it was chaos that developed in a predictable pattern: the far-right knuckleheads would refuse to back the House leadership no matter what, but because they were 'insurgents' they never had the responsibility of trying to actually fix things themselves. So they got to 'burn it all down' and screw up the legislative process, which of course allowed them to continue to complain loudly about how Washington's spending problem never got solved. . . . It was pathetic. It was irresponsible. But it was only the beginning."

And those are the words of the man who led House Republicans for nearly a decade, through 2015.

When Republicans took control of the House with the Tea Party wave of 2010, they owed their majority to a class of eighty-seven freshmen, most of them radicals steeped in the Tea Party. Among the majority Republicans' first acts was to repeal the "Gephardt Rule," which automatically increased the debt limit with each year's budget resolution. The rule's repeal invited a whole new era of brinkmanship by giving Republicans the ability to hold hostage the full faith and credit of the U.S. government.

And that's exactly what they did.

Ten days after Republicans took control, the new House majority leader, Eric Cantor, addressed the Republican caucus at a retreat in the Marriott in Baltimore's Inner Harbor. "I'm asking you to look at a potential increase in the debt limit as a leverage moment when the White House and President Obama will have to deal with us," Cantor told them, *The Washington Post* reported.

"Either we stick together and demonstrate that we're a team that will fight for and stand by our principles, or we will lose that leverage."

Cantor, who with Paul Ryan and Kevin McCarthy had recruited many of the radical newcomers, was preparing to play chicken with the federal government's finances, risking default to force Obama to accept massive spending cuts. Cantor directly contradicted Boehner, who had said two months earlier: "We're going to have to deal with it [the debt limit] as adults. Whether we like it or not, the federal government has obligations, and we have obligations on our part."

But the lunatics were now running the asylum. Republican senators Mike Lee of Utah and Jim DeMint of South Carolina, representing twenty GOP lawmakers, announced an ultimatum: cut spending back to 1966 levels—forty-five years earlier—or they would force the United States into default. "We want to make very clear: This is not just the best plan on the table for addressing the debt limit—this is the only plan," Lee warned.

These hostage takers, an informal "Default Caucus," disregarded warnings from Standard & Poor's, the conservative *Wall Street Journal* editorial board, and even antitax purist Grover Norquist.

Boehner had been trying to negotiate a "grand bargain" with Obama, trading massive spending cuts for tax increases. But Cantor torpedoed the talks in June. Boehner tried again, and Obama offered him a sweet deal: $4 trillion in spending cuts and reforms to Social Security, Medicare, Medicaid, and the tax code in exchange for tax increases worth only one third the spending cuts. But Boehner couldn't sell it to his caucus and blamed Obama for the failure. A bipartisan "Gang of Six" senators proposed a solution. No dice, said the Default Caucus. A McConnell proposal to punt the matter until after the 2012 election? Fuhgeddaboudit.

Default Caucus members, who had already grown accustomed to operating in a fact-free environment, declared (falsely) that the federal government wouldn't really go into default and that, even if it did, the consequences wouldn't be so dire. A Pew Research Center poll found that 65 percent of Tea Party supporters believed the default deadline could be ignored without major repercussions.

"There is no danger of a shortage of cash to pay the interest on our debt and to avoid a default," proclaimed new senator Pat Toomey, a Pennsylvania Republican. Large groups capitalizing on the Tea Party movement such as FreedomWorks and the Tea Party Patriots threatened Republican members with primary challenges if they compromised on the debt limit.

Boehner, out of options with just days before default, went on an arm-twisting campaign to get his insurgents to accept a $1 trillion increase in the debt ceiling in exchange for $1.2 trillion in cuts—but he had to pull his modest plan from the House floor in the face of certain defeat.

Finally, recognizing the Republicans were prepared to throw the economy into a tailspin, the White House surrendered. Obama agreed to spending cuts alone in exchange for extending the debt limit through the 2012 election.

Republicans celebrated their successful hostage taking. "I think some of our members may have thought the default issue was a hostage you might take a chance at shooting," McConnell said. "Most of us didn't think that. What we did learn is this: It's a hostage that's worth ransoming."

An embittered Boehner later called Cantor's sabotage of talks "a kick to the gut," and he condemned the hysteria of right-wingers that forced him to meet secretly with Obama: "Maybe they'd start questioning my place of birth."

The fun was just beginning.

Right after the debt limit standoff, Republicans tried the same hostage-taking technique with the Federal Aviation Administration, threatening to shut down the agency if Democrats didn't agree to rescind labor protections. This time, Democrats refused to surrender, and Republicans shot the hostage: the FAA went into partial shutdown for two weeks, at the cost of tens of thousands of jobs and hundreds of millions of dollars.

Republicans ran the same play in 2012 with the so-called fiscal cliff—a combination of huge tax increases and spending cuts scheduled to take place automatically at year end as an outgrowth of the 2011 debt limit deal. Their solution was a short-term stopgap, and even that was opposed by two thirds of House Republicans, including Cantor and McCarthy. Several panels, including the high-visibility Simpson-Bowles bipartisan presidential commission, had outlined major reforms needed to put the federal government's finances on a sustainable path, but they never got serious consideration.

The House even failed at the end of the 2011–12 term to take up a $60 billion hurricane relief bill for the Northeast, reeling from Superstorm Sandy. Why? Because Cantor and the insurgents demanded that the funds be taken away from other programs. Another hostage situation.

The next year was even worse, for it saw the arrival in Washington of Ted Cruz, the former George W. Bush acolyte who won election to the Senate from Texas as a Tea Party radical. He got right to work, leading an attempt to defund Obamacare after just a few weeks on the job. This failed, like the previous three dozen repeal attempts.

So Cruz got to work on a new plan to hold the nation's finances hostage to his desire to repeal Obamacare. "We need 41 Republicans in the Senate or 218 Republicans in the House to stand together, to join me" in saying that "we will not vote for a single continuing resolution that funds even a penny of Obamacare," Cruz told radio host Andrea Tantaros. He taunted "scared" Republicans who opposed him and dismissed as "cocktail chatter" the idea that a government shutdown would be bad for Republicans.

Cruz had the ability to threaten a shutdown because of the dysfunction in Congress; the failure to enact the annual appropriations bills meant that Congress had to pass a continuing resolution or the government would shut down on October 1, 2013. The Club for Growth, Heritage Action, FreedomWorks, and Norquist's Americans for Tax Reform all endorsed the hostage taking.

Days before the government's finances ran dry, Cruz tried to force a shutdown by giving an interminable speech on the Senate floor that would leave lawmakers with too little time to negotiate a solution. Some fellow Republicans pleaded with Cruz to stand down, fearing they would be blamed for the shutdown and still fail to repeal Obamacare. But Cruz wasn't having it.

"I intend to speak in support of defunding Obamacare until

I am no longer able to stand," he announced as he launched his twenty-one-hour speech. It was *Mr. Smith Goes to Washington* in reverse: instead of cleaning up government, he was kneecapping it.

"*Green Eggs and Ham* was my favorite book when I was a little boy," Cruz announced on the floor—and so he read it. He spoke of his affection for pancakes, White Castle restaurants, and black ostrich cowboy boots. He spoke endlessly—and mostly about himself.

Obama didn't cave in to the hostage takers' demands this time, and the government shut down—for sixteen days. Cruz tried releasing some of his hostages, offering to let a few government agencies reopen—but Obama didn't budge. Americans overwhelmingly (and accurately) blamed Republicans for the shutdown, by an even wider margin than they did during the 1995–96 shutdowns, and the Republican Party hit a record low in polling. McConnell, who had helped to end the debt limit and fiscal cliff fiascos, couldn't help this time—because he faced a Tea Party primary challenge at home.

Republican senator Lindsey Graham observed that "if you killed Ted Cruz on the floor of the Senate, and the trial was in the Senate, nobody would convict you." McCain labeled as "wacko birds" Cruz and Senator Rand Paul, the Kentucky Republican who gave his maiden speech in the Senate to denounce nineteenth-century statesman Henry Clay, "the Great Compromiser."

Finally, as the shuttered U.S. government approached yet another default deadline, Boehner surrendered. "This fight is over. Today," he told his caucus. He described Cruz variously as a "reckless asshole," "Lucifer in the flesh," a "miserable son of a bitch," and a "loudmouthed jerk." Boehner called Cruz's followers "knuckleheads" and the shutdown a "dumbass idea." Boehner observed: "[Y]ou can't govern by stunt, and eventually we couldn't govern at all."

It was true: they couldn't govern at all. Cruz forced another debt limit showdown in the Senate in 2014. Action on entitlements, climate change, and other crucial matters never had a chance of consideration. A bipartisan Gang of Eight senators drafted comprehensive immigration legislation that passed the Senate—but it was dead on arrival in the House. Cantor's attempt to persuade his far-right followers in the House to accept immigration legislation was a key factor in his primary defeat, the first time in history a House majority leader was defeated at the polls. Chaos reigned: one House Republican was indicted on tax-evasion charges and reelected, one resigned after a cocaine arrest, and a third was defeated after he was caught on video kissing a staffer.

The GOP of mid-decade was unrecognizable from a decade earlier. Even the Gipper himself would have been banished from this group as a RINO. Ronald Reagan presided over eighteen increases in the debt limit (he denounced debt "brinkmanship"), raised taxes eleven times, supported immigration "amnesty," signed a major expansion of Medicare, and accepted spending levels far above the Tea Party's ceiling.

Republican presidential candidate and commentator Mike Huckabee observed that "Reagan would have a very difficult, if not impossible time being nominated in this atmosphere," because he made deals and "compromised on things in order to move the ball down the field." Representative Duncan Hunter, a California Republican later imprisoned for campaign finance abuses, called Reagan a "moderate former liberal . . . who would never be elected today."

Bob Dole, the 1996 Republican presidential nominee, saw just how dramatically the party had shifted when he returned to the Senate floor in 2012 to urge the Senate to ratify a United Nations treaty on the disabled. Only eight Republicans defied pressure from right-wing groups and sided with Dole, a disabled World War II veteran. The treaty vote failed. Adding to Dole's humiliation, as the *Post*'s Paul Kane reported: many Republicans opposing the treaty cited a preposterous claim that it would somehow undermine homeschooling in the United States. The Republicans, tyrannized by the far-right fringe, were living a disaster of their own doing. Since the Supreme Court's conservative majority eviscerated campaign finance laws with its *Citizens United* decision in 2010, independent expenditures by outside groups increased sevenfold—from $143,659,091 in the 2008 election cycle to $1,002,145,869 in the 2012 cycle, the Center for Responsive Politics calculated. This gave huge (and often untraceable) influence to groups such as the Koch brothers' Americans for Prosperity and Karl Rove's Crossroads GPS.

Even the once respected Heritage Foundation played the game, forming "Heritage Action for America" to threaten lawmakers who strayed. These groups, which could fund right-wing primary challengers, exerted outside pressure on lawmakers to be ideologically pure. Among the many bills Heritage Action helped doom: a bipartisan attempt in 2013, embraced by Republican senator Pat Toomey of Pennsylvania, to expand background checks for gun purchases after the Sandy Hook Elementary School massacre. (At the state level, the Koch-backed American Legislative Exchange Council pushed legislators to enact cookie-cutter legislation such as voter ID laws and "stand your ground" laws protecting the use of deadly force.) Meanwhile, the Republican Study Committee in the House enforced ideological purity from within by coercing conservatives to vote as a bloc. Steve Scalise, elected RSC chief in 2012, vowed "to pull our leadership to the right"; Scalise eventually became the House Republican whip. When even the right-wing RSC proved insufficiently extreme, Congressman Jim Jordan, a voluble Ohio Republican, formed the Freedom Caucus in 2015 with future Trump White House staff chiefs Mick Mulvaney and Mark Meadows. The Freedom Caucus launched a mutiny against GOP leaders in June 2015, in an attempt to deny Obama the usual authority to negotiate trade deals.

All but about two dozen Republican seats in the House were safe seats—a result, in large part, of extreme partisan gerrymandering—so the only threat to most Republican lawmakers was from a primary challenge on the right. The rational response was to move as far right as possible. One who got that message too late was Dick Lugar, a legendary Republican senator from Indiana who shaped foreign policy, secured sanctions against South African Apartheid, brought democracy to the Philippines, and secured thousands of former Soviet nuclear warheads. He lost in a primary to Richard Mourdock, who attacked Lugar's bipartisanship and declared that "the time for being collegial is past" and "it's time for confrontation."

Boehner, facing a series of attempts to oust him as speaker, announced his retirement in September 2015. His successor, Paul Ryan, would follow the same path of failure over the next three years, for the same reasons.

"Incrementalism? Compromise? That wasn't their thing," Boehner wrote of the Republican insurgents. "A lot of them wanted to blow up Washington. . . . They wanted wedge issues and conspiracies and crusades." Boehner found his troops "radicalized by blind Obama hatred," he wrote. "I was living in Crazytown. . . . Every second of every day since Barack Obama became president I was fighting one batshit idea after another."

In the Senate, McConnell took a different tack. He knew he couldn't fight the "batshit" ideas of those radicalized by blind Obama hatred. So he joined them—and by doing so, kept his position as leader. He enabled dysfunction, and much worse, for his own job security.

After Obama's election in 2008, McConnell outlined his plan to fellow Republicans. "We have a new president with an approval rating in the 70 percent area. We do not take him on frontally," he said, according to an account by former Republican senator Robert Bennett in journalist Alec MacGillis's McConnell biography, *The Cynic*. "We find issues where we can win, and we begin to take him down, one issue at a time. We create an inventory of losses, so it's Obama lost on this, Obama lost on that."

In 2010, McConnell made his memorable declaration to the *National Journal:* "The single most important thing we want to achieve is for President Obama to be a one-term president." The same year, he told Carl Hulse of *The New York Times:* "I wish we had been able to obstruct more."

This wasn't terribly surprising. Back in 1994, McConnell announced his aspiration to end decades of bipartisan cooperation in the Senate, saying "I am a proud guardian of gridlock." He vowed to throw sand in the gears more frequently: "I think gridlock is making a big comeback in this country."

McConnell, a dour figure who walks with a slight limp from childhood polio, is a cunning leader who seems to have no principle other than amassing power. He switched sides on the minimum wage, withdrawal from Iraq, earmarks, abortion, labor and civil rights, and even campaign spending limits—all based on the requirements of the moment.

McConnell was a pioneer in the use of disinformation. With the help of Roger Ailes, who would go on to start Fox News, he won election to the Senate in 1984 by falsely attacking the Democratic incumbent as an absentee senator who enriched himself by giving paid speeches. In reality, McConnell's opponent had a 94 percent attendance record—and McConnell, not long after winning the seat, began enriching himself by giving paid speeches, McConnell biographer MacGillis recounted. McConnell, again with Ailes, won reelection six years later by portraying his Democratic challenger as having a drug problem.

Later, running the National Republican Senatorial Committee, Senate Republicans' campaign arm, he dramatically increased fundraising at the NRSC and counseled Senate Republicans to abandon the chamber's genteel traditions and instead to pummel Democratic colleagues with negative advertising.

After a four-year stint as the No. 2 Senate Republican, he became GOP leader in 2006, and the Senate GOP found itself in the unusual position of being led by a man with few major legislative achievements but rather a record of blocking agreement. He defeated legislation to regulate tobacco to prevent children from smoking, after striking a deal with tobacco lobbyists for the industry to run ads providing "political cover" for Republicans in exchange for them blocking legislation. A top congressional recipient of contributions from the pharmaceutical industry, he stymied efforts in both parties to reduce the cost of prescription drugs (a "socialist" scheme, he said). Same with bipartisan legislation on background checks for gun purchases. McConnell blocked, almost single-handedly, just about every attempt to police campaign spending, including his famous fight against the McCain-Feingold bill banning soft money in politics. His critics called him "Darth Vader" and the "Grim Reaper." He embraced the labels with pride.

In his memoir, former president Barack Obama describes McConnell's "shamelessness" in pursuit of power. Obama recalled a time when Vice President Biden tried to explain to McConnell the value of a piece of legislation McConnell had blocked. McConnell raised a hand to silence Biden and said, "You must be under the mistaken impression that I care." (McConnell derided Obama as the "professor," trying to have a discussion on the merits, which McConnell disdained.)

But most characteristic of McConnell was his adroitness at gumming up the works: forcing clerks to spend hours reading a bill aloud on the floor; opposing immigration legislation he'd encouraged; and asking for a vote on a debt ceiling proposal and then trying to filibuster it.

Senate Republicans put across-the-board "holds" on President Obama's nominees to executive and judicial positions. Republicans launched filibusters even against items they overwhelmingly supported, such as extending unemployment benefits. They refused to confirm officials to head key agencies unless the administration agreed to changes in law. McConnell in 2009 embraced legislation creating a deficit reduction task force, calling it "our best hope" and urging Obama's support. But when Obama actually did support it, McConnell joined a Republican filibuster to block the task force.

Under McConnell, Republican opposition to Obama was reflexive. Senate party unity votes—in which majorities of each party are on opposite sides—hit 72 percent in 2009 and 78.6 percent in 2010, shattering records going back to 1953 when *Congressional Quarterly* began measuring such a thing. This was gridlock by design—not to force compromise but to weaken the other side and thereby build GOP power.

In the entire history of the republic up to 2009, a total of sixty-eight judicial nominees had been blocked by Senate filibuster. Five years into Obama's term, McConnell's Republicans had blocked seventy-nine judicial nominees by filibuster—more than in the previous 225 years combined.

There had been skirmishes over judicial filibusters before. When Senate Republicans had threatened to abolish the filibuster (the nuclear option) in 2005, a compromise by the bipartisan "Gang of Fourteen" senators had averted the showdown. But in 2013, there was no compromise to be found. Democrats, facing

McConnell's boundless intransigence, invoked the nuclear option for presidential nominees other than Supreme Court justices.

When McConnell's Republicans took over the Senate majority in 2015, McConnell slowed confirmation of Obama's judicial nominees to a historic low. Only 28.6 percent of Obama's nominees were confirmed in the final two years of Obama's presidency, according to the Congressional Research Service—by far the lowest in the period going back to 1977 that the CRS examined. McConnell's actions gave Trump more than one hundred judicial vacancies to fill on day one (and the confirmation rate for Trump's judges shot all the way up to 83.8 percent).

The most famous of those vacancies was Scalia's seat on the Supreme Court. Ignoring precedent, McConnell devised a new principle to suit his situation: "We think the important principle in the middle of this presidential year is that the American people need to weigh in and decide who's going to make this decision. Not this lame duck president on the way out the door, but the next president."

Obama's nominee, Merrick Garland, never got a hearing. Most Republican senators refused even to meet him.

After Trump's election, McConnell hurriedly confirmed Trump nominee Neil Gorsuch to Scalia's seat. He did it by detonating the nuclear option and abolishing the filibuster—the very thing that, four years earlier, McConnell had said would mean "the end of the Senate," and would be "un-American" and a threat to "the future of our country."

McConnell called his Garland blockade "the most important decision I've made in my political career," and he boasted: "One of my proudest moments was when I looked Barack Obama in the eye and I said, 'Mr. President, you will not fill the Supreme Court vacancy.' "

Asked in 2019 what would happen if a Supreme Court justice died in 2020, with a Republican in the White House, McConnell broke into a broad grin. "Oh, we'd fill it," he said.

And so he did. Just eighty minutes after the first report of Justice Ruth Bader Ginsburg's death in September 2020, McConnell announced his intent to replace her as fast as possible, before the next president was sworn in. Even Trump showed more humanity at first, invoking the traditional Jewish expression for the dead.

After refusing to consider Garland more than eight months before a presidential election, McConnell jammed through a successor to Ginsburg eight *days* before a presidential election.

The court's naked partisanship, and McConnell's naked power grab, had a predictable effect. In 2000, before the *Bush v. Gore* decision, 62 percent of Americans approved of the Supreme Court. By 2021, that had fallen to 40 percent, an all-time low in Gallup's polling history. Disapproval reached a record-high 53 percent.

It was quite an achievement: not only had McConnell managed to destroy the self-proclaimed "world's greatest deliberative body," but he had also destroyed the credibility of the highest court in the land.

CHAPTER 13

Truth Isn't Truth

Sixteen days after President Donald Trump lost the 2020 election, his "personal lawyer," Rudy Giuliani, stood with other Trump defenders in the headquarters of the Republican National Committee, delivering the most fantastical claims.

Democrats rigged the voting machines!

Liberal billionaire George Soros was involved!

Deceased Venezuelan dictator Hugo Chávez was connected!

Trucks delivered ballots stuffed in garbage bags in the middle of the night!

Dead people voted!

Rounding out the inventive presentation, Giuliani cited a scene from the 1992 comedy film *My Cousin Vinny*.

The GOP's quarter-century war on facts had come to this: a gargantuan fabrication aimed at discrediting democracy itself, authored by the president's team, delivered from GOP headquarters—and carried live by Fox News. The *Washington Post* fact-checker, Glenn Kessler, saved his "Four Pinocchios" rating for the most egregious falsehoods, but after Giuliani's "truly bonkers" presentation he lamented: "This is one of those days when we wished we had more than Four Pinocchios."

As Giuliani delivered his lies, he began to perspire. The perspiration melted hair coloring that had been applied to his sideburns, causing a river of dark liquid to trickle down his cheek. It was as if his brain had liquefied from generating so much disinformation.

For Giuliani, it was the most humiliating episode since, well, twelve days earlier, when he stood outside Philadelphia's Four Seasons Total Landscaping, in the shadow of a porn shop, to level bogus allegations about Pennsylvania voter fraud—some of which had already been thrown out of court. The location, possibly chosen by Trump aides who confused it with the Four Seasons hotel, was never fully explained, but the landscaping business made a tidy sum after Giuliani's news conference by marketing T-shirts that said "Make America Rake Again" and "Lawn & Order."

The man once known as "America's mayor" had become a national joke.

Giuliani had a charmed career. In the 1980s, as U.S. attorney for the Southern District of New York, he policed Wall Street and cracked down on organized crime. In the 1990s, he was the popular two-term mayor of New York at a time when violent crime fell sharply. His handling of the 2001 attacks made him famous, an honorary Knight of the British Empire and *Time*'s Person of the Year. After making a killing in the private sector, he was the national front-runner for the 2008 Republican presidential nomination and might have prevailed but for a flawed strategy of gambling everything on the Florida primary.

But then, in 2016, Giuliani boarded the Trump train, becoming an outspoken defender of the candidate and president while playing on his access to gain foreign clients. He quickly went off the rails.

His downfall—variations of which countless respectable Republicans performed as they surrendered to Trump—is the story of how the GOP, after decades of assaulting facts, science, and expertise, became so immune to the sway of truth that it could be taken over by a charlatan whose only overlap with factual accuracy came via random chance.

This triumph of disinformation had been a long time in the making. Since the Vince Foster "murder" in the 1990s, Republican leaders had been feeding their voters a steady diet of fabrications: Troopergate. Iraq's weapons of mass destruction. Black helicopters. Death panels. Benghazi. Hillary Clinton's brain damage. Birtherism. They, and their allies on talk radio, the web, and Fox News, had conditioned their supporters to disbelieve anything that came from the media, from scientists, from experts, from Democrats, and from the U.S. government. GOP leaders' steady production of disinformation, aggravated by social media algorithms that spread falsehood and vitriol, had left the Republican electorate susceptible to all manner of conspiracy theories and propaganda. All that was needed was for an unprincipled demagogue to ply his wares.

Trump could not have happened without the acquiescence, and even the active support, of Republican elected officials and conservative opinion leaders, particularly Fox News hosts. One by one, a limitless cast of enablers swallowed hard, abandoned conscience, and embraced Trump's fantasies as fact, condoning, echoing, or even building upon his fabrications. Without this validation, the Republican electorate could not have solidified behind Trump.

There was, for example, Senator Lindsey Graham of South Carolina, who once called Trump a "jackass" who was "unfit for office." He became a prime validator of Trump's falsehoods, embracing the "no collusion" mantra and instead alleging (unfounded) "corruption" at the Justice Department and the FBI, a key part of the "deep state" conspiracy theory. Graham said he embraced Trump "to be relevant"—in exchange for his integrity.

Devin Nunes, with some help from the Trump White House, used his position as top Republican on the House Intelligence Committee to bolster Trump's misleading claims that the FBI had spied on Trump and based its Russia probe on information provided by Democrats. (Nunes later quit Congress to be CEO of Trump Media.)

After a meeting in which Trump, according to multiple witnesses, referred to African nations as "shithole countries," Republican senators Tom Cotton of Arkansas and David Perdue of Georgia covered for Trump, claiming they didn't hear that phrase.

Trump was obese, had heart disease, ate fast food, and didn't exercise, but the White House physician, Ronny Jackson, declared that he was in "excellent health" with "incredible cardiac fitness" and "if he had a healthier diet over the last 20 years, he might live to be 200 years old." (The doctor is now a Republican member of Congress.)

Trump's attorney general, Bill Barr, committed similar malpractice to promote Trump's alternate reality, but with much higher stakes. When special prosecutor Robert Mueller issued his damning report on the Trump campaign's Russia ties, Barr sat on it. Instead, he released a memo and gave a news conference in which he claimed that Mueller found "there was in fact no collusion" between the Trump campaign and Russia, and that Mueller's evidence was insufficient to merit charges of obstructing justice. But Mueller had reached no such conclusions, and he complained that Barr caused "public confusion" by missing the "substance of this office's work and conclusions."

Why would previously reputable figures throw aside their credibility and join Trump in fantasyland? The simple explanation is these Republican elites were opportunistically supporting claims they knew to be false because it furthered their personal ambitions or partisan aims. But it may be more complex than that: these elites weren't just deceiving others, but also themselves. Cognitive science has found that highly intelligent people are more susceptible to "identity-protective cognition," an unconscious process of "motivated reasoning" in which they use their intellect to justify rejecting facts inconsistent with their partisan identity. "The really upsetting finding is that the better you are at particular types of cognitive tests . . . the better you are at manipulating the facts to reflect your prior beliefs, the more able you are to cognitively shape the world so it fits with your values," David Hoffman, University of Pennsylvania law professor who studies cultural cognition, explained to me. We all slip into such "motivated reasoning" to some degree, but it became a particular problem on the right because of the Fox News influence and the weaponization of disinformation by Republican leaders.

The lying spread through Trump world like a cancer. Trump adviser Roger Stone was convicted on seven counts of lying to Congress, obstruction, and witness tampering related to lies he told about his communications with WikiLeaks about its release of emails that would damage Clinton's campaign in 2016. Trump pardoned him. Michael Flynn, Trump's national security adviser, pleaded guilty to lying to the FBI about his contacts with the Russian government. Trump pardoned him. Paul Manafort, Trump's campaign chairman, pleaded guilty to violating lobbying laws and witness tampering over his work for a pro-Russian Ukrainian politician, and a judge found that he had lied to prosecutors, the FBI, and a grand jury. Trump pardoned him. Campaign aide George

Papadopoulos pleaded guilty to lying to the FBI. Trump pardoned him. Trump advisers Rick Gates and Michael Cohen also pleaded guilty to lying to authorities—but, because they cooperated with prosecutors, Trump didn't pardon them.

During Manafort's sentencing, where his lawyers once again falsely represented the facts in the case, Judge Amy Berman Jackson offered this thought: "If people don't have the facts, democracy can't work. Court is one of those places where facts still matter."

Kirstjen Nielsen, Trump's homeland security secretary, boldly asserted that "we do not have a policy of separating families at the border. Period." She later stood next to Trump as he signed an order rescinding the policy they supposedly didn't have. Nielsen, under oath, also made the absurd claim that the cages used to hold migrant children at the border were not, in fact, cages. She also testified that "I actually do not know" if Norway (from which Trump wanted more immigrants) is a predominantly white country.

Administration officials often tried to corroborate Trump's false claims, "scrambling to reverse-engineer policies to meet Trump's sudden public promises—or to search for evidence buttressing his conspiracy theories and falsehoods," as *The Washington Post*'s Philip Rucker and Ashley Parker put it.

The White House set up a presidential commission to back up Trump's false claim of widespread voter fraud; it disbanded without finding any. He falsely said voters would receive a 10 percent tax cut before the midterm elections; aides tried to produce evidence that this was happening (it wasn't). Aides tried to substantiate his unfounded claim that "unknown Middle Easterners" were in a migrant caravan in Mexico. White House officials doctored a video to make it appear that CNN's Jim Acosta, who annoyed Trump with aggressive questioning at a news conference, had placed "his hands on a young woman" at the event.

Trump claimed that smugglers were binding and gagging migrant women with duct tape and that Muslim prayer rugs were found at the border. A senior Border Patrol official asked agents to produce evidence to support Trump's claims, but they came up empty—probably because the details cited came from the 2018 Benicio del Toro movie *Sicario: Day of the Soldado*.

During the 2016 campaign, Trump's Republican rivals shared

Trump's hostility to science. Scott Walker, the Wisconsin governor, wouldn't even endorse the theory of evolution. "I'm going to punt on that," he said. In 2017, Lamar Smith of Texas, the Republican chairman of the House Science Committee, announced at a hearing that "much of climate science today appears to be based more on exaggerations, personal agendas, and questionable predictions than on the scientific method."

Republicans also shared Trump's fondness for Obama conspiracy theories. During the 2016 campaign, Walker and fellow candidate Rick Santorum refused to say whether President Obama was Christian—a variation of the Birther libel—and candidate Chris Christie insisted, falsely, that Trump had not pursued the Birther allegations for years.

Because the disinformation preceded Trump in the GOP, it didn't end with his presidency. Republican lawmakers and governors devoted much of 2021 to raising doubts about the safety of the Covid-19 vaccines and endorsing conspiracy theories about public health efforts to contain the pandemic.

Representative Madison Cawthorn, a hotheaded Republican from North Carolina, said President Biden's attempts to boost vaccination rates with a door-to-door outreach campaign would lead to programs to "take your guns" and "take your Bibles." Representative Marjorie Taylor Greene, in one of the Georgia Republican's many Holocaust comparisons, sounded the alarm about "medical brown shirts showing up at their door ordering vaccinations" as part of a "human experiment." Representative Jason Smith, a Republican Senate candidate in Missouri, warned of "KGB-style" agents knocking on doors of unvaccinated Americans.

Meanwhile, Florida's Republican governor, Ron DeSantis, ordered schools in his state not to impose mask mandates; about half of Florida's public schools defied his order. Texas's Republican governor, Greg Abbott, also banned mask mandates and blocked local governments and even private businesses from requiring vaccination. Mississippi's Republican governor, Tate Reeves, called Biden "tyrannical" for requiring vaccines.

The Republican-controlled House in Ohio invited expert testimony from osteopath Sherri Tenpenny, who testified that the Covid vaccine made people magnetic. "I'm sure you've seen the pictures all over the Internet," she testified. "They can put a key on their forehead, it sticks."

Senator Ron Johnson, a Wisconsin Republican, promoted the use of ivermectin, a drug commonly used for deworming horses, as a Covid remedy (he earlier held a hearing promoting hydroxychloroquine for the same purpose). So did Rand Paul and Representative Louie Gohmert, a Texas Republican. The idea caused an increase in calls to poison control centers, and the Food and Drug Administration tried to stop the madness with a public service announcement: "You are not a horse."

Behind much of this craziness was Fox News, and in particular Tucker Carlson, who was now an angry, paranoid TV host whose prime-time show premiered on Fox News just days after the election of an angry, paranoid president. Carlson, with his wild conspiracy theories, soon eclipsed Hannity as Fox's top-rated host.

Carlson promoted the logical fallacy that anybody who got the vaccine and later died of any cause met their end *because* of the vaccine. He told his nearly three million viewers that Biden was trying to "force people to take medicine they don't want or need." He said students whose universities required the vaccine "shouldn't get the shot. . . . It's not good for them." (Fox News's corporate parent required employees to be vaccinated.) He alleged that the risk of the vaccine is "much higher than of Covid" and that "the most powerful people in America" were lying to the public about the vaccine. He claimed that the Covid death toll had been exaggerated and said that the military's vaccine requirement is an attempt to oust "sincere Christians" from service. He argued that the government uses the vaccine for "social control" and alleged that vaccine champion Bill Gates had "extraordinary powers" over people's bodies.

Carlson's lies undoubtedly killed people. Polling in August 2021 by the Pew Research Center found that 86 percent of Democratic voters had received a Covid vaccine, compared to only 60 percent of Republican voters. This correlated with media consumption: only 62 percent of Fox News viewers were vaccinated, an *Axios*/Ipsos poll found in July 2021, compared to 79 percent who watched ABC, CBS, and NBC and 83 percent who watched CNN and MSNBC.

Because the unvaccinated were eleven times more likely to die of Covid than the vaccinated, the disinformation spread by Carlson, by discouraging vaccination, almost certainly increased the death rate. A September 2021 analysis by *The New York Times* found that the Covid death rate was five times higher in counties where Trump won at least 70 percent of the vote than in counties where he received less than 32 percent. At that time, the five states with the highest per capita Covid death rates, and twelve of the highest fifteen, were governed by Republicans.

Trump himself followed Carlson's lead. Trump had promoted the vaccine constantly when it was being developed, voicing hope that it would be available by Election Day. When that didn't happen, Trump lost interest; he received the vaccine secretly before leaving office. But Trump saw that his base of support had turned decisively against the vaccine, and in July 2021, he joined them. "People are refusing to take the Vaccine because they don't trust [Biden's] administration, they don't trust the Election results, and they certainly don't trust the Fake News, which is refusing to tell the Truth," he wrote in a statement (he had been banned from Twitter months earlier).

Trump was often credited with leading Republican officials and voters into their post-truth existence, and he did plenty of that. But he just as often followed his base of support rather than leading it. He often merely amplified the conspiracy theories that his supporters believed. He held up a mirror to Republicans and reflected back what they wanted to hear.

"REPORT: THREE MILLION VOTES in Presidential Election Cast by Illegal Aliens; Trump May Have Won Popular Vote."

Thus announced conspiracy theorist Alex Jones's website, *InfoWars,* on November 14, 2016. Jones also claimed that at least "five states were stolen" by Hillary Clinton, and that four million dead people voted. Not quite two weeks later, the claim had made its way from the fringe to the president-elect. "In addition to winning the Electoral College in a landslide, I won the popular vote if you deduct the millions of people who voted illegally," Trump asserted.

Many of Trump's favorite conspiracies—climate change was a

myth, Obama wasn't born in America, Muslims in New Jersey celebrated 9/11, Clinton used drugs before a debate, Antonin Scalia was murdered, globalists were taking over the United States, vaccines caused autism, Ted Cruz's father helped assassinate JFK—were first promoted by Jones. Jones, who advised Trump privately, boasted (correctly) that Trump repeats his ideas "word for word." Trump, in turn, praised Jones's "amazing" reputation.

The Trump-Fox echo chamber worked similarly:

Fox News's morning show displayed a graphic alleging that 122 released "Gitmo prisoners reengaged in terrorism." Within an hour, Trump tweeted from the White House: "122 vicious prisoners, released by the Obama administration from Gitmo, have returned to the battlefield. Just another terrible decision!" (It turned out 113 of the 122 were released during the Bush administration.)

A *Fox & Friends* host called for Trump to block federal funding to universities that try to "silence conservative voices," after violent protests at the University of California at Berkeley over a speech by conservative provocateur Milo Yiannopoulos. Half an hour later, Trump tweeted: "If U.C. Berkeley does not allow free speech and practices violence on innocent people with a different point of view—NO FEDERAL FUNDS?"

Fox News's *O'Reilly Factor* cited statistics about crime in Chicago. An hour later, Trump tweeted the same statistics: "If Chicago doesn't fix the horrible 'carnage' going on, 228 shootings in 2017 with 42 killings (up 24% from 2016), I will send in the Feds!"

Fox News labeled Chelsea Manning, convicted for leaking classified information, an "ungrateful traitor" who had called President Barack Obama a "weak leader." Fourteen minutes later, according to CNN, Trump tweeted: "Ungrateful TRAITOR Chelsea Manning, who should never have been released from prison, is now calling President Obama a weak leader. Terrible!"

Fox's Tucker Carlson aired a bogus report alleging that Sweden had been trying to "cover up" an outburst of violence caused by Muslim immigrants. The next day, Trump told a crowd in Florida: "You look at what's happening last night in Sweden. Sweden? Who would believe this?" Baffled Swedes had no idea what the president of the United States was talking about.

Carlson falsely reported that a school shooting survivor quit a CNN town hall show after refusing a scripted question (in fact, the survivor's father doctored an email to make it appear that way). Trump tweeted out the bogus allegation after hearing it from Carlson.

Fox News had essentially created Trump as a political force. Beginning in 2011, Fox gave Trump a weekly segment on the *Fox & Friends* morning show. In addition, Trump was on Fox's evening and prime-time programs and *Fox News Sunday* forty-eight times between January 2013 and April 2015, the liberal watchdog Media Matters reported.

Trump appeared on Sean Hannity's show forty-one times in the first ten months of his 2016 campaign—at a time when Hannity was privately advising Trump's campaign, the Fox host admitted to *The New York Times*. Hannity even paid for a private jet during the campaign to fly Newt Gingrich to meet with Trump, CNN reported. Fox News's founder, Roger Ailes, also advised the Trump campaign. Fox executive Bill Shine became Trump's White House communications director, one of more than twenty people taking the revolving door between Fox and the Trump administration. And Steve Bannon, the head of Breitbart News and an ally of far-right nationalists, was the Trump campaign's CEO before becoming Trump's top strategist in the White House.

The work by Fox News to misinform the public on behalf of Trump gained unwanted attention in 2021 when the congressional committee investigating the January 6 attack on the Capitol released text messages sent to Trump's chief of staff, Mark Meadows, by various Fox News hosts. Brian Kilmeade wrote that Trump, by refusing to call off the insurrection, was "destroying everything you have accomplished." Laura Ingraham said "this is hurting all of us. He is destroying his legacy." Hannity said Trump should "ask people to leave the Capitol." But after the insurrection, Fox perpetuated Trump's phony version of the attack, characterizing it alternately as a false flag operation, a "mostly peaceful" protest, or the work of left-wing "antifa," a leaderless, decentralized "antifascist" network.

In the two weeks after Fox News declared Biden the victor in the 2020 election, Fox cast doubt on the election results at least 774 times, according to a calculation by Media Matters.

Fox did Trump another favor just before the 2020 election. Fox personalities, particularly Lou Dobbs, Ingraham, and Hannity, heavily promoted a false conspiracy theory during and after the 2016 campaign holding that Seth Rich, a young staffer with the Democratic National Committee, was murdered because he leaked damaging DNC emails about Clinton. (Police determined Rich was killed in a botched robbery; the emails had been hacked by Russia.) Fox agreed to pay millions of dollars to Rich's family—but stipulated that the settlement be kept secret until after the 2020 election, to avoid harming Trump politically.

But most Republican voters trusted the disinformation Fox produced for Trump's benefit. Two thirds of Republicans and Republican-leaning independents said they trusted Fox for political news, the nonpartisan Pew Research Center found in a 2020 poll. Only a third or fewer Republicans trusted any other news organization.

THE CROWD AT DONALD TRUMP'S inauguration was noticeably smaller than it had been for Barack Obama's inaugurals, and Trump didn't like that one bit. So he simply declared that there were 1.5 million people in attendance. Then he called the acting director of the National Park Service seeking photographic evidence to back up the preposterous figure, while ordering Sean Spicer, his new White House press secretary, to defend the nonsense in front of the cameras.

"This was the largest audience to ever witness an inauguration, period," announced a belligerent Spicer in a too-big suit jacket. "Both in person and around the globe." Spicer's reputation never recovered. Trump's pollster and "counselor" Kellyanne Conway defended Spicer's very public fib, saying he "gave alternative facts."

Alternative facts? It was a concept Trump's defenders would turn to again and again. Giuliani, defending Trump, would utter the phrase "truth isn't truth." Republican representative Mark Meadows of North Carolina, who would become Trump's last White House chief of staff, argued that "everybody has their impression of what truth is."

Shortly after Trump's inauguration, the new president visited the CIA in Langley, where he told officers that it had begun to rain during his inaugural address, but "God looked down and he said, we're not going to let it rain on your speech." Trump claimed that the rain "stopped immediately" as he spoke. "It was amazing. And then it became really sunny. And then I walked off and it poured right after I left."

I was there, in the sixth row, about forty feet from Trump, and I remembered the exact opposite: it began to rain when he started and tapered off toward the end. There wasn't a single ray of sunshine, before, during, or after the speech. Was I misremembering? I watched the time-lapse 360-degree video of the inauguration: not a single break in the clouds. I checked the satellite images from before, during, and after the address: a mass of unbroken cloud cover over the entire Washington region. I viewed the radar images: a band of rain approaching just before Trump's address, crossing the area while Trump spoke, then departing as he finished.

By then, Trump had a well-deserved reputation for spouting obvious falsehoods and easily disproved lies. A U.S. general executing Muslim prisoners with bullets dipped in pig blood? Apocryphal. He opposed the Iraq invasion "loud and strong" and "fought very, very hard" against going in? Audio from 2002 showed he supported the war. He "never mocked" a disabled reporter? The video showed otherwise. Never called John McCain a "loser"? Specifically, he said he didn't like McCain "because I don't like losers."

When Trump mistakenly tweeted a warning that a hurricane threatened Alabama (the National Weather Service had to issue a clarification), Trump famously redrew a government weather map with a black Sharpie to show Alabama in the storm's path. (He also pressured the National Weather Service to back up his false claim.)

It was difficult to be sure that Trump was lying; it seemed more that he didn't know the difference between fact and fiction. "Lying is second nature to him," Tony Schwartz, Trump's ghostwriter for *The Art of the Deal*, told *The New Yorker*'s Jane Mayer in 2016. "More than anyone else I have ever met, Trump has the ability to convince himself that whatever he is saying at any given moment is true, or sort of true, or at least ought to be true."

Trump gave insight into his way of thinking in a 2007 deposition when he was suing an author who claimed Trump's true net worth wasn't in the billions but less than $250 million. "My net worth fluctuates," Trump said, "and it goes up and down with the markets and with attitudes and with feelings, even my own feelings."

Of course, his "feelings" had nothing to do with his net worth. But now Trump was convincing millions to think the way he did.

There has always been what the late historian Richard Hofstadter called the "paranoid style" in U.S. politics: witch hunts, Illuminati, Red Scares. William Jennings Bryan promoted conspiracy theories. Richard Nixon believed in them. Americans, by nature, are more distrustful of authority, and what those in authority say, than citizens of other advanced democracies.

But the American electorate, at the dawn of the Trump age, was no more paranoid or predisposed to conspiracy thinking than it was in the past. Conservatives weren't inherently more conspiracy-minded than liberals. What changed is that, for the first time in U.S. history, a president and a major political party weaponized paranoia. Trump was the first president to promote conspiracy thinking from the bully pulpit, and the first to build a system in which elites—Republican Party leaders—validated paranoia. For the first time, America had "a president who has built a coalition by reaching out to conspiracy-minded people," Joseph Uscinski, a University of Miami political scientist who studies conspiracy theories, told me.

It is well established in political science that, for all their supposed contempt for their elected representatives, Americans take cues from political leaders. When leaders reject conspiracy theories, the public follows. But when Trump, as party leader, embraced conspiracy theories, Republican voters followed, some because of genuine belief but others because of partisan solidarity. Dartmouth College political scientist Brendan Nyhan told me that, because of Trump's amplification of fringe beliefs and his "grinding attack on factual evidence," "conspiracy theories and misinformation become yoked to partisanship in increasingly powerful ways."

Trump publicly embraced dozens of conspiracy theories:

Supreme Court justice Antonin Scalia was murdered. Rafael Cruz, Ted Cruz's father, was involved in the JFK assassination. MSNBC host Joe Scarborough, a former congressman, murdered one of his aides. Obama's wedding ring is inscribed "There is no god but Allah." The Hawaii official who verified Obama's birth certificate was murdered. A demonstrator who rushed the stage at one of Trump's rallies has ties to the Islamic State. Trump was being persecuted by the Internal Revenue Service because he's a "strong Christian." Global warming is a hoax created by the Chinese. Vaccines cause autism. Hillary Clinton "killed four Americans in Benghazi." Muslims in New Jersey celebrated on 9/11.

As a candidate and as president, Trump alleged that Democrats were in cahoots with so-called globalists such as George Soros to finance migrant caravans of MS-13 criminal gang members and violent antifa riots. He claimed a hurricane death toll in Puerto Rico had been faked. He repeatedly accused Obama of bugging his campaign and "spying" on him in "the biggest political crime and scandal in U.S. history," dubbed "Obamagate." (The Justice Department's inspector general concluded no such thing occurred.) Trump spread far-right paranoia about a deep state within the federal bureaucracy secretly undermining him. (The Trump-appointed FBI director, Christopher Wray, called the deep state allegations an "affront.") Trump, echoing Russian propaganda, claimed that Ukraine, not Russia, interfered in the 2016 U.S. election. (The FBI had "no information" implicating Ukraine, Wray said.)

During Trump's first impeachment by the House, in 2019, Fiona Hill, a Russia expert on the National Security Council, pleaded with lawmakers not to echo Putin's propaganda about Ukraine. "Based on questions and statements I have heard, some of you on this committee appear to believe that Russia and its security services did not conduct a campaign against our country and that perhaps, somehow, for some reason, Ukraine did," she testified. "This is a fictional narrative that has been perpetrated and propagated by the Russian security services themselves. . . . I refuse to be part of an effort to legitimize an alternative narrative that the Ukrainian government is a U.S. adversary." (It wasn't the first time GOP lawmakers showed such deference to the Kremlin.

Eight of them paid a kowtowing trip to Moscow for July 4th a year earlier—even as Russia was poisoning a former double agent in Britain—and posed for propaganda photos with Russian officials.)

Trump, when he wasn't promoting conspiracy theories himself, gave his support to the conspiracy theorists by retweeting them and inviting them to the White House. As he elevated conspiracy thinking, Trump also worked vigorously to discredit legitimate sources of information. He relentlessly attacked the national media as "fake news"—and that, too, became a defining belief for Republicans. In a July 2018 Quinnipiac University national survey, Americans overall trusted the media more than Trump to tell the truth, 54 percent to 34 percent. But among Republicans, 75 percent said they trusted Trump to tell the truth more than the media; only 16 percent trusted the media over Trump. Republican leaders had long used the media as a foil, but Trump took it to a new level, using the Stalinist label "enemy of the people" for the free press. It effectively neutralized the media's ability to call Trump on his untruths, because his supporters merely took that as confirmation of the media's vendetta against Trump.

Combined with Trump's enormous reach on social media (he could tweet disinformation to 100 million people at a time) and social media's susceptibility to disinformation (a BuzzFeed analysis found that fake news stories about the 2016 election generated more engagement on Facebook than the top election stories from nineteen major news outlets combined), his "fake news" attacks on the media freed him from accountability.

BEFORE HE ENTERED POLITICS, Trump was, above all else, a showman, and a charlatan. He claimed his Trump Tower had ten more floors than it did. He overstated his net worth by $4 billion. He pretended to be his own spokesman, "John Barron," to tout himself to reporters.

When I first covered him, in 1999, he was publicly flirting with challenging Pat Buchanan for the presidential nomination of Ross Perot's Reform Party. I flew with him on his 727 with a winged "T" on the tail and mirrored headboard on the bed. Roger Stone, the conspiracy theorist and longtime Trump adviser, was aboard, along with his dog. On our swing through Southern California I learned about Trump's positions: progressive on social issues such as gays in the military, in favor of campaign finance reform, universal health care, and more regulation, opposed to investing Social Security money in the stock market. Most of all, he preached tolerance—contrasting himself with Buchanan, who had made anti-Semitic and anti-immigrant statements.

To counter Buchanan, Trump announced that he hated intolerance because, in New York, "a town with different races, religions and peoples, I have learned to work with my brother man." On our trip, Trump underscored the point by touring the Simon Wiesenthal Center's Museum of Tolerance in Los Angeles. Buchanan, Trump charged, "seems to be a racist."

In 2011, Trump spoke at the annual Conservative Political Action Conference at the invitation of a gay Republican group. As late as 2013, Trump was still speaking out against conservatives. "The Republican Party is in serious trouble" as it gets "more and more conservative," he told CPAC then.

But Trump saw where the party was headed—and he utterly (and opportunistically) reinvented himself. Before launching his presidential run in 2015, he conveniently selected the precise basket of issues that Republican primary voters wanted to hear about: Repealing Obamacare. Anti-abortion. Antitax. Anti-China. Against Common Core education standards. Virulent in challenging President Obama's legitimacy. The thrice-married Trump claimed he was for traditional marriage. The developer who relied on (often undocumented) immigrant labor came out against immigrants. A hotelier whose properties offered guests copies of the Koran talked of banning Muslims from entering the United States.

Trump had become a political power largely by touting the Birther conspiracy theory on Fox News. He saw, through that experience, that there was a huge market among Republican voters for conspiracy and not a lot of regard for truth. Trump didn't cause Republicans to lose touch with the facts; he exploited the fact-challenged state the party already was in. Trump was a monster Republicans created.

In an October 2015 Republican presidential debate, CNBC's John Harwood listed some of Trump's absurd promises: make

Mexico pay for a border wall, deport eleven million people, cut taxes $10 trillion without increasing the deficit. "Let's be honest: Is this the comic book version of a presidential campaign?" Trump had also said he'd cut the then $19 trillion debt in half in eight years without cutting Social Security or Medicare (the debt soared by $8 trillion). He claimed the economy would grow at 4 percent a year and as high as 8 percent (actual: 1.6 percent).

Trump's mendacity was difficult to contextualize, but people tried. The *Washington Post*'s "Fact Checker" calculated during the campaign that Trump got the most untruthful rating 65 percent of the time, compared to Hillary Clinton's 15 percent. Later, in 2018, "Fact Checker" undertook to analyze all of Trump's statements in one rally and found that 76 percent of his utterances were false or suspect. During the first one hundred days of his presidency, Trump made 492 dubious claims. On the day before the 2020 election alone, he made 503 dubious claims. He had uttered 30,573 untruths over four years, or twenty-one a day.

He claimed "I have no relationship with Putin." (He had previously said "I do have a relationship" with Putin.) He said "13 Angry Democrats" working for independent counsel Robert Mueller were on a "witch hunt." (Mueller himself was a Republican, appointed by a Republican who was himself appointed by Trump.) He blamed Democrats for separating migrant parents and children at the border. (His own attorney general said the practice "inevitably" resulted from Trump's "zero tolerance" border policy.) After 2018 midterm elections gave Democrats control of the House, he called it "close to a complete victory" for him. His 2020 reelection effort involved, among other things, portraying Biden as senile, and claiming Biden would outlaw windows in homes and offices.

Trump's fondness for the phony was matched only by his distaste for science and expertise. Criticizing the Federal Reserve in 2018, he said: "I have a gut, and my gut tells me more sometimes than anybody else's brain can ever tell me." He claimed he was qualified to cast doubt on climate change science. Why? "My uncle was a great professor at MIT for many years, Dr. John Trump. And I didn't talk to him about this particular subject, but I have a natural instinct for science."

Trump dictated to his physician a letter for the doctor to release saying Trump would be "the healthiest individual ever elected to the presidency." And though the U.S. intelligence agencies concluded that Russia interfered in the 2016 election, Trump, standing beside Putin in Helsinki, said that he had "no reason" to disbelieve Putin's denials.

Former oil executive Rex Tillerson, after he was fired as Trump's first secretary of state, offered some thoughts on his old boss in 2018. "If our leaders seek to conceal the truth or we as people become accepting of alternative realities that are no longer grounded in facts, then we as American citizens are on a pathway to relinquishing our freedom," he said. "This is the life of non-democratic societies, comprised of people who are not free to seek the truth." Like so many others, alas, he couldn't manage to speak up when it still might have done some good.

TRUMP'S AFFECTION FOR ALTERNATIVE facts and his contempt for science came together with catastrophic results when the Covid-19 pandemic struck.

By February 10, 2020, Wuhan, China, had been sealed off for weeks, the virus-stricken *Diamond Princess* cruise ship was stranded off the coast of Japan, and cases of the novel coronavirus had already reached the United States. But Trump's budget director, Russell Vought, walked into the White House briefing room and assured the world that Covid-19 would not change Trump's rosy economic outlook. "Our view is that, at this point, coronavirus is not something that is going to have ripple effects," Vought said.

Trump had told Fox News's Sean Hannity that "we pretty much shut it down coming in from China" and that "we have it very much under control in this country." Treasury Secretary Steven Mnuchin called the situation "manageable." Markets plunged over the next couple of weeks as the deadly virus spread, but Trump, hosting online provocateurs Diamond and Silk at the White House, announced: "It's going to disappear. One day, it's like a miracle." He even knew when: in April 2020, the virus "miraculously goes away," he said.

At a Friday night rally in South Carolina on February 28,

Trump complained that Democrats were politicizing the virus, the way they did with Russian election interference. "And this is their new hoax," he said.

Trump later claimed he only meant Democrats' attempt to blame him was a hoax, but his son Eric later picked up the hoax theme, telling Fox News's Jeanine Pirro: "Guess what? After November 3 [Election Day] coronavirus will magically, all of a sudden, go away and disappear."

The disinformation had a lethal impact, because Republicans believed Trump's assurances. A Reuters-Ipsos poll early in the pandemic found that Republicans were half as likely as Democrats to say the virus posed an imminent threat. More Democrats than Republicans said they were taking steps such as changing travel plans. Similarly, a *Wall Street Journal*/NBC poll in March found that only 30 percent of Republicans planned to avoid large gatherings (versus 61 percent of Democrats) and Republicans were only a third as likely as Democrats to stop eating in restaurants.

Yet another poll, by the nonpartisan Pew Research Center, found that, among the majority of Republicans who had heard the conspiracy theory that "powerful people planned the coronavirus outbreak," half believed it to be true. The reason for the confusion: 75 percent of Republicans trusted that the White House presented accurate information. And so, by March, 71 percent of Republican primary voters suspected the virus had been exaggerated for political reasons, and barely half of Republicans accepted that the virus was not a hoax, an *Economist*/YouGov poll found.

Trump, ignoring scientific advice, advised Americans that taking a malarial drug, hydroxychloroquine, with the antibiotic azithromycin, would be a "phenomenal" Covid-19 remedy and "one of the biggest game changers in the history of medicine." The head of the federal government's Covid-19 vaccine efforts, Rick Bright, said such treatments "clearly lack scientific merit"—and Trump ousted him, while ordering the Veterans Administration to stockpile the drugs. An Arizona man died because he ate fish tank cleaner containing chloroquine.

Then Trump suggested injecting bleach into people's lungs. Observing that disinfectants quickly kill the virus on inanimate surfaces, Trump asked: "Is there a way we can do something like that by injection inside? Or almost a cleaning? . . . It would be interesting to check that." Government scientists dutifully promised to investigate the lung-bleaching plan. Maryland's governor reported that hundreds of people called a state hotline asking whether they should drink Clorox.

Sean Hannity, Rush Limbaugh, and other Trump allies amplified the disinformation. West Virginia governor Jim Justice recommended: "If you want to go to Bob Evans and eat, go to Bob Evans and eat." Oklahoma governor Kevin Stitt tweeted a photo of him with his children at a "packed" food hall. Senator John Cornyn, a Texas Republican, tweeted a photo of a Corona beer at a restaurant with the message "Don't Panic." Representative Devin Nunes, top Republican on the House Intelligence Committee, advised people to "go to your local pub."

Then there was Senator Rand Paul, the Kentucky Republican, who said "people should ask themselves whether this coronavirus 'pandemic' could be a big hoax"—even as his wife bought stock in a company with a promising Covid-19 drug. Several other Republican lawmakers made similar stock bets after receiving private briefings on the severity of the threat.

Ordinary Republicans, taking cues from their leaders, eschewed mask wearing and ignored public health restrictions. Trump even discouraged testing, saying, "If we stop testing right now, we'd have very few cases, if any."

The result? Before the pandemic, in October 2019, Johns Hopkins University rated the United States the country best prepared for an epidemic. But the United States had the world's worst response to the pandemic, and the greatest number of deaths. A year into the pandemic, *The Lancet* medical journal concluded that, of the then nearly 500,000 deaths in the United States, 40 percent were preventable. Trump's failure to do as the leaders of other advanced countries did caused some 200,000 Americans to die unnecessarily.

The government's top infectious disease expert, Tony Fauci of the National Institute for Allergy and Infectious Disease, said lives could have been saved if the Trump administration acted sooner; Trump responded by sharing a "#FireFauci" message. His administration forced Robert Redfield of the Centers for Disease Control to recant his (accurate) warning about a second wave of the virus. Trump political appointees tried to censor scientific updates from the CDC. Trump's campaign staffers tore down social distancing signs at a Trump rally. Republican governors of hard-hit states tampered with data and silenced public health experts.

But the worst moment came after Trump himself contracted the virus after a masks-off super-spreader event at the White House. He might have died if he had not been hospitalized and given cutting-edge treatments such as monoclonal antibodies (at the time unavailable to virtually all other Americans) and the antiviral remdesivir (rationed for ordinary Americans), in addition to oxygen and steroids.

Yet when he emerged from Walter Reed National Military Medical Center, he told Americans: "Don't be afraid of Covid," "Don't let it dominate your life," and "You're going to beat it." The then 229,000 dead, who didn't have access to Trump's treatments, no doubt would have disagreed.

AS HIS TERM WENT on, Trump increasingly used the bully pulpit to promote QAnon, a bizarre pro-Trump conspiracy theory with origins in "Pizzagate" holding that Satanists in the federal government deep state operated a pedophilia ring.

Among the QAnon beliefs: John F. Kennedy Jr. faked his death and masqueraded as bearded Trump supporter Vincent Fusca so that he could reveal his true identity at President Trump's Fourth of July celebration, where he was to replace Vice President Pence as Trump's running mate. North Korean dictator Kim Jong-un is a CIA puppet. The U.S. government is run by reptilian aliens. Liberal elites drink a substance called adrenochrome that they derive from the blood of children they hold in captivity as part of their pedophilia ring. And Austin Steinbart, a man many once believed to be "Q," had prophetic insight into the inner workings of the U.S. government because he received messages from his future self through quantum computing. (Steinbart got into legal trouble and was found in possession of a prosthetic penis called a Whizzinator used for falsifying drug tests, the Daily Beast's Will Sommer reported.)

QAnon began in late 2017 and hopped from platform to platform, as a supposed government official named "Q" issued coded predictions of sinister deep state machinations. "I heard that these are people that love our country," Trump said in 2020, noting that "they like me very much" and "it is gaining in popularity." Trump retweeted messages from scores of QAnon adherents, vastly boosting the movement's visibility. QAnon symbols surfaced at Trump events. Eric Trump, White House social media adviser Dan Scavino, and the House Intelligence Committee's Nunes all promoted QAnon theses, and Mike Flynn, the disgraced Trump national security adviser, issued a video of himself taking a QAnon oath. When GOP congressional candidate Laura Loomer (a self-styled "proud Islamophobe") became one of the several conspiracy theorists to win a GOP nomination in 2020, Trump responded: "Great going."

Trump's boosterism had proved persuasive. A May 2021 poll by the Public Religion Research Institute found that 23 percent of Republicans agreed that "the government, media and financial worlds in the U.S. are controlled by a group of Satan-worshipping pedophiles who run a global child sex trafficking operation." Other polls found that 25 to 30 percent of Republicans had a favorable view of QAnon supporters.

About two dozen QAnon adherents found their way onto ballots in 2020 as Republican nominees for Congress. And a couple of them prevailed. Representative Marjorie Taylor Greene of Georgia quickly made a name for herself with her support for the notion that various school shootings, the 9/11 attacks, and the Ronald Reagan assassination attempt were all faked. Another, Representative Lauren Boebert of Colorado, covered herself in a foil blanket on the House floor during President Biden's address to Congress (tin foil hats are so twentieth century!).

Among those swept up in the QAnon craziness was Trump's personal lawyer. Giuliani followed dozens of QAnon-tied accounts on Twitter, and the once reputable figure himself waded ever deeper into the fever swamps. When he took on the role of Trump's lawyer in the spring of 2018, the onetime lawman compared FBI agents to "stormtroopers" and called a law enforcement informant a "spy." He also pushed the debunked conspiracy theory that the

Clinton campaign colluded with Russia in the 2016 election. He even saw a conspiracy in his own typo: when he made a punctuation error in a tweet that created a link to an Indian website, he made the paranoid allegation that "Twitter allowed someone to invade my text."

Giuliani, who routinely pocket-tweeted and butt-dialed, became increasingly erratic, engaging in screaming matches with TV hosts: "Holy God! . . . You don't think there's a Deep State? . . . Of course I'm making sense! . . . You shouldn't be embarrassed for me. . . . Of course I'm aware of what I'm saying!" One moment he was saying "no one signed" a letter of intent for Trump to build a Moscow project; the next he was saying "of course" Trump signed the letter. Here he was saying Trump "fixer" Michael Cohen is "not going to lie"; there he was calling Cohen a "proven liar" who "lied all his life." Here he was promising "no collusion" with Russia; there he was saying "collusion is not a crime."

Turned down on his request to be secretary of state, Giuliani instead became Trump's lawyer—and bumbled his way through presidential scandals. In his pugilistic defense of Trump's hush-money payments to porn actress Stormy Daniels, Giuliani implicated Trump in a crime, live on cable news. In his attempt to defend Trump during the probe into Russia's manipulation of the 2016 presidential race, he stumbled into undermining Trump's claim that there was "no collusion" with Russia. Giuliani went to Ukraine to try to find dirt on Trump's likely Democratic opponent Joe Biden and Biden's son—and wound up becoming a central figure in Trump's impeachment for conditioning Ukraine's military aid on the country's help for Trump's campaign.

But Giuliani's lowest act was his last: trying to sell the public and the courts on the Big Lie, the proven falsehood that victory had been stolen from Trump in 2020 by massive fraud. Giuliani and fellow Trump defenders were laughed out of court, losing sixty-three of sixty-four cases (their one victory was in a case that didn't allege fraud) and earning rebukes from judges for sloppy work, errors, and demonstrable falsehoods. *The Washington Post* calculated that as of mid-December 2020, at least eighty-six judges (44 percent of them Republicans) had rejected the Trump lawyers' lawsuits. The Supreme Court wouldn't even entertain their wacky arguments.

Giuliani lifted allegations from affidavits that judges had already determined not to be credible. He made one allegation based on a doctored video. He misrepresented what had happened with the vote counts in Michigan, Georgia, and Pennsylvania. He falsely claimed the Detroit-area vote count had been decertified.

He claimed that Pennsylvania received more completed absentee ballots (2.6 million) than were requested (1.8 million). In fact, Pennsylvanians had requested 3.1 million absentee ballots. Giuliani went before a Pennsylvania judge and alleged "widespread, nationwide voter fraud, of which this is a part." Under questioning from the judge, Trump's lawyers admitted their complaint did not allege fraud.

He alternately claimed 65,000, 66,000, and 165,000 underage voters in Georgia. An audit by the (Republican) secretary of state found there were zero underage voters in 2020. He claimed 6,000 dead people voted in Georgia; the state probe found only two potential instances deserving more study.

And he echoed the zaniest of conspiracy theories. "You couldn't possibly believe," he said, "that the company . . . with control over our vote is owned by two Venezuelans who were allies of [Hugo] Chavez, are present allies of [Nicolás] Maduro, with a company whose chairman is a close associate and business partner of George Soros the biggest donor to the Democrat party, the biggest donor to antifa, and the biggest donor of Black Lives Matter."

Whoa. Chávez had been dead for seven years. Dominion Voting Systems, the target of the Trump allegations, is a U.S. company with no Venezuela or Soros ties. A different company, Smartmatic, was founded in Florida by Venezuelans, and the chairman of its parent company was on the board of Soros's Open Society Foundations. But Smartmatic's software was used only in Los Angeles— not in any of the states where Trump was contesting the outcome.

Months later, a defamation lawsuit brought by Dominion's chairman shook loose a Trump campaign memo showing the campaign knew the charges against Dominion to be bogus before Giuliani and friends made their wild allegations at the RNC.

Giuliani paid for his lies with his law license. In June 2021, a five-judge panel of the Supreme Court of New York's Appellate Division suspended him from practicing law pending a final ruling because "there is uncontroverted evidence that respondent communicated demonstrably false and misleading statements to courts, lawmakers and the public at large." The panel suspended Giuliani because his misconduct "immediately threatens the public interest."

"The seriousness of [Giuliani's] uncontroverted misconduct cannot be overstated," the panel concluded. "This country is being torn apart by continued attacks on the legitimacy of the 2020 election and of our current president, Joseph R. Biden. The hallmark of our democracy is predicated on free and fair elections. False statements intended to foment a loss of confidence in our elections and resulting loss of confidence in government generally damage the proper functioning of a free society."

Giuliani also had his law license suspended in Washington, and he faced a defamation lawsuit by Dominion and a civil action holding him responsible for the January 6 Capitol insurrection. In 2021, the U.S. Attorney's Office in Manhattan, the office he once led, seized Giuliani's mobile phones and computers as part of its investigation into whether he illegally lobbied the Trump administration for Ukrainian nationals while seeking dirt on the Bidens. One of Giuliani's associates pleaded guilty to campaign finance violations and another was convicted.

America's Mayor had come to ruin in the courts of law. But in the court of public opinion, he and his client, the former president, largely achieved their goals: they succeeded in convincing a majority of Republicans to reject the outcome of a free and fair election and instead to accept the Big Lie as an article of faith. An August 2021 survey by Yahoo! News found that 66 percent of Republicans still believed "the election was rigged and stolen from Trump," while only 18 percent acknowledged that "Joe Biden won fair and square."

The Republican electorate's slim tether to the truth, stretched by GOP leaders for a quarter century, had snapped. Giuliani and his client had shown beyond all doubt that Trump could fool most of his supporters all of the time.

CHAPTER 14

Very Fine People

On the eleventh and twelfth of August 2017, white suprema- cists held a coming-out party in the streets of Charlottesville, Virginia.

Donald Trump's successful presidential campaign, which echoed the words and themes of the racist alt-right and white nationalist fringe, emboldened many in those movements to step out of the shadows. In a show of force, hundreds of neo- Confederates and neo-Nazis descended on Thomas Jefferson's hometown to rally alongside former Klan leader David Duke and white nationalist Richard Spencer.

They had come at the invitation of a "pro-White" organizer and a member of the violent Proud Boys to oppose the threat- ened removal of a statue of Robert E. Lee, erected nearly a cen- tury earlier as a monument to white power at a time when KKK membership in Charlottesville was at its peak. Neo-Nazi groups had largely taken over the organizing, and on the night before the main event one hundred of the participants marched on the Uni- versity of Virginia campus carrying torches, giving Nazi salutes and chanting "Sieg Heil," the Nazi slogan "Blood and Soil," and "Jews will not replace us." They clashed violently with anti-Nazi counterdemonstrators.

The next morning, white supremacists dressed in fatigues and carrying semiautomatic rifles menaced worshippers at Charlot- tesville's Beth Israel synagogue during Shabbat services, and oth- ers paraded past the building, some carrying flags with swastikas, also chanting "Sieg Heil." The worshippers slipped out the back to avoid a confrontation.

During the main rally, two Virginia troopers monitoring the violent demonstration from the sky crashed their helicopter and perished. A twenty-two-year-old neo-Nazi from Ohio driving a Dodge Challenger encountered a crowd of peaceful counter-demonstrators. He backed up his car and then plowed it into the group, killing Heather Heyer, thirty-two, and injuring nineteen others. The murderer, James Fields Jr., would get life in prison.

The racist violence stunned the nation. And then President Trump spoke—in defense of the neo-Nazis. "You had a group on one side that was bad, and you had a group on the other side that was also very violent, and nobody wants to say that," the president said from the lobby of Trump Tower in New York. He said the anti-Nazi demonstrators didn't have a permit and "were very, very violent." Those marching among the white supremacists had been treated "absolutely unfairly" by the press, Trump said, and there "were very fine people, on both sides."

Very fine people on both sides. Thus did the president of the United States draw a moral equivalence between Nazis and those who opposed Nazis. And he wasn't done. He argued that "not all of those people were White supremacists" but rather were there only to oppose the removal of Lee's statue. "I wonder, is it George Washington next week?" Trump asked. After equating Nazis with anti-Nazis, he equated the father of the country with the man who led an armed rebellion against that country in defense of slavery.

It was just the sort of response that would please a former KKK grand wizard. "Thank you President Trump for your honesty & courage to tell the truth about #Charlottesville & condemn the leftist terrorists," David Duke tweeted.

In the national outcry that followed, even many of Trump's usual enablers—Paul Ryan, Kevin McCarthy, Mitch McConnell, Lindsey Graham—couldn't abide Trump's "fine people on both sides" stance. Both Presidents Bush spoke out. Trump disbanded his corporate advisory panels after eight members quit in protest.

But Trump's treasury secretary, Steve Mnuchin (who is Jewish), and his homeland security secretary, Kirstjen Nielsen, disgraced themselves by defending his statements, and Trump counselor Kellyanne Conway called Trump's words "darn near perfection." Jerry Falwell Jr. attested that Trump "does not have a racist bone in his body." And Trump's boosters on *Fox & Friends* gave him a pass: "He could cure cancer tomorrow," host Todd Piro said, and "people in the media are going to attack him." Within a couple of weeks, the GOP again unified behind Trump, who declared that he had spoken "perfectly." And, for a guy whose political survival required stoking racial fears, he had.

TRUMP MADE IT SAFE for America to hate again. He pulled white supremacists from the dark shadows, brought them into the White House, and fanned racial rage. But he was building on what had long been under way in the GOP, from the Southern Strategy to the Republican overtures to the militias in the 1990s, to Birtherism and the Tea Party's racist backlash against Obama, to the party's turn against immigration.

The GOP's autopsy after the 2012 presidential loss had concluded that the party would be doomed by changing demographics if it did not reach out to voters of color. That is true, in the long run, as people of color become a majority in the United States in the 2040s, and a majority of the electorate a decade or two later. But Trump was doubling down on the Republicans' bet on white grievance: in the short run, less-educated white Americans, afraid of losing their dominant status to a growing immigrant and minority population, would show up to vote in higher numbers than Americans of color.

J. D. Vance, the conservative author of *Hillbilly Elegy,* accurately described Trump's rise in a private message in February 2016 to a former Yale Law School roommate who later made their exchange public: "I think the entire party has only itself to blame . . . We are, whether we like it or not, the party of lower-income, lower-education white people, and I have been saying for a long time that we need to offer those people SOMETHING . . . or a demagogue would. We are now at that point. Trump is the fruit of the party's collective neglect." Back then, Vance said he couldn't decide whether Trump was "America's Hitler" or just a "cynical asshole." But Vance became a Trump supporter and, as a Trump-endorsed Senate candidate from Ohio in 2022, campaigned by stoking racist fears of immigrants.

Much of the post-2016 commentary attributed Trump's surprise victory to economic anxiety; in reality it was *racial* anxiety. Extensive research documented that race and racial attitudes became the single most important factor driving "affective polarization" (the antipathy members of each party feel for members of the other), more than religion, culture, class, or ideology. Research by Nicholas Valentino and Kirill Zhirkov at the University of Michigan found that "these changes in race and ethnicity . . . drive most of the affective polarization we have witnessed over the last 30 years." American voters have developed "highly racialized mental images of political parties," and white voters "who thought of the Democratic Party as Black reported clear affective preference for the Republican Party." This "ethnicization" of political parties has been associated elsewhere with instability and bad governance—and the same is now occurring in the United States.

Likewise, researchers from San Francisco State University and the liberal think tank Demos, writing in *The Nation,* reported on regression analyses comparing voters' presidential preferences with their reaction to being told that the United States will become a minority-majority nation. The likelihood of supporting Trump increased sharply among those with negative views of racial diversity. This was new; there was no similar effect seen among supporters of John McCain in 2008 or Mitt Romney in 2012.

The parties had been realigning themselves according to race and racial attitudes for decades, but the Obama presidency, and the Trump-led racial backlash against it, dramatically accelerated the trend—drawing those with racial resentment into the Republican Party and repelling those who welcome a multiracial America. Conversely, racial liberalism drove preference for the Democratic Party (among voters of all colors) more than other factors.

The emphasis on fear, on the threat to traditional white dominance, inevitably built a more racist GOP. Consider one standard question on racial attitudes in which people are asked to agree or disagree with this statement: "It's really a matter of some people not trying hard enough; if Blacks would only try harder, they could be just as well off as whites." In 2012, 56 percent of white Republicans agreed with that statement, according to the American National Election Studies. The number grew in 2016 with Trump's rise, to 59 percent. And in June 2020, an astonishing 71 percent of white Republicans agreed, according to polling done by Christopher Parker of the University of Washington. The liberalization on race among Democrats is even more striking. In 2012, 38 percent agreed that African Americans didn't try hard enough. In 2016, that dropped to 27 percent. And in 2020? Just 13 percent.

Trump recognized intuitively that racial animus is a potent motivator. White evangelicals are only about 15 percent of the U.S. population, but they were more like 25 percent of the electorate in 2020—and about 40 percent of Trump's vote. (This, despite the evangelical magazine *Christianity Today* labeling Trump and his Twitter invective "a near perfect example of a human being who is morally lost and confused.") White evangelicals were always active voters, but that turnout was extraordinary. Why? A Southwestern Baptist Theological Seminary graduate who runs the Public Religion Research Institute, Robert P. Jones, told me that Trump inspired white Christians, "not despite, but through appeals to white supremacy," attracting them not because of economics or morality, but because "he evoked powerful fears about the loss of white Christian dominance." (White evangelicals had abandoned the Democratic Party after the Voting Rights Act and became a political force in the early 1970s in large part to defend the ban on interracial dating at Bob Jones University; they didn't embrace abortion as an issue until 1979.)

The Public Religion Research Institute's American Values Survey from September 2020 found overwhelming majorities of white evangelical Protestants saying that police killings of African Americans were "isolated incidents," and that Confederate flags and monuments are symbols of southern pride rather than racism. Majorities of white evangelicals also perceived discrimination against Christians and whites, and rejected the idea that a history of slavery and longtime discrimination makes it difficult for Black Americans to succeed.

A similar effect happened with women. Though the "gender

gap" (in which women vote more Democratic) was thought to benefit Democrats, Trump managed to tap gender animus in the same way he tapped racial animus—by making men feel threatened that they were losing power to women. Dan Cassino, a political scientist at Fairleigh Dickinson University, found that in 2016 a perceived threat to male identity and masculinity led to increased support for Trump among men. Cassino found that when he "primed" poll respondents by asking whether their spouses earned more than them before asking them about their presidential preference, support for Trump over Hillary Clinton jumped 24 percentage points among men. (Confirming that it was a gender effect, there was no such change in a hypothetical Trump versus Bernie Sanders contest.) In the 2016 election, Trump lost women by 12 points—but he offset that disadvantage by winning men by a dozen points. In other words, Trump could gain votes not just by frightening white voters about racial minorities but also by frightening men about women. There was cunning behind his crudeness.

For Trump, the bigotry came easily; unlike other policies he adopted out of expediency, the racism, misogyny, and demonization of religious minorities, immigrants, and the disabled had been with him from the start.

In early December 2015, I opened a column with a simple declarative. "Let's not mince words: Donald Trump is a bigot and a racist." It prompted a blizzard of anti-Semitic replies from irony-immune Trump supporters. I had traced his racism to a quarter century earlier, when he took out ads in New York newspapers calling for the death penalty for five Black and Latino teens who were accused of assaulting the Central Park jogger. The young men were later cleared by DNA evidence and the confession of a serial rapist—and Trump called their wrongful-conviction settlement a "disgrace." Similarly, he fought Indian gaming interests by claiming Native Americans were under mob control, were cocaine traffickers, or were "so-called Indians."

Later, Trump led the Birther movement challenging President Obama's Americanness; used vulgar expressions to refer to women; called for rounding up and deporting eleven million undocumented immigrants; kicked out a prominent Latino journalist from a news conference and said the U.S.-based Spanish-language Univision "takes its marching orders" from Mexico and "cares far more about Mexico than it does about the U.S."; mocked Asian accents; proposed banning Muslims from entering the country, forcing those here to register in a database, and saying he would "strongly consider" closing mosques; falsely claimed thousands of Muslims in New Jersey celebrated the 9/11 attacks; tweeted bogus statistics asserting that most killings of whites are done by Blacks; approved of the roughing up of a Black demonstrator at one of his events; and publicly mocked the movements of a *New York Times* journalist who had a chronic condition limiting mobility.

Trump let stand a claim that Obama was a Muslim and that Muslims were "a problem" for America. He hesitated to disavow David Duke. He circulated social media messages from white supremacists, including an image previously on an anti-Semitic message board of a Star of David atop a pile of cash, phony crime statistics that originated with neo-Nazis, and an image of Nazi soldiers superimposed on an American flag next to Trump's likeness. He ran an ad linking prominent Jews to a secret "global power structure." He quoted Mussolini and said "half" of all undocumented immigrants are criminals.

A white nationalist wound up on the list of Trump delegates to the Republican National Convention. Trump claimed that an American-born judge, Gonzalo Curiel, could not impartially judge a case involving Trump because the judge was "Mexican" and "I'm building a wall" on the Mexican border. Trump told Jewish Republicans, "You're not going to support me, because I don't want your money."

Journalists documented racial ugliness at Trump rallies: Trump's personal bodyguard punching a pro-immigration demonstrator in the head, and Trump supporters assaulting or shouting at Black demonstrators ("shoot him!," "Sieg Heil," "light the motherfucker on fire"), at Latino protesters ("motherfucking tacos—go back to Mexico"), at the mention of Hillary Clinton ("Hang that bitch"), and at the mention of Obama ("He's a monkey!").

Trump gave a top campaign (and later White House) role to Steve Bannon, a nationalist who called the Civil War the "war of Southern Independence," found "zero evidence" of racial motive in the shooting of unarmed Black teen Trayvon Martin, and warned that "cities could be washed away in an orgy of de-gentrification." His website, Breitbart News, wrote about "Muslim Rape Culture," a "Dangerous Faggot Tour," the gay pride flag as a "symbol of anti-Christian hate, and the belief that women 'Just Suck at Interviews.'" Breitbart had a special tag for "Black crime" and called for roundups of worshippers in mosques.

Trump also hired "alt-right" figures Stephen Miller and Sebastian Gorka, who wore to an inaugural ball a medal from the Hungarian nationalist organization Vitezi Rend, an anti-Semitic group that claimed Gorka was one of its own. Trump officials canceled a grant to a group, Life After Hate, that rehabilitated neo-Nazis, and proposed eliminating the "Countering Violent Extremism" program, arguing that the focus on right-wing extremism was misguided.

It's no coincidence that hate crimes rose 42 percent from 2015 to 2020, when such crimes reached a twelve-year high, according to FBI data, even though fewer law enforcement agencies reported the crimes. The Anti-Defamation League reported roughly a doubling of anti-Semitic incidents between 2015 and 2019, to a record level. And Americans saw their country being torn apart by race. As recently as 2013, 70 percent of Americans believed there were good relations between white and Black people, Gallup polling found. That plunged among both Black and white Americans as Trump rose in 2015, and by 2021, only 42 percent said relations were good.

TRUMP MADE THE BIGOTRY in the Republican Party far more overt, but he didn't invent it. As with his assault on facts and science, he merely exploited the animus in the GOP that predated his run.

Before there was Trump, there was Representative Steve Pearce, a New Mexico Republican who opined that "the wife is to voluntarily submit, just as the husband is to lovingly lead and sacrifice." And before there was Trump, there was Steve King. King had made his name promoting "Western civilization" and opposing bilingualism. He supported racist leaders abroad, and he argued that "demographics are our destiny. We can't restore our civilization with somebody else's babies." He pushed to end the constitutional guarantee of "birthright citizenship" and he thwarted President George W. Bush's attempts at comprehensive immigration reform.

Trump saw the growing power of King's politics with the Tea Party success in 2010, and in 2011 Trump praised King for "doing great work in the House." For King's reelection in 2014, Trump also taped a robocall for his "friend." Trump returned for a King-hosted event in January 2015, at which he expressed his "great respect" for King, "a great guy" who "doesn't get fair press."

Finally, after years of GOP leadership ignoring the remarks and enabling him, Republican Leader Kevin McCarthy stripped King of his committee assignments in January 2019, for saying to *The New York Times,* "White nationalist, White supremacists . . . how did that language become offensive?" But by that time, King's themes had been fully co-opted by the White House.

At a hearing in April 2015 on ending birthright citizenship, Republicans brought in to testify University of Texas law professor Lino Graglia, who had said that Black and Latino Americans are "not academically competitive with Whites," are less "academically competent," and come from a "culture that seems not to encourage achievement." A few months later, Republicans interrupted a routine debate on an appropriations bill when their floor leader raised an unrelated amendment to protect the sale and display of the Confederate battle flag at national parks and monuments— a reaction to a move by South Carolina to remove the symbol of hatred from its statehouse grounds after a neo-Confederate massacred nine Black worshippers in a Charleston church. Days after that, Obama, traveling in Oklahoma City, was greeted at his hotel by ten demonstrators waving the Confederate battle flag.

In early 2015, Giuliani, before his embrace of Trump, declared at a dinner that "I do not believe that the president loves America" and that Obama "wasn't brought up the way you were brought up and I was brought up, through love of this country." GOP presidential candidate Scott Walker, seated near Giuliani at the dinner, declined to disagree with Giuliani, saying "I'm not going to comment on what the president thinks." Asked if Obama was a Christian, Walker said, "I don't know." Another GOP presidential candidate, Louisiana governor Bobby Jindal, said "the gist" of what Giuliani said was true.

Candidate Ted Cruz added that Obama was "an apologist for radical Islamic terrorists." Rupert Murdoch's *New York Post* at the time published a photo of a blindfolded Obama and the words "Islamic Terror? I just don't see it." The conservative activist Dinesh D'Souza, tweeting a photo of Obama jokingly taking a selfie, added the message: "YOU CAN TAKE THE BOY OUT OF THE GHETTO . . . Watch this vulgar man show his stuff, while America cowers in embarrassment."

Once Trump joined the presidential scrum, the other candidates didn't reject his hatred; they echoed and even one-upped Trump. Cruz joined Trump at a rally organized by Frank Gaffney, who, among other things, alleged that the Muslim Brotherhood had infiltrated the Obama administration, hosted a well-known white nationalist on his radio show, hailed a "wonderful" white nationalist magazine, and was denounced by the Anti-Defamation League for promoting "the threat of an Islamic takeover of the U.S."

After terrorist attacks in Paris in November 2015, candidates Cruz and Jeb Bush both floated the idea of admitting Christian refugees from Syria but not Muslims. "Wake up and smell the falafel," a like-minded Mike Huckabee, former Arkansas governor, said. Mike McCaul, the GOP chairman of the House Homeland Security Committee, introduced legislation giving Christians priority over Muslims, and several Republican governors moved to ban Syrian Muslims from their states. Candidate Ben Carson compared refugees to "rabid dogs" and argued that the United States shouldn't "put a Muslim in charge of this nation" because Islam was inconsistent with the Constitution.

Jindal joined the effort to end birthright citizenship for U.S.-born children of undocumented immigrants. Bush used the pejorative term "anchor baby." The candidates celebrated an Indiana law, signed by Governor Mike Pence, that allowed businesses to refuse service to gay people. Candidate Rick Santorum compared the Supreme Court ruling legalizing same-sex marriage to the *Dred Scott* decision calling Black Americans property, not citizens.

Cruz, during the campaign, mocked Trump's "New York values." The concern that he was using "New York" as a euphemism for "Jewish" was confirmed when Cruz later said that the Yiddish "chutzpah" was "a New York term."

The bigotry trickled down. Trump's campaign chair in Mahoning County, Ohio, resigned after telling *The Guardian* in a video interview that there wasn't "any racism until Obama got elected" and that if you're Black and unsuccessful "it's your own fault." Representative Robert Pittenger, a North Carolina Republican, said civil rights protesters in Charlotte, North Carolina, "hate white people because White people are successful and they're not."

A New Hampshire legislator said a Democratic congresswoman would lose because she's "ugly as sin." Another New Hampshire legislator said men earn more than women because "they don't mind working nights and weekends" or "overtime and outdoors." An Arizona GOP official said women on Medicaid should be sterilized. An Idaho legislator suggested a gynecological exam could be done by having a woman swallow a camera.

Had Republican officeholders stood up to Trump's bigotry, they might have stopped him. Instead, they validated him. Republican National Committee chairman Reince Priebus called Trump's campaign "a net positive for everybody" (and became Trump's first chief of staff in the White House). When the *Access Hollywood* tape threatened to derail Trump's campaign, evangelical leaders vouched for him. Ralph Reed, the former Christian Coalition power broker, said the issue "ranks pretty low" on evangelical Christians' "hierarchy of their concerns." Jerry Falwell Jr. dismissed the boasting about sexual assaults as "dumb comments on a videotape 11 years ago." Fox News's Sean Hannity, meanwhile, preached: "King David had 500 concubines for crying out loud."

The validation continued after Trump's election, along with a new tendency to imitate Trump's style.

In the early days of the Trump presidency, Senate Republican

Leader Mitch McConnell infamously silenced Elizabeth Warren on the Senate floor when the Massachusetts Democrat read from a Coretta Scott King letter criticizing attorney general nominee Jeff Sessions. "She was warned. She was given an explanation. Nevertheless, she persisted," said McConnell, who delivered no rebuke when male senators read the same letter. During the Brett Kavanaugh sexual assault controversy, successful GOP Senate candidate Kevin Cramer of North Dakota declared the women's allegations "absurd," and Representative Ralph Norman, a South Carolina Republican, joked at a debate that "Ruth Bader Ginsburg came out saying she was groped by Abraham Lincoln."

House Speaker Paul Ryan, though at times calling out Trump's racism, allowed the $100 million Congressional Leadership Fund (which he endorsed and raised funds for) to run a plainly racist ad in upstate New York showing doctored images of a Black Democratic congressional candidate rapping. The ad accused the Black man of "extreme New York City values." The same Ryan-backed group used false charges in another ad to accuse an Asian American Democrat running in Ohio of "selling out Americans."

In West Virginia, self-described "Trumpier than Trump" Senate GOP candidate Don Blankenship attacked McConnell's Asian American father-in-law as a "Chinaperson" and his wife's relatives as a "China family."

Testifying at a congressional hearing, Ryan Zinke, Trump's secretary of the interior, greeted Representative Colleen Hanabusa, a Hawaii Democrat and fourth-generation American, by saying "konnichiwa," a Japanese greeting.

Representative Jim Jordan, top Republican on the House Oversight Committee, spelled the name of Tom Steyer, a billionaire of Jewish descent, as "$teyer." House Republican Leader Kevin McCarthy added two other Jewish names and tweeted that "we cannot allow Soros, Steyer, and Bloomberg to BUY this election!" (He deleted it amid an uproar.)

Trump's commerce secretary, billionaire Wilbur Ross, tried to put a citizenship question on the census to deter Latinos from responding. The architect of the plan had written that it would "be advantageous to Republicans and Non-Hispanic Whites." But Ross lied to Congress about the plan, and the administration's solicitor general, Noel Francisco, presented the same falsehood to the Supreme Court; both claimed, falsely, that the citizenship question was added to help enforce the Voting Rights Act.

Trump adviser Roger Stone had proposed that a top Clinton adviser who was Muslim could be a "terrorist agent." On social media, Donald Trump Jr. likened Syrian (Muslim) refugees to a bowl of Skittles, asking if "I told you just three would kill you, would you take a handful?" (Trump Jr. also mocked Brett Kavanaugh's sexual assault accusers with a crayon drawing posted on Instagram.)

Trump spokesman Spicer apologized after calling Nazi death camps "Holocaust centers" and suggesting that Adolf Hitler didn't gas "his own people." Trump's second secretary of state, Mike Pompeo, hosted the previously shunned Hungarian foreign minister, following his government's reelection on a campaign of anti-Semitism and anti-Muslim demagoguery. Breitbart News, which had been run by Trump's campaign chief, Steve Bannon, referred to Bill Kristol as a "renegade Jew." Trump supporter Alex Jones, the conspiracy theorist and radio host Trump praised, went on a diatribe about "the Jewish mafia in the United States." Donald Trump Jr. (who joked in 2016 about "warming up the gas chamber") shared the slander that Soros was a Nazi collaborator in his youth.

Representative Marjorie Taylor Greene, a QAnon-admiring Georgia Republican and a Trump clone elected in 2020, claimed that the neo-Nazi violence in Charlottesville was really an "inside job," and shared a video from a Holocaust denier denouncing "Zionist supremacists" who are "breeding us out of existence in our own homelands," and speculated that wealthy Jewish interests set forest fires in California using lasers from space. All but eleven House Republicans voted against sanctioning her for her remarks. (Some Republicans pointed to anti-Semitic comments by Democratic congresswoman Ilhan Omar—she said support for Israel was "all about the Benjamins," or $100 bills—but there was a crucial difference: fellow Democrats denounced such remarks, and Omar apologized.)

During the pandemic, Florida governor Ron DeSantis, a Trump protégé, blamed the virus's spread on "overwhelmingly

Hispanic" workers and racial justice street protests. In Wisconsin, the Supreme Court's conservative chief justice, Patience Roggensack, argued that a spike in the pandemic was among meatpacking workers (mostly Latino), and not "the regular folks." During racial justice protests, Senator Tom Cotton, an Arkansas Republican, declared that there was no "structural racism" in law enforcement and called for the military to quash demonstrations.

And in Texas, the Republican Party chairs in several counties and the Texas agriculture commissioner shared postings on social media saying George Floyd, the unarmed Black man murdered by police in Minneapolis, was a "brutal criminal" who faked asphyxiation as part of a "staged event" to counter the "rising approval rating of President Trump"; placing a quote about justice from Rev. Martin Luther King Jr. over the image of a banana; and alleging that Soros was paying protesters in an attempt to "start the race war."

On and on it went:

A pro-Trump Republican U.S. Senate candidate in Missouri posted a statement saying he expects his wife to have dinner waiting for him each night and denouncing "nail-biting manophobic hell-bent feminist she devils who shriek."

A Republican state representative in Kansas alleged that marijuana was illegal because "the African Americans, they were basically users and they responded the worst off to those drugs."

A Trump appointee to AmeriCorps resigned after CNN uncovered his past remarks, saying "I just don't like Muslim people." A Trump appointee at Homeland Security resigned over comments linking Black people to "laziness" and "promiscuity."

Representative Mo Brooks, Republican of Alabama, said Obama and Democrats launched a "war on whites" and threatened to remove undocumented immigrants by doing "anything short of shooting them."

Representative Jeff Duncan, a South Carolina Republican, spoke of immigration policy as "allowing any kind of vagrant, or animal . . . to come in."

David Bossie, Trump's former deputy campaign manager, told a Black man on TV that "you're out of your cotton-picking mind." (Facing suspension, he apologized.)

The acting head of the Environmental Protection Agency, Andrew Wheeler, was found to have "liked" a 2013 social media post showing Barack Obama and Michelle Obama looking longingly at a banana held by a white hand.

Seth Grossman, the Republican nominee for a competitive House seat in New Jersey, was found on video saying that "the whole idea of diversity is a bunch of crap," that Kwanzaa was a "phony holiday" created by "Black racists," that Islam is a cancer, and that Black oppression was "exaggerated."

When Fox News executive Bill Shine was tapped for a Trump White House job, his wife's Twitter account, which contained tweets defending racists, was deleted.

In a special class was Giuliani. Years earlier, in 1992, he had led a mob of (white) off-duty New York police officers in a City Hall riot full of racist invective during his successful bid to oust the city's first Black mayor, David Dinkins. Now he was doing much the same on the national level.

Giuliani, the president's lawyer, retweeted a message calling George Soros, the Jewish American billionaire and a major funder of progressive causes, the "anti-Christ." He claimed that the Black Lives Matter movement, a response to police brutality, was "inherently racist" and "anti-American." He made the absurd claim that Black children have "a 99 percent chance" of killing each other. At the 2020 GOP convention, he said of racial justice protests: "BLM and antifa sprang into action and in a flash hijacked the protests into vicious, brutal riots." He countered the Black Lives Matter slogan by saying "All Lives Matter" and he alleged that Democrats would release prisoners and "go to war with the police." Joe Biden, Giuliani said, is "a Trojan horse with Bernie [Sanders], AOC [Alexandria Ocasio-Cortez], [Nancy] Pelosi, Black Lives Matter, and his party's entire left wing just waiting to execute their pro-criminal, anti-police socialist policies."

THE SHEER VOLUME OF Trump's bigotry was overwhelming. Other politicians might have been undone by uttering any one of his offensive statements. But the frequency of Trump's outrages against women, Black and Asian Americans, Latinos, Muslims, and Jews had a numbing effect. People lost their sense of outrage from repetition.

With distance, it's worth recalling just a few of his greatest hits.

He became famous for his depictions of women over the years: "fat pig," "dog," "slob," "disgusting animal," "bimbo," "piece of ass." He publicly imagined a woman giving him oral sex and spoke amorously of his daughter. During the campaign, he boasted publicly about his penis size and called Clinton "nasty woman" when she refused to sit silently during their debate and "disgusting" for taking a bathroom break during a debate. When Fox News's Megyn Kelly questioned him forcefully in a debate, he countered with an image of menstruation: "You could see there was blood coming out of her eyes, blood coming out of her wherever." Of Republican primary challenger Carly Fiorina, he said: "Look at that face! Would anyone vote for that?" When the *Access Hollywood* video emerged showing him boasting about sexually assaulting women ("grab 'em by the pussy," "when you're a star they let you do it"), he offered a rare apology—but later suggested the recording was a fake. When Michigan's governor, Gretchen Whitmer, criticized him, Trump called her that "woman governor" and "Half Whitmer."

Trump's oft-repeated campaign appeal to Black voters in 2016 went like this: "To the African American community, I say what the hell do you have to lose? You're living in poverty. Your schools are no good. You have no jobs. . . . You get shot walking to the store."

When Black football players took a knee during the national anthem to highlight racial injustice, Trump said they "shouldn't be in this country" and suggested NFL team owners should say "get that son of a bitch off the field." He mocked the intelligence of Black representative Maxine Waters, Black broadcaster Don Lemon, and Black basketball star LeBron James. He told the audience at one rally to "look at my African American over here."

He attacked Black lawmaker Elijah Cummings's Baltimore congressional district as "a disgusting, rat and rodent infested mess." He attacked Black lawmaker John Lewis's Atlanta congressional district as "in horrible shape and falling apart (not to mention crime infested)." He attacked "the Squad" of four Democratic congresswomen: two Black, one Latina, and one Palestinian American. Trump claimed they "originally came from countries whose governments are a complete and total catastrophe. Why don't they go back and help fix the totally broken and crime infested places from which they came?" Three of the four were born in the United States.

Trump's language inspired his supporters at one rally to chant "send her back!" in reference to Somali-born Representative Ilhan Omar, a Minnesota Democrat and one of the Squad foursome. Republican officials were quick to say the racist chant was "offensive," but they offered no criticism of Trump's similar words. In fact, Mitch McConnell said "the president is onto something" with his attack on the Squad. By contrast, Representative Justin Amash of Michigan, a conservative who quit the GOP in protest, said the "send her back" chant "is the inevitable consequence of President Trump's demagoguery."

In a private meeting with multiple witnesses, Trump said he wanted fewer Haitian immigrants (he claimed they "all have AIDS") and more Nordic ones. "Why are we having people from all these shithole countries come here?" he remarked, referring to African countries. But no worries. "I am the least racist person," Trump claimed, again and again. Trump famously kicked off his 2016 campaign with an attack on Mexican immigrants: "They're bringing drugs. They're bringing crime. They're rapists. And some, I assume, are good people." He campaigned on the nonsense claim that Mexico would pay for his border wall, and he closed his campaign warning about "bad hombres."

It worked in 2016—so in 2018 Trump declared that "many" immigrants are "stone-cold criminals," that certain immigrants are "animals" rather than people. He created a zero-tolerance border policy that led in 2018 to children being seized from their parents' arms and warehoused, often in chain link enclosures.

Trump then fabricated a border "emergency" by claiming an unstoppable "caravan" of criminals and gang members was headed through Mexico toward the U.S. border. He ordered troops to the border and said he thought they should be able to fire on unarmed people. The migrant caravan, destitute people on foot, largely dissolved before reaching the United States, and the few who remained went through normal processing. But that didn't stop Republican candidates, and Trump's GOP, from using race-baiting ads in the midterms. One showed a Mexican man who killed two police officers, accompanied by the message: "Democrats let him into our country. Democrats let him stay." The killer came to the United States during the presidency of George W. Bush.

Trump had dismissed Hurricane Maria, which devastated Puerto Rico, saying it wasn't "a real catastrophe like Katrina," and he claimed the death toll in the thousands had been falsified. He finally visited the island and tossed "beautiful, soft" paper towels at the desperate survivors ("they want everything to be done for them," he said of the Puerto Ricans).

Early in his presidential campaign, Trump used a fake accent and broken English to describe his dealings with Asian negotiators. As president, he made loops around his eyes with his fingers to mock the eyeglasses worn by a visiting delegation from China. Things took a more sinister turn when the Covid-19 pandemic spread. Trump referred to the contagion as the "Kung Flu" and the "China virus," and he darkly suggested that the World Health Organization, a "tool of China," conspired with China to hide the danger of the virus from the world: "I have a feeling they knew exactly what was going on." (Never mind that Trump had previously thanked China for "their efforts and transparency" and said "they're doing a very good job" with the virus.)

Trump asked a Texas-born Asian American at one event: "Are you from South Korea?" He also mocked those with Indian accents, including imitating India's prime minister, Narendra Modi. Trump managed to antagonize American Indians, too, with his mockery of Senator Elizabeth Warren's claim of Native American ancestry. He called her "Pocahontas" and, with a reference to the Trail of Tears forced Indian relocation, tweeted: "See you on the campaign TRAIL, Liz!"

Nobody suffered more of Trump's bigotry than Muslims. "Donald J. Trump is calling for a total and complete shutdown of Muslims entering the United States until our country's representatives can figure out what is going on," his campaign announced in December 2015. His website touted a policy of "PREVENTING

MUSLIM IMMIGRATION." Trump lawyer Rudy Giuliani said Trump asked him to take the "Muslim ban" and "show me the right way to do it legally." The son of national security adviser Michael Flynn praised the "Muslim ban" on Twitter.

As president, Trump retweeted anti-Muslim videos. After a Muslim American man killed forty-nine in an Orlando gay nightclub, Trump claimed "thousands of shooters like this" in the American Muslim community, hidden by their coreligionists, were prepared to do the same and speculated that the trouble could be "in their religion." He suggested that Omar, who is Muslim, was one of the members of Congress who "hate our country."

During the campaign, Trump tweeted and retweeted messages from neo-Nazis and appeared on their radio shows. After an October 13 speech in which Trump warned that Hillary Clinton "meets in secret with international banks to plot the destruction of U.S. sovereignty" and that "a global power structure" is conspiring against ordinary Americans, the Anti-Defamation League urged Trump to "avoid rhetoric and tropes that historically have been used against Jews." Trump's response? He issued a closing ad for his campaign repeating offending lines from that speech, this time illustrated with images of prominent Jews: financier George Soros (accompanying the words "those who control the levers of power"), Federal Reserve chair Janet Yellen (with the words "global special interests"), and Goldman Sachs CEO Lloyd Blankfein (following the "global power structure" quote).

Trump also spoke of "blood suckers" who backed international trade. Asked to call off supporters who were increasingly threatening violence against a Jewish journalist, Trump said "I don't have a message" for them.

Once Trump became president, his White House excised any mention of Jews from a statement on the Holocaust. Trump claimed that Jews who vote Democratic (nearly 80 percent of them) have "a total lack of knowledge or great disloyalty"—reviving the anti-Semitic dual-loyalty slander.

AFTER TRUMP'S 2016 WIN, prominent white supremacists exulted. David Duke boasted that "our people have played a HUGE role in electing Trump" and the head of the neo-Nazi site Daily Stormer bragged that "we did this." They saw the appointment of Steve Bannon as top Trump strategist as evidence that Trump would be repaying the debt.

"We have a psychic connection, or you can say a deeper connection, with Donald Trump in a way that we simply do not have with most Republicans," Richard Spencer told *The New York Times* at the time. "We've crossed the Rubicon in terms of recognition" for white nationalists. "America was, until this last generation, a white country designed for ourselves and our posterity. It is our creation, it is our inheritance, and it belongs to us."

Politico quoted Spencer saying the alt-right was "a head without a body" and "the Trump movement was a body without a head." Now, "I think, moving forward, the alt-right can, as an intellectual vanguard, complete Trump." And the *Los Angeles Times* quoted Spencer saying that Trump's election was an "awakening" and that "we're not quite the establishment now, but I think we should start acting like it."

Trump earned praise from Spencer, David Duke, and the neo-Nazi Daily Stormer for his talk about Charlottesville and "shithole" countries and a border wall. He flew to Nashville to visit the tomb of Andrew Jackson and took up the campaign to prevent Harriet Tubman from replacing the man nicknamed "Indian killer" on the $20 bill. The Daily Stormer, which now proclaimed itself "the new face of the Republican Party," called it "fitting" for Trump to honor this "White supremacist extremist."

Trump also embraced the language of white supremacists in talking about immigrants "breeding" like insects. Trump appointee Carl Higbie resigned from his post at AmeriCorps after the publishing of his earlier complaints that Black women think "breeding is a form of government employment." Spencer's National Policy Institute had warned of white "displacement by the subject race through differential fertility rates and interracial breeding." Alex Jones's *InfoWars,* which Trump touted, had published headlines saying things such as "Top Imam: Muslim Migrants Should Breed with Europeans to 'Conquer Their Countries.'"

Trump further tugged the heartstrings of white nationalists with his vows to preserve Confederate symbols as part of "our proud American heritage." He claimed that the "culture of our great country [was] being ripped apart with the removal of our beautiful statues" of Confederate heroes (the statues had been erected long after the Civil War as symbols of resilient white power). Trump held an event at the White House to highlight murders committed by illegal immigrants, and participants used the forum to direct people to a website touting white nationalist claims of "genocide" and a "Holocaust" being perpetrated against white Americans, and a convoluted conspiracy theory about attempts to lure "new citizens for the country to replace us, the American people."

Trump stocked his administration with white nationalists and their allies. The chief White House economic adviser hosted a publisher of white nationalists. A White House speechwriter participated in a white nationalist conference. A homeland security adviser exchanged emails with white nationalists using Nazi terminology.

All over the country, white supremacists crawled out of the cracks. A candidate with ties to white nationalists became the 2018 GOP Senate nominee in Virginia (with Trump's endorsement). In California, the Republican facing Democratic representative Mark DeSaulnier, John Fitzgerald, had appeared on neo-Nazi podcasts, claimed the Holocaust is a lie, and alleged an international Jewish conspiracy. In Illinois, a Republican congressional nominee, Arthur Jones, had a campaign website that mixed anti-Semitic propaganda and support for Trump, and had pictures of him speaking at a neo-Nazi rally for Trump in 2016 and making a Nazi salute with other "White patriots." Russell Walker, Republican nominee for a North Carolina State House seat, was a white supremacist whose personal website was "littered with the n-word" and stated that Jews are "satanic," Vox reported. Running in the Republican primary for Speaker Paul Ryan's congressional seat in Wisconsin was Paul Nehlen, who called himself "pro-White" and was booted from Twitter for racism. A town manager in Maine was ousted for promoting racial segregation and "pro-White" views. Neo-Nazi Patrick Little ran as a Republican in the California Senate primary, blaming his loss on fraud by "Jewish supremacists," according to the website Right Wing Watch.

When House Democrats held a hearing in 2019 on the rise of

white nationalism, Republicans invited as their witness Candace Owens, a woman Richard Spencer called "the last stand of implicit White identity," and who inspired the man who massacred Muslims at a New Zealand mosque, according to the killer. Trump retweeted a TV clip in which one of his allies, Representative Matt Gaetz of Florida, accused the left of "cultural genocide," an echo of white nationalists' claims of "white genocide." Trump tweeted (and deleted, but never disavowed) a video in which a man shouts "White power." He threatened to veto a defense bill if it removed the names of Confederate generals from U.S. military bases. Facebook took down Trump campaign ads because they used a Nazi symbol. Trump attacked NASCAR for banning the Confederate flag.

White supremacy was out in the open, and it didn't retreat to the shadows after Trump's presidency. The proposed America First Caucus in the House, devoted to honoring "Anglo Saxon political traditions," never got off the ground (founders got cold feet), but Republican legislators in Tennessee and Colorado spoke favorably of the three-fifths compromise that counted Black Americans as less than whole people. A well-known white nationalist and Holocaust denier who favored segregation arranged a fundraiser for Representative Paul Gosar, an Arizona Republican. The invitation said the fundraiser, by the group America First, was "authorized by Gosar for Congress Committee," and Gosar appeared to confirm its authenticity in a tweet: "Not sure why anyone is freaking out. I'll say this: there are millions of Gen Z, Y and X conservatives. They believe in America First." (Gosar had appeared at a gathering of the same group previously and stood by as the same white nationalist bemoaned the loss of America's "White demographic core.") Gosar later claimed, vaguely, that "there's no fundraiser scheduled on Friday" (the invitation said the date hadn't yet been determined).

And Republicans everywhere concocted a new, race-based attack against a fictitious menace. The supposed danger was critical race theory, an academic theory that examines the origins and structure of racism. But Republicans claimed it was a direct threat to white people. It holds that "the United States is rotten to its core," Senator Josh Hawley, a Missouri Republican who encouraged the January 6 insurrectionists, alleged. "In our American flag, they see propaganda, and in our family businesses, they see White supremacy. . . . They pit Whiteness and Blackness against each other in a manner that reduces every American, no matter their character or creed, to their racial identity alone."

Claiming, with zero evidence, that it was the "animating ideology" of the Biden administration, Hawley asserted that the ideology holds "that subjects like mathematics are inherently racist, that the Christian faith is oppressive," and "that the nuclear family perpetuates racism."

The white nationalists had a new slogan! In state legislatures and school board meetings in red states across the country, they mobilized against a new, phantom threat to the white race. It got bad enough that in September 2021, the National School Boards Association asked for assistance from the Justice Department and the FBI to protect the safety of school board members against sometimes violent protesters opposing Covid-19 safety protocols and the supposed critical race theory threat.

Thanks to overtures by Trump, amplification by Fox News, and quiescence of leaders of the Republican Party, the "very fine people" of Charlottesville 2017 were now very much in the GOP mainstream. Republicans had allowed themselves to become the party of white nationalism—and put themselves on a collision course with democracy and civil society.

CHAPTER 15

Sabotage

President Volodymyr Zelensky, the reformist leader of Ukraine, had reason to panic.

Weeks earlier, President Trump had suddenly and without explanation put a hold on $400 million in security assistance Ukraine desperately needed to keep invading Russian forces at bay. The new Ukrainian president was also desperate for the international validation of an official White House meeting, which Trump had dangled but delayed.

On the morning of July 25, 2019, Trump made it all perfectly clear to Zelensky: he was being shaken down.

"The United States has been very, very good to Ukraine," Trump told him by phone from the White House residence. "I wouldn't say that it's reciprocal necessarily because things are happening that are not good."

You got such a nice country. Shame if something happened to it.

Zelensky thanked Trump for the military support and said he wanted to buy more Javelin antitank missiles.

"I would like you to do us a favor though," Trump responded. He then referred to a debunked right-wing conspiracy theory holding that a Democratic National Committee server was in Ukraine, part of a false Russian propaganda claim that Ukraine interfered in the 2016 election to help Hillary Clinton, not Russia, to help Trump.

The desperate Zelensky promised to do as Trump demanded,

offering to work with Trump's designated dirt digger, Rudy Giuliani. "We will meet once he comes to Ukraine," the desperate president promised.

Trump moved on to the second part of his shakedown: getting Zelensky to announce an investigation into Hunter Biden, the son of Trump's likely Democratic opponent, Joe Biden, and the involvement of both men with a Ukrainian company, Burisma. "There's a lot of talk about Biden's son," Trump said. "Biden went around bragging that he stopped the prosecution [of Burisma] so if you can look into it. It sounds horrible to me."

Zelensky voiced the words that Trump aides, before the call, had coached him to say: "I . . . ensure you that we will be very serious about the case and will work on the investigation."

Trump, then dangling the prospect of a White House visit, told the Ukrainian: "I will tell Rudy and Attorney General [Bill] Barr to call."

It was a breathtaking abuse of power. The president of the United States withheld congressionally approved military aid from an ally under Russian invasion to force that ally to assist Trump's reelection campaign by announcing investigations into Trump's likely opponent and the Democratic Party. As details dribbled out, it only got worse.

Trump removed the anticorruption ambassador to Ukraine, Marie Yovanovitch (he vowed darkly to Zelensky that "she's going to go through some things"), so that she wouldn't interfere with the efforts by Giuliani and his colleagues to manipulate Ukraine's government to Trump's political advantage. She was publicly defamed by Sean Hannity and other Trump allies and was led to believe her personal safety was in jeopardy.

Trump's own national security adviser, John Bolton, called the arrangement a "drug deal" and Giuliani "a hand grenade who's going to blow everybody up." Trump sidelined the State Department and its diplomatic corps—even telling the ambassador to the European Union and the special representative for Ukraine negotiations that they had to "talk to Rudy" to get their marching orders.

Once exposed, Trump and his defenders went to extraordinary lengths to slander and punish the diplomats, civil servants, and military officers in the U.S. government who revealed what had happened. He refused to comply with an impeachment investigation launched by the House, ignoring or defying subpoenas for documents and witnesses and ordering others to do the same. "I have an Article II, where I have the right to do whatever I want as president," was Trump's misreading of the Constitution. And Republicans in the House and the Senate supported his efforts to vitiate Congress's constitutional powers. The lone House Republican who condemned Trump, Representative Justin Amash of Michigan, was driven from the party.

In the Senate trial, the lead impeachment manager, Adam Schiff, spoke passionately—and presciently: "We must say enough—enough! He has betrayed our national security, and he will do so again. He has compromised our elections, and he will do so again. You will not change him. You cannot constrain him. He is who he is. Truth matters little to him. What's right matters even less, and decency matters not at all."

In all the Senate, only one Republican had the integrity to say "enough."

I was one of the few in the gallery when Senator Mitt Romney of Utah, the 2012 Republican presidential nominee, took the floor at 2 p.m. on February 5, 2020, after the closing arguments in Trump's trial. "I swore an oath before God to exercise impartial justice," Romney said to a nearly empty chamber. "I am profoundly religious. My faith is at the heart of who I am." Then Romney, on the verge of tears, paused for a full twelve seconds to pull himself together. This was no ordinary speech. Reporters stampeded into the gallery.

"The grave question the Constitution tasks senators to answer is whether the president committed an act so extreme and egregious that it rises to the level of a high crime and misdemeanor. Yes, he did."

There were gasps in the chamber. "It was a flagrant assault on our electoral rights, our national security and our fundamental values," Romney went on. "The president is guilty of an appalling abuse of public trust."

At that moment, he was the last Republican in Congress to recognize that there was an obligation greater than partisanship. Romney said he received pressure to "stand with the team." He said he would "hear abuse from the president." But, he said, "were I to ignore the evidence . . . for the sake of a partisan end, it would, I fear, expose my character to history's rebuke and the censure of my own conscience."

Romney's speech had noble echoes of Margaret Chase Smith's heroic 1950 "Declaration of Conscience" against the demagoguery of Joe McCarthy and her "Four Horsemen of Calumny" speech. "We are Republicans. But we are Americans first," the Maine Republican said. Smith got six Republican senators to join in her condemnation of McCarthy's "selfish political exploitation," beginning the long march toward McCarthy's censure in 1954.

But this time, nobody joined Romney's declaration of conscience. Trump had abused his office for personal, political gain, compromised national security, shaken down an embattled ally, corrupted the Justice Department, sidelined the State Department and the Defense Department, and thumbed his nose at Congress. And only one Republican senator had the moral fiber to object.

Eleven months almost to the day before Trump would attempt a coup to overturn his reelection defeat, Schiff had asked the senators: "What are the odds if left in office that he will continue trying to cheat? I will tell you: 100 percent. A man without character or ethical compass will never find his way."

Trump wasn't the only one without character or ethical compass. With their votes to acquit, congressional Republicans showed that the entire party had lost its way.

DURING THE IMPEACHMENT HEARINGS, Yovanovitch, who braved gunfire in Moscow, the violence of Somalia's civil war, an attack on the U.S. embassy in Uzbekistan, and ten trips to the front line of Ukraine's war with Russia before Trump unceremoniously ousted her, asked lawmakers how they could accept the horrors that had been committed. "How could our system fail like this?" she asked. "How is it that foreign corrupt interests could manipulate our government? . . . Such conduct undermines the U.S., exposes our friends and widens the playing field for autocrats like President Putin."

How? Because Republicans put party before country. They were sworn to support and defend the Constitution. But instead they used their power to sabotage the institutions and structures of American government—for the advancement of Trump's short-term interests. Republicans defended Trump through the *Access Hollywood* tapes and the Stormy Daniels scandal (in which he paid hush money to a porn actress alleging an affair). They abandoned principles and acquiesced to his military pullout from Syria, his inexplicable solicitude toward Moscow, his blunderbuss trade wars, and his phony "emergencies" that usurped congressional power. Now they were acquiescing to compromising national security in the name of partisanship.

The framers assumed that a man such as Trump would never be elected president. "Talents for low intrigue and the little arts of popularity may alone suffice to elevate a man" to low office, it says in Federalist Paper No. 68, "but it will require other talents and a different kind of merit to . . . make him a successful candidate for the distinguished office of president of the United States. It will not be too strong to say, that there will be a constant probability of seeing the station filled by characters preeminent for ability and virtue."

Alexander Hamilton never met Donald Trump.

The founders had been inspired by the philosophy of Baron de Montesquieu, who wrote about the centrality of character to democracy. "Not much probity is needed for maintaining or sustaining a monarchical government or a despotic government," he wrote. "But in a popular state, one more recourse is necessary, which is virtue."

The Ukraine scandal was unusual in that it laid waste to so many democratic institutions all at once. But the assaults were, by then, routine. Sometimes it was through cunning. Other times, mere bumbling. But the effect was a sustained, four-year attack on the foundation of democracy. Again and again, Trump and his enablers managed to break the rules, written and unwritten, under which American democracy had functioned for generations. Missing was any sense of character, of probity, of virtue.

He pressured Israel not to allow two Democratic members of Congress to enter the country. He threatened to cut off highway funds, disaster aid, and later pandemic relief to states governed by Democrats and claimed the "absolute" right to relocate criminals to jurisdictions governed by Democrats. He unilaterally "ordered" U.S. businesses to pursue disinvestment from China. And he assaulted Americans' sense of decorum and decency: he publicly labeled Ted Cruz a "pussy," promised to "bomb the shit out of ISIS," and as president made "bullshit," "motherfucker," "ass," and "son of a bitch" all part of the presidential vocabulary.

In the process, he hacked away at all the institutions that protected us as a people. And Republicans facilitated the sabotage.

JUST WEEKS ON THE job, Trump upended alliances that had kept order in the world since the Second World War. He called NATO "obsolete" and threatened to abandon the alliance and go his "own way." He chewed out the prime minister of Australia and cut off their phone call. At a gathering of world leaders, he physically shoved the prime minister of Montenegro. Trump announced that he wanted to buy Greenland from Denmark, and when the Danish prime minister understandably called the idea "absurd," Trump canceled a visit to Copenhagen and called the prime minister "nasty."

In no particular order, he insulted the leaders of Britain, Germany, France, Belgium, Canada, and the European Union. He shared sensitive Israeli intelligence with Russia. He falsely accused South Africa (a "crime-ridden mess") of "large scale killing" of white farmers. He told a crowd that there had been immigrant violence "last night in Sweden." (Swedes reported no such thing.) He threatened North Korea's dictator on Twitter with his "bigger & more powerful" nuclear button (the two later "fell in love," Trump said). Speaking at the United Nations, he boasted that "my administration has accomplished more than almost any administration in the history of our country." The assembled world leaders laughed at him.

Occasionally, congressional Republicans protested Trump's crockery smashing. But Republicans had already set a precedent for partisan sabotage of foreign affairs. When the Obama administration negotiated a nuclear agreement with Iran and European allies, House Speaker John Boehner invited Israeli prime minister Benjamin Netanyahu to criticize the deal before a joint session of Congress (Obama wasn't consulted), and forty-seven Republican senators wrote directly to Iran's leaders warning that Republicans opposed the agreement and would try to undo it.

Visiting France, Trump canceled a trip to visit a World War I U.S. military cemetery at the place where two thousand U.S. Marines died—because it was raining. Two days later, he skipped a Veterans Day visit to Arlington National Cemetery—because he was "extremely busy." Later, he did visit a U.S. military cemetery in France—and used the gravestones of the fallen as the backdrop for a TV interview in which he attacked Democrats.

Trump famously suggested Vietnam POW John McCain was a "loser" and resisted lowering flags when he died. According to *The Atlantic* magazine, Trump described fallen soldiers as "losers" and "suckers," labeled U.S. generals warmongers, and recoiled at the idea of seeing wounded veterans in a military parade. Trump claimed that "I know more about ISIS than the generals do." He likewise disparaged U.S. intelligence agencies for their "bad decisions" and accused them of acting like Nazis. Standing with Vladimir Putin in Helsinki, he accepted Putin's denials over the U.S. intelligence community's findings that Russia was the country that interfered in the 2016 elections: "I don't see any reason why it would be."

Trump squabbled with the Gold Star parents of a U.S. soldier killed in Iraq because they criticized him at the Democratic convention in 2016. He intervened to defend a Navy SEAL convicted of a war crime—and forced the Navy secretary to resign when the secretary objected to Trump's threat to "good order and discipline."

When judges struck down his first attempt at a travel ban from certain Muslim countries, Trump lashed out at one of them, a George W. Bush appointee, as a "so-called judge" and said to "blame him" if "something happens." The next year, when a judge struck down a Trump attempt to dismiss asylum claims, Trump called the decision "a disgrace" and the judge "an Obama judge."

Trump pardoned Joe Arpaio, the Arizona sheriff imprisoned for ignoring a court order. He told aides they could seize private land and ignore environmental regulations as they built a southern border wall, offering to pardon any of them who were convicted of crimes.

Just three months into the job, Trump fired FBI director James Comey for refusing to drop the investigation into Russia's election interference. It had echoes of Richard Nixon's "Saturday Night Massacre," when Nixon ousted the Watergate prosecutor, setting off resignations and outrage. But this time, Republicans lined up behind Trump. McConnell, on the Senate floor the next day, defended the firing.

Trump claimed the FBI's "reputation is in tatters—worst in history" and that special prosecutor Robert Mueller's Russia probe was "rigged," "phony," "dishonest," and a partisan "witch hunt." He declared those investigating him guilty of "treason."

Republicans in Congress supported and amplified Trump's baseless claims, alleging an "anti-Trump bias" at the FBI and threatening to hold Comey's (Trump-appointed) successor, Christopher Wray, in contempt of Congress.

Disregarding the congressional power of the purse, Trump raided the Pentagon budget to finance his border wall. He stocked his administration with "acting" officials in key positions to avoid Senate confirmation and to escape its advice-and-consent powers. Congressional Republicans supported the White House's defiance, and McConnell vowed to be in "total coordination" with the White House during Trump's first impeachment trial so there would be "no difference between the president's position and our position."

After a campaign in which Trump cynically vowed to "drain the swamp" of political corruption in Washington, he used his presidency to funnel millions of taxpayer dollars to his own businesses, pressured federal agencies and international organizations to do business with his personal enterprises, invited foreign governments to pay millions of dollars to his businesses, and ran out the clock on releasing his tax returns, which would have revealed conflicts of interest.

He routinely traveled as president to his properties in Ireland, Scotland, Virginia, New Jersey, and Florida, and encouraged other officials to do the same, channeling his businesses a fortune in taxpayer dollars from the Secret Service and others. When it was the

United States' turn to host the G-7 meeting, he tried to hold it at his Doral golf resort in Miami. The Chinese government fast-tracked trademarks for presidential daughter Ivanka Trump's businesses. Presidential son-in-law Jared Kushner invited investors and creditors to the White House that later provided funds to his family businesses.

The self-dealing was contagious. Steve Bannon, who had been Trump's top strategist, was arrested aboard a Chinese billionaire's yacht for defrauding donors to a private effort to build Trump's wall on the Mexican border. Trump pardoned him. EPA administrator Scott Pruitt got a sweetheart deal from a lobbyist on a condo rental, had a $43,000 soundproof phone booth built in his office, had his security detail use lights and sirens to take him to social events, dispatched the same security detail to fetch him scented lotion from Ritz-Carlton hotels, and used his office to get seats at the Rose Bowl, take his family to Disneyland, and try to get his wife a Chick-fil-A franchise.

Interior Secretary Ryan Zinke spent tens of thousands of taxpayer dollars on private flights, commissioned a commemorative coin with his name on it, and assigned a staffer to hoist a special flag whenever he entered agency headquarters.

Trump and his appointees used the federal government as Trump's personal property. The Justice Department intervened in a defamation lawsuit against Trump brought by a woman claiming Trump raped her years earlier. DOJ claimed Trump was "acting within the scope of his office as President" when he denied the assault. During the pandemic, Trump gave his friends (Chris Christie, Ben Carson, Giuliani) lifesaving antibody cocktails unavailable to the public. Trump used the White House itself to stage the 2020 Republican National Convention, and Secretary of State Mike Pompeo used an official trip to Israel as a backdrop for his convention speech.

Newt Gingrich advised Trump simply to ignore laws against using public office for personal enrichment, suggesting on NPR that Trump say "I pardon them if anybody finds them to have behaved against the rules." Trump did pardon many, but he had other methods, too. He fired the State Department's inspector general who was looking into possible improprieties by Pompeo.

He replaced the acting inspector general at the Transportation Department who was investigating allegations of favoritism by transportation secretary Elaine Chao benefiting her husband, Senate GOP Leader McConnell.

By the end of Trump's term, his former campaign chairman, personal lawyer, national security adviser, chief strategist, and at least six other close aides were arrested or convicted.

Presidential counselor Kellyanne Conway was found by the Office of Special Counsel to have violated the Hatch Act (which forbids government employees from using their positions for partisan activism) thirteen times. In eight years of the Obama administration, only two violations were found—by all officials, combined.

Congressional Republicans and conservative leaders took ethical cues from the Trump administration. Wayne LaPierre, head of the National Rifle Association, filed for bankruptcy protection for the gun group after New York's attorney general filed suit accusing NRA leadership of taking tens of millions of dollars from the organization for trips to the Bahamas, private jets, and other personal use. Jerry Falwell Jr. resigned as president of the evangelical college Liberty University, which he had used as a forum to vouch for Trump's moral integrity and religious bona fides, after acknowledging a multiyear affair in which he was accused of watching his wife have sex with a pool boy.

Representative Duncan Hunter, a California Republican and co-chairman of the Trump caucus in the House, was convicted and sentenced to prison for using campaign funds for private school tuition, jewelry, vacations, and more. Trump pardoned him. Representative Chris Collins, a New York Republican, was sentenced to twenty-six months in prison on charges related to insider trading—from the White House lawn. Trump pardoned him, too.

Senator Richard Burr, a North Carolina Republican, dumped stock a day after senators were scheduled to receive a private briefing on the coming pandemic. Five other Republican senators and a Democrat were linked to similarly suspicious trades.

Representative Blake Farenthold, a Texas Republican, resigned over his use of public funds to settle a sexual harassment lawsuit. Representative Pat Meehan, a Pennsylvania Republican, resigned after word got out of a sexual harassment settlement with a staffer the married congressman called his "soul mate." Representative Tim Murphy, another Pennsylvania Republican, resigned over allegations that he urged his mistress to seek an abortion. Arizona Republican representative Trent Franks resigned when a former aide alleged that he offered her $5 million to have his child as a surrogate. And Representative Jim Jordan of Ohio, a chief Trump defender, battled allegations by seven former Ohio State wrestlers that he turned a blind eye to sexual misconduct when serving as a coach.

Then there was McConnell. As Trump protected Elaine Chao by removing the person investigating her, her husband, McConnell, protected Trump by repeatedly blocking bipartisan attempts to build up U.S. election systems to avoid a repeat of the 2016 Russian interference that had benefited Trump's campaign. This earned him the nickname "Moscow Mitch" from MSNBC's Joe Scarborough, and I called him a "Russian asset"—not a spy or traitor, but of great help to Moscow. McConnell flew into a rage on the Senate floor, denouncing this "McCarthyism."

His umbrage might have been more persuasive if he hadn't used his power to block sanctions against a Russian oligarch with close ties to Putin; three months later, a Russian aluminum giant owned in part by the oligarch announced a $200 million investment in McConnell's Kentucky. "Completely unrelated," McConnell claimed. Naturally.

Trump also undermined the government's capacity to function. Just fifteen months into the Trump presidency, 61 percent of the appointees who began with Trump on day one had already departed, *The Washington Post* calculated. A quarter of his core cabinet members were gone. He was on his third national security adviser. After two years in the White House, he was on his fifth deputy national security adviser and Health and Human Services secretary and his third attorney general and his second secretary of state, defense secretary, and press secretary.

By October 2020, turnover had reached 90 percent among cabinet and top White House staff, the Brookings Institution calculated. He was on his fourth chief of staff, fourth press secretary, sixth communications director, and fourth national security adviser.

With the more reputable figures disinclined to associate themselves with Trump's mayhem, he staffed his administration with exotic characters and personal friends. In an echo of George W. Bush's appointment of "Brownie" at FEMA and nomination of Harriet Miers to the Supreme Court, Trump, after sacking his first attorney general, installed Matthew Whitaker, who previously hawked hot tub seats for a business that shut down after reaching a $26 million settlement for defrauding customers. Dan Scavino, Trump's onetime golf caddie, became White House director of social media. Hope Hicks, a former model who helped with Ivanka's fashion line, became White House communications director. Keith Schiller, Trump's former bodyguard, became head of Oval Office operations. Lynne Patton, who among other things planned Eric Trump's wedding, became a senior official at the Department of Housing and Urban Development.

Robin Bernstein, Trump friend and a founding member of Trump's Mar-a-Lago, was named ambassador to the Dominican Republic, even though she spoke only "basic" Spanish. Trump tapped Sam Clovis to be chief scientist at the Agriculture Department, even though he was not a scientist but a talk show host. Trump named the former manager of a Meineke Car Care branch to be assistant to the secretary of energy for energy efficiency and renewable energy. He also named a country club "cabana attendant" and a scented-candle developer to be confidential assistants at the Agriculture Department.

A leaked memo from the British ambassador to Washington, Kim Darroch, observed: "We don't really believe this administration is going to become substantially more normal; less dysfunctional; less unpredictable; less faction riven; less diplomatically clumsy and inept." He was forced to resign.

One hire, of businessman Anthony Scaramucci to be White House communications director, was so bad that Scaramucci had to be fired ten days later—sixteen days before his formal start date. Among other things, "Mooch" accused White House staff chief Reince Priebus of a felony and of being a paranoid schizophrenic, and he launched into a profanity-laced tirade about his White House colleagues with *The New Yorker*'s Ryan Lizza.

In private, or after quitting or being fired, Trump advisers routinely badmouthed the boss. Secretary of State Rex Tillerson never quite denied calling Trump a "moron." Preibus told author Chris Whipple to "take everything you've heard" about chaos in the White House "and multiply it by 50." In Bob Woodward's account, Defense Secretary Jim Mattis said Trump had the understanding of "a fifth- or sixth-grader," National Economic Council chief Gary Cohn described him as a "professional liar," lawyer John Dowd told the president that he was "not really capable" of answering a prosecutor's questions, and White House chief of staff John Kelly called him an "idiot." But not one of them had the courage to say so, publicly, in real time.

THE CONSTITUTION REQUIRES THE chief justice to preside over the impeachment trial of a sitting president. So it was entirely fitting that John Roberts was forced to sit in the Senate presiding officer's chair, day after day, witnessing with his own eyes the mess he and his colleagues on the Supreme Court had made of the U.S. political system. The living consequences of the Roberts Court's decisions, and their corrosive effect on the functioning of American democracy, were plain to see.

Ten years to the day before Trump's impeachment trial began, the Supreme Court had released its *Citizens United* decision, plunging the country into the era of super PACs and unlimited, unregulated, secret campaign money from billionaires and foreign interests. *Citizens United,* and the resulting rise of the super PAC, led directly to this impeachment: Lev Parnas and Igor Fruman, the two convicted Giuliani associates at the center of the scandal (they conspired with a corrupt Ukrainian official to oust Marie Yovanovitch and they attempted to force Ukraine's president to announce investigations into Biden and the Democrats), first got to know Trump officials by funneling massive contributions, some of disguised origins, to the president's super PAC.

The Roberts Court's decisions led to this moment in indirect ways, as well. Fourteen states had new voting restrictions in place for the first time in the 2016 election (and twenty had done so since 2010), including strict photo ID requirements, cutbacks in early voting, and new restrictions on registration, all designed by Republican legislatures to reduce the Democratic vote. The Leadership Conference Education Fund, a civil rights group, found that counties previously covered by the Voting Rights Act because of past abuses had now closed down at least 868 polling places, disproportionately in minority communities. Purges of voting rolls disenfranchised countless more eligible voters. Zoltan Hajnal, a University of California at San Diego political scientist, estimated that millions of would-be voters had been deterred. It's entirely possible that there never would have been a President Trump without the Supreme Court's assault on voting rights.

The High Court's decision in 2014's *McCutcheon v. Federal Election Commission* further surrendered campaign finance to the wealthiest. The court had come to equate money with free speech (by letting candidates and then contributors spend unlimited sums), making it so that the more wealth and wealthy friends a candidate had, the more "speech" he got. And Trump had a lot of both.

The combined effect of the campaign finance rulings was to eliminate the traditional culling of candidates in a "money primary," in which poorly performing candidates saw their fundraising dry up and had to drop out of the race. But the money primary no longer applied, because a large number of nonviable candidates were artificially kept in the race by a beneficent billionaire, or even a friendly multimillionaire or two, who contributed to super PACS. Fifteen White House hopefuls had super PACS operating in their name, insulating them from pressure to drop out. The practical effect was to prevent Republicans from rallying behind one alternative to Trump.

Republicans, with no way to push weak candidates from the race, watched as Trump mowed down rivals, one at a time. He was the Frankenstein monster created by the Roberts Court's campaign finance system in which money trumps all.

Other decisions played a role, too. The Supreme Court's 2018 *Janus* decision hobbled the ability of labor unions to counter wealthy donors, while the 2019 *Rucho v. Common Cause* ruling blessed partisan gerrymandering, expanding antidemocratic tendencies. Conservative justices didn't even try to conceal their partisan motives. Justice Samuel Alito wanted to approve partisan gerrymandering in Wisconsin, where it allowed Republicans to hold more than 60 percent of the state assembly while getting less than half the vote. So he ambushed the lawyer arguing against the Wisconsin plan with the last question of the argument, telling him that "the seminal article by your expert" found that the partisan benefits "are small and decay rapidly."

What Alito said was categorically false. I spoke with the expert he cited, and he told me Alito had referred to the wrong study, one that was two decades out of date. But the lie had been planted. And the decision ultimately blessed partisan gerrymandering.

The cumulative consequence of these decisions: falling confidence in government, and a growing perception that Washington had become a "swamp" corrupted by political money, which fueled Trump's victory. The Republican Party could stop neither Trump's hostile takeover of the party nor the takeover of the congressional GOP ranks by far-right candidates. The Center for Responsive Politics, a watchdog group, found in 2018 that House Republicans in the most competitive seats got almost all their campaign funds from large contributors (often people who donate $2,700 or $5,400) and political action committees. Only a tiny fraction of funds came from those who give $200 or less. (Democrats got twice as much of their contributions from small donors.) The financial might of extreme outside groups and donors led lawmakers on both sides, but particularly Republicans, to give their patrons what they wanted: partisan conflict over collaboration and ideological purity at the cost of a functioning government.

Roberts had been warned about this sort of thing. The late Justice John Paul Stevens, in his *Citizens United* dissent, wrote: "Americans may be forgiven if they do not feel the Court has advanced the cause of self-government today."

Justice Stephen Breyer, in his *McCutcheon* dissent, warned that the campaign finance system post–*Citizens United* would be "incapable of dealing with the grave problems of democratic legitimacy." After the Ukraine shakedown, America faced a crisis of democratic legitimacy: a president who had plainly abused his office and broken the law, a legislature too paralyzed to do anything about it—and a chief justice coming face-to-face with the system he broke.

Republicans in Congress recognized that the Supreme Court was insulating their power from the public will. That's why Senate Majority Leader Mitch McConnell effectively stole a Supreme Court seat by refusing for nearly a year to consider Obama's eminently qualified nominee, Merrick Garland. That's why McConnell used the nuclear option to abolish the filibuster after Trump's election so Republicans could quickly elevate Neil Gorsuch to the seat that rightfully should have gone to Garland. That's why, in an act of breathtaking hypocrisy, he rushed through the confirmation of Amy Coney Barrett in just days at the end of Trump's term after Ruth Bader Ginsburg's death. And that's why Republicans, in between those two events, waged an all-out fight to confirm Brett Kavanaugh despite credible accusations of sexual misconduct. Kavanaugh isn't the most ideological justice on the bench, but he's hands down the most partisan.

Even without the Supreme Court's help, congressional Republicans had been undermining their own institution long before Trump arrived. Well before Trump, the Republican congressional caucus had become ungovernable. Six months into Republicans' unified control of Congress in 2015, John Boehner was already facing a "motion to vacate the chair"—essentially, a vote of no confidence—from his own caucus. He survived that, but he was finding it impossible to lead. Boehner tried just about everything to placate the hard right, even agreeing to create a select committee to investigate Planned Parenthood, despite the fact that three committees were already investigating the group and the chairman of one of the committees said he had no evidence that the group broke the law.

In late September 2015, Boehner announced that he would retire. After four and a half years in misery, perpetually badmouthed and badgered by the Freedom Caucus and other conservative malcontents, he announced his retirement singing "Zip-A-Dee-Doo-Dah." Eric Cantor would have replaced Boehner, but he had already been ousted in a primary by a more extreme version of himself. House Majority Leader Kevin McCarthy wanted the job but withdrew because conservatives rebelled against him.

Reluctantly, House Ways and Means Committee chairman Paul Ryan, Mitt Romney's 2012 running mate, agreed to take the job. He opened with an optimistic message of bipartisanship, telling lawmakers "we are all in the same boat." But the craft immediately took on water—and just two and a half years later, Ryan announced that he was abandoning ship.

At the other end of Pennsylvania Avenue, Trump was disengaged from what happened on Capitol Hill, and he contributed mixed signals, confusion, and sabotage, mainly by Twitter. His supporters in Congress tried to honor his erratic pronouncements, and the result was thorough dysfunction.

In September 2017, for example, Trump rescinded the Obama-era Deferred Action for Childhood Arrivals program, or DACA, that gave legal protection to the Dreamers—undocumented immigrants who were brought to the United States as children and knew no other home. Trump told lawmakers to replace the program with a "bill of love" that would protect the Dreamers and promised to sign whatever bill landed on his desk.

Republicans and Democrats complied. But at the last minute, Trump rejected the compromise—forcing the government to shut down because the agreement was part of a bill funding the government. With the government shuttered for the first time since 2013, Trump refused to say what bill he would support, or even to engage in negotiations. The shutdown went on for three days before a bipartisan group of senators reached an agreement to reopen the government—without input from Trump. The government reopened, but immigration remained unaddressed.

The whole thing repeated itself a year later, on a much larger scale. After Democrats took the House in the 2018 midterm, Trump called incoming House Speaker Nancy Pelosi and Senate Democratic Leader Chuck Schumer to the White House to negotiate border security. Instead, he launched into a televised tirade. "Look, we have to have the wall," he bellowed. "This is a national emergency." Then Trump threatened them: "If we don't get what we want one way or the other. . . . I will shut down the government, absolutely." He went on: "I will be the one to shut it down. I'm not going to blame you for it . . . I will take the mantle of shutting down."

And that's exactly what he did. Trump, having shut the government down, issued self-pitying tweets. "I am alone (poor me) in the White House. . . . I am in the White House, waiting." Even a few Republicans scolded Trump for forcing a government shutdown over one tenth of 1 percent of the federal budget. Senator Bob Corker, a Tennessee Republican, called it "juvenile." (Trump responded with a misspelled Twitter attack on Corker.)

After Pelosi suggested he postpone his State of the Union address until after the shutdown, Trump responded by grounding the government airplane that was supposed to take Pelosi to see U.S. troops in Afghanistan. Finally, after a thirty-five-day closure—the longest shutdown in U.S. history—Trump surrendered to an agreement opening the government without funding for his border wall.

Trump then turned around and declared an "emergency" so that he could repurpose other funds to build his wall without congressional approval. "I didn't need to do this," he freely admitted, undermining the so-called emergency.

Matters were no better in the Senate. Even before Trump, Republican senators had become expert in bringing government to a halt. Rand Paul of Kentucky held up Obama's nominee to run the CIA with a thirteen-hour filibuster. Paul, Ted Cruz of Texas, and Marco Rubio of Florida blocked the Senate from designating conferees to negotiate a budget with the House. Cruz bottled up a $1.1 trillion spending bill. Paul single-handedly blocked the 9/11-era Patriot Act from being reauthorized, causing it to lapse for several days.

During the Trump presidency, Senate Republicans continued their relentless investigations of the now former Obama administration. Senate Judiciary Committee chairman Lindsey Graham used his high office, in the middle of the pandemic, to circumvent decades-old rules and give himself unilateral power to issue subpoenas to Obama administration national security officials John

Brennan, James Clapper, James Comey, Susan Rice, and others. He vowed that "their day is coming." Republicans used the same hearing to renew their quest to do yet more probing into Hillary Clinton's and the DNC's emails from the 2016 campaign.

McConnell directly subverted the Obama administration's authority, explicitly urging states (in a *Lexington Herald-Leader* op-ed) to refuse to implement a major new power plant regulation issued by the U.S. government. After the pandemic struck, McConnell, though he supported initial rounds of relief to the states, declared in late April 2020 that states should file for bankruptcy rather than receive emergency funds. He then said in May that he didn't feel "the urgency of acting immediately." Finally, in October 2020, the Trump White House worked directly with House Democrats to pass another Covid relief package—but McConnell stepped in to block it, warning the White House not to strike a deal before the election.

McConnell continued the sabotage after the election. Asked after the January 6 insurrection whether he was concerned that many Republicans believed Trump's Big Lie about the election, McConnell replied, twice: "One hundred percent of my focus is on stopping this new administration." He even blocked a bipartisan effort to create a commission to investigate the January 6 insurrection—telling colleagues, as *Politico* reported at the time, that it "could hurt the party's midterm election message." Partisanship before country.

BY THE END OF Trump's impeachment trial for the Ukraine shakedown, investigators had documented that Trump sent Giuliani to Ukraine for dirt on Biden; that he directed two U.S. ambassadors to work with Giuliani; that he fired an anticorruption ambassador to Ukraine; that he told Vice President Mike Pence not to go to Zelensky's inauguration; that he had his chief of staff withhold Ukraine's military assistance; that he refused a White House meeting with Ukraine's president; that he ignored his advisers' anticorruption talking points; that he asked the Ukrainian president for "a favor" and for an investigation into his opponent, Biden; that he asked China to do similarly; and that he blocked investigators from discovering more. And he was still doing it! Even as Trump was being impeached and tried, Giuliani went back to Ukraine in his ongoing quest for dirt on Biden.

On top of all that, Attorney General Barr, the nation's top law enforcement official, facilitated Trump's misbehavior. Barr, the same man who misled the public about the content of the Mueller report, traveled to Italy in search of evidence that would discredit the Trump-Russia investigation. He testified to Congress that "I think spying did occur" against Trump's campaign in the Russia probe, echoing Trump's bogus claim and earning a public contradiction by FBI director Wray. Barr even appointed a prosecutor who launched a criminal investigation into the FBI and other officials who ran the Trump-Russia probe.

A few Republicans freely admitted that Trump was guilty as charged. Senator Lamar Alexander, a Tennessee Republican, said the impeachment managers' case has "been proven." Added Alexander: "It was inappropriate for the president to ask a foreign leader to investigate his political opponent and to withhold United States aid to encourage that investigation." Alexander voted to acquit anyway.

To defend Trump, congressional Republicans resorted to character assassination. They questioned the loyalty of one witness, Army Lt. Col. Alexander Vindman, an Iraq veteran with a Purple Heart who had come to the United States as a three-year-old Jewish refugee from the Soviet Union. They accused him of having a "conflict" because of his ethnic origins.

A week earlier, the White House slimed another witness—career diplomat, decorated officer in Vietnam, and West Point graduate William B. Taylor Jr.—as a "radical unelected bureaucrat." Taylor had been handpicked for the Ukraine posting by the Trump administration after Trump sacked Marie Yovanovitch.

Emblematic of the ugliness was Republican representative Matt Gaetz of Florida, who defended Trump by mocking Biden's son Hunter's drug addiction. "It's a little hard to believe that [Ukraine's] Burisma hired Hunter Biden to resolve their international disputes when he could not resolve his own dispute with

Hertz rental car over leaving cocaine and a crack pipe in the car," declared Gaetz, who had a DUI arrest of his own and would soon be in a scandal over alleged sex with an underage girl.

But the chutzpah prize went to Ken Starr. He fretted to conservative writer Byron York about "the evils of impeachment," and said the country needed "a reasoned and deliberate conversation about some lesser kind of response." Funny, he proposed no such "lesser kind of response" two decades earlier.

Trump received word that he had been impeached during a campaign rally in Michigan. He used the occasion to ridicule Representative Debbie Dingell, a Michigan Democrat who had recently lost her husband, John Dingell, the longest-serving member of the House in history. He mocked her gratitude to Trump for extending funeral honors to her husband, and then he speculated that the deceased was "looking up" from hell. The crowd cheered.

The next morning, it was business as usual. Trump was tweeting:

"Democrats . . . will feel the almighty wrath of God!"

"No Nads Nadler [Jerry Nadler, chairman of the House Judiciary Committee] needs to Shut the H3LL Up."

"The Democrats are the ANTITHESIS of what it means to be an American."

"Our Government was working . . . to overthrow an [sic] duly elected President!"

The morning after his acquittal in the Senate, Trump attended the National Prayer Breakfast, where political opponents always set aside differences. House Speaker Nancy Pelosi urged the assembled to "raise our voices in prayer as one." House Minority Leader Kevin McCarthy prayed for his colleagues, including Pelosi.

Then there was Trump. He complained that he was "put through a terrible ordeal by some very dishonest and corrupt people." Trump later gathered Republican lawmakers in the East Room of the White House, the chamber where Abraham Lincoln met Ulysses S. Grant and where John F. Kennedy and six other presidents lay in state.

There, Trump disparaged Pelosi's faith, saying "I doubt she prays at all." The Republican lawmakers laughed.

There, he said that Romney, a devout man (and the lone vote to convict Trump), "used religion as a crutch" and told Utahns: "I'm sorry about Mitt Romney." The Republican lawmakers laughed.

There, Trump described his political opponents and government bureaucrats as "bad," "dirty," "horrible," "evil," "sick," "corrupt," "scum," "leakers," "liars," "vicious," "mean," "lowlifes," "non-people," "stone-cold crazy," and "the crookedest, most dishonest, dirtiest people I've ever seen." The list bore a striking resemblance to the list of epithets Gingrich proposed to label Democrats with a quarter century earlier.

In what was billed by the White House as an address to the nation, Trump declared to every American man, woman, and child that the case against him "was all bullshit."

The Republican lawmakers laughed at the vulgarity and applauded the speech with whoops and cheers—in the same way they had laughed, shrugged, averted their gaze, or even applauded as Trump assaulted everything that made American government function.

They are the Republican Party, and they approved this message.

CHAPTER 16

Trial by Combat

My daughter was a toddler when Comet Ping Pong opened in what was then my neighborhood in Northwest Washington. We'd stop in often for brick-oven pizza and read a picture book we just bought at Politics & Prose a few doors down. In front, the cavernous place was invariably jammed with young kids and their parents. In back, there was a birthday-party room and another with table tennis, errant balls pinging and ponging every which way. And there was good enough beer to make the noise and commotion tolerable.

On November 8, 2016, Donald Trump was elected president. On December 4, 2016, a man walked into Comet Ping Pong with an AR-15, a .38 revolver, and a knife, and fired several rounds before surrendering to police. The two events were closely related.

The gunman had come, according to the police account, because "he had read online that the Comet restaurant was harboring child sex slaves and that he wanted to see for himself if they were there"—and he had come "armed to help rescue them."

And who had planted the bizarre idea that a popular family pizza joint was the hub of a Satanic pedophile ring?

On November 2, retired General Michael Flynn, the man Trump had picked to be his national security adviser, tweeted: "U decide: NYPD Blows Whistle on New Hillary Emails: Money Laundering, Sex Crimes w Children, etc. . . . MUST READ!" It linked to a disreputable website.

The notion that Comet was part of the child sex crimes scandal was heavily promoted by Trump ally Alex Jones, the radio conspiracy theorist who often touted (and was touted by) Trump. Trump had praised Jones's "amazing" reputation and called Jones after winning the presidency to thank him for his support. Jones promoted the Comet Ping Pong allegation, and the gunman, a Facebook fan of Jones, later told *The New York Times* he had listened to Jones's radio show.

"When I think about all the children Hillary Clinton has personally murdered and chopped up and raped, I have zero fear standing up against her," Jones said in a November 4, 2016, video. "Yeah, you heard me right. Hillary Clinton has personally murdered children."

Twenty years earlier, it was Vince Foster. Now she was chopping up children?

The only "evidence" for the insane slander linking the pizza restaurant to a pedophilia ring was that the owner of Comet had offered to host a fundraiser for Clinton. The rest was all invention. But within a few days, the hashtag #pizzagate was trending on Twitter, and the lie was spreading across 4chan and Reddit. Jack Posobiec, who worked with a group called Citizens4Trump and who had ties to longtime Trump adviser Roger Stone and white nationalist leader Richard Spencer, escalated the hoax further. He went to Comet, crashed a child's birthday party, and streamed his search online.

Death threats poured in. Comet workers were threatened with a "public lynching" for the nonexistent pedophile ring. "I pray someone comes to Comet pizza with automatic weapons and kills everyone inside," said one such threat. "I just may cut your throat. . . . I truly hope someone blows your brains all over Comet pizza."

Even after the confused twenty-eight-year-old gunman fired shots inside the family restaurant in his attempt to "self-investigate 'Pizza Gate,'" as he told police, those close to Trump continued to perpetuate the slander. Posobiec said the gunman episode was a false flag operation to conceal the pedophile ring. And Michael Flynn Jr., son of the incoming national security adviser and a member of Trump's transition team, tweeted: "Until #Pizzagate proven to be false it'll remain a story." Flynn Jr. said there were too "many 'coincidences.'"

The capital had already been on edge before the gunman visited Comet. Two weeks earlier, some three hundred white supremacists and neo-Nazis gathered in Washington at the invitation of Richard Spencer's National Policy Institute to celebrate Trump's victory. At the gathering, in the Ronald Reagan Building a few blocks from the White House, attendees shouted "Heil" and "Lügenpresse," a Nazi term that means "lying press." Some of the few hundred attendees applauded mention of the neo-Nazi site *Daily Stormer*. Reality TV personality Tila Tequila tweeted an image of herself and others giving a Nazi salute and the misspelled words "Seig heil!"

They clashed with counterdemonstrators in downtown Washington and again when they held a private dinner at a family restaurant, Maggiano's, in residential Northwest Washington—about a mile from Comet. At Maggiano's, Spencer proposed a jocular toast: "Let's party like it's 1933." The white supremacists applauded.

There was truth in the jest. The Reichstag burned in 1933, bringing about the end of Weimar Germany and the ascent of Hitler. The blundering Trump was no Hitler, but he had the autocrat's disdain for the rule of law, the autocrat's instinct to blame minorities for the nation's ills, and the autocrat's embrace of violence as a political tool. And now this distinctly antidemocratic figure was the president-elect, enjoying the near-unanimous support and validation of Republican officeholders.

This moment had been a long time coming. Two decades earlier, John McCain had admonished the party, and the country: "Patriotism is another way of saying service to a cause greater than self-interest." But over and over again, Republican leaders chose self-interest over country. They abandoned their principles of limited government, of being international champions of freedom. They played on racial fears, they demonized opponents as un-American, they knowingly championed egregious falsehoods, and they sabotaged the smooth functioning of the government—all because it suited their political self-interest. Gingrich impugned his opponents' loyalty to country to gain power, Bush and Rove squandered the unity of 9/11 to expand power, Palin and the Tea Party crowd spread lies and racism and winked at violence to cut down their opponents. McConnell sabotaged the Senate and discredited the Supreme Court because it maximized his power.

After so many years of choosing power over principle, self-interest over country, Republican leaders had lost their way. They stood for nothing but gaining and holding power. Then, in 2015, along came a man who showed them a way to gain and hold power. They swallowed what was left of their integrity, and they followed him.

THE POISON HAD BEEN building long before Trump. As with the war on truth, the stoking of racial animus, and the assaults on the institutions of government, Republicans had been cozying up to the violent and undermining democracy when Trump was still firing people on *The Apprentice*. As in the other cases, he saw where the Republican Party was, and he exploited it.

Up until the time of the Republican Revolution of 1994, Americans had a relatively neutral view of those in the other party. In 1994, only 21 percent of Republicans had a "very unfavorable" view of the Democratic Party—but by 2016, that antipathy had nearly tripled, to 58 percent, the Pew Research Center found. Democrats underwent a corresponding growth in their distaste for Republicans, from 17 percent in 1994 to 55 percent in 2016. Measured on what social scientists call a "feeling thermometer," the number of people with a "very cold" view of opposing partisans also roughly tripled over that time. The once common practice of split-ticket voting (nearly half of congressional districts in 1984 chose one party for president and another for Congress) had vanished (under 4 percent of districts did so in 2020).

Discrimination against those of the other party extended beyond politics and into personal relationships and nonpolitical behaviors. Americans increasingly lived in neighborhoods with like-minded partisans, married fellow partisans, and disapproved of their children marrying someone from the other party, and they were more likely to choose partners based on partisanship than physical or personality attributes. Party affiliation had become the single deepest divide in American society, greater than race, gender, region, education, or anything else.

"Unlike race, gender and other social divides where group-related attitudes and behaviors are constrained by social norms, there are no corresponding pressures to temper disapproval of political opponents," Stanford and Princeton researchers Shanto Iyengar and Sean Westwood concluded in 2014. "If anything, the rhetoric and actions of political leaders demonstrate that hostility directed at the opposition is acceptable, even appropriate. Partisans therefore feel free to express animus and engage in discriminatory behavior toward opposing partisans."

At the same time, social media amplified the dehumanizing and violent rhetoric. And the Supreme Court, by allowing unlimited, unidentifiable funds to flow into politics, weakened the major political parties so they could no longer police their own ranks. Round after round of partisan redistricting had put almost all House members in safe seats where the only threat comes from primaries. Primary voters tend to favor extreme candidates—who, once in Congress, defied their party leaders and refused compromise.

Growing partisan hatred. Weakening clout of party leaders. A misinformed electorate and a torrent of well-funded disinformation. It was a dry forest, just waiting for a spark.

Yet even at this stage had prominent Republicans countered or condemned Trump's violent, antidemocratic rhetoric in large numbers, they could have lowered the temperature. Instead, they acquiesced, and then echoed and imitated him.

His GOP presidential rivals were saying similar things. Scott Walker likened public sector unions to Islamic State terrorists. Chris Christie talked about his wish to punch a teachers union in its collective face. Ted Cruz said the Obama administration was becoming the "world's leading financier of radical Islamic terrorists." Mike Huckabee talked about Obama marching Israelis to the "door of the oven" and suggested he would use federal troops to block abortions. Rand Paul declared that highly taxed people are "half-slave" and released videos of him setting the tax code on fire, using a chain saw on it, and putting it in a wood chipper. Ben Carson called America "very much like Nazi Germany," labeled Obamacare the worst thing since slavery, and said a Muslim should not be president.

Trump surrogate Scottie Nell Hughes asked on CNN about the

possibility of violence at the Republican convention, said: "Riots aren't necessarily a bad thing." Another surrogate, Omarosa Manigault, defended violence against demonstrators at Trump events: "You get what's coming to you." *Slate*'s Ben Mathis-Lilley tallied twenty violent incidents at Trump events by Trump supporters, including protesters hit with pepper spray by Trump backers, and instances of demonstrators being sucker-punched, shoved, and choked. Among the violent: Trump's campaign manager. Trump's campaign promoted the endorsement of rocker Ted Nugent, who said Clinton and Obama should be "tried for treason and hung."

Trump adviser Roger Stone was on record saying Clinton should be "executed." Al Baldasaro, a surrogate for Trump on veterans issues, said in a radio interview that Clinton should be "put in the firing line and shot for treason." In August 2016, Stone proposed that Trump claim Clinton was trying to steal the election. Asserting that there is already "widespread voter fraud," Stone said Trump should say that "we will have a constitutional crisis, widespread civil disobedience, and the government will no longer be the government." Stone promised Breitbart that Clinton's inauguration "will be a bloodbath"—though dialed down his incitement by saying he meant a "rhetorical" one.

If there were any doubt Stone had Trump's ear, two days later Trump said, "I'm afraid the election's going to be rigged." Talk of voter fraud became dominant at his events, and his supporters expressed expectations of violence if Trump lost. In a debate with Clinton, Trump refused to commit to accepting the election results, saying, "I will keep you in suspense."

Republican leaders normalized the violent, antidemocratic rhetoric because of short-term political considerations. "Trump can hit the right chord," Ward Baker, executive director of the National Republican Senatorial Committee, wrote in a September 2016 memo. "We can't afford to depress the GOP vote," he added. "Spending full time attacking our nominee will ensure that the GOP vote is depressed. That will only serve to topple GOP candidates at every level. Maintain the right amount of independence, but avoid piling on the nominee."

Reince Priebus, the Republican National Committee chairman, announced his moral flexibility, telling CBS's John Dickerson that his "role is to basically be 100 percent behind" the eventual nominee. House Speaker Paul Ryan often criticized Trump for betraying conservatism, but, asked if he could support Trump, Ryan also went morally supine, saying he would back "whoever the Republican nominee is." Trump presidential rivals Ted Cruz, Marco Rubio, and John Kasich said the same. And were it not for McConnell's efforts to rally big Republican contributors behind Trump, there probably wouldn't have been a President Trump.

Refusing to commit to honoring the election results was a fundamental departure from democratic tradition, and an unmistakable step toward the authoritarian. The underlying atmosphere of violence and intimidation Trump cultivated was a further departure, and a hallmark of authoritarians the world over. Yet Republican leaders acquiesced to both, out of short-term political expediency.

This political calculation to wink at Trump's authoritarianism would repeat itself endlessly through Trump's presidency. When Trump announced his plan to circumvent Congress and build his border wall by executive fiat, dozens of Republicans spoke out against the "emergency" action—more than enough to override a presidential veto. They had, after all, called it "tyranny" when Obama used executive actions to circumvent Congress in a much more limited way. But, as usual, Republicans acquiesced to Trump's usurpation. House Minority Leader Kevin McCarthy explained the cave-in to Trump: "Well, times change as it moves forward."

Trump lawyer Rudy Giuliani warned that if Trump were to be impeached, "the American people would revolt." Trump son Eric declared that Democrats "are not even people." Newt Gingrich spoke of a "deep-state spear aimed at destroying." Wayne LaPierre, head of the National Rifle Association, warned the Conservative Political Action Conference of a "tidal wave" of "European-style socialists bearing down upon us," creating a "captive society," eliminating "resistance," expunging the "fundamental concept of moral behavior," and leaving Americans "just a short hop to the systematic destruction of our most basic freedoms."

Hours after a mass shooting in El Paso, Senate Republican Leader Mitch McConnell's campaign tweeted a photo of fake tombstones bearing the name of McConnell's Democratic Senate challenger, Amy McGrath, among others. McGrath protested that McConnell used "imagery of the death of a political opponent (me)." Around the same time, young men (apparently volunteers) wearing "Team Mitch" campaign T-shirts posed in an Instagram photo groping and choking a cardboard cutout of Democratic Representative Alexandria Ocasio-Cortez.

TRUMP SEEMED PROUD OF his ability to bring out the worst in people.

During the 2016 campaign, Trump sat down at Washington's Trump International Hotel with authors Bob Woodward and Robert Costa and reflected on the distress his presidential candidacy fomented. "I bring rage out," he said. "I always have."

Four rage-filled years later, America was aflame. Federal authorities attacked peaceful racial justice protesters outside the White House with pepper balls, flash-bangs, and rubber bullets, clearing Lafayette Square in part so that Trump, accompanied by the chairman of the Joint Chiefs of Staff in battle fatigues, could stage a photo op outside St. John's Episcopal Church holding a Bible.

A Trump supporter sent pipe bombs to prominent Democrats and media outlets. Republican members of Congress were shot while playing baseball. A gunman massacred worshippers in a Pittsburgh synagogue. A white supremacist killed a woman at the Charlottesville march of neo-Nazis. And as racial justice demonstrators poured into the streets to protest the police killing of another Black man, George Floyd, masses poured into the streets to vent their anger—most peacefully, some violently.

And Trump continued to escalate tensions. He taunted demonstrators with a phrase from segregation days: "When the looting starts, the shooting starts." He spoke of "vicious dogs" and "ominous weapons" awaiting protesters and the need to "dominate" them. He celebrated the "good people" who invaded the Michigan capitol carrying guns to intimidate the legislators and to defy public health rules during the pandemic. He urged gun rights supporters to "LIBERATE MICHIGAN!; LIBERATE

MINNESOTA!; LIBERATE VIRGINIA." Fourteen men, many members of an antigovernment paramilitary group, were arrested in October 2020 as part of an alleged plot to kidnap Michigan governor Gretchen Whitmer, a Democrat. "Kidnapping plots and death threats endanger not just individuals, but democracy itself," Whitmer wrote in a victim's impact statement.

The year 2019, the FBI reported, was the deadliest year for domestic terrorism since the Oklahoma City bombing of 1995. Hate crimes in the United States were up 30 percent (hate crimes against Muslims alone were up 67 percent in 2015, when Trump's campaign debuted). Various white supremacist and antigovernment groups and movements—the Proud Boys, "boogaloo" followers, and adherents of the QAnon conspiracy theories—were engaging in violence coast to coast. Domestic violent extremists, as the FBI called them, were killing more people in the United States than international terrorists. In eighteen months between 2020 and 2021, the FBI nearly tripled its domestic terrorism caseload, from 1,000 investigations to 2,700 investigations. "The violence in 2020 is unlike what we have seen in quite some time," Christopher Wray, the Trump-appointed FBI director, said of domestic terrorism.

Researchers at Britain's University of Warwick found that the rise in anti-Muslim hate crimes since Trump's campaign has been concentrated in counties with high Twitter usage, and that these counties did not previously experience consistently more anti-Muslim hate crimes.

Trump spoke of shooting unarmed migrants at the border. He shared violent videos on Twitter. He praised a congressman for assaulting a journalist, routinely described the press as the "enemy of the people," and often induced crowds to menace the "enemy" journalists in the room. He told supporters to "knock the crap" and "knock the hell" out of protesters, fantasized about punching one, and offered to pay legal defenses of those who did. He said a Black Lives Matter protester at his event "should have been roughed up."

Trump encouraged police aggression, urging cops, "please, don't be too nice" when throwing "thugs" into "the back of a paddy wagon," and he suggested not "protecting their head." His administration rescinded reforms that kept surplus military weapons from going to local police with inadequate training. And it disparaged the Justice Department's decades-old practice of investigating and remediating police misconduct.

The vitriol flowing from Trump's speeches and Twitter stream—"crooked," "corrupt," "dirty," "disgrace," "sham," "horrendous," "socialist," "communist," "whack job," "crazed lunatic," "vicious," "raging left-wing mob," "sabotage," "dumbest human beings"—fueled fury. "We have reason to be angry, folks," he told his supporters. He also imagined his supporters resorting to violence: "We have the toughest people," but "hopefully" it won't come to that. While stoking rage in his supporters, he celebrated his opponents suffering such "derangement" that "people actually go see psychiatrists."

He warned his supporters that *they* would be the victims of violence, saying that Democrats "will overturn everything that we've done, and they'll do it quickly and violently—and violently." He portrayed Democrats as lawless and inhuman, on a "ruthless mission" to "demolish and destroy," to "replace freedom with socialism," to launch "an assault on the sovereignty of our country . . . and the safety of every single American," and to invite in immigrants who "carve you up with a knife."

The effect was measurable. The National Opinion Research Center at the University of Chicago, which has conducted an annual survey of the national mood since 1972, found in 2020 that the proportion of people describing themselves as "very happy" had plummeted to 14 percent—compared with the survey's previous record low of 29 percent, recorded after the 2008 financial crisis. This was despite 36 percent declaring themselves "satisfied" with their financial situation, the highest in the study's history.

For the first time in half a century, there was "a disconnect between financial satisfaction and overall happiness," David Sterrett, senior researcher for the study, told me. Driving the unhappiness was the social and political environment.

After the 2016 election, well-being measures among Democratic constituencies and independents dropped in Gallup surveys—*and there was no corresponding jump in the sense of well-being among Republicans or among whites*. After past elections, constituencies of the winning party typically reported higher levels of happiness. But after Trump's election, the overall sense of well-being among Americans worsened—and stayed worse. Gallup called it an "obvious Trump effect."

Trump brought out the rage—and Americans had responded with a combustible combination of venom and despair.

Trump, during the campaign, fantasized about Clinton being assassinated (disarm her security detail and "let's see what happens to her") as well as her judicial nominees: "If she gets to pick her judges, nothing you can do, folks. Although, the Second Amendment people, maybe there is."

He speculated that he could shoot somebody on Fifth Avenue without losing support. He retweeted to his followers a video clip doctored to show him driving a golf ball off the tee and between the shoulder blades of Hillary Clinton, knocking the former secretary of state and Democratic presidential nominee to the ground.

Trump warned that "you would have riots" and "bad things would happen" if he were denied the GOP nomination. Trump promised to bring back the form of torture known as waterboarding and "much worse," figuring terrorism suspects "deserve it" even if it doesn't work. He said the military would obey if he issued (illegal) orders to torture detainees or to kill noncombatant relatives of terrorists. His acceptance speech at the 2016 Republican National Convention was a dystopic nightmare ("violence," "chaos," "humiliation," "disasters," "ruins," "crushed," "ripped apart," "poverty and violence at home, war and destruction abroad") and an authoritarian solution: "I alone can fix it."

In the first week of 2017 after Trump's election win, the Anti-Defamation League saw a proliferation of racist and anti-Semitic vandalism, and the Southern Poverty Law Center received four hundred allegations of instances of hate-based intimidation and harassment. Trump claimed he was "very surprised" to learn of violence and threats being made in his name, and said on CBS's *60 Minutes* that those responsible should "stop it." But he didn't hold himself responsible. Asked by *The Wall Street Journal* if any of his campaign rhetoric had gone too far, he replied: "No. I won."

———

IN EARLY 2016, TRUMP retweeted a quote to his millions of followers: "It is better to live one day as a lion than 100 years as a sheep." The man who coined that phrase: Mussolini. Informed of the provenance of the quote he shared, Trump replied on NBC's *Meet the Press*: "It's a very good quote. . . . [W]hat difference does it make whether it's Mussolini or somebody else?" The imitation of the fascist dictator didn't end there. Trump had supporters at one rally raise their hands in a loyalty pledge that the former head of the ADL called a "fascist gesture." He banned news organizations he didn't like from his events. He threatened publishers and broadcasters with boycotts and antitrust actions. He vowed to "open up" libel laws to restrict the First Amendment to curtail criticism of him.

Trump said he would consider forcing Muslims in the United States to register in a database. And he used many of the fascist's tools: a contempt for facts, spreading a pervasive sense of fear and overwhelming crisis, portraying his backers as victims, assigning blame to foreign or alien actors, and suggesting only his powerful personality could transcend the crisis.

A quantitative analysis of Trump's speeches by *The New York Times* found that Trump echoes what historians said were "the appeals of some demagogues of the past century" in his repetition of "divisive phrases, harsh words and violent imagery." I asked Factbase, a data analytics company that analyzes language with artificial intelligence, to do a sentiment analysis of Trump's speech compared with that of his predecessors. It found that Trump's rhetoric was twice as extreme as that of all predecessors over the past century. Trump's rhetoric was also about twice as extreme as the most extreme members of Congress.

Such rhetoric is a hallmark of totalitarianism. "It's using emotion to circumvent reason, to overwhelm reason," Jason Stanley, a Yale philosopher specializing in language and author of the book *How Fascism Works*, told me. "He wants to get the situation such that it's a crisis and there's such fear and suspicion that the only happiness, the delivery, is winning over his enemies," Stanley said. Hence, the lavish praise of and great love for his supporters and the unalloyed vitriol toward foreigners, racial minorities, elites, and socialists.

"Goebbels talks about propaganda being best when it appeals to straightforward emotion: fear, suspicion, anger, and then it would be culminated with 'we're winning,' 'we're going to get them,'" Stanley said. A speech of this method was often very long, "with extremes of paranoia and then praise of 'us,' 'our' greatness, and a desire for revenge for lost greatness. . . . When our emotions are being overwhelmed, it's because people are trying to manipulate us and drive us toward a desired goal."

Trump admired and befriended autocrats the world over. He claimed a "great relationship" with Rodrigo Duterte of the Philippines, known for his extralegal killing squads. He called North Korea's Kim Jong-un, leader of the most repressive regime on earth, "very open," "very honorable," and a "smart cookie." He called Egypt's Abdel Fattah al-Sissi, who violently cracked down on dissidents, a "fantastic guy" who was "very close to me." He admired the "very high marks" given to Turkey's Recep Tayyip Erdoğan, known for jailing opponents. China's premier, Xi Jinping, was a "great gentleman" and a "very good man." And Russia's Vladimir Putin, with whom he had "positive chemistry," was "getting an A" in leadership, by Trump's grading.

Trump particularly admired Xi's successful move to abolish term limits. "He's now president for life—president for life—and he's great," Trump said at a closed-door fundraiser, audio of which leaked to CNN. "And look, he was able to do that. I think it's great. Maybe we'll have to give that a shot someday." His audience cheered and applauded the line, which Trump later called a "joke."

Another time, Trump declared that "I find China, frankly, in many ways, to be far more honorable than Cryin' Chuck [Schumer] and Nancy [Pelosi]. I really do. . . . I think that China is actually much easier to deal with than the opposition party." A government that holds a million members of religious minorities in concentration camps, has over time exterminated tens of millions of people, and illegally steals technology from and launches cyber attacks on the United States is . . . honorable?

Similarly, Trump defended Putin against accusations that the Russian dictator killed journalists: "You think our country is so innocent?" and "I think that our country does plenty of killing, too." Earlier, Trump saluted Iraq's Saddam Hussein for being "damn good at killing terrorists" and said the Chinese government's Tiananmen Square massacre "shows you the power of strength."

Trump's attacks on the press as "fake news" and the "enemy of the people" did tangible damage, at home and abroad. Threats against journalists rose with Trump's rise. Around the time of Trump's election, *The Washington Post*'s executive editor, Marty Baron, noted that when Trump refers to journalists as "the lowest form of life," "scum," and the enemy, "it is no wonder that some members of our staff [at the *Post*] and at other news organizations received vile insults and threats of personal harm so worrisome that extra security was required."

"Rope, Tree, Journalist," read one email I received. "Some assembly required." To this slogan, made popular by T-shirts Trump supporters wore at his rallies, my would-be hangman added his offer: "I will assemble for you." This bit of, er, gallows humor was far from the worst of the sort of correspondence my colleagues and I had been receiving at the time. After *The Washington Post* reported about the Comet gunman and the nonsense conspiracy theory, the reporters involved received emails and tweets saying "I hope the next shooter targets you lying sacks of s— in the media," "God has a plan better than death," and "it would also be a shame if someone took a gun to" the *Post*.

Trump's White House rescinded White House press passes of journalists it didn't like, including CNN's Jim Acosta (and me). Worse, Trump succeeded in discrediting the free press in his supporters' eyes. By mid-2018, a Quinnipiac University survey found, a plurality of Republicans said it was more accurate to describe the media as "the enemy of the people" than as an important part of democracy.

Montana Republican congressman Greg Gianforte pleaded guilty in 2017 to assaulting a journalist. He was sentenced to community service and anger management classes. Trump celebrated the assault, telling a rally crowd, "Any guy that can do a body slam, he's my kind of—he's my guy."

Upon hearing that, one man in the crowd looked at CNN's Jim Acosta "and ran his thumb across his throat," Acosta reported. A man arrested in 2018 for threatening to kill *Boston Globe* employees referred to the newspaper as "enemy of the people."

In June 2018, a deranged man walked into the newsroom of the *Capital Gazette* in Annapolis, Maryland, with smoke grenades and a shotgun, killing five. He had a long-standing grudge against the newspaper since its long-ago coverage of a harassment case he was involved in—and the grudge extended to the paper's coverage of Trump. "Referring to @realDonaldTrump as 'unqualified,' " he tweeted at the newspaper in 2015, "@capgaznews could end badly (again)."

Trump's attacks on journalists had an even more profound effect overseas. Reporters Without Borders outlined the "growing animosity towards journalists" worldwide: murders of journalists swelling and the killers escaping justice in nine out of ten cases. As U.S. officials under Trump stopped protesting the abuse of journalists abroad, strongmen around the world accelerated a crackdown on journalists as "terrorists"—several imprisoning journalists for the crime of producing "fake news."

In 2018, a year in which murders of journalists worldwide doubled, according to the Committee to Protect Journalists, Saudi operatives flew to Istanbul, where they kidnapped, killed, and used a bone saw to dismember journalist Jamal Khashoggi, a Virginia-based contributor to *The Washington Post*. U.S. intelligence quickly determined that the operation was approved at the highest levels of the Saudi regime, and a declassified intelligence report eventually concluded that the killers reported directly to Saudi Crown Prince Mohammed bin Salman.

But Trump claimed that "we may never know" whether the Saudi crown prince was involved, and he refused to hold the repressive regime accountable. A few months later, billionaire Tom Barrack, Trump friend, informal adviser, and chairman of the president's inaugural committee, defended the Saudi government's murder of Khashoggi. "Whatever happened in Saudi Arabia, the atrocities in America are equal or worse than the atrocities in Saudi Arabia," Barrack said at a conference in the region. He added: "For us to dictate what we think is the moral code there. . . . I think is a mistake." (After I inquired, Barrack belatedly issued a written statement saying the Khashoggi killing "was atrocious and is inexcusable.")

Who knows how many other murders of journalists were

inspired by Trump's assaults on the press? Strongmen in Russia, China, Syria, Venezuela, the Philippines, Turkey, and elsewhere all echoed Trump's "fake news" phrase as they cracked down on press freedoms, imprisoned journalists, or worse.

Trump had the autocrat's disdain for other democratic customs. He mused about serving "at least for 10 or 14 years" rather than the two-term limit required by the Constitution, and he retweeted a message arguing that, because of the Russia probe, he should have "two years added to his first term as payback for time stolen by this corrupt failed coup." He complained about the pesky presence of judges to hear asylum cases: "They step on our land, we have judges. It's insane." He claimed that "it's embarrassing for the country to allow protesters." His Justice Department went to court—twice—to prosecute a woman because she laughed at Jeff Sessions, the attorney general, during his confirmation hearing.

Trump urged the postmaster general to double the rate it charged Amazon, apparently to punish it for coverage by *The Washington Post,* owned by Amazon founder Jeff Bezos. That same postmaster general, a major Trump donor, disrupted and slowed postal operations on the eve of the 2020 election, which relied on mail-in voting. Trump blocked lawmakers from getting intelligence briefings about foreign attempts to interfere in the election.

After he noticed that Democrats didn't applaud much during his State of the Union address, Trump called them "un-American" and asked: "Can we call that treason?" He accused administration officials of "treason" when they criticized him. He called news coverage of his summit with North Korea "almost treasonous." He said an FBI agent who investigated him committed a "treasonous act." He called the entire Mueller investigation "treason." Also guilty of treason: Republicans who didn't support him, Barack Obama, Bill Clinton, Hillary Clinton, various Obama administration officials, and Trump's own deputy attorney general. A Trump appointee, Michael Caputo, accused CDC scientists of "sedition" during the pandemic.

Trump assigned himself "the absolute right" to send illegal immigrants to sanctuary cities. He claimed the "absolute authority" to overrule governors on stay-at-home orders, to interfere in criminal proceedings for cronies, to close the southern border, to fire Robert Mueller, and to end, by executive fiat, the constitutional guarantee of birthright citizenship. "And yes," he said, "I do have an absolute right to pardon myself." Trump aide Stephen Miller said on CBS's *Face the Nation* that judges could not interfere with Trump: "[T]he powers of the president to protect our country are very substantial and will not be questioned." Trump's lawyers claimed before the Supreme Court that he had "absolute immunity" from state legal proceedings, which the court said "runs up against . . . 200 years of precedent."

Trump tweeted the words of a racist conspiracy theorist who said Israelis view Trump like "the King of Israel" and "the second coming of God." Trump said he took a tough trade stance against China because "I am the chosen one." His aides likened him to Queen Esther, King David, Moses, and other biblical figures; more than one said God wanted Trump to be president. Trump thought it proper that Americans "sit up at attention" for him.

He declared that he could unilaterally revoke the Constitution's guarantee of citizenship for anyone born in the United States. He threatened to shut down Twitter because it pointed out he was factually inaccurate, and to overrule state governors by sending in U.S. troops to police U.S. citizens on U.S. soil. He threatened to withhold pandemic aid to states whose governors were not "appreciative" of him.

TWO WEEKS BEFORE THE midterm elections in 2018, a domestic employee of liberal billionaire George Soros went to the mailbox of his estate in Katonah, New York, and found a bubble-wrapped package. Inside was a pipe bomb.

In the next couple of days, similar explosive devices were intercepted on their way to Barack Obama, Hillary Clinton, Joe Biden, Senators Kamala Harris and Cory Booker, former Obama administration officials Eric Holder, John Brennan (care of CNN), and James Clapper, and others.

All thirteen intended victims had one thing in common: they were frequent targets of Trump's wrath.

The trail quickly led to Cesar Sayoc, a Florida bodybuilder

with mental health troubles. A lawyer for his family went on CNN and said Sayoc "found a father in Trump."

"He was attracted to the Trump formula of . . . reaching out to these types of outsiders, people who don't fit in, people who are angry at America, telling them they have a place at the table and it's OK to get angry," the lawyer said.

Thankfully, nobody was hurt—the bombs were later found to be inoperative—and Sayoc was sentenced to twenty years in prison.

In October 2018, a madman, armed with an AR-15-style rifle and at least three handguns, walked into the Tree of Life Synagogue in Pittsburgh and slaughtered eleven people during Shabbat services. It was the deadliest anti-Semitic attack in U.S. history. The gunman, though rejecting Trump for being insufficiently nationalist, embraced on social media the themes Trump has popularized: the "globalist" danger, immigrant "invaders that kill our people," and an "infestation" of undesirables. He was motivated by Trump-inspired paranoia about a caravan coming from Mexico (a conspiracy theory making the rounds alleged that Soros, a Jew, was funding it), and he wanted to kill Jews because they were helping settle refugees in the United States.

Trump, reading from a teleprompter after the massacre, denounced anti-Semitism. But he proceeded with a political rally mere hours later, riling up the crowd over the very caravan that inflamed the killer.

In the national and state capitals, Trump backers practiced a new politics of intimidation.

During impeachment hearings in the House in October 2019, Trump instructed Republicans to "get tougher and fight." A couple of days later, two dozen House Republicans, led by Louisiana representative Steve Scalise, the No. 2 Republican leader, met in the Capitol basement and literally used their bodies to stop the proceedings. They rushed past Capitol Police and burst into the secure meeting room of the House Permanent Select Committee on Intelligence—where the day's witness was about to begin her closed-door testimony. The intruders shouted grievances about the process and defenses of the president—one reportedly got in Chairman Adam Schiff's face—forcing Schiff and the witness to abandon the room. The lawmakers brought their cell phones into the secure facility, making it an easy target for foreign surveillance.

A few months later, after the pandemic struck, Trump supporters staged an "American Patriot Rally" at the state capitol in Lansing, Michigan. Demonstrators, several armed with military-style guns, then marched into the statehouse, stared down the police, and entered the Senate gallery with their guns, menacing the lawmakers, one of whom put on a bulletproof vest. They chanted "our house" and "let us in," and they carried signs displaying the Confederate flag and nooses and likening the governor to Hitler. "Tyrants Get the Rope," proclaimed some signs.

In what would later be seen as a precursor of the January 6 attack on the U.S. Capitol, Trump egged on the invaders ("save your great 2nd amendment. It is under siege!"). The president tweeted that Governor Whitmer, a frequent Trump target, should "put out the fire" by making "a deal" with the armed mob. "These are very good people, but they are angry," he wrote.

Another target of Trump's constant attacks who received death threats was Anthony Fauci, who had been the government's top infectious disease official since the Reagan administration. He had to get a Secret Service detail because of threats to him, his wife, and his children, and he had to be sprayed down by a hazmat crew after opening a letter filled with powder.

Republicans justified the growing glorification of violence in their own ranks with what had come to be known as "whataboutism"—what about the Democrats? They portrayed their opponents as the ones fomenting violence, pointing, for example, to (Black) Senator Cory Booker telling people to "get up in the face of some congresspeople," and (Black) Congresswoman Maxine Waters saying that people who see Trump cabinet members should "create a crowd, and you push back on them, and you tell them they're not welcome anywhere." They also howled about Schumer's warning that conservative justices would "pay the price" for their abortion rulings (he said the next day that "I should not have used the words I used"). That these examples weren't at all equivalent didn't bother the whataboutists.

A month after the armed occupation of the Michigan capitol came another, bigger opportunity for Trump to "bring rage out," as he liked to do. George Floyd was killed in Minneapolis when a police officer pressed his knee to Floyd's neck for nearly nine minutes—all on suspicion of using a counterfeit $20 bill, a misdemeanor. This was the sort of police brutality they were talking about two years earlier when, in response to Trump repeatedly encouraging police to handle suspects less gently, the NAACP said he was "encouraging police officers to disregard the safety of individuals in their custody." Black Lives Matter protests erupted in cities across the country following the Floyd killing. Trump decided to use the limited violence at mostly peaceful racial justice demonstrations as a foil for his reelection. Americans witnessed in real time on TV the violent clearing of peaceful protests in Lafayette Square by federal police. (An inspector general later found that the clearing, though planned for other reasons, was hastened for Trump's appearance.) In Portland, Oregon, federal police used batons, tear gas, and rubber bullets on moms in bicycle helmets. Unidentified federal officers, defying duly elected state and city leaders, threw civil rights demonstrators into unmarked vans without charges. Trump's acting homeland security secretary, Chad Wolf, told his agents to "go out and proactively arrest individuals."

The administration called the demonstrators in Portland and Seattle "sick and deranged Anarchists & Agitators" who "hate our country" and seek to "destroy our American cities, and worse." Trump's Justice Department labeled New York, Portland, and Seattle "anarchist jurisdictions." (Reuters reported that federal prosecutors produced no evidence linking the people arrested in Portland protests to antifa or anarchists.) Trump celebrated the case of a Missouri couple who came out of their home brandishing guns and shouting at nonviolent racial justice demonstrators.

Just as he sent the military to the border in 2018 to focus anger on the "caravan," he now used federal police against racial justice demonstrators. Oregon's governor, Democrat Kate Brown, said Trump's "dictatorship"-style use of "secret police" was "adding gasoline to a fire" that had been dying. At a racial justice protest in Kenosha, Wisconsin, a seventeen-year-old who had been in the front row of a Trump rally earlier in the year shot and killed two demonstrators and injured a third. Trump leaped to the gunman's defense.

In Portland, a group with white supremacist ties called Patriot Prayer staged a caravan of armed counterdemonstrators to confront the Black Lives Matter protests. Trump retweeted a video showing the pro-Trump demonstrators shooting paintballs and firing pepper spray into the crowd, adding that the "big backlash going on in Portland cannot be unexpected." Soon after that, one of the pro-Trump demonstrators, carrying bear spray and a baton, was shot and killed by a self-proclaimed antifa militant who was himself later shot by police.

In Provo, Utah, anti-mask demonstrators, some wearing Trump 2020 paraphernalia, stormed a county commission meeting, forcing its adjournment. In Tulsa, anti-mask protesters, some in MAGA gear, taunted, threw water, and waved money at a Black minister reading the Bible through a bullhorn and calling for reparations.

The right-wing militia group Oath Keepers (whose founder was later indicted for seditious conspiracy in the January 6 insurrection) produced a November 2020 video in which a leader of the group quoted Paul Gosar (the Republican congressman from Arizona who produced an anime video of himself killing a Democratic colleague) as telling the group that a civil war had already begun. "We just haven't started shooting at each other yet."

AS THE 2020 ELECTION approached, Trump turned darker and darker. Invited at a presidential debate to condemn white supremacists and militias, Trump instead made common cause with the Proud Boys, which the FBI labels an extremist group with ties to white nationalism. Trump suggested they "stand back and stand by"—presumably, for further violence when needed. Proud Boys leaders turned that into a new slogan. Wrote one of the group's leaders: "That's my President!"

By the fall of 2020, Trump and his Republican allies had conditioned their supporters to expect voter fraud in elections—and Republicans in state government had become more brazen in their voter suppression efforts. They blocked rehabilitated felons from getting voting rights restored, fought ballot drop boxes, purged voting rolls, and closed polling places. In one majority-Black Georgia county, for example, an official recommended by Republican secretary of state and gubernatorial candidate Brian Kemp proposed closing 78 percent of polling places in the county. Republicans and allied groups devoted some $20 million to wage more than three hundred court fights across the country either to strike down election rules that encourage higher voter turnout or to fight lawsuits aimed at easing voting, according to the Center for Public Integrity.

Trump fought bitterly against mail-in voting during the pandemic, and admitted that he opposed it because it would increase "levels of voting" to the point where "you'd never have a Republican elected."

When early voting opened, Trump supporters tried to intimidate those who showed up. In Virginia, Trump supporters descended on a polling station, waving Trump signs and flags, chanting and forming a gauntlet through which voters had to walk. When *The New York Times* reported that the effort was connected to the Republican National Committee co-chairman, the Virginia GOP responded mockingly from its official Twitter account: "Quick! Someone call the waaaambulance!" Trump told his followers to "go into the polls" and "watch very closely," and some supporters stood outside polling places carrying guns. Trump got the national intelligence director to declassify unverified information about his political opponents, and he threatened to invoke the Insurrection Act to "put down" election night unrest.

In September 2020, the eminent Yale historian of twentieth-century totalitarianism Timothy Snyder told me that the moment was similar to the burning of Germany's Reichstag in 1933 before the Nazi takeover. "It's an election surrounded by the authoritarian language of a coup d'état," he said. "It's going to be messy."

The world was about to find out just how messy.

Hours after the polls closed on Election Day, Trump was trailing in both the popular and electoral vote. "A big WIN!" he declared, tweeting: "We are up BIG, but they are trying to STEAL the Election. Votes cannot be cast after the Poles [*sic*] are closed!"

He further declared that "we already have" won, and "we hereby claim" the electoral votes of states he had not actually won. "There's tremendous corruption and fraud going on."

In the following days, his supporters formed mobs outside polling offices where ballots were being tabulated, demanding "STOP THE COUNT!" in states where Trump was ahead (Pennsylvania) and, conversely, "COUNT THE VOTES" in states where he was behind (Arizona). The president fired off tweets ("Ballot Counting Chaos," "secretly dumped ballots") trying to discredit the election.

He had lost the election by six million votes, 4 percentage points, and an electoral vote margin his own team called "historic" and a "landslide" when he was the victor by a similar margin in 2016. He lost the recounts. He lost the vote certifications, by Republican and Democratic officials alike. His own attorney general said "we have not seen fraud on a scale that could have effected a different outcome." Christopher Krebs, the head of the Cybersecurity and Infrastructure Security Agency in the Department of Homeland Security, called the election "the most secure in American history." Trump fired him. He failed in every single postelection ballot-counting challenge. Judges scolded his lawyers: "like Frankenstein's Monster . . . haphazardly stitched together," "simply not how the Constitution works," "inadmissible hearsay within hearsay," "generalized speculation," "your submission is defective."

But Trump wouldn't relent. He tried, and failed, to get state legislators to throw out the results. He called Brad Raffensperger, Georgia's Republican secretary of state, and told him to "find 11,780 votes . . . Fellas, I need 11,000 votes. Give me a break." Even the Murdoch-owned *New York Post* urged Trump to stop "cheering for an undemocratic coup" and avoid being the "King Lear of Mar-a-Lago, ranting about the corruption of the world."

Trump's team arranged a protest in Washington on November 14—and Trump took his motorcade to pay the protesters a visit. Trump supporters unfurled a huge "TRUMP LAW AND ORDER" banner in Washington's newly named Black Lives Matter Plaza. Clashes erupted. A man was stabbed. Some were arrested on gun charges.

Trump backers held a similar rally four weeks later, two

days before the Electoral College would formalize Trump's loss. Michael Flynn and Alex Jones rallied the crowd. "Wow!" Trump tweeted. "Thousands of people forming in Washington (D.C.) for Stop the Steal. Didn't know about this, but I'll be seeing them! #MAGA." Trump flew above the crowd in Marine One. Below, at least four people were stabbed at an assembly point for the Proud Boys.

Fueling the Big Lie was Fox News, which, in the nine days after Biden's victory, cast doubt on the outcome or publicized conspiracy theories about results no fewer than 574 times, according to Media Matters.

Krebs, the U.S. election security chief Trump fired, pleaded with his fellow Republicans to stop the disinformation—which provoked death threats against him and election officials around the country. "This is not the America I recognize, and it's got to stop," he testified to Congress in mid-December. "I would appreciate more support from my own party, the Republican Party, to call this stuff out and end it." He added: "Democracy in general is fragile. . . . If a party fails to participate in the process and instead undermines the process, we risk losing that democracy."

But Republican lawmakers were having none of it. They encouraged their party's voters to believe that Trump had won the election.

"The election in many ways was stolen," announced Senator Rand Paul.

Senator Rick Scott of Florida said his constituents think the election outcome is no "different than what Maduro is doing" in Venezuela's dictatorship.

Senator Josh Hawley of Missouri said his constituents felt "disenfranchised" and that "the election had been rigged."

Representative Jim Jordan of Ohio, a leader of House conservatives, joined a "Stop the Steal" rally in Pennsylvania and shouted into a bullhorn that "our elections should have integrity." He later cast doubt on Biden's victory ("somehow the guy who never left his house wins the election?"), and complained about "the fraud" and "the unconstitutional fashion" of the elections and an "end-run around the Constitution." He declared that "sixty million Americans think it was stolen" and that "it's time for us to fight."

Senator Ron Johnson of Wisconsin, while acknowledging that "the conclusion has collectively been reached" that there wasn't enough fraud to change the outcome, held a hearing to demonstrate the opposite. He complained about "fraud," "irregularities," "violations of election laws," "fraudulent votes and ballot stuffing," and "corruption of voting machines and software." He brought in Ken Starr, who testified about a "clear violation of the law."

McConnell, the Senate Republican leader, refused for six weeks to acknowledge Biden's win, declining to refer to Biden as "president-elect" and voting against the customary joint inaugural resolution because it affirmed Biden's win. ABC News's Jonathan Karl later reported that McConnell privately urged Barr to refute Trump's unfounded claims of voter fraud. McConnell wouldn't do it himself, because "we need the president in Georgia" for two Senate runoff elections, McConnell told Barr. "And so we cannot be frontally attacking him right now."

That craven decision gave momentum to those such as Cruz, Hawley, and just-arrived Senator Tommy Tuberville of Alabama, who planned to raise objections when it came time for Congress to certify the Electoral College vote on January 6.

"We will not take it anymore, and that's what this is all about," Trump told a sea of MAGA fans and Proud Boys on the Ellipse outside the White House at noon on January 6. From behind bulletproof glass, he told them: "If you don't fight like hell, you're not going to have a country anymore."

Trump worked the crowd into a frenzy with his claim that victory had been stolen from him by "explosions of bullshit."

"Bullshit! Bullshit!" the mob chanted.

Trump instructed his supporters to march to the Capitol—"and I'll be there with you"—to "demand that Congress do the right thing" and not count the electoral votes of swing states he lost. "You'll never take back our country with weakness, you have to show strength and you have to be strong," he admonished them, with instructions to make themselves heard "peacefully and patriotically." Wink, wink.

"We're going to the Capitol," he told the mob.

At the same event, Donald Trump Jr. delivered a political

threat to lawmakers who didn't vote to reject the election results: "We're coming for you."

And then there was Giuliani. "Let's have trial by combat," he told the crowd. "I'm willing to stake my reputation, the president is willing to stake his reputation, on the fact that we're going to find criminality" in the election.

It would later emerge that Giuliani, Flynn, Stone, and others were coordinating this last-ditch assault on democracy from a war room in the luxury Willard Hotel, where Abraham Lincoln stayed before his first inauguration, while the Confederates were coordinating an earlier assault on American democracy.

Trump's mob, riled by the president and his men, marched to the Capitol and breached the barricades. They overpowered Capitol Police, climbed scaffolding, scaled walls, shattered glass, busted into the Senate chamber and stood at the presiding officer's desk, and broke into Speaker Nancy Pelosi's hastily abandoned office. They marauded about the Rotunda and Statuary Hall wearing MAGA hats, carrying Confederate flags, posing for souvenir photos, and scribbling graffiti ("Murder the Media").

Police rushed legislative leaders to safety. They barricaded doors to the House chamber and drew guns to protect lawmakers sheltering inside. They fired tear gas at the attackers. Shots were fired inside the Capitol; a bloodied woman who was wheeled out later died. The District of Columbia declared a curfew. And even then it took Trump nearly three hours before he released a video telling those ransacking the Capitol to "go home"—even as he glorified the violence by saying "these are the things and events that happen when a sacred landslide election victory is so unceremoniously & viciously stripped away from great patriots."

Americans would later see the grotesque images: of the insurrectionists using poles with U.S. flags attached to beat Capitol Police officers and to smash Capitol windows; an officer screaming in pain as he was crushed and beaten; the domestic terrorists using a metal barricade with a Trump "Drain the Swamp" banner on it to break down the doors of the House chamber; the invaders ransacking senators' desks on the Senate floor; the makeshift noose and gallows meant for Vice President Mike Pence because he didn't cooperate with Trump's coup attempt; an officer firing a lethal shot as an insurrectionist broke through the last barrier separating the mob from lawmakers hiding on floors, under desks.

An organizer of the attack identified Representatives Andy Biggs and Paul Gosar, both Arizona Republicans, and Representative Mo Brooks of Alabama as people who "schemed up" the seditious moment. During the attack, QAnon-admiring Representative Lauren Boebert of Colorado tweeted about Pelosi's evacuation from the House chamber—helpful information for any would-be assassin. Hawley famously pumped his fist in solidarity with the mob on January 6.

Kevin McCarthy reached Trump by phone and demanded that he call off the riot, according to an account given by Representative Jaime Herrera Beutler, a Washington Republican. Trump replied: "Well, Kevin, I guess these people are more upset about the election than you are."

The Capitol Police called desperately for help from the D.C. National Guard. It took three hours and nineteen minutes for the Army to grant permission for the Guard to help—either a catastrophic failure of military command or a deliberate decision by Trump loyalists at the Pentagon to prevent the Capitol from being defended.

Seven lives were lost in the attack and its aftermath. One hundred forty police officers were wounded. A force of some twenty thousand troops—the first of its kind since the Civil War—came to Washington to defend the capital from pro-Trump rioters during Biden's inauguration.

It was the first time the Capitol, the seat of American government, was sacked since the British did it in the War of 1812. Yet even after the bloody insurrection was quelled, 147 Republican lawmakers—including fully two thirds of the House GOP caucus—returned to the Capitol that night and voted to overturn the will of the people.

The coup had failed, but the Republican Party had cast its lot with the would-be autocrat.

Conclusion

Just how close the United States had come to the unthinkable didn't become fully clear until much later. In early 2022, the House select committee appointed to investigate the January 6 insurrection uncovered a draft executive order prepared for Trump but, mercifully, never signed. Citing vague authorities under the Constitution and the National Emergencies Act, the December 16, 2020, draft order asserted the fiction that there had been "systemic fraud" in the election and ordered the secretary of defense to seize voting machines and other "national critical infrastructure supporting federal elections." It was, in essence, a proposed military takeover to invalidate the election.

It also emerged that Giuliani and other Trump advisers had hatched a scheme to install fake Trump electors in seven swing states, thereby subverting the Electoral College and handing the presidency to Trump. Meeting in or near state capitols, the phony electors signed fake, forged election certificates designed to replace the real ones sent to Congress by the states. Meanwhile, Ginni Thomas, the activist wife of Supreme Court justice Clarence Thomas, texted with White House chief of staff Meadows about her "hope" that the "Biden crime family" as well as elected officials, bureaucrats, and journalists would be taken to "barges off GITMO to face military tribunals for sedition."

Happily, the plots all failed to alter the outcome. Trump boycotted Biden's inauguration and instead, in one final abuse, took

Air Force One on a joy ride, doing a flyover of his Mar-a-Lago club in Florida.

But the reprieve was temporary. The Republican Party, corrupted by its taste of the authoritarian, had passed the point of no return. Trump was gone, at least for the moment. But Trumpism endured.

This wasn't surprising. Republicans had created the conditions that made it possible for Trump to rise, and those conditions still existed when he departed. In fact, they were much worse, because for five years Republican lawmakers had endorsed and enabled Trump's conspiracy theories, his wooing of white supremacists, his taste for the autocratic, and his sabotage of the institutions of government. The habits would prove impossible to shake.

After some initially recoiled at the Trump-provoked insurrection, Republican leaders quickly got in line behind the former president. House GOP leader Kevin McCarthy at first charged that "the president bears responsibility" for the attack and should "accept his share of responsibility, quell the brewing unrest," and be the subject of a censure resolution. After a pilgrimage to Mar-a-Lago, McCarthy eventually recanted his criticism, claiming Trump was unaware of the January 6 attack and wanted to "make sure to stop" it.

McConnell, on the Senate floor, had said that "the mob was fed lies" and "they were provoked by the president and other powerful people, and they tried to use fear and violence to stop" the election certification. But McConnell postponed the Senate impeachment trial and then assured Trump's acquittal by proclaiming on the eve of the vote that the senators "lack jurisdiction"—because Trump, thanks to McConnell's delay, was no longer in office.

Instead, congressional Republicans moved to purge the few in their ranks who spoke out against Trump's attempted coup. House Republicans, with McCarthy's backing, ousted Congresswoman Liz Cheney of Wyoming, the former vice president's daughter, from her position as the No. 3 Republican leader over her criticism of Trump's election lies. Minutes before she was ousted, she told her GOP colleagues that "we cannot both embrace the 'big lie' and embrace the Constitution."

A defiant Cheney said on the House floor that "I will not sit back and watch in silence while others lead our party down a path that abandons the rule of law and joins the former president's crusade to undermine our democracy." On the nearly empty floor, her powerful words were met with silence.

McCarthy also blocked the formation of a bipartisan, independent commission to examine January 6—even though it had been negotiated by his own point man, the top Republican on the Homeland Security Committee, and even though it was nearly identical to the commission proposal Republicans had previously introduced. McConnell helped defeat the commission by announcing his opposition before the House vote.

After Republicans blocked a January 6 commission, Pelosi formed a January 6 congressional committee—which McCarthy promptly sabotaged by appointing Jim Jordan, who worked closely with Trump on January 6 and had been part of the "Stop the Steal" action. When Pelosi objected, McCarthy boycotted the committee entirely.

Instead, the outcast Cheney joined the committee as its vice chair. At its first hearing, she challenged her Republican colleagues: "Will we be so blinded by partisanship that we throw away the miracle of America? Do we hate our political adversaries more than we love our country?"

The Republicans' answer to those questions is now clear, and ominous.

Fox News spent a chunk of Biden's inaugural week perpetrating the fabrication that the left was proposing "reeducation camps" to "reprogram" Trump supporters. "Are they going to set up a concentration camp?" asked one Fox News host.

Fox's Tucker Carlson made a three-part "documentary" that suggested January 6 may have been instigated by far-left activists, that it was a false flag operation run by the FBI, that the rioters were being held as "political prisoners," and that January 6 was being used to deny Trump voters their constitutional rights. In Congress, Greene and Gaetz joined in accusing the FBI of orchestrating January 6.

Paul Gosar, the Arizona congressman, claimed that Ashli Babbitt, the insurrectionist shot dead by Capitol Police on January 6 as she breached the final barrier protecting lawmakers, was "executed" by a police officer "lying in wait" for her. (Trump himself claimed Babbitt was "murdered.") Gosar described the insurrectionists as "peaceful patriots."

Representative Andrew Clyde of Georgia called the January 6 insurrection a "normal tourist visit." (Trump claimed his supporters were "hugging and kissing" police, not beating them with flagpoles.)

Representative Mo Brooks of Alabama falsely proclaimed: "Evidence growing that fascist ANTIFA orchestrated Capitol attack with clever mob control tactics."

Republican lawmakers began referring to the January 6 defendants as "political prisoners." Twenty-one House Republicans voted against a proposal to award the Congressional Gold Medal to police officers who defended the Capitol on January 6.

By early 2022, the Justice Department had brought cases against 791 people for their January 6 actions, according to a George Washington University tally, and 281 have been convicted. The founder of the extremist Oath Keepers militia and ten others were charged with "seditious conspiracy." The former national chairman of the Proud Boys has also been indicted on conspiracy charges. Trump suggested he would pardon them all if he were returned to power—while the RNC officially labeled the insurrection "legitimate political discourse." Republicans had landed emphatically on the side of the seditionists.

And it wasn't just about January 6. The illiberalism that infected the party now caused the same pathologies to recur in Trump's absence: conspiracy theories, white nationalism, violent language, and creeping authoritarianism.

In Arizona, Trump supporters launched a so-called audit of the election results, involving a group called the Cyber Ninjas and examining ballots with UV light to see "if there's bamboo in the paper" in support of a wacky conspiracy theory that forty thousand fake ballots were surreptitiously flown in from Asia. Several jurisdictions followed Arizona's "audit" example.

The Texas Republican Party promoted a new slogan, "We are the Storm"—an echo of the QAnon term for when Trump's enemies will face mass executions. Hawaii's Republican Party praised QAnon believers and promoted a Holocaust denier.

By early 2022, ten Republican-controlled states had enacted what are known as "memory laws" in totalitarian countries. Under the guise of combating the phantom threat of critical race theory, such gag laws restrict what can be taught about race in American history so that white students need not feel "discomfort." Egged on by Republican officials' claims, right-wing activists went on a spree of book banning at schools across the country, the vast majority about race, gender, and sexuality. Florida, which set off a rush in Republican-run states to enact "don't say gay" legislation banning teaching about sexual orientation or gender identity, even banned 28 math textbooks for allegedly promoting critical race theory or other "prohibited topics."

Also by early 2022, nineteen states had enacted thirty-four laws restricting voting and compromising election integrity; the Brennan Center for Justice, a voting rights group, found an "unprecedented" effort at disenfranchisement. A Georgia law made it illegal for anybody to offer food or drink—even water—to voters waiting in long lines. Such lines exist primarily in Black precincts, because Republicans have reduced the number of polling places and hours of voting in those areas.

Texas Republicans passed a bill that banned drive-through and twenty-four-hour voting (both used disproportionately by voters of color), imposed new limits on voting by mail, blocked election officials from distributing mail-ballot applications unless specifically requested, gave partisan poll watchers more leeway to influence vote counting, and put in place new rules and paperwork requirements that will deter people from helping others vote or register. The new Texas law caused fully 12.4 percent of all ballots to be rejected in the state's March 2022 primaries—an order of magnitude higher than in previous elections—with Democrats slightly more likely than Republicans to have ballots tossed.

Republicans in Congress, for their part, blocked the Democrats' attempt to protect voting rights against such incursions. Republicans also blocked action on an attempt to restore provisions of the 1965 Voting Rights Act gutted by the Supreme Court's conservative majority in 2013. (McConnell justified the GOP obstruction by saying "African American voters are voting in just as high a percentage as Americans"; he later said he misspoke.)

And the Supreme Court upheld new Arizona laws that banned a number of voting practices used disproportionately in minority communities.

Republican-controlled states used redistricting to take some 40 percent of competitive House seats off the table—protecting GOP lawmakers from the growing number of voters of color. Republicans, for example, redrew maps to give themselves both of Texas's new congressional seats (even though most of the population growth was in Democratic-leaning communities of color), and they reduced the number of competitive House seats from six to one. Democrats could win by a landslide 57 percent in Texas and would still control no more than 37 percent of the state's congressional seats, the Brennan Center calculates.

In Congress, McCarthy has kept House Republicans unified in defense of members such as Gosar (found to have ties to white nationalists and produced a cartoon video of himself killing a Democratic colleague) and Greene (spoke at a white-nationalist conference, "liked" social media comments recommending "a bullet to the head" of Pelosi and proposing that FBI agents should be executed for helping the fictional deep state, and posted an image of herself with an AR-15 next to photos of Democratic colleagues). Neither did Representative Madison Cawthorn, a North Carolina Republican, face consequences for saying that "if our election systems continue to be rigged and continue to be stolen then it's going to lead to one place and that's bloodshed."

Democratic lawmakers (and the rare Republicans who work with Democrats) have endured an unnerving volume of violent threats. And the authoritarians keep marching. Former Trump national security adviser Michael Flynn told a gathering of QAnon followers in Texas that a military coup "should happen here" in the United States (he later qualified that call to sedition). Former Trump lawyer Sidney Powell told the same assembly that Trump could be "reinstated."

In Florida, Republican governor Ron DeSantis proposed to create his own police force, an "Office of Election Crimes and Security," that could be used to intimidate voters. In Virginia, Republican governor Glenn Youngkin created a tip line so that parents could serve as informants and report teachers teaching anything "divisive." In Texas, Republican governor Greg Abbott signed an abortion ban incentivizing private citizens to sue people they suspect performed or aided an abortion, and anti-abortion activists set up a tip line so informants could report people they suspect. Missouri's legislature is taking up legislation allowing private citizens to sue anyone who helps a resident get an abortion out of state. In such gestures are the beginnings of a Stasi state.

When Vladimir Putin's Russia invaded democratic Ukraine in February 2022, indiscriminately targeting civilians, Trump called the dictator's unprovoked attack "genius" and "savvy." Fox's Carlson and some GOP lawmakers and candidates have parroted Kremlin propaganda justifying the invasion. In April 2022, 63 House Republicans—30 percent of the caucus—voted against a resolution affirming support for NATO as Russia's brutal attack continued. Most Republicans, while opposing Putin, have spent more time blaming Biden for the invasion, for his response to the attack, and for higher gas prices.

As they look to the midterm elections of 2022, Republicans have turned to a familiar guide: Newt Gingrich. The former speaker told *The Washington Post* he is serving as a consultant to Kevin McCarthy and his leadership team. Republicans have come full circle: the man who started American politics down the road to destruction is returning to see his work completed.

No sooner had this been announced than Gingrich, on Fox News, threatened to imprison lawmakers serving on the January 6 committee, saying they're "going to face a real risk of going to jail" after Republicans take over Congress.

Throwing political opponents in jail for investigating an attack on the U.S. Capitol? Replied Liz Cheney: "This is what it looks like when the rule of law unravels."

Death threats. Gag laws. Book banning. Secret informants. Voter suppression and election intimidation. Vows to imprison political opponents.

In retrospect, how we got into this mess is obvious: Republican leaders have been weakening democracy's defenses for a quarter century.

How we get out of this mess is less clear. The lure of power has induced Republican leaders to abandon the compact of democracy. And the reflexive, tribal politics they nurtured means a large chunk of the electorate has joined them in abandoning the American experiment.

There are any number of things we could do, as a country, to restore democratic institutions, and faith in them: restoring and protecting voting rights; cracking down on social media disinformation; reining in the corruption unleashed by *Citizens United;* reforming the Supreme Court; rebuilding civics education; rescuing local newspapers. But any of these remedies presupposes that both major American political parties are operating on the level. We don't have that now. The Republican Party is not a good-faith actor in the democratic system. So there's not much we can do but ride it out—and vote as if our way of life is at stake, for surely it is.

Democrats, as well as small-d democrats, are despairing. There is a danger in 2022 that Republicans will assert that the typical backlash against an incumbent president's party during midterm elections is instead a validation by the voters of its antidemocratic ways. That raises the risk of a nightmare scenario in 2024: Republicans lose the presidential election but a Republican Congress declares the GOP candidate the victor. J. Michael Luttig, a retired appellate judge and a longtime conservative intellectual leader, warns starkly that Republicans will "overturn the 2024 election if Trump or his anointed successor loses again."

Months after the January 6 insurrection, I checked back with Timothy Snyder, the Yale historian of totalitarianism who accurately predicted Trump's attempted coup. "We're looking almost certainly at an attempt in 2024 to take power without winning the election," he told me. The antidemocratic actions of Republican-controlled state legislatures "are all working toward the scenario in 2024 where they lose by 10 million votes but they still appoint their guy."

History warns that this move toward the authoritarian will bring greater violence. Republicans are "digging themselves ever deeper into becoming a party which only wins by keeping other people from voting, and that's a downward spiral," Snyder said.

A quarter century after a truck bomb set by an antigovernment extremist decimated Oklahoma City, Republicans have lit a fuse under democracy itself.

We have, as Americans, endured threats to democracy before. During the 1790s, it wasn't at all clear the new country would survive foreign invasion or internal division. The 1810s brought more of the same. The divisions of the 1850s exploded into the Civil War, followed by the instability of Reconstruction. The 1890s were filled with farmer revolts, strikes, massive immigration, war with Spain, an economic depression, and the expansion of Jim Crow. The 1930s brought the Great Depression and the threat of fascism abroad and at home. And then there were the assassinations and upheaval of the late 1960s.

The good news: things will get better in the long run with the rise to political dominance of the millennials and Gen Z, who have grown up in, and overwhelmingly favor, a multicultural America. The source of political rage, the older white backlash as the United States becomes majority-minority, will in the long run be quashed because there is no stopping that demographic transition. The transition to a white-minority country is inevitable.

The bad news: things will get worse before they get better, as less-educated, rural, white Americans, their anxiety stoked by Republican leaders, grow more desperate over their loss of power. The question is whether, and to what extent, our democratic institutions and instincts will survive the transition.

I've told this story of how one of America's two major political parties swerved off the path of democracy in hopes that rising generations will, in time, find in it a roadmap to get the United States back on course.

Acknowledgments

I could not have written this book without the enthusiastic support of Fred Hiatt, my mentor, teacher, North Star, and boss for the last thirteen years. Fred, the longtime editorial page editor of *The Washington Post,* died unexpectedly at the end of 2021, leaving a gaping hole in American journalism and in the hearts of the many who loved him for his courage and decency.

Among Fred's many gifts was his eye for talent, and his two deputies, Ruth Marcus and Karen Tumulty, have done a magnificent job since his death running the place under the most difficult circumstances. I'm lucky to have as my editors at *The Post* Michael Larabee and Drew Goins, who counsel me with judgment, skill, and endless patience. I also appreciate Nancy Szokan, Jim Downie, Autumn Brewington, Michael Duffy, Becca Clemons and her team, Trey Johnson and his team, and the others in the *Post* Opinions section who make it all happen.

This book draws on my reporting from Washington over the last twenty-seven years, and naming all those who taught and guided me would take another book. From the *Wall Street Journal* Washington bureau of Alan Murray and Jill Abramson, to the *New Republic* of Marty Peretz and Chuck Lane, to *The Washington Post* of Gene Robinson, Maralee Schwartz, Liz Spayd, Mike Abramowitz, Susan Glasser, Steve Ginsberg, Len Downie, and Marcus Brauchli, I've had the honor of working with the best.

Writing a book during the pandemic meant never being in the same room with my editor, Kristine Puopolo, Doubleday's editorial director of nonfiction. But her unerring judgment and deft touch improved my work at every step of the process: conceptualizing, organizing, writing, and editing. I'm in awe of her abilities. I'm grateful that she and Bill Thomas chose to do this project with me. Carolyn Williams, Fred Chase, Nora Reichard, Michael Goldsmith, Lindsay Mandel, John Fontana, Maria Carella, Peggy Samedi, and Dan Novack at Doubleday made the production process a pleasure.

I've known my agent, Rafe Sagalyn, for nearly the entire time period covered by this book, and through all that time he has shown remarkable patience and aplomb dealing with this columnist's tangled relationship with long-form journalism. I've benefited, as well, from advice from Bob Kaiser, Al Kamen, Kim Ghattas, Eric Liu, John Wertheim, and "bubbe and zayde" (as they are known in my house), Rosa DeLauro and Stan Greenberg.

Remember this name: Erin Doherty. You'll be hearing more of it in the years to come, I predict. She's an extraordinary talent, now with Axios news, and I was lucky enough to convince her to be my researcher for this book. She was indispensable in seeking out information new and old, with a keen eye for the telling detail and a hugely impressive work ethic. Erin is going places. I also salute the talented Aidan Stretch, who took time out of his gap year before Yale to gather helpful data for me.

My daughter, Paola Milbank, and my stepchildren, Sadie and Jasper Delicath, kept me sane and centered throughout the difficult balancing of book, column, pandemic, and insurrection. As glum as I am about short-term prospects for the country and the world, I am optimistic about the long term, because I know they and their generation have what it takes to clean up the mess we're leaving them. That's why I dedicated this book to them.

Finally, I would be nowhere at all without my wife, Anna Greenberg, my best source and my best friend. She's also my secret weapon. A former Harvard political science professor who now runs a renowned Democratic polling firm, she has an unparalleled ability to spot trends, to see the big picture, and to cut through clutter. Anna challenges me, inspires me, encourages me, and nurtures me. This book, like everything else I do, is better because of her.

Notes

INTRODUCTION

2   mostly false allegations: Julian Zelizer, *Burning Down the House: Newt Gingrich and the Rise of the New Republican Party* (Penguin, 2021).

2   promised land: Rally, "Republican Contract with America Rally," C-SPAN, September 27, 1994. https://www.c-span.org/video/?60472-1/republican-contract-america-rally.

4   civil war: Barbara F. Walter, *How Civil Wars Start* (Crown, 2022).

4   "lethal threat": Report, "Homeland Threat Assessment," Department of Homeland Security, October 2020. https://www.dhs.gov/sites/default/files/publications/2020_10_06_homeland-threat-assessment.pdf.

6   "political traditions": Alan Fram, "New Conservative Group Would Save 'Anglo-Saxon' Traditions," Associated Press, April 17, 2021.

6   provoked threats: Brittany Shammas, "School Boards Are 'Under an Immediate Threat,' Organization Says in Request for Federal Help," *The Washington Post,* September 30, 2021.

10   "right thing": Dana Milbank, "Trump Will Lose, or I Will Eat This Column," *The Washington Post,* October 2, 2015.

11   "Trump Party": Cristiano Lima, "Boehner: 'There Is No Republican Party. There's a Trump Party.'" *Politico,* May 31, 2018. https://www.politico.com/story/2018/05/31/john-boehner-republican-trump-party-615357.

CHAPTER 1: SHOOTING AT MELONS

14   Foster's death: David Von Drehle and Howard Schneider, "Foster's Death a Suicide," *The Washington Post,* July 1, 1994.

14   *Wall Street Journal:* Michael Kinsley, "The Journal and Vincent Foster," *The Washington Post,* July 29, 1993.

14   before his death: Stephen Labaton, "A Report on His Suicide Portrays a Deeply Troubled Vince Foster," *The New York Times,* October 11, 1997.

14   Investigators deduced: "Whitewater: The Foster Report," *The Washington Post,* 1998. https://www.washingtonpost.com/wp-srv/politics/special/whitewater/docs/fosterviii.htm.

14   "mistakes from ignorance": Michael Isikoff and Dan Balz, "Foster Note Reveals an Anguished Aide," *The Washington Post,* August 11, 1993.

15   special order speech: "In-Depth Investigative Report on Vince Foster Suicide,"

Congress, *Congressional Record,* August 2, 1994. https://www.govinfo.gov/content/pkg/CREC-1994-08-02/html/CREC-1994-08-02-pt1-PgH102.htm.

15 "foul play": "Whitewater: The Foster Report, 1993 Park Police Investigation," *The Washington Post,* 1998. https://www.washingtonpost.com/wp-srv/politics/special/whitewater/docs/fosterii.htm.

16 "self-inflicted gunshot": "Whitewater: The Foster Report, Congressional Inquiries," *The Washington Post,* 1998. https://www.washingtonpost.com/wp-srv/politics/special/whitewater/docs/fosterii.htm.

16 "cries of conspiracy": Dan E. Moldea, *A Washington Tragedy: How the Death of Vincent Foster Ignited a Political Firestorm* (Regnery, 1998).

16 grassy knoll: Michael E. Miller, "JFK Assassination Conspiracy Theories: The Grassy Knoll, Umbrella Man, LBJ and Ted Cruz's Dad," *The Washington Post,* October 27, 2017.

16 "I'm not convinced": R. H. Melton, and Ann Devroy, "Gingrich Not Convinced Foster Death Was Suicide," *The Washington Post,* July 26, 1995.

17 "Arkansas Project": Brooks Jackson, "Who Is Richard Mellon Scaife?," CNN, April 27, 1998. https://www.cnn.com/ALLPOLITICS/1998/04/27/scaife.profile/.

17 "Rosetta stone": Robert G. Kaiser, "Scaife Denies Ties to 'Conspiracy,' Starr," *The Washington Post,* December 17, 1998.

17 "died mysteriously": Kevin Drum, "Tea Party: Old Whine in New Bottles," *Mother Jones,* September–October 2010. https://www.motherjones.com/politics/2010/09/history-of-the-tea-party/.

17 launch Newsmax: Sarah Ellison, Jonathan O'Connell, and Josh Dawsey, "Chris Ruddy and Newsmax Went All-In on Trump. Now They Might Pay a Price for It," *The Washington Post,* May 6, 2021.

17 "Foster was murdered": "The Attack Machine," *The New York Times,* November 12, 1995.

18 "involved in a murder": Russell Watson, "Vince Foster's Suicide: The Rumor Mill Churns," *Newsweek,* March 20, 1994. https://www.newsweek.com/vince-fosters-suicide-rumor-mill-churns-185900.

18 Chris Lehane: Chris Lehane, "Yeah, I Wrote the Vast Right-Wing Conspiracy Memo," *Politico,* April 27, 2014. https://www.politico.com/magazine/story/2014/04/chris-lehane-right-wing-conspiracy-memo-106059/.

18 "currently investigating": Robert O'Harrow Jr. and Michael Kranish, "After Investigating Clinton White House and Vincent Foster's Death, Brett Kavanaugh Had a Change of Heart," *The Washington Post,* August 2, 2018.

19 "discrepancy list": "Discrepancy List: Brett Kavanaugh," Archives, May 30, 1995. https://www.archives.gov/files/research/kavanaugh/releases/docid-70105372.pdf.

20 killed himself: Philip Weiss, "Clinton Crazy," *The New York Times Magazine,* February 23, 1997.

20 "keep them together": Dale Russakoff and Dan Balz, "After Political Victory, A Personal Revolution," *The Washington Post,* December 19, 1994.

20 "Without C-SPAN": Cokie Roberts and Steven V. Roberts, "The Real Conservative Revolution," *The Baltimore Sun,* January 17, 1995.

21 congressional pay raise: Jack Anderson and Dale Van Atta, "In Campaign, Mum's the Word on Pay," *The Washington Post,* October 5, 1990.

21 twenty-two overdrafts: Clifford Krauss, "The House Bank; Committee Names All Who Overdrew at the House Bank," *The Washington Post,* April 17, 1992.

21 "truth is transactional": Peter Baker, *The Breach: Inside the Impeachment and Trial of William Jefferson Clinton* (Simon & Schuster, 2000).

21   Office of Technology Assessment: Ed O'Keefe, "When Congress Wiped an Agency Off the Map," *The Washington Post,* November 29, 2011.

21   "not the truth": "Hon. Jennifer Dunn of Washington in the House of Representatives," *Congressional Record,* June 29, 1999. https://www.govinfo.gov/content/pkg/CREC-1999-06-29/html/CREC-1999-06-29-pt1-PgE1427-2.htm.

22   "promoting homosexuality": Mary Jacoby, "Signs Hint Christian Coalition Influence Has Peaked," *Chicago Tribune,* September 13, 1996.

22   "paint my face": Thomas B. Edsall, "Christian Political Soldier Helps Revive Movement," *The Washington Post,* September 10, 1993.

23   "other news outlets": "White House Assails Gingrich Allegation on Brown," *The Washington Post,* June 6, 1996.

23   "nuclear attack": Don van Natta Jr., "Republican Pitch Plays on Nuclear Fears," *The New York Times,* September 4, 1999.

23   "he'd be gone": Edward Walsh, "Panel Split Over 'Scumbag' Comment," *The Washington Post,* April 22, 1998.

23   mandatory AIDS testing: "Congressman Proposes Mandatory Universal AIDS Testing," UPI, March 18, 1987. https://www.upi.com/Archives/1987/03/18/Congressman-proposes-mandatory-universal-AIDS-testing/4478543042000/.

23   razor to the barber: "Dan Burton Exits Stage Right," MSNBC, January 31, 2012. https://www.msnbc.com/rachel-maddow-show/dan-burton-exits-stage-right-msna33320.

23   Clintons' cat: James Warren, "Stamping Out Socks' Mail," *Chicago Tribune,* January 8, 1995.

23   "personal friends": Jonathan Weisman, "Burton Releases New Tapes of Hubbell to Counter Foes Democratic Colleague Alleged Bid to Mislead with First Transcripts," *The Baltimore Sun,* May 5, 1998.

24   Burton's "circus": George Lardner Jr. and Juliet Eilperin, "Burton Apologizes to GOP," *The Washington Post,* May 7, 1998.

24   "lying to the press": Christopher Ruddy, *The Strange Death of Vincent Foster: An Investigation* (Free Press, 2002).

24   "Foster's alleged affair": Tom Hamburger, Robert Barnes, and Robert O'Harrow Jr., "Senate Democrats Want to Know Whether Kavanaugh Crossed Line During Clinton Probe," *Chicago Tribune,* August 22, 2018.

24   Linda Tripp: Amy Goldstein and Rene Sanchez, "Tripp's Curious Path to the Pentagon," *The Washington Post,* February 7, 1998.

25   "Foster committed suicide": Glenn Kessler, "No, Donald Trump, There's Nothing 'Fishy' About Vince Foster's Suicide," *The Washington Post,* May 25, 2016.

25   "Vince Foster nonsense": Alex Swoyer, "Bill Clinton Takes Jab at Brett Kavanaugh over Vince Foster Probe," *The Washington Times,* May 7, 2019.

25   "utterly preposterous": Michael Isikoff, "The Strange Case of Christopher Ruddy," *Slate,* October 19, 1997. https://slate.com/culture/1997/10/the-strange-case-of-christopher-ruddy.html.

25   "planning suicide": Leigh Ferrara, "Conspiracy Watch: Bill and Hill's Thrill Kill," *Mother Jones,* 2008. https://www.motherjones.com/politics/2008/01/conspiracy-watch-bill-and-hills-thrill-kill/.

26   "On this date": Harriet Gutter, "Facebook Post," September 5, 2018. https://www.facebook.com/photo.php?fbid=10217476285321916&set=a.1114153336915&type=3&theater.

26   "haunts me": "Tucker Carlson and Ken Starr Revive Vince Foster Conspiracy Theory," Media Matters, September 10, 2018. https://www.mediamatters.org/

tucker-carlson/tucker-carlson-and-ken-starr-revive-vince-foster-conspiracy
-theory.

26   "muddy trail": Dana Milbank, "The Crazy Face of Trump's GOP," *The Washington Post,* July 18, 2016.

26   "we killed Vince Foster": Eric Garcia, "Olson Says Clinton–Vince Foster Remarks Were 'a Step Too Far,'" *Roll Call,* June 21, 2017. https://www.rollcall.com/2017/06/21/olson-says-clinton-vince-foster-remarks-were-a-step-too-far/.

26   "very serious": Jose A. Del Real and Robert Costa, "Trump Escalates Attack on Bill Clinton," *The Washington Post,* May 23, 2016.

26   Sheila Foster Anthony: Sheila Foster Anthony, "Vince Foster Was My Brother," *Pittsburgh Post-Gazette,* May 27, 2016.

CHAPTER 2: PERSONAL DESTRUCTION

28   "If Monica Lewinsky says": Brett M. Kavanaugh, Memorandum, Office of the Independent Counsel, August 15, 1998. https://www.archives.gov/files/research/kavanaugh/releases/kavanaugh8.15.98.pdf.

29   "genital-to-genital contact": Monica Lewinsky, Testimony, July 30, 1998. https://www.govinfo.gov/content/pkg/CDOC-105hdoc310/pdf/CDOC-105hdoc310.pdf.

29   "On four occasions": Monica Lewinsky, Testimony, August 6, 1998. https://www.govinfo.gov/content/pkg/CDOC-105hdoc310/pdf/CDOC-105hdoc310.pdf.

31   list of about sixty-five words: "Language: A Key Mechanism of Control," GOPAC, September 1990. https://web.archive.org/web/20130902053532/http://web.utk.edu/~glenn/GopacMemo.html.

32   "encourage you to be nasty": Michael Oreskes, "Political Memo; For G.O.P. Arsenal, 133 Words to Fire," *The New York Times,* September 9, 1990.

33   "moral coward": Newt Gingrich, Speech to College Republicans, June 24, 1978. https://www.pbs.org/wgbh/pages/frontline/newt/newt78speech.html.

33   "corrupt left-wing machine": Craig Shirley, *Citizen Newt: The Making of a Reagan Conservative* (Thomas Nelson, 2017).

33   "dictator": Jeffrey Goldberg, "When Gingrich Accused Reagan of Losing the Cold War," *The Atlantic,* January 25, 2012. https://www.theatlantic.com/politics/archive/2012/01/when-gingrich-accused-reagan-of-losing-the-cold-war/252009/.

33   Neville Chamberlain's appeasement: Tip O'Neill Jr., "The Speaker's Words Are Ordered Taken Down," C-SPAN, May 10, 1984. https://www.c-span.org/video/?93662-1/speakers-words-ordered#.

33   coddling communist governments: Julian Zeliger, *Burning Down the House: Newt Gingrich, the Fall of a Speaker, and the Rise of the New Republican Party* (Penguin, 2020).

33   "destructive of the values": James Salzar, "Gingrich's Language Set New Course," *The Atlanta Journal-Constitution,* July 5, 2016.

33   "ruthless, corrupt": Steven V. Robert, "The Foreign Policy Tussle," *The New York Times,* January 24, 1988.

33   "empty House": Craig Shirley, *Citizen Newt: The Making of a Reagan Conservative* (Thomas Nelson, 2007).

34   "Daffy Dukakis": McKay Coppins, "The Man Who Broke Politics," *The Atlantic,* October 17, 2018.

34   "chameleon-like actions": Sheryl Gay Stolberg, "Gingrich Stuck to Caustic Path in Ethics Battles," *The New York Times,* January 26, 2012.

34   "values of the left": David Beers, "Newt Gingrich: Master of Disaster," *Mother Jones,* September 1, 1989. https://www.motherjones.com/politics/1989/09/master-disaster/.

34   "Grotesque," "loony": John Harwood, "Newt Gingrich: GOP's Bare Knuckles Battler," *St. Petersburg Times,* July 27, 1989.

34   "non-incest": John K. Wilson, *Newt Gingrich: Capitol Crimes and Misdemeanors* (Common Courage, 1996).

34   "enemy of normal Americans": Godfrey Sperling, "Sen. McGovern: How Clinton Can Fight Back," *The Christian Science Monitor,* January 3, 1995.

34   "corrupt congressional leadership": Newt Gingrich, Address to the Conservative Political Action Conference, February 20, 1992.

34   "tax collector for the welfare state": Helen Dewar, "Republicans Wage Verbal Civil War," *The Washington Post,* November 19, 1984.

34   "declaration of war": Howell Raines, "GOP Figure Irked by House Forecast," *The New York Times,* March 6, 1982.

34   "scale and a duration": Sheryl Gay Stolberg, "Gingrich Stuck to Caustic Path in Ethics Battles," *The New York Times,* January 26, 2012.

35   "guerilla movement": Julian Zeliger, *Burning Down the House: Newt Gingrich, the Fall of a Speaker, and the Rise of the New Republican Party* (Penguin, 2020).

35   "fatherly advice": Dan Balz and Charles R. Babcock, "Gingrich, Allies Made Waves and Impression," *The Washington Post,* December 20, 1994.

35   "you get attention": David Osborne, "The Swinging Days of Newt Gingrich," *Mother Jones,* November 1, 1984. https://www.motherjones.com/politics/1984/11/newt-gingrich-shining-knight-post-reagan-right/.

35   Dick Armey: "Armey Calls 'Fag' Reference Slip of Tongue," Associated Press, January 28, 1995. https://apnews.com/article/c643119f69b806f67461d5ab22eba251.

35   "my own expert, my mother": Elspeth Reeve, "Barney Frank's Best Video Moments," *The Atlantic,* November 28, 2011. https://www.theatlantic.com/politics/archive/2011/11/barney-franks-best-video-moments/335025/.

35   "I am Dick Armey": Ben White and Beth Berselli, "Armey Upsets Gays with Off-Color Joke," *The Washington Post,* August 5, 2000.

36   "White House dog": Molly Ivins, "It Ain't Funny, Rush," *The Washington Post,* October 14, 1993.

36   "Fold those": Anne Smith, "Limbaugh Returned to 'Testicle Lockbox'; Claimed Clinton 'Reminds Men of the Worst Characteristics of Women,'" Media Matters for America, February 15, 2008. https://www.mediamatters.org/rush-limbaugh/limbaugh-returned-testicle-lockbox-claimed-clinton-reminds-men-worst-characteristics.

36   "Rush was right": Kevin Merida, "Rush Limbaugh Saluted as a 'Majority Maker,'" *The Washington Post,* December 11, 1994.

36   "threatens this president": Michael Kelly, "The President's Past," *The New York Times Magazine,* July 31, 1994.

37   "people in this country": "What Palin's Trump Speech Says About the State of the Conservative Movement," *The Rush Limbaugh Show,* January 20, 2016. https://www.rushlimbaugh.com/daily/2016/01/20/what_palin_s_trump_speech_says_about_the_state_of_the_conservative_movement/.

37   *Dirty Little Secrets:* Larry Sabato and Glenn R. Simpson, *Dirty Little Secrets: The Persistence of Corruption in American Politics* (Times Books, 1996).

38   confidence in Congress: "Confidence in Institutions," Gallup, n.d. https://news.gallup.com/poll/1597/confidence-institutions.aspx.

38   "played golf": Craig Shirley, *Citizen Newt: The Making of a Reagan Conservative* (Thomas Nelson, 2007).

38   "Ethics Committee": Julian Zelizer, *Burning Down the House: Newt Gingrich and the Rise of the New Republican Party* (Penguin, 2021).

38   "mindless cannibalism": William J. Eaton, "Wright Resigns, Urges End to This 'Mindless Cannibalism': Speaker Declares Innocence in Impassioned House Speech," *Los Angeles Times,* June 1, 1989.

39   "comity and compassion": Timothy McNulty and Brendan McNulty, *The Meanest Man in Congress: Jack Brooks and the Making of an American Century* (NewSouth Books, 2019).

39   "junior member of Congress": "Gingrich Should Cool It, GOP Minority Leader Says: Whip Urged to Be More Responsible," *Los Angeles Times,* June 1, 1989.

39   "trashing the institution": Adam Clymer, "Michel, G.O.P. House Leader, to Retire," *The New York Times,* October 5, 1993.

39   "Liberal Closet": Ann Devroy and Tom Kenworthy, "GOP Aide Quits over Foley Memo," *The Washington Post,* June 8, 1989.

39   "little boys": Richard Cohen, "Foul Rumor," *The Washington Post,* June 8, 1989.

39   "wreck Congress": "Clinton Signs Law Expanding Business Aid," Associated Press, October 27, 1994. https://www.csmonitor.com/1994/1027/27022.html.

39   speaking fees: Larry J. Sabato and Glenn R. Simpson, *Dirty Little Secrets: The Persistence of Corruption in American Politics* (Times Books, 1996).

39   never published: Zelizer, *Burning Down the House.*

39   stakes in several matters: "Gingrich Says He Mishandled Book Deal," *The New York Times,* March 26, 1995.

40   funds from a nonprofit: "In the Matter of Representative Newt Gingrich," House Report, House Select Committee on Ethics (105th), 1997–1998. https://www.congress.gov/congressional-report/105th-congress/house-report/1.

40   "I apologize": Transcript, Newt Gingrich, *The Washington Post,* January 8, 1997.

40   Justice John Paul Stevens: *Clinton v. Jones,* Justice John Paul Stevens, May 27, 1997. https://casetext.com/case/clinton-v-jones.

40   twelve-year affair: Gennifer G. Flowers, "Declaration of Gennifer G. Flowers," *The Washington Post,* March 13, 1998.

41   sexual harassment case: *Paula Corbin Jones v. William Jefferson Clinton and Danny Ferguson,* United States District Court for the Eastern District of Arkansas Western Division, May 1994. https://www.washingtonpost.com/wp-srv/politics/special/pjones/docs/complaint.htm.

41   *The Breach:* Peter Baker, *The Breach: Inside the Impeachment and Trial of William Jefferson Clinton* (Scribner, 2012).

41   "sexual relations": "Grounds for Impeachment, No. 1," *The Washington Post,* n.d. https://www.washingtonpost.com/wp-srv/politics/special/clinton/icreport/7groundsi.htm#L6.

41   twenty-seven years in prison: Don van Natta Jr., "Judge Finds Starr's Aides Did Not Abuse Lewinsky," *The New York Times,* December 4, 1998.

42   Lewinsky in a deposition: "Deposition of Monica S. Lewinsky," August 26, 1998. http://www.tep-online.info/laku/usa/clinton/clinlew3.htm.

42   "obstruction of justice": McKay Coppins, "The Man Who Broke Politics," *The Atlantic,* November 2018. https://www.theatlantic.com/magazine/archive/2018/11/newt-gingrich-says-youre-welcome/570832/.

42   anti-Clinton talking points: Peter Baker, "Bitter Divisions Ensured Show-down," *The Washington Post,* September 17, 2000.

42   "Democratic cop-out": Juliet Eilperin, "DeLay Mobilizes Hill Effort with Aim of Clinton Resignation," *The Washington Post,* August 28, 1998.

43   Gallup poll: "Clinton Receives Record High Job Approval Rating After Impeachment Vote and Iraq Air Strikes," Gallup, December 24, 1998. https://news.gallup.com/poll/4111/clinton-receives-record-high-job-approval-rating-after-impeachment-vot.aspx.

43   "willing to lead": Guy Gugliotta and Juliet Eilperin, "Gingrich Steps Down in Face of Rebellion," *The Washington Post,* November 7, 1998.

43   "strayed from my marriage": CBSNews.com Staff, "A Revelation from Liv-ingston," December 17, 1998. https://www.cbsnews.com/news/a-revelation-from-livingston/.

43   high school wrestlers: Monica Davey, Julie Bosman, and Mitch Smith, "Den-nis Hastert Sentenced to 15 Months, and Apologizes for Sex Abuse," *The New York Times,* April 27, 2016.

44   married man: Bob Fick, "2nd GOP Conservative Admits Affair," Associated Press, September 11, 1998. https://apnews.com/article/a28b4de3da45326a94bf75e2afd7d33e.

44   extramarital affairs: David Stout, "Hyde Admits to Affair with Married Woman," *The New York Times,* September 17, 1998.

44   Mark Souder: Carl Hulse, "Citing Affair, Republican Gives Up House Seat," *The New York Times,* May 18, 2010.

44   Mark Sanford: Jim Rutenberg, "Mark Sanford's Breakup Post Caught His Fiancée Off Guard," *The New York Times,* September 13, 2014.

44   John Ensign: Frank James, "Sen. John Ensign's Parents Gave His Ex-Mistress $96,000," NPR, July 9, 2009. https://www.npr.org/sections/thetwo-way/2009/07/sen_john_ensigns_parents_gave.html.

44   "guidepost as to how they should live": David Osborne, "The Swinging Days of Newt Gingrich," *Mother Jones,* November 1, 1984. https://www.motherjones.com/politics/1984/11/newt-gingrich-shining-knight-post-reagan-right/.

44   affair with Callista Bisek: Beth Berselli and Paul Farhi, "How and What Newt Told Marianne," *The Washington Post,* August 14, 1999.

44   open marriage or a divorce: James V. Grimaldi, "Marianne Gingrich, Newt's Ex-Wife, Says He Wanted 'Open Marriage,'" *The Washington Post,* January 19, 2012.

44   "American Culture": Video, "The Demise of American Culture," C-SPAN, May 12, 1999. https://www.c-span.org/video/?123231-1/demise-american-culture.

45   "how people treat people": Grimaldi, "Marianne Gingrich, Newt's Ex-Wife, Says He Wanted 'Open Marriage.'"

45   "Nazi Germany": Andy Barr, "Gingrich Nazi Comparisons Rebuked," *Polit-ico,* May 20, 2010. https://www.politico.com/story/2010/05/gingrich-nazi-comparisons-rebuked-037573.

45   "secular fascism": Seth Abramovitch, "Newt Gingrich Calls Obama's Com-ments on Trayvon Martin 'Disgraceful,'" *The Atlantic,* March 24, 2012. https://www.theatlantic.com/politics/archive/2012/03/gingrich-calls-obamas-comments-trayvon-martin-disgraceful/330172/.

45   "400 years": Howard Fineman, "Newt Gingrich Marches into Political Battle, Firing Fascist Analogies and Apocalyptic Warnings," *HuffPost,* December 6, 2017. https://www.huffpost.com/entry/newt-gingrich-political-battle-fascists-apocalypse_n_1119507.

45   "negative nature": Jeremy W. Peters, "Gingrich Attacks the News Media and Creates a Stir," *The New York Times,* January 20, 2012.

45   "destructive political memo": David Corn, "Donald Trump's Politics of Hate Began with a 'Cynical and Evil' GOP Memo," *Mother Jones,* July 18, 2019. https://www.motherjones.com/politics/2019/07/donald-trumps-politics-of-hate-began-with-a-cynical-and-evil-gop-memo/.

CHAPTER 3: A DYSFUNCTIONAL FAMILY

47   "it's petty": John E. Yang, "Underlying Gingrich's Stance Is His Pique About President," *The Washington Post,* November 16, 1995.

47   "avoid the shutdown": Katharine Q. Seelye, "Battle Over the Budget: The Leader; Snub on Clinton Plane Had Consequences, Gingrich Says," *The New York Times,* November 16, 1995.

47   once-in-a-century insult: John K Wilson, *Newt Gingrich: Capitol Crimes and Misdemeanors* (Common Courage, 1996).

47   "25-hour trip": Wilson, *Newt Gingrich.*

47   "white with horror": Godfrey Sperling, "Open Mouth, Insert Breakfast," *The Christian Science Monitor,* April 21, 1998. https://www.csmonitor.com/1998/0421/042198.opin.column.1.html.

48   "CRY BABY": Lars-Erik Nelson, "Cry Baby," New York *Daily News,* November 16, 1995.

48   "one too many interceptions": Michael Duffy and Nancy Gibbs, "Fall of the House of Newt," *Time,* November 16, 1998. https://www.cnn.com/ALLPOLITICS/time/1998/11/09/gingrich.html.

49   *Si Monumentum Requiris:* "Wren's Epitaph," *The New York Times,* January 31, 1982.

49   703 bills: "Statistics and Historical Comparison," GovTrack. https://www.govtrack.us/congress/bills/statistics.

49   American Enterprise Institute: Thomas E. Mann and Norman J. Ornstein, *It's Even Worse Than It Looks: How the American Constitutional System Collided with the New Politics of Extremism* (Basic Books, 2012).

50   Tuesday-to-Thursday workweek: Al Kamen, "Notes to the Grindstone," *The Washington Post,* December 4, 1998.

51   "they choose, we lose": "Health-Care Ad War Destined to Escalate," Knight-Ridder/*Chicago Tribune,* February 21, 1994.

51   "force a crisis": Julian Zeliger, *Burning Down the House: Newt Gingrich, the Fall of a Speaker, and the Rise of the New Republican Party* (Penguin, 2020).

51   action to the Holocaust: John Herbers, "House Makeup Apparent Despite Disputed Races," *The New York Times,* November 9, 1984.

52   "denouncing the Democrats": Craig Shirley, *Citizen Newt: The Making of a Reagan Conservative* (Thomas Nelson, 2017).

52   "parliamentary pyrotechnics": Julian Zelizer, *Burning Down the House: Newt Gingrich and the Rise of the New Republican Party* (Penguin, 2021).

52   "not overfunded, but underfunded": Janet Hook and Edwin Chen, "Gingrich Calls for Study of Campaign Financing," *Los Angeles Times,* November 3, 1995.

53   Congressional "earmarks": Jonathan Karl and Gregory Simmons, "Newt Gingrich: Big Spender," ABC News, December 15, 2011. https://abcnews.go.com/Politics/newt-gingrich-big-spender/story?id=15163688.

53   raise soft money: "The Soft Money Explosion," *The New York Times,* May 28, 2000.

53   hire Republicans: Sheilah Kast, "The K Street Project and Tom DeLay," NPR,

January 14, 2006. https://www.npr.org/templates/story/story.php?storyId=51 57988.

53   pressure on individual lobbyists: John Cassidy, "The Ringleader," *The New Yorker,* July 24, 2005. https://www.newyorker.com/magazine/2005/08/01/the -ringleader?reload.

53   "Third World humanitarian aid effort": Michael Weisskopf and David Maraniss, "Forging an Alliance for Deregulation," *The Washington Post,* March 12, 1995.

54   "help me draft": Larry J. Sabato and Glenn R. Simpson, *Dirty Little Secrets: The Persistence of Corruption in American Politics* (Times Books, 1996).

54   "is relevant": Ann Devroy and John F. Harris, "The President Is Relevant," *The Washington Post,* April 19, 1995.

54   "Gettysburg in the Civil War": Senate Session, C-SPAN, September 7, 1995. https://www.c-span.org/video/?67041-1/senate-session.

55    $750 billion overall cut: Ronald Brownstein and Dan Balz, *Storming the Gates: Protest Politics and the Republican Revival* (Little, Brown, 1996).

55   "chickenshit operation": Bob Woodward, *The Choice* (Simon & Schuster, 1996).

56   public posturing: Steven M. Gillon, *The Pact: Bill Clinton, Newt Gingrich, and the Rivalry That Defined a Generation* (Oxford University Press, 2008).

56   "our endgame": Gillon, *The Pact.*

56   "our nation's history": Gillon, *The Pact.*

56   "till Doomsday": Edward Walsh, "For Livingston, the Time Is Now," *The Washington Post,* November 7, 1998.

56   "stay the course": David Maraniss and Michael Weisskopf, "GOP Lost Control of Members and Public Perception," *The Washington Post,* January 19, 1996.

56   "the damn phone": Gillion, *The Pact.*

56   senator is concerned: Jerry Gray, "2 Sides in Senate Disagree on Plan to End Furloughs," *The New York Times,* January 1, 1996.

57   "test of manhood": Major Garrett, *The Enduring Revolution: The Inside Story of the Republican Ascendancy and Why It Will Continue* (Three Rivers Press, 2006).

57   "bug-eyed zealots": Mary Thornton, "Simpson: the 'Anglo' Behind The Immigration Bill," *The Washington Post,* October 19, 1986.

57   "adult leadership": Gillion, *The Pact.*

57   "conscious decision": John E. Yang, "For Embattled Gingrich, Something to Celebrate," *The Washington Post,* August 1, 1997.

58   "exercise in futility": Rachel Weiner, "Gingrich Run Could Bring Up Bad Memories for Former Colleagues," *The Washington Post,* December 9, 2011.

58   "deceit": Doherty and Katz, "Firebrand GOP Class of '94 Warms to Life on the Inside."

58   "cave[d] in": Carroll J. Doherty and Jeffrey L. Katz, "Firebrand GOP Class of '94 Warms to Life on the Inside," *CQ News,* January 4, 1998. https://www .cnn.com/ALLPOLITICS/1998/01/26/cq/freshmen2.html.

58   "turned": William Greider, "Newt Gingrich: Dead Man Talking," *Rolling Stone,* October 3, 1996. https://www.rollingstone.com/politics/politics-news/ newt-gingrich-dead-man-talking-67498/?

58   "circular firing squad": James Carney, "Attempted Republican Coup: Ready, Aim, Misfire," *Time,* July 28, 1997. https://www.cnn.com/ALLPOLITICS/ 1997/07/21/time/gingrich.html.

58   "roadkill on the highway": Katie Couric, Transcript, "Congressman Peter King Discusses His Criticism of Newt Gingrich," NBC News, April 2, 1997.

58   "dysfunctional family": John E. Yang, "Session Changes Gingrich," *The Washington Post,* November 15, 1997.

59   "some talents": Edward Walsh, "For Livingston, the Time Is Now," *The Washington Post,* November 7, 1998.

59   "situation the way it is": Peter Baker, *The Breach: Inside the Impeachment and Trial of William Jefferson Clinton* (Scribner, 2000).

59   "into the bathroom": Mara Liasson, "Conservative Advocate," *NPR,* May 25, 2001.

59   disillusioned revolutionaries: Dana Milbank, "Whatever Happened to the Class of 1994?," *The New York Times Magazine,* January 17, 1999.

CHAPTER 4: BLACK HELICOPTERS

60   Branch Davidian: Tracey McVeigh, "Dead Man Talking," *The Guardian,* April 22, 2001.

60   "Kill the sons of bitches": Richard Cohen, "The Salute That Wasn't," *The Washington Post,* May 4, 1995.

60   "bearing arms": Richard Bottoms, "Liddy's Lethald Advice," FAIR, July 1, 1995. https://fair.org/home/liddys-lethal-advice/.

60   "groin area": Howard Kurtz, "Gordon Liddy on Shooting from the Lip," *The Washington Post,* April 26, 1995.

61   "armed revolution": Leslie Jorgenson, "AM Armies; Government 'Cleansing,'" FAIR, March 1, 1995. https://fair.org/extra/am-armies/.

61   "culture of violence": Colman McCarthy, "In Ignorance, Bashing the Indigent," *The Washington Post,* January 31, 1995.

61   "tyranny everywhere": Elspeth Reeve, "A Quarter Century of Gingrich Dirt," *The Atlantic,* October 30, 2013. https://www.theatlantic.com/facebook -instant/article/334717/.

61   "enemy of normal": Howard Kurtz, "Spin Cycles," *The Washington Post,* February 26, 1995.

61   "aid and comfort": Eric Bailey and Peter M. Warren, "Congress Loses One of Its Leading Characters," *Los Angeles Times,* November 23, 1996.

61   "Clinton better watch out": Steven Greenhouse, "Helms Takes New Swipe at Clinton, Then Calls It a Mistake," *The New York Times,* November 23, 1994.

61   "armed agency officials": Timothy Egan, "Terror in Oklahoma: In Congress; Trying to Explain Contacts with Paramilitary Groups," *The New York Times,* May 2, 1995.

62   "bloody fiasco": Kevin Merida and Marilyn W. Thompson, "Raid Rumor Fueled Fears in Militias," *The Washington Post,* April 25, 1995.

62   "second violent American revolution": Garry Willis, "It's His Party," *The New York Times Magazine,* August 11, 1996.

62   "federal juggernaut": Tracey McVeigh, "The McVeigh Letters: Why I Bombed Oklahoma," *The Guardian,* May 6, 2001.

63   "That's grotesque!": "Query Gets Angry Response from Gingrich," *The Washington Post,* April 23, 1995.

63   "condemn any group": Tim Russert, *Meet the Press,* May 7, 1995.

64   "openly anti-state": Kathleen Belew, *Bring the War Home: The White Power Movement and Paramilitary America* (Harvard University Press, 2008).

65   nascent internet: Mark Potok, "Rage on the Right," Southern Poverty Law Center, March 2010. https://www.splcenter.org/fighting-hate/intelligence-report/2010/rage-right.

65   "racial quota": Thomas B. Edsall, "Helms Makes Race an Issue," *The Washington Post,* November 1, 1990.

66   "racial slur implications": Craig Shirley, *Citizen Newt: The Making of a Reagan Conservative* (Thomas Nelson, 2017).

66   "southern prejudice": Dale Russakoff and Dan Balz, "After Political Victory, A Personal Revolution," *The Washington Post,* December 19, 1994.

66   party was racist: Julian Zelizer, *Burning Down the House: Newt Gingrich and the Rise of the New Republican Party* (Penguin, 2021).

66   "morally repulsed": Zelizer, *Burning Down the House.*

66   "liberal welfare state": David S. Broder, "Malarkey from Newt Gingrich," *The Washington Post,* April 23, 1989.

66   "violent crimes": Shirley, *Citizen Newt.*

66   "Dukakis-Jackson administration": Myra MacPherson, "Newt Gingrich, Point Man in a House Divided," *The Washington Post,* June 12, 1989.

67   "multicultural nihilistic hedonism": A. J. Apple, "G.O.P. Is Flirting with Dangers of Negativism," *The New York Times,* August 19, 1992.

67   "cannot survive": Peter Overby, "Revisiting Newt Gingrich's 1997 Ethics Investigation," NPR, December 8, 2011. https://www.npr.org/2011/12/08/143333594/revisiting-newt-gingrichs-1997-ethics-investigation.

67   "established a playbook": David Nakamura, "With Kristen Clarke, Republicans Follow Playbook in Opposing Democratic Nominees to Justice Dept.'s Civil Rights Post," *The Washington Post,* May 24, 2021.

67   "Thug Basketball Association": Andrew Seifter, "Limbaugh on the NBA: 'Call It the TBA, the Thug Basketball Association . . . They're Going in to Watch the Crips and the Bloods,'" Media Matters, December 10, 2004. https://www.mediamatters.org/rush-limbaugh/limbaugh-nba-call-it-tba-thug-basketball-association-theyre-going-watch-crips-and.

67   "all have casinos": Media Matters Staff, "Limbaugh on 'Holocaust' of 'Indians': 'They Have Casinos—What's to Complain About?'" Media Matters, September 25, 2009. https://mediamatters.org/rush-limbaugh/limbaugh-holocaust-indians-they-all-have-casinos-whats-complain-about.

68   "furthest thing from a racist": Clarence Page, "Rush Limbaugh Can Dish It Out, But He Sure Can't Take It," *Chicago Tribune,* May 5, 1993.

68   racist newsletters: Jerry Markon and Alice Crites, "Ron Paul Signed Off on Racist 1990s Newsletters, Associates Say," *The Washington Post,* January 27, 2012.

68   White Citizens' Councils: Jack Anderson and Michael Binstein, "Lawmakers Keeping Gun PAC's Cash," *The Washington Post,* February 29, 1996.

68   "non-Jewish whites": Patrick Buchanan, *Suicide of a Superpower: Will America Survive to 2025?* (Thomas Dunne Books, 2011).

68   "great courage": Jeff Cohen, "Patrick J. Buchanan: In His Own Words; Presidential Hopeful's Writings and Comments Shed Light on His Claims That Mainstream Media Have Distorted His Views," *The Baltimore Sun,* October 3, 1999.

68   "interracial marriage": Jack Anderson and Michael Binstein, "Party Unity and Buchanan," *The Washington Post,* March 11, 1996.

68   "philosophical ayatollah": Bruce Lambert, "D'Amato Calls Buchanan a Divisive 'Philosophical Ayatollah,'" *The New York Times,* May 5, 1996.

69   "private message": Terry Kelleher, "He Starred in Watergate, He Eats Rats and Liberals," *Newsday,* May 10, 1995.

69   "gun owners of New Hampshire": Kevin Merida, "Under Fire, Buchanan Aide Leaves," *The Washington Post,* February 16, 1996.

69   "represent the normal American": Anderson and Binstein, "Lawmakers Keeping Gun PAC's Cash."

70   "ban on so-called 'assault weapons'": Dana Milbank, "Whatever Happened to the Class of 1994," *The New York Times Magazine,* January 17, 1999.

70   "pushing people": D. F. Oliveria, "Chenoweth Condemns Bombing After Putting Foot in Mouth," *The Spokesman-Review,* April 25, 1995. https://www.spokesman.com/stories/1995/apr/25/chenoweth-condemns-bombing-after-putting-foot-in/.

70   written permission: Melissa Healy, "Oklahoma City: After the Bomb, Slower Approach to Anti-Terrorism Laws Urged," *Los Angeles Times,* May 1, 1995.

70   "protect themselves": Lane Crothers, *Rage on the Right: The American Militia Movement from Ruby Ridge to Homeland Security* (Rowman & Littlefield Publishers, 2003).

70   Idaho salmon: "Helen Chenoweth Says Idaho Sockeye Is Not Endangered," Associated Press, August 28, 1994. https://lmtribune.com/helen-chenoweth-says-idaho-sockeye-is-not-endangered/article_e00d4447-62f3-57b9-8d25-9d50d636acfd.html.

70   "We have democracy": Chad Pergram, "The Freshmen Visit Willy Wonka and the Chocolate Factory," Fox News, December 24, 2015.

71   "a signal": "Idahoan Wants Fred to Drop Their Guns," *Deseret News,* May 8, 1995.

71   "interested in violence": Janet Hook, "Militias Have Forged Ties to Some Members of Congress: Capitol Hill: Anti-Government Groups Are an Important Political Force in Some Areas—and Are Treated as Such," *Los Angeles Times,* April 28, 1995.

71   "responsible, reasonable, lawful": Dan Morgan, "Militias Flexing More Muscle in the Political Process," *The Washington Post,* May 1, 1995.

72   "legitimate political dialogue": Todd S. Purdum, "Terror in Oklahoma: The President; Shifting Debate to the Political Climate, Clinton Condemns 'Promoters of Paranoia,'" *The Washington Post,* April 25, 1995.

72   "domestic terrorism": Todd Gregory, "Rush: 'President Clinton's Ties to the Domestic Terrorism of Oklahoma City Are Tangible,' Blames the 'Waco Invasion,'" Media Matters, April 19, 2010. https://www.mediamatters.org/rush-limbaugh/rush-president-clintons-ties-domestic-terrorism-oklahoma-city-are-tangible-blames-0.

72   "stretch of the imagination": Francis X. Clines, "Terror in Oklahoma: Talk Radio; President Is Criticized by Oklahoma Senators," *The New York Times,* April 26, 1995.

73   "emblem of irresponsibility": William F. Buckley Jr., "Goldwater, the John Birch Society and Me," *The Wall Street Journal,* February 27, 2008. https://www.wsj.com/articles/SB120413132440097025.

CHAPTER 5: SWIFT BOATING

74   "as Americans": George W. Bush, "President Delivers State of the Union Address," January 29, 2002. https://georgewbush-whitehouse.archives.gov/news/releases/2002/01/20020129-11.html.

74   "spirit of unity": Richard L. Berke, "Bush Adviser Suggests War as Campaign Theme," *The New York Times,* January 19, 2002.

75   "strengthening America's military": Mark Halperin, "Rove: Republicans Benefit from War Credentials," ABC News, January 6, 2006. https://abcnews.go.com/Politics/story?id=121248&page=1.

75   two dozen fundraisers: Dana Milbank, "Bush Turns More Partisan with Coming of Elections," *The Washington Post,* May 19, 2002.

75   "Focus on War and Economy": Kenneth B. Mehlman, "The 2002 Challenge,"

PowerPoint, June 4, 2002. https://static01.nyt.com/packages/pdf/politics/14 rov.1.pdf.

76 "very good footing": Tom Daschle, Senate floor speech, September 25, 2002.

76 "hit again": David E. Sanger and David M. Halbfinger, "Cheney Warns of Terror Risk if Kerry Wins," *The New York Times,* September 8, 2004.

76 "defending our homeland": Julie Davis Hirschfeld and David L. Greene, "Daschle Seeks Bush Apology on Patriotism," *The Baltimore Sun,* September 26, 2002.

76 "Economy Fades": Dana Milbank, "In President's Speeches, Iraq Dominates, Economy Fades," *The Washington Post,* September 25, 2002.

77 "divide this nation": David Stout, "Senate Leader Denounces Bush Remarks on Security as Partisan," *The New York Times,* September 25, 2002.

79 enabler of Osama bin Laden: Lou Cannon and Carl M. Cannon, *Reagan's Disciple: George W. Bush's Troubled Quest for a Presidential Legacy* (PublicAffairs, 2008).

79 "'dirty tricks'": "GOP Probes Official as Teacher of Tricks," *The Washington Post,* August 10, 1973.

79 "Free beer": "Chronology Karl Rove's Live and Political Career," *Frontline,* PBS, n.d. https://www.pbs.org/wgbh/pages/frontline/shows/architect/rove/cron.html.

80 *Bush's Brain:* Wayne Moore and James Slater, *Bush's Brain: How Karl Rove Made George W. Bush Presidential* (John Wiley & Sons, 2003).

81 "armies of compassion": Dan Balz, "'Armies of Compassion' in Bush's Plans," *The Washington Post,* April 25, 1999.

81 "instability": James B. Stockdale, "John McCain in the Crucible," *The New York Times,* November 26, 1999.

81 *Boy genius:* Lou Dubose, Jan Reid, and Carl M. Cannon, *Boy Genius: Karl Rove, the Brains Behind the Remarkable Political Triumph of George W. Bush* (PublicAffairs, 2003).

82 "sire children": Jennifer Steinhauer, "Confronting Ghosts of 2000 in South Carolina," *The New York Times,* October 19, 2007.

82 "own opinion": Robert Draper, *Dead Certain: The Presidency of George W. Bush* (Free Press, 2007).

83 force if necessary: Steve Turnham, "Police Called During House Meeting," CNN, July 21, 2003. https://www.cnn.com/2003/ALLPOLITICS/07/18/house.disarray/index.html.

83 bad Catholic: Helen Dewar and Dana Milbank, "Cheney Dismisses Critic with Obscenity; Clash with Leahy About Haliburton," *The Washington Post,* June 25, 2004.

83 upset victory: Jeffrey Gettleman, "The 2002 Elections: Georgia; an Old Battle Flag Helps Bring Down a Governor," *The New York Times,* November 7, 2002.

83 "all these problems": Carl Hulse, "Lott's Praise for Thurmond Echoed His Words of 1980," *The New York Times,* December 11, 2012. https://www.nytimes.com/2002/12/11/us/lott-s-praise-for-thurmond-echoed-his-words-of-1980.html.

84 "Free at last": John Tierney, "Midterm Elections: Voted, Noted, Counted and Quoted," *The Atlanta Journal-Constitution,* November 10, 2002.

84 "aid terrorists": Terry Frieden, "Justice Defends Ashcroft's Congressional Testimony," CNN, December 7, 2001. http://www.cnn.com/2001/ALLPOLITICS/12/07/inv.ashcroft.testimony/.

84 "comfort to our enemies": Ron Fournier, "Would We Rally Behind Obama

After the Next 9/11?," *The Atlantic*, August 11, 2014. https://www.theatlantic .com/politics/archive/2014/08/would-we-rally-behind-obama-after-the-next -911/461304/.

84   "confronting evil": Judy Woodruff, *Inside Politics*, CNN, September 25, 2002. https://transcripts.cnn.com/show/ip/date/2002-09-25/segment/00.

84   "want us to do": Dan Balz, "Bush and GOP Defend White House Response," *The Washington Post*, May 18, 2002.

85   "air strikes in October": James Carney, "General Karl Rove, Reporting for Duty," *Time*, September 29, 2002. http://content.time.com/time/nation/ article/0,8599,356034,00.html.

85   "marketing point of view": "Quotation of the Day," *The New York Times*, September 7, 2002.

85   "visit soon": James Carney, "General Karl Rove, Reporting for Duty," *Time*, September 29, 2002. http://content.time.com/time/nation/article/0,8599,3560 34,00.html.

85   "campaigning openly": Scott McClellan, *What Happened: Inside the Bush White House and Washington's Culture of Deception* (PublicAffairs, 2008).

85   "have to do this": Ronald Brownstein and Emma Vaughn, "Timing Entwined War Vote, Election," *Los Angeles Times*, November 28, 2005.

85   "somebody else to act": Dana Milbank, "Democrats Question Iraq Timing; Talk of War Districts from Election Issues," *The Washington Post*, September 16, 2002.

86   "breaking his oath": Mary McGrory, "Dirty-Bomb Politics," *The Washington Post*, June 20, 2002.

86   "voted against": Jill Zuckerman, "Senator Faces GOP Barrage," *Chicago Tribune*, October 24, 2002.

86   "political battlefield": Max Cleland, *Heart of a Patriot: How I Found the Courage to Survive Vietnam, Walter Reed and Karl Rove* (Simon & Schuster, 2010).

86   "it was factual": Karl Rove, *Courage and Consequence: My Life as a Conservative in the Fight* (Threshold Editions, 2010).

86   "attacking the president": Mike Allen, "Bush Ad Criticizes Democrats on Defense," *The Washington Post*, November 22, 2003.

87   "America is the problem": "Remarks by Sen. Miller to the Republican National Convention," *The Washington Post*, September 1, 2004.

87   "dishonored his country": Dana Milbank and Thomas B. Edsall, "Bush-Cheney Lawyer Advised Anti-Kerry Vets," *The Washington Post*, August 25, 2004.

87   "enemy for free": Glen Justice and Jim Rutenberg, "The 2004 Campaign: Advertising; Kerry Is Filing a Complaint Against Swift Boat Group," *The New York Times*, August 21, 2004.

87   denied involvement: Glen Justice and Eric Lichtblau, "Bush's Backers Donate Heavily to Veteran Ads," *The New York Times*, September 11, 2004.

88   "good friend": Dan Balz and Thomas B. Edsall, "Lawyer Quits Bush-Cheney Organization," *The Washington Post*, August 26, 2004.

88   "damaged Kerry's campaign": Rove, *Courage and Confidence*.

88   "cowards cut and run": Jason Deparle, " 'Mean Jean' Goes to Washington, and Invites a Firestorm," *The New York Times*, November 20, 2005.

88   "war on terror": Charles Babington, "From GOP, Zero Tolerance for Democratic War Critics," *The Washington Post*, May 16, 2004.

88   "loyal opposition": Dana Milbank, "Reprise of the Grand Old Party Line," *The Washington Post*, September 13, 2006.

89   "hearts of our troops": Brendan Nyhan, "Republican Attacks on Dissent Since 9/11." https://www.brendan-nyhan.com/blog/gop-dissent-attacks.html.

CHAPTER 6: CULTURE OF DECEPTION

90   "Major combat operations": Dana Milbank and Claudia Deane, "Hussein Link to 9/11 Lingers in Many Minds," *The Washington Post,* September 6, 2003.

91   "greeted as liberators": Transcript for September 14, NBC News. https://www.nbcnews.com/id/wbna3080244.

91   "limited period": George Tenet, *At the Center of the Storm: My Years at the CIA* (HarperCollins, 2007).

91   "Facts Are Malleable": Dana Milbank, "For Bush, Facts Are Malleable," *The Washington Post,* October 22, 2002.

93   half of it: Dana Milbank, "Karl Rove Sets the Record Straight—Sort Of," *The Washington Post,* March 7, 2010.

94   "overplayed or completely wrong": Scott McClellan, *What Happened: Inside the Bush White House and Washington's Culture of Deception* (PublicAffairs, 2008).

95   long-range missiles: Walter Pincus and Dana Milbank, "Bush Clings to Dubious Allegations About Iraq," *The Washington Post,* March 18, 2003.

95   "preparations for hijackings": "Bin Ladin Determined to Strike in US," August 6, 2001. Declassified and Approved for Release April 10, 2004. https://irp.fas.org/cia/product/pdb080601.pdf.

96   master prevaricators: Ron Suskind, *The Price of Loyalty: George W. Bush, the White House and the Education of Paul O'Neill* (Simon & Schuster, 2004).

96   "no financial interest": John King, "Cheney Aide Rejects Halliburton Questions," CNN, September 16, 2003. https://www.cnn.com/2003/ALLPOLITICS/09/16/cheney.halliburton/index.html.

96   "alternative reality": James Moore and Wayne Slater, *The Architect* (Crown, 2006).

96   "Absolutely not": Karl Rove, *Courage and Consequence: My Life as a Conservative in the Fight* (Threshold, 2010).

97   "Thirty days": Jonathan Topaz, "Rove Disputes Clinton Remarks," *Politico,* May 13, 2014. https://www.politico.com/story/2014/05/karl-rove-hillary-clinton-remarks-106621.

97   closed the door: Richard A. Clarke, *Against All Enemies: Inside America's War on Terror* (Free Press, 2004).

98   "pay a price": Tenet, *At the Center of the Storm.*

98   "lead to Baghdad": Richard N. Perle, "How the CIA Failed America," *The Washington Post,* May 11, 2007.

98   "pretty well confirmed": Transcript, "Text: Cheney on Bin Laden Tape," *The Washington Post,* December 9, 2001. https://www.washingtonpost.com/wp-srv/nation/specials/attacked/transcripts/cheneytext_120901.html.

98   "very confident": Walter Pincus and Dana Milbank, "Al Qaeda–Hussein Link Is Dismissed," *The Washington Post,* June 17, 2004.

99   "overwhelming": "Cheney Blasts Media on al Qaeda-Iraq Link," CNN, June 18, 2004. https://www.cnn.com/2004/ALLPOLITICS/06/18/cheney.iraq.al.qaeda/.

99   "major blow": Greg Miller, "No Proof Connects to 9/11, Busy Says," *Los Angeles Times,* September 18, 2003.

99   "war on terror": George W. Bush, "Mission Accomplished Speech," May 1, 2003. https://www.cnn.com/2003/US/05/01/bush.transcript/.

99   "no credible evidence": Walter Pincus and Dana Milbank, "Al Qaeda–Hussein Link Is Dismissed," *The Washington Post,* June 17, 2004.

99   role in the attacks: "Washington Post Poll: Saddam Hussein and the Sept. 11 Attacks," *The Washington Post,* September 6, 2003.

99   "Seventy percent": Clarke, *Against All Enemies.*

99   "systematic effort": Byron York, *The Vast Left Wing Conspiracy: The Untold Story of the Democrats' Desperate Fight to Reclaim Power* (Crown Forum, 2006).

100   "enhancing its capabilities": Al Gore, "Vice President Speaks at VFW 103rd National Convention," August 26, 2002. https://georgewbush-whitehouse .archives.gov/news/releases/2002/08/20020826.html.

100   "intelligence community's belief": Tenet, *At the Center of the Storm.*

100   "pursuing nuclear weapons": Dick Cheney and Wolf Blitzer, "Interview with Dick Cheney," *CNN Late Night Edition,* March 24, 2002.

100   "graver threat": "In Their Own Words: Iraq's 'Imminent' Threat," Center for American Progress, January 29, 2004. https://www.americanprogress.org/ article/in-their-own-words-iraqs-imminent-threat/.

100   "seeking nuclear weapons": George W. Bush, "Bush Addresses Nation on Iraq," CNN Live Event/Special, October 7, 2002.

101   "significant quantities": George W. Bush, "Text of President Bush's 2003 State of the Union Address," *The Washington Post,* January 28, 2003.

101   "no doubt": George W. Bush, "President Bush's Speech on Iraq," *The New York Times,* March 17, 2003.

101   "reconstituted nuclear weapons": Wolf Blitzer, "Did the Bush Administration Exaggerate the Threat from Iraq," CNN, July 8, 2003. https://www.cnn.com/ 2003/ALLPOLITICS/07/08/wbr.iraq.claims/.

101   "resumed nuclear activities": Mohamed ElBaradei, "The Status of Nuclear Inspections in Iraq: An Update," International Atomic Energy Agency, March 7, 2003. https://www.iaea.org/newscenter/statements/status-nuclear -inspections-iraq-update.

101   "Wrong": Harold Meyerson, "Inconvenient Facts . . ." *The Washington Post,* July 17, 2003. https://www.washingtonpost.com/archive/opinions/2003/07/ 17/inconvenient-facts/b364656d-9e78-4c08-8bf7-97dfb8e6ab15/.

101   "Andy shook his head": Tenet, *At the Center of the Storm.*

101   "facts and conclusions": Julian Borger, "Colin Powell's UN Speech: A Decisive Moment in Undermining US Credibility," *The Guardian,* October 18, 2021. https://www.theguardian.com/us-news/2021/oct/18/colin-powell-un-security -council-iraq.

101   "garbage": Tenet, *At the Center of the Storm.*

102   "slam dunk": "Woodward: Tenet told Bush WMD case a 'slam dunk,'" CNN, April 19, 2004. https://www.cnn.com/2004/ALLPOLITICS/04/18/woodward .book/.

102   "intentionally misused": Tenet, *At the Center of the Storm.*

102   "never saw anything": Dana Milbank, "White House Fires Back at O'Neill on Iraq," *The Washington Post,* January 13, 2004.

102   "a bigger market": Suskind, *The Price of Loyalty.*

102   "poisonous atmosphere": Paul R. Pillar, "Intelligence, Policy, and the War in Iraq," *Foreign Affairs,* March/April 2006. https://www.foreignaffairs.com/ articles/iraq/2006-03-01/intelligence-policy-and-war-iraq.

102   "never seemed satisfied": Tenet, *At the Center of the Storm.*

102   "blindly accept": Tenet, *At the Center of the Storm.*

102   "persnickety": Tenet, *At the Center of the Storm.*

103   Valerie Plame: Joseph C. Wilson, "What I Didn't Find in Africa," *The New York Times,* July 6, 2003. https://www.nytimes.com/2003/07/06/opinion/what-i-didn-t-find-in-africa.html.

103   "repeat a lie": Elisabeth Bumiller, "In Ex-Spokesman's Book, Harsh Words for Bush," *The New York Times,* May 28, 2008. https://www.nytimes.com/2008/05/28/washington/28mcclellan.html.

103   "amount of sympathy": Dana Milbank, "Free-Fall for the Fall Guy," *The Washington Post,* March 7, 2007.

104   "whiff of gunpowder": Reuters Staff, "Factbox: Iraq War, the Notable Quotes," Reuters, March 11, 2018. https://www.reuters.com/article/us-iraq-war-quotes/factbox-iraq-war-the-notable-quotes-idUSL212762520080311.

104   "use of force in Iraq": Reuters Staff, "Factbox: Iraq War, the Notable Quotes."

104   "going through Paris": Peter Baker, *Days of Fire: Bush and Cheney in the White House* (Anchor, 2014).

104   "deserved better": Baker, *Days of Fire.*

104   "coalition of the willing": "Bush: Join 'Coalition of Willing,'" CNN, November 20, 2002. http://edition.cnn.com/2002/WORLD/europe/11/20/prague.bush.nato/.

104   "old Europe": John Hooper and Ian Black, "Anger of Rumsfeld Attack on 'Old Europe,'" *The Guardian,* January 23, 2003.

104   "freedom fries": "Threats and Responses: Washington Talk; An Order of Fries, Please, but Hold the French," *The New York Times,* March 12, 2003.

104   "arrival ceremonies": Dana Milbank, "Curtains Ordered for Media Coverage of Returning Coffins," *The Washington Post,* October 21, 2003.

105   "turned a corner": Thomas E. Ricks, "Cheney Stands by His 'Last Throes' Remark," *The Washington Post,* June 20, 2006.

105   "spin, hide, shade, and exaggerate": McClellan, *What Happened.*

105   "culture of deception": McClellan, *What Happened.*

105   political gain: Transcript, CNN, November 7, 2005. http://edition.cnn.com/TRANSCRIPTS/0511/07/lol.03.html.

106   "not authorized": "Report to the President," Commission on the Intelligence Capabilities of the United States Regarding Weapons of Mass Destruction, March 31, 2005. https://govinfo.library.unt.edu/wmd/report/report.html#overview.

106   "partisan exercise": Randall Mikkelsen, "Bush Misused Iraq Intelligence: Senate Report," Reuters, June 5, 2008. https://www.reuters.com/article/us-iraq-usa-intelligence/bush-misused-iraq-intelligence-senate-report-idUSN0540864220080605.

106   "turned out not to be true": Devan Cole, "Trump in 2008: It'd Be 'Wonderful' if Pelosi Impeached Bush over Iraq," CNN, December 19, 2019. https://www.cnn.com/2019/12/19/politics/donald-trump-impeachment-nancy-pelosi-george-w-bush/index.html.

CHAPTER 7: A HECKUVA JOB

107   escape the commotion: Dexter Filkins and Dana Canedy, "Counting the Vote: Miami-Dade County; Protest Influenced Miami-Dade's Decision to Stop Recount," *The New York Times,* November 24, 2000.

108   "Let us in!": Dan Rather, "Republican Hassling Leads Miami-Dade County Election Officials to Abandon Hand Count," CBS News, November 22, 2000.

108   "Brooks Brothers Riot": Dexter Filkins and Dana Canedy, "Counting the Vote: Miami-Dade County; A Wild Day in Miami, with an End to Recounting and Democrats Going to Court," *The New York Times,* November 23, 2000.

108 "consideration is limited": Linda Greenhouse, "Bush v. Gore: A Special Report; Election Case a Test and a Trauma for Justices," *The New York Times,* February 20, 2001.

109 "piece of shit": Evan Thomas, *First: Sandra Day O'Connor* (Random House, 2019).

109 "grossly derelict": Katharine Q. Seelye, "Divided Civil Rights Panel Criticizes Florida Election," *The New York Times,* June 5, 2001.

110 "voters intimidated": John Ashcroft, "Prepared Remarks of Attorney General John Ashcroft Voting Integrity Symposium," Justice Department, October 8, 2002. https://www.justice.gov/archive/ag/speeches/2002/100802 ballotintegrity.htm.

111 "gettable middle": Jeffrey Marcus, "Dowd Sees Undecideds Breaking for Bush," *The Washington Post,* September 1, 2004.

111 "*motivation* rather than *persuasion*": Robert Draper, *Dead Certain: The Presidency of George W. Bush* (Free Press, 2008).

111 International Criminal Court: Eric Pianin, "U.S. Aims to Pull Out of Warming Treaty," *The Washington Post,* March 28, 2001.

111 smaller cut: Frank Bruni and Allison Mitchell, "Bush Pushes Hard to Woo Democrats over to Tax Plan," *The New York Times,* March 4, 2001.

111 "compassionate conservativism": John Dilulio, "John Dilulio's Letter," *Esquire,* October 24, 2002. https://www.esquire.com/news-politics/a2880/dilulio/.

112 "groundless and baseless": Howard Kurtz, "Ron Suskind, the Confident Confidant," *The Washington Post,* December 9, 2002.

112 "political operative": Scott McClellan, *What Happened: Inside the Bush White House and Washington's Culture of Deception* (PublicAffairs, 2008).

112 "mature party": John McCain, "White House, McCain Respond to Jeffords' Party Switch," CNN, May 24, 2001. https://transcripts.cnn.com/show/bn/date/2001-05-24/segment/02.

112 "Hastert Rule": Charles Babington, "Hastert Launces a Partisan Policy," *The Washington Post,* November 27, 2004.

113 "closed" rules: Thomas E. Mann and Norman J. Ornstein, *The Broken Branch: How Congress Is Failing America and How to Get it Back on Track* (Oxford University Press, 2008).

113 "nuclear option": David D. Kirkpatrick, "Rove and Frist Reject Democrats' Compromise over Bush's Judicial Nominees," *The New York Times,* April 27, 2005.

113 lockstep partisanship: Dana Milbank and Jim VandeHei, "Bush's Strong Arm Can Club Allies Too; Lawmakers, Activists Say Tactics for Enforcing Loyalty Are Tough and Sometimes Vindictive," *The Washington Post,* March 21, 2003.

113 Club for Growth: Club for Growth, Open Secrets, https://www.opensecrets.org/orgs//summary?id=D000000763.

114 "RINOs": Anna Palmer and Alexander Burns, "Inside Club for Growth's Art of War," *Politico,* April 7, 2014. https://www.politico.com/story/2014/04/inside-the-club-for-growths-art-of-war-105415.

114 purity police: Scorecard, Heritage Action for America, https://heritageaction.com/scorecard.

114 "right direction": Brian Rosenwald, "They Just Wanted to Entertain," *The Atlantic,* August 21, 2019. https://www.theatlantic.com/ideas/archive/2019/08/talk-radio-made-todays-republican-party/596380/.

115   "deficits don't matter": Ron Suskind, *The Price of Loyalty: George W. Bush, the White House, and the Education of Paul O'Neill* (Simon & Schuster, 2004).

115   "gaming of the system": Suskind, *The Price of Loyalty.*

115   "torture memos": U.S. Department of Justice, Office of Legal Counsel, "Memorandum for William J. Haynes II, General Counsel of the Department of Defense," March 14, 2003. https://nsarchive2.gwu.edu/torturingdemocracy/documents/20030314.pdf.

115   hospital room: Dan Eggen and Paul Kane, "Gonzales Hospital Episode Detailed," *The Washington Post,* May 16, 2007.

115   Michael Brown: Matthew Davis, "FEMA 'Knew of New Orleans Danger,'" BBC News, October 11, 2005. http://news.bbc.co.uk/2/hi/americas/4331330.stm.

116   unaware of events: U.S. House of Representatives, "A Failure of Initiative; Final Report of the Select Bipartisan Committee to Investigate the Preparation for and Response to Hurricane Katrina," 2006. https://www.nrc.gov/docs/ML1209/ML12093A081.pdf.

116   "heckuva job": Eric Garcia, "What 'Brownie' Regrets,'" *The Atlantic,* August 28, 2015. https://www.theatlantic.com/politics/archive/2015/08/what-brownie-regrets/446280/.

116   "incomplete to insulting": Michael A. Fletcher and Charles Babington, "Miers, Under Fire from Right, Withdrawn as Court Nominee," *The Washington Post,* October 28, 2005.

116   ousting Iglesias: "Fired U.S. Attorneys," *The Washington Post,* 2007. https://www.washingtonpost.com/wp-dyn/content/graphic/2007/03/06/GR2007030600062.html.

116   redraw congressional maps: Adam Nagourney, "Texas Court Overturns Conviction of DeLay," *The New York Times,* September 19, 2013.

117   "important to the president": Lee Hockstader, "Texas Democrats Trying Fight, Not Flight, over Districts," *The Washington Post,* July 1, 2003.

118   "air interdiction": Jeffrey Smith, "In Texas Feud, a Plane Tale of Intrigue," *The Washington Post,* June 7, 2003.

119   "permanent majority": Janet Hook, "GOP Seeks Lasting Majority," *Los Angeles Times,* July 21, 2003.

119   Ruth's Chris Steak House: Jan Reid and Lou Dubose, "The Man with the Plan," *Texas Monthly,* August 2004. https://www.texasmonthly.com/news-politics/the-man-with-the-plan/.

119   federal government: Julie Mason and Karen Masterson, "King of the Hill, Dauntless Style Marks Delay's Surge to Power," *The Houston Chronicle,* June 22, 2003.

119   "consciously done": Eric Lipton and Ian Urbina, "In 5-Year Effort, Scant Evidence of Voter Fraud," *The New York Times,* April 12, 2007.

119   "sole purpose": Linda Greenhouse, "Justices Uphold Most Remapping in Texas by G.O.P," *The New York Times,* June 29, 2006.

120   "suppress the Detroit vote": Chip Reid, "Voter Suppression Charges on the Rise," NBC News, October 13, 2004. https://www.nbcnews.com/id/wbna6242175.

120   voter suppression party: Jo Becker, "GOP Challenging Voter Registrations," *The Washington Post,* October 29, 2004.

120   "account for fraud": "Sounding the Alarm," *The Hotline,* May 22, 2012. https://global.factiva.com/redir/default.aspx?p=sa&an=HTLN000020120523e85m00010&cat=a&ep=ASE.

CHAPTER 8: BRIDGES TO NOWHERE

121   "parameters of international discourse": Susan Schmidt and James V. Grimaldi, "The Fast Rise and Steep Fall of Jack Abramoff," *The Washington Post,* December 29, 2005.

121   yoga instructor: Dana Milbank, "One Committee's Three Hours of Inquiry, in Surreal Time," *The Washington Post,* June 23, 2005.

122   gambling clients: Henry Foster and Adam Cohen, "The Right Hand of God," *Time,* May 15, 1995. http://content.time.com/time/covers/0,16641,19950515 ,00.html.

122   jailed his political opponents: Tom Hamburger and Peter Wallsten, "Abramoff Bragged of Ties to Rove," *Los Angeles Times,* February 15, 2006.

122   Susan Ralston: Jack Abramoff, *Capital Punishment: The Hard Truth About Washington Corruption from America's Most Notorious Lobbyist* (WND Books, 2011).

122   resign from the House: Andrea Seabrook, "Facing Long Odds in Texas, DeLay Opts Out," NPR, April 4, 2006. https://www.npr.org/templates/story/ story.php?storyId=5323575.

123   "lobbyists go wild": Matthew Continetti, *K Street Gang: The Rise and Fall of the Republican Machine* (Doubleday, 2006).

123   public financing: Peter Overby, "Decade Brought Change to Campaign Finance," NPR, December 25, 2009. https://www.npr.org/templates/story/ story.php?storyId=121872329.

124   16,000 percent: "Total Outside Spending by Election Cycle, Excluding Party Committees," Open Secret, n.d. https://www.opensecrets.org/outside spending/cycle_tots.php.

124   ban soft money: "Money-in-Politics Timeline," Open Secrets, n.d. https:// www.opensecrets.org/resources/learn/timeline.

124   "dark money": "Super PACs," Open Secrets, n.d. https://www.opensecrets .org/political-action-committees-pacs/super-pacs/2020.

125   "frozen food containers": Philip Shenon, "FBI Contends Lawmaker Hid Bribe in Freezer," *The New York Times,* May 22, 2006.

125   bribe menu: Brian Ross, "From Cash to Yachts: Congressman's Bribe Menu," ABC News, March 2, 2006. https://abcnews.go.com/Politics/story?id=1667 009&page=1.

125   "word is out": David Maraniss and Michael Weisskopf, "Speaker and His Directors Make the Cash Flow Right," *The Washington Post,* November 27, 1995.

126   "not a shrewd business decision": Jill Abramson, "Republicans Are Irked at Industry Group's Hiring of Democrat," *The New York Times,* October 14, 1998.

126   "desire to get things done": "Lawmaker Warned About Playing Politics," Associated Press, May 17, 1999. https://www.oklahoman.com/article/2653642/ lawmaker-warned-about-playing-politics.

127   "K Street meetings": Maeve Reston, "Santorum Denies Ties to 'K Street Project,'" *Pittsburgh Post-Gazette,* January 26, 2006. https://old.post-gazette .com/pg/06026/644541.stm.

127   maximum contributions: Lou Dubose, "Broken Hammer?," *Salon,* April 8, 2005. https://www.salon.com/2005/04/08/scandals/.

127   hot tub party: Sam Tanehaus, "Tom DeLay's Hard Drive," *Vanity Fair,* July 2004. https://www.vanityfair.com/news/2004/07/tom-delay-200407.

127   "appearance of impropriety": John Bresnahan, "Ethics Panel Hands DeLay Second Rebuke in a Week," *Roll Call,* October 6, 2004. https://www.rollcall .com/2004/10/06/ethics-panel-hands-delay-second-rebuke-in-a-week/.

128   "temper your future actions": Ted Barrett, "House Ethics Committee Admonishes DeLay Again," CNN, October 7, 2004. https://www.cnn.com/2004/ALLPOLITICS/10/07/delay.ethics/.

128   sexually explicit online messages: Brian Ross, Rhonda Schwartz, and Maddy Sauer, "Three More Former Pages Accuse Foley of Online Sexual Approaches," ABC News, October 5, 2006. https://web.archive.org/web/20061011091337/http:/blogs.abcnews.com/theblotter/2006/10/three_more_form.html.

128   "serial child molester": Liam Stack, "Dennis Hastert, Ex-House Speaker Who Admitted Sex Abuse, Leaves Prison," *The New York Times,* July 18, 2017.

129   Toward Tradition: Dana Milbank, "One Committee's Three Hours of Inquiry, in Surreal Time," *The Washington Post,* June 23, 2005.

129   "big deal": Peter Overby, "Joining the Club Proves Difficult for Lobbyist," NPR, July 7, 2005. https://www.npr.org/templates/story/story.php?storyId=4734647.

130   "sent out emails": Jack Abramoff, *Capitol Punishment: The Hard Truth About Washington Corruption from America's Most Notorious Lobbyist* (WND Books, 2011).

130   "Bridge to Nowhere": Liz Ruskin, "Stevens Says He'll Quit if Bridge Funds Diverted," *Anchorage Daily News,* October 21, 2005.

130   Enron scandal: James Moore and Wayne Slater, *Bush's Brain: How Karl Rove Made George W. Bush Presidential* (John Wiley & Sons, 2003).

131   "good friends": Joe Stephens, "Bush 2000 Adviser Offered to Use Clout to Help Enron," *The Washington Post,* February 17, 2002.

131   "religious nuts": David Kuo, "Putting Faith Before Politics," *The New York Times,* November 16, 2006.

131   "corporate accounts": "Ralph Reed's Rehabilitation," MSNBC, February 9, 2012. https://www.msnbc.com/rachel-maddow-show/ralph-reeds-rehabilitation-msna33181.

131   "the wackos": Jim Galloway and Alan Judd, "Reed's Fees All Paid by Casino," *The Atlanta Journal-Constitution,* November 3, 2005.

131   "serious swat": Adam Zagorin, Karen Tumulty, and Masimo Calabresi, "An Unholy Alliance?" *Time,* October 23, 2005. http://content.time.com/time/subscriber/article/0,33009,1122014,00.html.

131   "ping Karl": Ken Herman, "Report Details Reed's Role as Go-Between: Abramoff Sought Contact with Rove," *The Atlanta Journal-Constitution,* September 30, 2006.

131   "election year": Report, "Gimme Five—Investigation of Tribal Lobbying Matters," *Committee on Indian Affairs, One Hundred Ninth Congress,* September 5, 2006. https://www.govinfo.gov/content/pkg/CRPT-109srpt325/html/CRPT-109srpt325.htm.

132   "helping the pro-family forces": Continetti, *K Street Gang.*

132   "a bad version": Report, "Gimme Five—Investigation of Tribal Lobbying Matters."

133   "dearest friends": Staff reports, "The Abramoff Affair: Timeline," *The Washington Post,* n.d. https://www.washingtonpost.com/wp-dyn/content/custom/2005/12/28/CU2005122801176.html.

133   "got the invitation": Alex Gibney, *Casino Jack and the United States of Money,* Jigsaw Productions, Participant Media, 2010.

134   "wealthy Indian gaming tribes": Susa Schmidt, "A Jackpot from Indian Gaming Tribes," February 22, 2004.

134   "plain stupid": Continetti, *The K Street Gang.*

134   "did not consider": Abramoff, *Capitol Punishment.*

CHAPTER 9: A DEEP-SEATED HATRED OF WHITE PEOPLE

136   Fifteen times: William Douglas, "Tea Party Protesters Scream 'Ni****' at Black Congressman," McClatchy, June 16, 2015. https://www.mcclatchydc .com/news/politics-government/article24577294.html.

136   spat on him: Lee Hill, "GOP Pressured to End 'Tea Party Racism,'" NPR, March 25, 2010. https://www.npr.org/sections/tellm2011/01/25/03/gop _pressured_to_end_tea_party.html.

136   "back of the bus": Steve Benen, "Calling Out the Loathsome," *Washington Monthly*, March 21, 2010. https://washingtonmonthly.com/2010/03/21/ calling-out-the-loathsome/.

137   Tea Party rallies: Ashley Fantz, "Obama as Witch Doctor: Racist or Satirical," CNN, September 18, 2009. http://www.cnn.com/2009/POLITICS/09/ 17/obama.witchdoctor.teaparty/index.html.

137   "undocumented worker": Dana Milbank, "Republican Lawmakers Stir Up the 'Tea Party' Crowd," *The Washington Post,* March 22, 2010.

137   "got cussed": Dana Milbank, "A Message That Fits the GOP to a T," *The Washington Post,* July 22, 2010.

138   "long time coming": Barack Obama, "Transcript of Barack Obama's Victory Speech," NPR, November 5, 2008. https://www.npr.org/templates/story/story .php?storyId=96624326.

138   "hatred for white people": Michael Calderone, "Fox's Beck: Obama Is 'a Racist,'" *Politico,* July 28, 2009. https://www.politico.com/blogs/michael calderone/0709/Foxs_Beck_Obama_is_a_racist.html.

138   "outside our comprehension": Adam Serwer, "Birtherism of a Nation," *The Atlantic,* May 13, 2020. https://www.theatlantic.com/ideas/archive/2020/05/ birtherism-and-trump/610978/.

138   "You lie!": "Rep. Wilson Shouts, 'You Lie' to Obama During Speech," CNN, September 2009. https://www.cnn.com/2009/POLITICS/09/09/joe.wilson/.

138   Jimmy Carter: Gwen Ifill, "Transcript: Debate on Race Emerges as Obama's Policies Take Shape," September 16, 2009. https://www.pbs.org/newshour/ show/debate-on-race-emerges-as-obamas-policies-take-shape.

139   "certification of live birth": Martha M. Hamilton, "The Obama Birth Certificate: A Timeline," PolitiFact, April 27, 2011. https://www.politifact.com/ article/2011/apr/27/obama-birth-certificate-timeline/.

139   "show his birth certificate": Gabriella Schwarz, "Trump Again Questions Obama's Birthplace," CNN, March 23, 2011. https://politicalticker.blogs.cnn .com/2011/03/23/trump-again-questions-obamas-birthplace/.

139   "really concerned": Melody Johnson, "Fox Goes Birther," Media Matters for America, March 28, 2011. https://www.mediamatters.org/fox-friends/fox -goes-birther.

139   "birth certificate is missing": "Trump Claims Obama Birth Certificate 'Missing,'" CNN, April 25, 2011. https://ac360.blogs.cnn.com/2011/04/25/trump -claims-obama-birth-certificate-missing/?hpt=ac_mid.

139   "long-form": Alan Silverleib, "Obama Releases Original Long-Form Birth Certificate," CNN, April 27, 2011. http://www.cnn.com/2011/POLITICS/04/ 27/obama.birth.certificate/.

140   "terrible student": Glenn Kessler, "A Look at Trump's 'Birther' Statements," *The Washington Post,* April 28, 2011.

140   "history of lying": Jim Rutenberg, "The Man Behind the Whispers About Obama," *The New York Times,* October 12, 2008.

140   madrassa in Indonesia: Ben Smith and Byron Tau, "Birtherism: Where It All

Began," *Politico,* April 22, 2011. https://www.politico.com/story/2011/04/birtherism-where-it-all-began-053563.

141   "not an American": Halimah Abdullah, "Why Politicians Lie and Why We Want to Believe Them," CNN, June 1, 2012. https://www.cnn.com/2012/05/31/politics/why-politicians-lie/index.html.

141   "fair game": Dana Milbank, "Sarah Palin, the Political Mother of Trump," *The Washington Post,* May 11, 2016.

141   "natural born citizen": Dana Milbank, "Getting Creative with the Constitution," *The Washington Post,* February 25, 2011.

141   Obama was a Muslim: "Little Voter Discomfort with Romney's Mormon Religion," Pew Research Center, July 26, 2012. https://www.pewforum.org/2012/07/26/2012-romney-mormonism-obamas-religion/.

141   Mitt Romney: Kasie Hunt, "Mitt: Obama Born Here, Period," *Politico,* April 12, 2011. https://www.politico.com/story/2011/04/mitt-obama-born-here-period-053073.

141   "closer look": Ryan Struyk, "67 Times Donald Trump Tweeted About the 'Birther' Movement," ABC News, September 16, 2016. https://abcnews.go.com/Politics/67-times-donald-trump-tweeted-birther-movement/story?id=42145590.

142   "founder of ISIS": Tal Kopan, "Donald Trump: I Meant That Obama Founded ISIS, Literally," CNN, August 12, 2016. https://www.cnn.com/2016/08/11/politics/donald-trump-hugh-hewitt-obama-founder-isis/index.html.

142   "right time": Andrew Prokop, "Trump Fanned a Conspiracy About Obama's Birthplace for Years. Now He Pretends Clinton Started It," *Vox,* September 16, 2016. https://www.vox.com/2016/9/16/12938066/donald-trump-obama-birth-certificate-birther.

143   "Growth and Opportunity Project": Republican National Committee, "Growth and Opportunity Project," March 18, 2013. https://online.wsj.com/public/resources/documents/RNCreport03182013.pdf.

144   "too hard": Sheila McLaughlin, "Boehner Mocks GOP Colleagues on Immigration Reform," *The Cincinnati Enquirer,* April 24, 2014. https://www.cincinnati.com/story/news/politics/2014/04/24/boehner-mocks-colleagues-immigration-reform/8101699/.

144   "bigot": Eric Bradner, "First on CNN: Top Jeb Bush Adviser Leaves GOP, Will Vote for Clinton If Florida Close," CNN, August 2, 2016. https://www.cnn.com/2016/08/01/politics/sally-bradshaw-jeb-bush-donald-trump-florida/index.html.

144   voter registration rates: "The Effects of Shelby County v. Holder," Brennan Center for Justice, August 6, 2018. https://www.brennancenter.org/our-work/policy-solutions/effects-shelby-county-v-holder.

145   "current conditions": Adam Liptak, "Supreme Court Invalidates Key Part of Voting Rights Act," *The New York Times,* June 25, 2013.

145   "umbrella in a rainstorm": Vann R. Newkirk, "How *Shelby County v. Holder* Broke America," *The Atlantic,* July 10, 2018. https://www.theatlantic.com/politics/archive/2018/07/how-shelby-county-broke-america/564707/.

145   disenfranchised: Kevin Morris, Myrna Perez, and Jonathan Brater, "Purges: A Growing Threat to the Right to Vote," Brennan Center for Justice, July 20, 2018. https://www.brennancenter.org/our-work/research-reports/purges-growing-threat-right-vote.

145   "Islam is peace": Transcript, "Newscast: Bush assembling international coalition against terrorism, hunting for bin Laden," NBC News, September 17, 2001.

145 "enemy of America": Backgrounder, "The President's Quotes on Islam," The White House, President George W. Bush, September 20, 2001. https://georgewbush-whitehouse.archives.gov/infocus/ramadan/islam.html.

146 "family-man": Transcript, "Newscast: McCain camp to tone down negative attacks on Obama," NBC News, October 11, 2008.

146 "Barack Hussein Obama": Joe Garofoli, "Veiled Racism Seen in New Attacks on Obama," San Francisco Chronicle, October 9, 2008.

146 "palling around with terrorists": Janell Ross, "Sarah Palin Called Black Lives Matter Protesters 'Dogs.' Here's Why She Doesn't Get the Benefit of the Doubt," The Washington Post, September 10, 2015.

146 some of the same support: Jim Rutenberg and Serge F. Kovaleske, "Paul Disowns Extremists' Views but Doesn't Disavow the Support," The New York Times, December 25, 2011.

146 "spell the word 'vote'": Joan Walsh, "Too Much Tea Party Racism," Salon, March 20, 2010. https://www.salon.com/2010/03/20/tea_party_racism/.

146 "emancipation thing": Alexander Zaitchik, "New Report Examines 'Tea Party Nationalism,' Charts Extremist Ties," Southern Poverty Law Center, October 20, 2010. https://www.splcenter.org/hatewatch/2010/10/20/new-report-examines-tea-party-nationalism-charts-extremist-ties.

147 "Chicago hood": Mark Potok, "TeaParty.org Founder Labels Obama with Racial Terms," Southern Poverty Law Center, May 28, 2010. https://www.splcenter.org/hatewatch/2010/05/28/teapartyorg-founder-labels-obama-racial-terms.

147 "quickly into slavery": Dana Milbank, "Civil Rights' New 'Owner': Glenn Beck," The Washington Post, August 29, 2010.

147 song on air: Rush Limbaugh, "Barack the Magic Negro." https://www.youtube.com/watch?v=5_FAJUFutyw.

147 punishment for slavery: Igor Volsky, "Rush Limbaugh: Obama Wants Americans to Get Ebola as Payback for Slavery," ThinkProgress, October 6, 2014. https://archive.thinkprogress.org/rush-limbaugh-obama-wants-americans-to-get-ebola-as-payback-for-slavery-ddf50bfc8056/.

147 "half-breed": Terence Samuel, "The Racist Backlash Obama Has Faced During His Presidency," The Washington Post, April 22, 2016.

147 "given platforms": Kate Zernike, "N.A.A.C.P. Report Raises Concerns About Racism Within Tea Party Groups," The New York Times, October 20, 2010.

148 "tried for treason": Dana Milbank, "The GOP's Animal Planet," The Washington Post, September 1, 2012.

148 "racial animus": Eric Holder, "U.S. Still 'Afraid' of Race," ABC News, July 15, 2014. https://abcnews.go.com/ThisWeek/video/eric-holder-us-afraid-race-24542622.

148 "roll their eyes": Peter Grier, "Obama and Race: Why Eric Holder's Words Stirred Such Anger," The Christian Science Monitor, July 15, 2014.

148 "lived that life": Frank James, "Sotomayor's 'Wise Latina' Line Maybe Not So Wise," NPR, May 27, 2009. https://www.npr.org/sections/thetwo-way/2009/05/sotomayors_wise_latina_line_ma.html.

148 "Latina woman racist": Huma Khan and Jake Tapper, "Newt Gingrich on Twitter: Sonia Sotomayor 'Racist,' Should Withdraw," ABC News, May 27, 2009. https://abcnews.go.com/Politics/SoniaSotomayor/story?id=7685284.

149 "better off as slaves": Ralph Ellis and Greg Botelho, "Rancher Says He's Not Racist, Still Defiant over Grazing Battle," CNN, April 25, 2004. https://www.cnn.com/2014/04/24/politics/cliven-bundy-interview/index.html.

149 "marijuana across the desert": Gene Demby, "Steve King Doubles Down,"

NPR, July 26, 2013. https://www.npr.org/sections/codeswitch/2013/07/26/205885068/steve-king-doubles-down.

149   "fascist book": Jeremy Diamond, "Rep. Steve King on Garland Attack: 'We Knew This Was Coming,'" CNN, May 5, 2015. https://www.cnn.com/2015/05/05/politics/steve-king-garland-islam-free-speech/index.html.

149   "country great again": Sharyn Jackson, "Trump: King Has 'the Right Views,'" *The Des Moines Register,* October 18, 2014.

150   targeting Latino drivers: Colin Dwyer, "Ex-Sheriff Joe Arpaio Convicted of Criminal Contempt," NPR, July 31, 2017. https://www.npr.org/sections/the-two-way/2017/07/31/540629884/ex-sheriff-joe-arpaio-convicted-of-criminal-contempt.

150   "Allah sort it out": James Arkin, "Palin: 'Let Allah Sort It Out,'" *Politico,* August 31, 2013. https://www.politico.com/story/2013/08/sarah-palin-let-allah-sort-it-out-096128.

150   *Duck Dynasty* patriarch: Ann Oldenburg, "Sarah Palin Rallies Fans, Defends 'Duck Dynasty,'" *USA Today,* December 19, 2013.

150   "good idea": Ed Kilgore, "McConnell Thinks Obama Was Reparations Enough," *New York,* June 19, 2019. https://nymag.com/intelligencer/2019/06/mcconnell-thinks-obamas-election-was-reparations-enough.html.

151   "revere my family": Helen Dewar, "Senate Bows to Braun on Symbol of Confederacy," *The Washington Post,* July 23, 1993.

151   "matter to rest": Barack Obama, "Remarks by the President at the White House Correspondents Association Dinner," White House, May 1, 2011. https://obamawhitehouse.archives.gov/the-press-office/2011/05/01/remarks-president-white-house-correspondents-association-dinner.

CHAPTER 10: DEATH PANELS

153   "jaw is dropping": Angie Drobnic Holan, "Sarah Palin Falsely Claims Barack Obama Runs a 'Death Panel,'" PolitiFact, August 10, 2009. https://www.politifact.com/factchecks/2009/aug/10/sarah-palin/sarah-palin-barack-obama-death-panel/.

154   "dead right": Don Gonyea, "From the Start, Obama Struggled with Fallout from a Kind of Fake News," NPR, January 10, 2017. https://www.npr.org/2017/01/10/509164679/from-the-start-obama-struggled-with-fallout-from-a-kind-of-fake-news.

154   "put to death": Angie Drobnic Holan, "PolitiFact's Lie of the Year: 'Death Panels,'" PolitiFact, December 18, 2009. https://www.politifact.com/article/2009/dec/18/politifact-lie-year-death-panels/.

154   "cynical and irresponsible": Barack Obama, "President's Address to a Joint Session of Congress on September 9, 2009, Relative to Health Care Legislation," *Congressional Record,* September 9, 2009. https://www.govinfo.gov/content/pkg/CRECB-2009-pt16/html/CRECB-2009-pt16-Pg21203-6.htm.

155   "dictated by fact-checkers": James Bennet, "'We're Not Going to Let Our Campaign Be Dictated by Fact-Checkers,'" *The Atlantic,* August 28, 2012. https://www.theatlantic.com/politics/archive/2012/08/were-not-going-to-let-our-campaign-be-dictated-by-fact-checkers/261674/.

155   "denied care": Emily Pierce, "GOP Leaders Refuse to Name Obamacare Board Members," *CQ Roll Call,* May 9, 2013. https://www.rollcall.com/2013/05/09/gop-leaders-refuse-to-name-obamacare-board-members/.

155   *Vox* poll: Sarah Kliff, "Today in Obamacare: Liberals Are Taking Back the Term 'Death Panels,'" *Vox,* February 22, 2017. https://www.vox.com/policy-and-politics/2017/2/22/14700282/obamacare-death-panels-grassley.

156   Fast and Furious: Sari Horwitz, "Inspector General Critical of Justice Dept., ATF in 'Fast and Furious' Operation," *The Washington Post,* September 19, 2012.

156   "creating a situation": Dana Milbank, "In Congress, Blowing Gunsmoke," *The Washington Post,* June 20, 2012.

156   "covering up a crime": Dana Milbank, "GOP-Style Jobs Program," *The Washington Post,* June 27, 2012.

156   "no evidence": Report, "A Review of ATF's Operation Fast and Furious and Related Matters," U.S. Department of Justice, Office of the Inspector General, September 2012. https://oig.justice.gov/reports/2012/s1209.pdf.

156   sixty-four thousand pages: Bill Chappell, "Newly Released 'Fast and Furious' Documents Include a Slam on Issa," NPR, December 5, 2014. https://www.npr.org/sections/thetwo-way/2014/11/05/361550503/newly-released-justice-documents-includes-a-slam-on-issa.

157   "Obama's Watergate": Ben Smith, "Issa Won't Investigate 'Obama's Watergate,'" *Politico,* January 2, 2011. https://www.politico.com/blogs/ben-smith/2011/01/issa-wont-investigate-obamas-watergate-031815.

157   "corrupt presidents": Ruth Marcus, "Which Darrell Issa Would Run House Oversight Panel?" *The Washington Post,* October 27, 2010. https://www.washingtonpost.com/wp-dyn/content/article/2010/10/26/AR2010102605215.html?tid=a_inl_manual.

157   "winners and losers": Dana Milbank, "Darrell Issa and the Overblown Scandals," *The Washington Post,* June 28, 2013.

157   Washington headquarters: Connor Simpson, "Issa Says IRS Scrutiny Was Directed by Washington," *The Atlantic,* June 2, 2013. https://www.theatlantic.com/politics/archive/2013/06/issa-says-irs-scrutiny-was-directed-washington/314695/.

157   "enemies list": Dana Milbank, "Accuse and Ask Questions Later," *The Washington Post,* June 3, 2013.

158   "acted on": Dana Milbank, "Rep. Darrell Issa's Subpoena Mania," *The Washington Post,* June 23, 2014.

158   "career employee": Dana Milbank, "IRS Hearings Are Another Republican Circus," *The Washington Post,* April 9, 2014.

158   "security cables": House Hearing, "Hearing Before the Committee on Foreign Affairs House Representatives," Congress, January 23, 2013. https://www.govinfo.gov/content/pkg/CHRG-113hhrg78250/html/CHRG-113hhrg78250.htm.

159   "cable from Clinton": Glenn Kessler, "Issa's Absurd Claim That Clinton's 'Signature' Means She Personally Approved It," *The Washington Post,* April 26, 2013.

159   "sharply contradicts": Zachary Pleat, "Wash. Post's Fact Checker Further Discredits Fox-Promoted GOP Smear Against Clinton," Media Matters for America, April 26, 2013. https://www.mediamatters.org/fox-nation/wash-posts-fact-checker-further-discredits-fox-promoted-gop-smear-against-clinton?redirect_source=/blog/2013/04/26/wash-posts-fact-checker-further-discredits-fox/193787&page=1.

159   "stand down order": Glenn Kessler, "Issa's 'Suspicions' That Hillary Clinton Told Panetta to 'Stand Down' on Benghazi," *The Washington Post,* February 21, 2014.

159   "Department of Defense asset": Glenn Kessler, "Rep. Darrell Issa Disputes His Four-Pinocchio Ratings," *The Washington Post,* March 3, 2014.

159   "to be substantiated": Report, "Of the U.S. Senate Select Committee on Intel-

ligence Review of the Terrorist Attacks on U.S. Facilities in Benghazi, Libya," U.S. Senate, January 15, 2014. https://www.intelligence.senate.gov/sites/default/files/publications/113134.pdf.

159   1,100 segments: Rob Savillo and Hannah Groch-Begley, "REPORT: Fox's Benghazi Obsession by the Numbers," Media Matters for America, September 9, 2014. https://www.mediamatters.org/sean-hannity/report-foxs-benghazi-obsession-numbers.

159   "catch-phrase": Leon Neyfakh, "Benghazi, Episode 5: Greatest Hits," *Fiasco Benghazi,* July 22, 2021. https://podcasts.apple.com/us/podcast/benghazi-ep-5-greatest-hits/id1568510339?i=1000526768995.

160   "prevent it from ever happening again": Tom Kertscher, "In Context: Hillary Clinton's 'What Difference Does It Make' Comment," PolitiFact, May 8, 2013. https://www.politifact.com/article/2013/may/08/context-hillary-clintons-what-difference-does-it-m/.

160   "14 days": Jon Greenberg, "Says President Obama Waited Two Weeks to Call the Attack in Libya 'Terror,'" PolitiFact, October 17, 2012. https://www.politifact.com/factchecks/2012/oct/17/mitt-romney/romney-says-obama-waited-14-days-call-libya-attack/.

160   probed Benghazi: David M. Herszenhorn, "House Benghazi Report Finds No New Evidence of Wrongdoing by Hillary Clinton," *The New York Times,* June 28, 2016.

160   revisit Benghazi anew: Russell Berman, "John Boehner Forges Ahead on the House Benghazi Probe," *The Atlantic,* November 24, 2014. https://www.theatlantic.com/politics/archive/2014/11/john-boehner-forges-ahead-on-benghazi-probe/383200/.

160   "away from Gowdy": Dana Milbank, "Meet the Chief Prosecutor in the GOP's Benghazi Show Trial," *The Washington Post,* May 7, 2014.

161   "morally reprehensible": Dana Milbank, "Two Years, $7 Million, Still No Smoking Gun on Clinton and Benghazi," *The New York Times,* June 28, 2016.

161   "secret effort": Elspeth Reeve, "What Benghazi Truthers Are Looking For," *The Atlantic,* May 20, 2013. https://www.theatlantic.com/politics/archive/2013/05/what-benghazi-truthers-are-looking/315370/.

161   "serious brain injury": Katie Glueck, "Rove: Clinton Might Have Brain Injury," *Politico,* May 12, 2014. https://www.politico.com/story/2014/05/karl-rove-hillary-clinton-brain-injury-106613.

162   "numbers are dropping": E. J. Dionne Jr., "Kevin McCarthy's Truthful Gaffe on Benghazi," *The Washington Post,* September 30, 2015.

162   "mandatory service": Steven Thomma, "Secret Camps and Guillotines? Groups Make Birthers Look Sane," McClatchy D.C. Bureau, June 15, 2015. https://www.mcclatchydc.com/news/politics-government/article245531 26.html.

162   "secret getaway": Mark Knoller, "Conspiracy Theories Abound After Obama Ditches the Press," CBS News, April 14, 2010. https://www.cbsnews.com/news/conspiracy-theories-abound-after-obama-ditches-the-press/.

162   takeover of the world: Larry Keller, "Fear of FEMA," Southern Poverty Law Center, March 2, 2010. https://www.splcenter.org/fighting-hate/intelligence-report/2010/fear-fema.

162   "Tree of Revolution": "Beck's 'Tree of Revolution' Links Obama, SEIU, ACORN, SDS, Che Guevara," Media Matters for America, September 18, 2009. https://www.mediamatters.org/glenn-beck/becks-tree-revolution-links-obama-seiu-acorn-sds-che-guevara.

163   "circle of crazy": John Boehner, *On the House: A Washington Memoir* (St. Martin's Press, 2021).

163   "waged the attacks": "Romney Criticizes Obama Response to Libya, Egypt Attacks," Reuters, September 11, 2012. https://www.reuters.com/article/uk -usa-campaign-romney-obama/romney-criticizes-obama-response-to-libya -egypt-attacks-idUKBRE88B03K20120912.

164   "Jeep manufacturing": Katie Glueck, "Trump Rips Auto Exec's 'Filthy' Mouth," *Politico,* November 2, 2012. https://www.politico.com/story/2012/ 11/trump-rips-auto-execs-filthy-mouth-083235.

164   "post-truth politics": James Fallows, "Three 'Post-Truth' Related Items," *The Atlantic,* August 31, 2012. https://www.theatlantic.com/politics/archive/ 2012/08/three-post-truth-related-items/261853/.

164   "reality matter?": David Corn, "Hate Trumps History: A Reality TV Star Wins the White House in a Broken America," *Mother Jones,* November 9, 2016. https://www.motherjones.com/politics/2016/11/hate-trumps-history -reality-tv-star-wins-white-house-broken-america/.

164   "Sovietize": Igor Volsky, "Blow by Blow: A Comprehensive Timeline of the GOP's 4-Year Battle to Kill Obamacare," *ThinkProgress,* March 23, 2014. https://archive.thinkprogress.org/blow-by-blow-a-comprehensive-timeline-of -the-gops-4-year-battle-to-kill-obamacare-5dd069a5518a/.

164   "funneled out": Jason Stanley, "Speech, Lies and Apathy," *The New York Times,* August 30, 2012.

165   "new Gestapo": "Maine Governor LePage Apologizes for 'Gestapo' Comment," Reuters, July 9, 2012. https://www.reuters.com/article/us-usa-maine -politics/maine-governor-lepage-apologizes-for-gestapo-comment-idUSBRE 8681DK20120709.

165   "trains to concentration camps": Associated Press, "Idaho Pol: Health Care Like Holocaust," *Politico,* January 31, 2013. https://www.politico.com/ story/2013/01/idaho-sen-sheryl-nuxoll-compares-health-care-to-holocaust-0 86984.

165   sign ups: "Campfield Blog Post Condemned by GOP, Dem Leaders," Associated Press, May 6, 2014. https://www.washingtontimes.com/news/2014/may/ 5/campfield-blog-post-condemned-by-gop-dem-leaders/.

165   "individual liberty": Rebecca Ballhaus, "Explaining 'Fugitive Slave Act' Claim Highlighted by Obama," *The Wall Street Journal,* September 26, 2013. https://www.wsj.com/articles/BL-WB-40669.

165   "racist tax": Sarah Kliff, "Rep. Ted Yoho: Tanning Tax Is a Racist Tax— Against White People," *The Washington Post,* August 5, 2013.

165   "end of prosperity": Conor Friedersdorf, "How Right-Wing Media Saved Obamacare," *The Atlantic,* March 27, 2017. https://www.theatlantic.com/ politics/archive/2017/03/the-right-wing-media-helped-obamacare-in-spite-of -itself/520851/.

165   "most dangerous piece": Jonathan Weisman, "Boehner Seeking Democrats' Help on Fiscal Talks," *The New York Times,* September 12, 2013.

165   "death knell": Luke Johnson, "Rick Santorum Says U.S. Moving Towards Fascist Italy," *HuffPost,* December 14, 2011. https://www.huffpost.com/entry/ rick-santorum-2012-health-care_n_1148682.

165   "never recover": Ashley Parker, "Conservatives with a Cause: 'We're Right,'" *The New York Times,* October 1, 2013.

165   "kills women": Aaron Blake, "Bachmann: Obamacare 'Literally Kills' People," *The Washington Post,* March 21, 2013.

165   "die sooner": Glenn Thrush, "Coburn: 'You're Gonna Die Sooner' Under

Dem Plan," *Politico,* December 1, 2009. https://www.politico.com/blogs/on-congress/2009/12/coburn-youre-gonna-die-sooner-under-dem-plan-023162.

166 require microchips: Aaron Sharockman, "Obamacare Is . . . the Largest Tax Increase in the History of the World," PolitiFact, June 28, 2012. https://www.politifact.com/factchecks/2012/jun/28/rush-limbaugh/health-care-law-not-largest-tax-increase-us-histor/.

166 "Question Your Sex Life": Betsy McCaughey, "Obamacare Will Question Your Sex Life," *New York Post,* September 15, 2013. https://nypost.com/2013/09/15/obamacare-will-question-your-sex-life/.

166 "paid only by the plan": James Fallows, "A Triumph of Misinformation," *The Atlantic,* January 1995. https://www.theatlantic.com/magazine/archive/1995/01/a-triumph-of-misinformation/306231/.

167 "Nothing in this Act": Fallows, "A Triumph of Misinformation."

167 "enforcing uniformity": Betsy McCaughey, "Ruin Your Health with the Obama Stimulus Plan," *Congressional Record,* February 2009. https://www.govinfo.gov/content/pkg/CRECB-2009-pt3/html/CRECB-2009-pt3-Pg3517.htm.

167 "clinical guidelines": "Agency for Healthcare Research and Quality," U.S. Government Publishing Office, n.d. https://www.govinfo.gov/content/pkg/USCODE-2011-title42/html/USCODE-2011-title42-chap6A-subchapVII.htm.

167 "monitor treatments": Phillip Longman, "The Republican Case for Waste in Health Care," *Washington Monthly,* March 11, 2013.

167 "guiding decisions your doctor": Steve Benen, "Remember the Last Time McCaughey Lied?," *Washington Monthly,* August 22, 2009. https://washingtonmonthly.com/people/steve-benen/?post_page=2108.

167 "counseling session": Paul West, "GOP Rides Wave of Ire," *The Baltimore Sun,* August 16, 2009. https://www.baltimoresun.com/news/bs-xpm-2009-08-16-0908150142-story.html.

168 "decline nutrition": Catharine Richert, "McCaughey Claims End-of-Life Counseling Will Be Required for Medicare Patients," PolitiFact, July 23, 2009. https://www.politifact.com/factchecks/2009/jul/23/betsy-mccaughey/mccaughey-claims-end-life-counseling-will-be-requi/.

168 "trivialization of abortion": "EDITORIAL: No 'Final Solution,' but a Way Forward," *The Washington Times,* November 23, 2008. https://www.washingtontimes.com/news/2008/nov/23/no-final-solution-but-a-way-forward/.

168 "pay parents": George Neumayr, "Nancy Pelosi's Modest Proposal," *The American Spectator,* January 27, 2009. https://spectator.org/42265_nancy-pelosis-modest-proposal/.

CHAPTER 11: DON'T RETREAT—RELOAD

169 "Don't Retreat": Igor Volsky, "Blow by Blow: A Comprehensive Timeline of the GOP's 4-Year Battle to Kill Obamacare," *ThinkProgress,* March 23, 2014. https://archive.thinkprogress.org/blow-by-blow-a-comprehensive-timeline-of-the-gops-4-year-battle-to-kill-obamacare-5dd069a5518a/.

169 "Second Amendment remedies": Jennifer Epstein, "Angle Defends Herself, Tea Party," *Politico,* January 12, 2011. https://www.politico.com/story/2011/01/angle-defends-herself-tea-party-047475.

169 "tyrannical government": Greg Sargent, "Sharron Angle Floated Possibility of Armed Insurrection," *The Washington Post,* June 25, 2010.

170 "firing line": Eric Zimmerman, "Steele: Put Pelosi on the 'Firing Line,'" *The Hill,* March 24, 2010. https://thehill.com/blogs/blog-briefing-room/news/88783-steele-put-pelosi-on-the-firing-line.

170   "drop by": Alex Isenstadt, "Perriello Tries to Woo Tea Party," *Politico*, September 1, 2010. https://www.politico.com/story/2010/09/perriello-tries-to-woo
-tea-party-041672.

170   "break their windows": James Ridgeway, "Giffords's Office Was Vandalized by Followers of Former Militia Leader," *Mother Jones*, January 8, 2011. https://www.motherjones.com/crime-justice/2011/01/giffordss-office-was
-vandalized-followers-former-militia-leader/.

170   phone threat: Jake Sherman and Marin Cogan, "The Backlash: Reform Turns Personal," *Politico*, March 24, 2010. https://www.politico.com/story/2010/03/
the-backlash-reform-turns-personal-034907.

170   threatening letter: Brian Montopoli, "Anthony Weiner's Office Receives Threatening Letter Containing White Powder," CBS News, March 25, 2010. https://www.cbsnews.com/news/anthony-weiners-office-receives-threatening
-letter-containing-white-powder/.

170   coffin to the office: "Health Care Reform Anger Takes a Nasty, Violent Turn," CNN, March 26, 2010. http://www.cnn.com/2010/POLITICS/03/25/
congress.threats/index.html.

170   "remain vigilant": Scott Wong, "Senate Sergeant at Arms: Warning 'Confusing,'" *Politico*, September 9, 2011. https://www.politico.com/blogs/on
-congress/2011/09/senate-sergeant-at-arms-warning-confusing-039059.

171   "dead man": Robert Costa, "Context," *National Review*, March 26, 2010. https://www.nationalreview.com/corner/context-robert-costa/.

171   "violence and threats": Jake Sherman, "Hoyer: Members Are at Risk," *Politico*, March 24, 2010. https://www.politico.com/story/2010/03/hoyer-members
-are-at-risk-034953.

171   "kill your children": Michael Cooper, "Accusations Fly Between Parties over Threats and Vandalism," *The New York Times*, March 25, 2010.

171   "fanning the flames": "Rattled Dems Move Forward Amid Threats," CBS News, March 25, 2010. https://www.cbsnews.com/news/rattled-dems-move
-forward-amid-threats/.

171   "inflame these situations": Chris Good, "Cantor Accuses Democrats of Using Threats, Violence to Score Points," *The Atlantic*, March 25, 2010. https://
www.theatlantic.com/politics/archive/2010/03/cantor-accuses-democrats-of
-using-threats-violence-to-score-points/38024/.

171   "Congress on Your Corner": Colleen Curry, "Rep. Gabrielle Giffords Rejected Staff Request to Skip Meeting Where She Was Shot," ABC News, November 11, 2011. https://abcnews.go.com/US/gabby_giffords/rep-gabrielle
-giffords-rejected-staff-request-skip-meeting/story?id=14881689.

172   "outbursts of violence": Kenneth P. Vogel and Jonathan Martin, "Giffords Downplayed Threats," *Politico*, January 8, 2011. https://www.politico.com/
story/2011/01/giffords-downplayed-threats-047258.

172   "Victory in November": David Weigel, "Meanwhile, in Arizona," *Slate*, April 16, 2012. https://slate.com/news-and-politics/2012/04/meanwhile-in
-arizona.html.

172   "what is on your mind": Philip Rucker and Marc Fisher, "Tucson Shootings: How Gabrielle Giffords's Event for Constituents Turned to Tragedy," *The Washington Post*, January 10, 2011.

173   permanently injuring his leg: Melissa Bell and James Buck, "Updated: List of Injured Victims in Arizona Shooting Released by Pima County Sheriff," *The Washington Post*, January 14, 2011.

173   erroneously reported: Alicia C. Shepard, "NPR's Giffords Mistake: Relearning the Lesson of Checking Sources," NPR, January 11, 2011. https://www

.npr.org/sections/publiceditor/2011/01/11/132812196/nprs-giffords-mistake
-re-learning-the-lesson-of-checking-sources.

173 false report: Gabrielle Giffords and Mark Kelly, *Gabby: A Story of Courage, Love and Resilience* (Scribner, 2012).

174 "whole Tea Party": Meredith Shiner and Carrie Budoff Brown, "Liberals Blame Palin," *Politico,* January 8, 2011. https://www.politico.com/story/2011/01/liberals-blame-palin-047252.

174 "blood libel": Glenn Kessler, "Palin's Use of 'Blood Libel' and Reagan Comment in Statement on Tucson," *The Washington Post,* January 12, 2011.

174 "time to retreat": Zeke Miller, "Palin to Republicans on Debt Limit: Don't Retreat, 'Reload,'" *Business Insider,* July 14, 2011. https://www.businessinsider.com/palin-on-debt-limit-dont-retreat-reload-2011-7.

174 "Don't retreat": Paul Bond, "Sarah Palin Brings Back Controversial 'Reload' Line at Breitbart Tribute," *Hollywood Reporter,* June 16, 2012. https://www.hollywoodreporter.com/news/politics-news/sarah-palin-revisits-reload-inspire-conservative-bloggers-338469/.

175 paramilitary groups tripling: "U.S. Right-Wing Groups, Militias Surge: Study," Reuters, March 4, 2010. https://www.reuters.com/article/us-usa-politics-patriots/u-s-right-wing-groups-militias-surge-study-idUSTRE6234JT20100304.

175 "radical-right ideas": Mark Potok, "The Year in Hate and Extremism," Southern Poverty Law Center, March 10, 2015. https://www.splcenter.org/fighting-hate/intelligence-report/2015/year-hate-and-extremism-0.

175 gun confiscation: "Rage Grows in America: Anti-Government Conspiracies," Anti-Defamation League, November 2009. https://www.adl.org/sites/default/files/documents/assets/pdf/combating-hate/Rage-Grows-In-America.pdf.

175 "angry white guys": "Stuck in the Center-Right with You," The Hotline, October 13, 2009.

176 "scared to death": Chris Cillizza, "The Fix: Joe Wilson and the Laws of Political Chaos," *The Washington Post,* September 11, 2009.

176 "brush fires": Dana Milbank, "Hard to Say He's Sorry," *The Washington Post,* September 11, 2009.

176 "blood of patriots": Transcript, "Monday, March 22, 2010," NBC News, March 23, 2010. https://www.nbcnews.com/id/wbna36004440.

176 "toward civil war": Dana Milbank, "Gun-Toting Protesters Stick to their Bricks," *The Washington Post,* April 20, 2010.

177 "kind of fun": Kent Bush, "History May Be on GOP's Side in November," *The Register-Mail,* March 24, 2010. https://www.galesburg.com/story/news/2010/03/24/kent-bush-history-may-be/47882949007/.

177 "this rancor": William Douglas, "Tea Party Protesters Scream 'N-Word' at Black Congressman," McClatchy Washington Bureau, March 20, 2010.

177 "socialist policies": Dana Milbank, "Despite Peril, GOP Accepts Tea Party," *The Washington Post,* July 24, 2010.

177 "gangster government": Dana Milbank, "Michele Bachmann's Alternative Universe," *The Washington Post,* January 28, 2011.

178 "conservative media darling": John Boehner, *On the House: A Washington Memoir* (St. Martin's Press, 2021).

178 "Tea Party activists": Michael O'Brien, "Boehner: No Difference in Beliefs Between GOP and Tea Partiers," *The Hill,* February 4, 2010. https://thehill.com/blogs/blog-briefing-room/news/79725-boehner-no-difference-in-beliefs-between-gop-and-tea-partiers.

178 "no daylight": Jennifer Epstein, "Boehner: I'm with the Tea Party," *Politico,*

April 7, 2011. https://www.politico.com/story/2011/04/boehner-im-with-the
-tea-party-052722.

178 "Tea Partier": Dana Milbank, "Tea Partiers Get Audience with RNC Chairman but Not a Shared Public Stage," *The Washington Post,* February 17, 2010.

178 Tea Party movement: Dana Milbank, "What Republican Establishment?" *The Washington Post,* September 19, 2010.

178 "dabbled into witchcraft": Ryan Creed, "Christine O'Donnell: 'I Dabbled in Witchcraft,'" ABC News, September 18, 2010. https://abcnews.go.com/News/christine-odonnell-dabbled-witchcraft/story?id=11671277.

178 party check: Dana Milbank, "Tea Time for the Grand Old Party," *The Washington Post,* September 21, 2010.

179 "tipping point": Dana Milbank, "Quoth the Craven," *The Washington Post,* July 27, 2011.

179 "break you": Alexandra Petri, "A Grimm Apology," *The Washington Post,* February 1, 2014.

179 "car we takin'?": Dana Milbank, "Quoth the Craven," *The Washington Post,* July 27, 2011.

179 "revival stuff": Dana Milbank, "Eric Cantor Tries a Civil Approach to the Health-Care Debate," *The Washington Post,* September 22, 2009.

180 "no compromise": Dana Milbank, "GOP Could Use Some Adults," *The Washington Post,* March 9, 2011.

180 "time for compromise": Michael O'Brien, "Boehner: 'Not a Time for Compromise,'" *The Hill,* October 27, 2010. https://thehill.com/blogs/blog-briefing-room/news/126153-boehner-this-is-not-a-time-for-compromise.

180 "crazier Republicans": "Human Events: Sen. Bob Corker Denies Obamacare Reports—Sen. Bob Corker (R-TN) News Release," U.S. Government Publishing Office, October 20, 2010.

180 "donate today": Dana Milbank, "A Tea Party of Populist Posers," *The Washington Post,* October 20, 2010.

181 "legitimate rape": John Eligon and Michael Schwirtz, "Senate Candidate Provokes Ire with 'Legitimate Rape' Comment," *The New York Times,* August 19, 2012.

181 "transvaginal ultrasounds": Lucy Madison, "Virginia Gov. Bob McDonnell Signs Virginia Ultrasound Bill," CBS News, March 7, 2012. https://www.cbsnews.com/news/virginia-gov-bob-mcdonnell-signs-virginia-ultrasound-bill/.

181 "almost treasonous": Dana Milbank, "Ben Bernanke Smiles in the Face of Critics," *The Washington Post,* January 25, 2012.

181 Export-Import Bank: Dana Milbank, "A Case Study in Republicans' Rapid Radicalization," *The Washington Post,* June 3, 2015.

182 "unjust law": Dana Milbank, "Lawbreaker Kim Davis and the Lawless Ted Cruz," *The Washington Post,* September 4, 2015.

182 "uphold the law": Rachel Kleinman, "Jeb Bush Seeks Middle Ground on Clerk's Same-Sex Marriage Stand," NBC News, September 3, 2015. https://www.nbcnews.com/politics/2016-election/jeb-bush-seeks-middle-ground-clerks-same-sex-marriage-stand-n421516.

183 militia members: Ashley Fantz, Joe Sutton, and Holly Yan, "Armed Group's Leader in Federal Building: 'We Will Be Here as Long as It Takes,'" CNN, January 4, 2016. https://www.cnn.com/2016/01/03/us/oregon-wildlife-refuge-protest/index.html.

183 "got a shotgun": Ed Pilkington, "Cliven Bundy Saga Forces Republicans into Awkward U-Turn from Far Right," *The Guardian,* April 25, 2014.

183 "really suspicious": Arit John and Abby Ohlheiser, "A List of Cliven Bundy's Supporters, Now That We Know He's a Pro-Slavery Racist," *The Atlantic,* April 24, 2014. https://www.theatlantic.com/politics/archive/2014/04/a-list-of -cliven-bundys-supporters-now-that-we-know-hes-a-pro-slavery-racist/361154/.

184 "media people": Dana Milbank, "Andrew Breitbart and the Rifts on the Right," *The Washington Post,* April 21, 2011.

185 "stage for violence": Teddy Davis and Steven Portnoy, "Rush Limbaugh, Bill Clinton Square Off: Who's Encouraging Domestic Terror," ABC News, April 16, 2010. https://abcnews.go.com/Politics/rush-limbaugh-bill-clinton -set-stage-violence/story?id=10396718.

185 "hummus": Dana Milbank, "Bill O'Reilly's Threats," *The Washington Post,* November 10, 2010.

185 Obama to Hitler: Jim Edwards, "Beck Compares Obama to the Nazis; Ad Boycott List Reaches 46; Viewers at 3M," CBS News, August 28, 2009. https:// www.cbsnews.com/news/beck-compares-obama-to-the-nazis-ad-boycott-list -reaches-46-viewers-at-3m/.

185 "national security force": Glenn Beck and Shepard Smith, "New Republic: America's Future Series; Beck Discusses Radical Political Groups Associated with Obama White House, with Massive Federal Funding, and Says They Have Control of the Government, Democratic Party," Fox News, August 27, 2009.

185 "coup going on": Dana Milbank, "Beck's Rhetoric of Violence," *The Phila-delphia Inquirer,* August 3, 2010.

185 armor-piercing bullets: Conor Friedersdorf, "Fox's Rambling Man," *The Atlantic,* February 3, 2011. https://www.theatlantic.com/daily-dish/archive/ 2011/02/foxs-rambling-man/176285/.

186 concentration camps: Dana Milbank, "Glenn Beck's Gun-Toting Followers," *The Washington Post,* August 1, 2010.

186 "domestic extremist killers": Mark Potok, "The Year in Hate and Extrem-ism," Southern Poverty Law Center, February 17, 2016. https://www.splcenter .org/fighting-hate/intelligence-report/2016/year-hate-and-extremism.

CHAPTER 12: WACKO BIRDS AND RINOS

187 weekend of hunting: Eva Ruth Moravec, Sari Horwitz, and Jerry Markon, "The Death of Antonin Scalia: Chaos, Confusion and Conflicting Reports," *The Washington Post,* February 14, 2016.

187 "brilliant": Kyle Balluck, "Sanders: Scalia a 'Brilliant, Colorful,' Member of the Court," *The Hill,* February 13, 2016. https://thehill.com/blogs/ballot-box/ presidential-races/269387-sanders-scalia-a-brilliant-colorful-and-outspoken -member.

187 "dedicated public servant": CBS News, "Swift Social Media Reaction to Jus-tice Scalia's Death," February 13, 2016. https://www.cbsnews.com/news/swift -social-media-reaction-to-justice-scalias-death/.

188 "joy for life": "The Death of Justice Scalia: Reactions and Analysis," *The New York Times,* February 13, 2016.

188 "voice in the selection": Burgess Everett and Glenn Thrush, "McConnell Throws Down the Gauntlet: No Scalia Replacement Under Obama," *Politico,* February 13, 2016. https://www.politico.com/story/2016/02/mitch-mcconnell -antonin-scalia-supreme-court-nomination-219248.

188 "any prognostication": Dana Milbank, "The Ugly Political Spectacle Around Justice Scalia's Death," *The Washington Post,* February 15, 2016.

188 longest vacancy: Ron Fournier, "Behind the Supreme Court Stalemate," *The*

Atlantic, February 16, 2016. https://www.theatlantic.com/politics/archive/2016/02/the-supreme-court-stalemate/463026/.

189 "sight unseen": Dana Milbank, "Republicans' Supreme Court Contortions," *The Washington Post,* February 17, 2016.

189 "be a test": Barack Obama, "Remarks by President Obama at U.S.-ASEAN Summit Press Conference," U.S. Embassy and Consulates in Indonesia, February 17, 2016. https://id.usembassy.gov/remarks-by-president-obama-at-u-s-asean-summit-press-conference/.

189 one hundred days: NCC Staff, "On This Day: Senate Rejects Robert Bork for the Supreme Court," *Constitution Daily,* October 23, 2021. https://constitutioncenter.org/blog/on-this-day-senate-rejects-robert-bork-for-the-supreme-court/.

190 "insurgent outlier": Thomas E. Mann and Norman J. Ornstein, *It's Even Worse Than It Looks* (Basic Books, 2012).

190 "critical occasions": Mann and Ornstein, *It's Even Worse Than It Looks.*

191 average confirmation: Partnership for Public Service, "Why Reducing the Number of Senate-Confirmed Positions Can Make Government More Effective," Center for Presidential Transition, August 9, 2021. https://presidentialtransition.org/publications/unconfirmed-reducing-number-senate-confirmed-positions/.

191 trust by Americans: "Public Trust in Government: 1958–2021," Pew Research Center, May 17, 2021. https://www.pewresearch.org/politics/2021/05/17/public-trust-in-government-1958-2021/.

191 hostage takers: Carl Hulse and David M. Herszenhorn, "Trying to Avoid Economic Calamity, Lawmakers Grope for Resolution," *The New York Times,* September 30, 2008.

191 "break their arms": Patrick O'Connor and John Bresnahan, "Boehner's Gamble: Could It Cost Him His Job?" *Politico,* September 30, 2008. https://www.politico.com/story/2008/09/boehners-gamble-could-it-cost-him-his-job-014107.

192 "Sean Hannity": John Boehner, *On the House: A Washington Memoir* (St. Martin's Press, 2021).

192 "leverage moment": Lori Montgomery et al., "Origins of the Debt Showdown," *The Washington Post,* n.d. https://www.washingtonpost.com/business/economy/origins-of-the-debt-showdown/2011/08/03/gIQA9uqIzI_story.html.

193 "as adults": Naftali Bendavid, "Boehner Warns GOP on Debt Ceiling," *The Wall Street Journal,* November 18, 2010. https://www.wsj.com/articles/BL-WB-26171.

193 "only plan": Dana Milbank, "Dangerous Dealings with the Default Caucus," *The Washington Post,* July 22, 2011.

193 "grand bargain": Dana Milbank, "John Boehner's Bind," *The Washington Post,* July 11, 2011.

194 "shortage of cash": Dana Milbank, "Default Deniers Say It's All a Hoax," *The Washington Post,* May 18, 2011.

194 spending cuts: NPR staff and wire services, "Obama Signs Bill to Raise Debt Ceiling," NPR, August 2, 2011. https://www.npr.org/2011/08/02/138916516/senate-takes-up-debt-limit-bill-passage-likely.

194 "chance at shooting": David A. Farenthold, Lori Montgomery, and Paul Kane, "In Debt Deal, the Triumph of the Old Washington," *The Washington Post,* August 3, 2011.

194 rescind labor protections: Dana Milbank, "The FAA Shutdown and the New Rules of Washington," *The Washington Post,* August 4, 2011.

195   Superstorm Sandy: Dana Milbank, "Defined by a Sandy Sidestep," *The Washington Post,* January 2, 2013.

195   "penny of Obamacare": Dana Milbank, "Itching for a Shutdown," *The Washington Post,* July 31, 2013.

196   "able to stand": Dana Milbank, "Ted Cruz Is Filibusted," *The Washington Post,* September 24, 2013.

196   "killed Ted Cruz": Catherine Treyz, "Lindsey Graham Jokes About How to Get Away with Murdering Ted Cruz," CNN, February 26, 2016. https://www.cnn.com/2016/02/26/politics/lindsey-graham-ted-cruz-dinner/index.html.

196   "wacko birds": Kevin Cirilli, "McCain Apologizes for 'Wacko Birds,'" *Politico,* March 16, 2013. https://www.politico.com/story/2013/03/john-mccain-apologizes-for-wacko-birds-088942.

196   "fight is over": Boehner, *On the House.*

196   "reckless asshole": Boehner, *On the House.*

196   "govern by stunt": Boehner, *On the House.*

197   kissing a staffer: Paige Lavender, "Married GOP Rep. Caught Kissing Staffer in Surveillance Video," *HuffPost,* April 7, 2014. https://www.huffpost.com/entry/vance-mcallister-affair_n_5106908.

197   expansion of Medicare: Dana Milbank, "The New Party of Reagan," *The Washington Post,* July 19, 2011.

197   "very difficult": Bill Hemmer, "Interview with Mike Huckabee," Fox News, May 6, 2011.

197   "moderate former liberal": Dana Milbank, "The New Party of Reagan," *The Washington Post,* July 19, 2011.

197   the *Post*'s Paul Kane: Paul Kane, "Bob Dole Got a Front-Row Seat—and a Big Snub—as the GOP Moved on from His View of American Leadership," *The Washington Post,* December 11, 2021.

197   independent expenditures: "Total Outside Spending by Election Cycle, Excluding Party Committees," Open Secrets, n.d. https://www.opensecrets.org/outsidespending/cycle_tots.php.

198   cookie-cutter legislation: Trini Parti, "'Dark Money': ALEC Wants Image Makeover," Politico, July 30, 2015.

198   "leadership to the right": Erik Wasson and Russell Berman, "GOP Rep. Scalise Elected RSC Chairman, Pledges to Pull Leadership 'to the Right,'" *The Hill,* November 15, 2012. https://thehill.com/policy/finance/268261-scalise-will-head-republican-study-committee.

198   Freedom Caucus: Timothy B. Lee, "The House Freedom Caucus, Explained," *Vox,* October 9, 2015. https://www.vox.com/2015/10/9/9488835/house-freedom-caucus-explained.

198   Dick Lugar: Dana Milbank, "Richard Mourdock's Ads of Mass Destruction," *The Washington Post,* May 4, 2012.

199   "Incrementalism": Boehner, *On the House.*

199   "take him on": Alec MacGillis, *The Cynic: The Political Education of Mitch McConnell* (Simon & Schuster, 2014).

199   "one-term president": Dana Milbank, "Mitch McConnell, the Man Who Broke America," *The Washington Post,* April 7, 2017.

199   "obstruct more": Carl Hulse, "Despite Flurry of Achievement, No Reveling for Democrats," *The New York Times,* August 15, 2010.

199   "proud guardian": Sean Sullivan and Marc Fisher, "A Leader Skilled at Blocking Looks to Build," *The Washington Post,* July 1, 2017.

200   "shamelessness": Barack Obama, *A Promised Land* (Crown, 2020).

201   party unity votes: "Standing Together Against Any Action," *Congressional*

Quarterly Almanac, n.d. https://library.cqpress.com/cqalmanac/file.php
?path=Party%20Unity%20Tables/2014_Party_Unity.pdf.

202 final two years: "Judicial Nomination Statistics and Analysis: U.S. Circuit and
District Courts, 1977–2020," Congressional Research Service, May 18, 2021.
https://sgp.fas.org/crs/misc/R45622.pdf.

202 nuclear option: Jane C. Timm, "McConnell Went 'Nuclear' to Confirm Gorsuch, but Democrats Changed Senate Filibuster Rules First," NBC News,
June 28, 2018. https://www.nbcnews.com/politics/donald-trump/mcconnell
-went-nuclear-confirm-gorsuch-democrats-changed-senate-filibuster-rules
-n887271.

202 "Supreme Court vacancy": Ron Elving, "What Happened with Merrick Garland in 2016 and Why It Matters Now," NPR, June 29, 2018. https://www
.npr.org/2018/06/29/624467256/what-happened-with-merrick-garland-in-2016
-and-why-it-matters-now.

202 "we'd fill it": Amber Phillips, "'Oh, We'd Fill It': How McConnell Is Doing a
180 on Supreme Court Vacancies in an Election Year," *The Washington Post,*
May 29, 2019.

203 "greatest deliberative body": Paul Kane, "On the Death of the Senate and Its
Long History as the World's Greatest Deliberative Body," *The Washington
Post,* January 31, 2017.

CHAPTER 13: TRUTH ISN'T TRUTH

204 "This is one of those days": Glenn Kessler, "Fact-Checking the Craziest News
Conference of the Trump Presidency," *The Washington Post,* November 19,
2020.

205 "Make America Rake Again": Nick Corasaniti, tweet, November 9, 2020.
https://twitter.com/nytnickc/status/1325795553146441736?lang=en.

205 *Time*'s Person of the Year: Eric Pooley, "Mayor of the World: Person of the
Year 2001," *Time,* December 31, 2001. http://content.time.com/time/specials/
packages/article/0,28804,2020227_2020306,00.html.

206 "unfit for office": Mark Leibovich, "How Lindsey Graham Went from Trump
Skeptic to Trump Sidekick," *The New York Times,* February 25, 2019.

206 "no collusion": Dana Milbank, "Trump Is a Knight Errant Just Looking for
His Windmill," *The Washington Post,* April 7, 2019.

206 FBI had spied on Trump: Karoun Demirjian, Greg Miller, and Philip Rucker,
"Nunes Admits Meeting with Source of Trump Surveillance Documents on
White House Grounds," *The Washington Post,* March 27, 2017.

206 based its Russia probe on information: Charlie Savage, "How a Trump Decision Revealed a G.O.P. Memo's Shaky Foundation," *The New York Times,*
July 22, 2018.

206 "shithole countries": Ali Vitali, Kasie Hunt, and Frank V. Thorp, "Trump
Referred to Haiti and African Nations as 'Shithole' Countries," NBC News,
January 11, 2018. https://www.nbcnews.com/politics/white-house/trump
-referred-haiti-african-countries-shithole-nations-n836946.

206 "excellent health": Dan Merica, "Dr. Ronny Jackson's Glowing Bill of Health
for Trump," CNN, January 16, 2018. https://www.cnn.com/2018/01/16/
politics/dr-ronny-jackson-donald-trump-clean-bill-of-health/index.html.

207 "there was in fact no collusion": Alan Neuhauser, "Barr Says Mueller Report
Found 'No Collusion,'" *U.S. News & World Report,* April 18, 2019. https://
www.usnews.com/news/national-news/articles/2019-04-18/attorney-general
-barr-says-mueller-report-found-no-collusion.

207   "public confusion": Joshua Barajas, "Read Mueller's Letter to William Barr About Russia Report: 'There Is Now Public Confusion,'" *PBS NewsHour,* May 1, 2019. https://www.pbs.org/newshour/politics/read-muellers-letter-to -william-barr-about-russia-report-there-is-now-public-confusion.

208   "democracy can't work": Katelyn Polantz, Veronica Rocha, Meg Wagner, and Brian Ries, "Paul Manafort Sentenced," CNN, March 13, 2019. https://www.cnn.com/politics/live-news/paul-manafort-sentencing-dc/h _c3686eb818d9f27b5c4471a94d057884.

208   "policy of separating families at the border": "DHS Sec. Kirstjen Nielsen Denies Family Separation Policy Exists, Blames Media," CBS News, June 18, 2018. https://www.cbsnews.com/news/dhs-sec-kirstjen-nielsen-denies-family -separation-policy-exists-blames-media/.

208   "scrambling to reverse-engineer policies": Philip Rucker and Ashley Parker, "'In the Service of Whim': Officials Scramble to Make Trump's False Assertions Real," *The Washington Post,* October 23, 2018.

208   "unknown Middle Easterners": Linda Qiu, "Trump's Evidence-Free Claims About the Migrant Caravan," *The New York Times,* October 22, 2018. https:// www.nytimes.com/2018/10/22/us/politics/migrant-caravan-fact-check.html.

208   White House officials doctored a video: Christopher Brito, "White House Accused of Sharing 'Doctored' Video of CNN Reporter, Intern Exchange," CBS News, November 8, 2018. https://www.cbsnews.com/news/jim-acosta -sarah-sanders-cnn-reporter-white-house-intern-video-doctored/.

209   "I'm going to punt on that": Jonathan Topaz, "Walker 'Punts' on Evolution Question," *Politico,* February 11, 2015. https://www.politico.com/story/2015/ 02/scott-walker-avoids-evolution-question-115117.

209   "based more on exaggerations, personal agendas": "Lamar Smith Says He Won't Be Seeking Reelection," Associated Press, November 2, 2017. https:// apnews.com/article/e5e2431549984746939bbd39f46a7845.

209   "take your guns": Celine Castrunuovo, "Cawthorn: Biden Door-to-Door Vaccine Strategy Could Be Used to 'Take' Guns, Bibles," *The Hill,* July 9, 2021. https://thehill.com/homenews/house/562372-cawthorn-biden-door-to-door -vaccine-strategy-could-be-used-to-take-guns-bibles.

209   "KGB-style": Jason Smith, Twitter, July 17, 2021. https://twitter.com/jason smithmo/status/1416559177737064451.

209   impose mask mandates: Shawna Chen and Oriana Gonzalez, "DeSantis Issues Order Barring Florida Schools from Mandating Masks," *Axios,* July 30, 2021. https://www.axios.com/covid-masks-florida-schools-desantis-1ed7d9c7-817a -47a9-8b62-06f2f056030d.html.

209   "tyrannical": Leah Willingham, "Mississippi Governor Calls Biden Vaccine Mandate 'Tyranny,'" Associated Press, September 10, 2021. https://apnews .com/article/joe-biden-health-coronavirus-pandemic-mississippi-tate-reeves -546dfb92122b16daa903622c59e92032.

209   osteopath Sherri Tenpenny: Andrea Salcedo, "A Doctor Falsely Told Lawmakers Vaccines Magnetize People: 'They Can Put a Key on Their Forehead. It Sticks,'" *The Washington Post,* June 9, 2021.

210   Tucker Carlson: Charlotte Alter, "Talking with Tucker Carlson, the Most Powerful Conservative in America," *Time,* July 15, 2021. https://time.com/ 6080432/tucker-carlson-profile/.

210   "force people to take medicine": Tiffany Hsu, "Despite Outbreaks Among Unvaccinated, Fox News Hosts Smear Shots," *The New York Times,* July 11, 2021.

210   Pew Research Center: Alec Tyson et al., "Majority in U.S. Says Public Health Benefits of COVID-19 Restrictions Worth the Costs, Even as Large Shares Also See Downsides," Pew Research Center, September 15, 2021. https://www .pewresearch.org/science/2021/09/15/majority-in-u-s-says-public-health -benefits-of-covid-19-restrictions-worth-the-costs-even-as-large-shares-also -see-downsides/.

210   Fox News viewers: Harry Enten, "How Fox News Viewers Are Less Likely to Get Vaccinated," CNN, July 26, 2021. https://www.cnn.com/2021/07/25/ politics/fox-news-viewers-analysis/index.html.

211   September 2021 analysis: David Leonhardt, "U.S. Covid Deaths Get Even Redder," *The New York Times,* November 8, 2021.

211   "don't trust": Caitlin Owens, "Prominent Republicans Find New Enthusiasm for COVID-19 Vaccines," *Axios,* July 22, 2021. https://www.axios.com/ republicans-coronavirus-vaccines-resistance-trump-a02544f7-c3ee-443a -a2f7-ab9c83e86c98.html.

211   "Three Million Votes": Dana Milbank, "Trump's 'News' Source: Alien Lizards, Fluoride Mind Control and Voter Fraud," *The Washington Post,* November 28, 2016.

212   "Gitmo prisoners": Jenna Johnson, "Trump's Split Screen: A Two-Hour Virtual Conversation Between the President and 'Fox & Friends,'" *The Washington Post,* March 7, 2017.

212   "silence conservative voices": Ashley Hoffman, "Donald Trump Said He Doesn't Watch Cable News. His Tweets Show He Does," *Time,* December 11, 2017.

212   school shooting survivor: John Kruzel, "School Shooting Survivor Claims CNN Asked Him to Read 'Scripted' Question," PolitiFact, February 23, 2018. https://www.politifact.com/article/2018/feb/23/school-shooting-survivor -claims-cnn-asked-him-read/.

213   Trump appeared: Dana Milbank, "Sean Hannity, Trump's Spin 'Doctor,'" *The Washington Post,* August 22, 2016.

213   private jet: Dana Bash and Dylan Byers, "Sources: Sean Hannity Flew Gingrich to Trump Meeting," CNN, July 13, 2016. https://www.cnn.com/2016/ 07/13/politics/newt-gingrich-sean-hannity-fox-news-donald-trump/index .html.

213   "destroying everything": Dartunnoro Clark, "Fox News Hosts, Donald Trump Jr. Asked Meadows to Get Trump to Call Off Rioters, House Panel Reveals," NBC News, December 13, 2021. https://www.nbcnews.com/politics/ congress/fox-news-hosts-texted-meadows-jan-6-saying-trump-needed -n1285921.

213   "hurting all of us": Clark, "Fox News Hosts, Donald Trump Jr. Asked Meadows to Get Trump to Call Off Rioters, House Panel Reveals."

213   "people to leave": Nicholas Wu and Kyle Cheney, "'He's Got to Condemn This . . . ,": "Panel Releases Urgent Jan. 6 Texts from Donald Trump Jr., Lawmakers and Fox Hosts," *Politico,* December 13, 2021. https://www.politico .com/news/2021/12/13/hes-got-to-condemn-this-shit-panel-releases-urgent -jan-6-texts-from-trump-jr-lawmakers-524188.

213   "mostly peaceful": Adam Serwer, "Fox Hosts Knew—and Lied Anyway," *The Atlantic,* December 16, 2021. https://www.theatlantic.com/ideas/archive/ 2021/12/mark-meadows-january-6-texts-fox-news-anchors/621032/.

214   simply declared: Dana Milbank, "In Trump's Mind, It's Always 'Really Sunny,' and That's Terrifying," *The Washington Post,* January 27, 2017.

214   "This was the largest audience": Glenn Kessler, "Spicer Earns Four Pinoc-

chios for False Claims on Inauguration Crowd Size," *The Washington Post,* January 22, 2017.

214 "truth isn't truth": Rebecca Morin and David Cohen, "Giuliani: 'Truth Isn't Truth,'" *Politico,* August 19, 2018. https://www.politico.com/story/2018/08/ 19/giuliani-truth-todd-trump-788161.

214 "their impression": Christal Hayes and Courtney Subramanian, "GOP Dismisses First Impeachment Hearing as Boring: 'Everybody Has Their Impression of What Truth Is,'" *USA Today,* November 13, 2019. https://www .usatoday.com/story/news/politics/2019/11/13/trump-impeachment-hearing -meadows-gop-dismiss-boring-testimony/4180459002/.

215 "really sunny": Donald Trump, "Remarks by President Trump and Vice President Pence at CIA Headquarters," The White House, January 21, 2017. https:// trumpwhitehouse.archives.gov/briefings-statements/remarks-president-trump -vice-president-pence-cia-headquarters/.

215 Trump famously redrew a government weather map: Matthew Cappucci and Andrew Freedman, "President Trump Showed a Doctored Hurricane Chart. Was It to Cover Up for 'Alabama' Twitter Flub?," *The Washington Post,* September 5, 2019.

215 "Lying is second nature to him": Jane Mayer, "Donald Trump's Ghostwriter Tells All," *The New Yorker,* July 18, 2016. https://www.newyorker.com/ magazine/2016/07/25/donald-trumps-ghostwriter-tells-all.

216 "My net worth fluctuates": Dana Milbank, "Trump's Not a Liar. He's a Madman," *The Washington Post,* May 29, 2018.

216 "paranoid style": Dana Milbank, "The Great American Crackup Is Underway," *The Washington Post,* July 17, 2020.

217 Democrats were in cahoots: Dana Milbank, "Trump's 'News' Source: Alien Lizards, Fluoride Mind Control and Voter Fraud," *The Washington Post,* November 28, 2016.

217 deep state: Dana Milbank, "A Dispatch from Deep State Command," *The Washington Post,* October 6, 2017.

217 "conduct a campaign": Transcript, "Fiona Hill and David Holmes Testimony in Front of the House Intelligence Committee," *The Washington Post,* November 26, 2019.

218 "to Moscow for July 4th": Dana Milbank, "Opinion: Eight Republicans Pick the Worst Possible Place to Celebrate July 4," *The Washington Post,* July 6, 2018.

218 Quinnipiac University: Philip Bump, "Three-Quarters of Republicans Trust Trump over the Media," *The Washington Post,* July 25, 2018.

218 social media's susceptibility: Craig Silverman, "This Analysis Shows How Viral Fake Election News Stories Outperformed Real News on Facebook," *BuzzFeed News,* November 16, 2016. https://www.buzzfeednews.com/article/ craigsilverman/viral-fake-election-news-outperformed-real-news-on-facebook.

219 "work with my brother man": Dana Milbank, "Donald Trump Is the Monster the GOP Created," *The Washington Post,* July 8, 2015.

220 "the comic book version of a presidential campaign": Elliot Smilowitz, "CNBC Anchor Asks if Trump Is Running 'Comic Book Version' of a Campaign," *The Hill,* October 28, 2015. https://thehill.com/blogs/ballot-box/gop -primaries/258482-cnbc-anchor-trump-running-comic-book-version-of-a -campaign.

220 *Post*'s "Fact Checker": Michelle Ye Hee Lee, Glenn Kessler, and Leslie Shapiro, "100 Days of Trump Claims," *The Washington Post,* February 21, 2017.

220 "I have a gut": Philip Rucker, Josh Dawsey, and Damian Paletta, "Trump

Slams Fed Chair, Questions Climate Change and Threatens to Cancel Putin Meeting in Wide-Ranging Interview with the Post," *The Washington Post,* November 27, 2018.

221 "healthiest individual ever elected": Dana Milbank, "This Is What Happens When a Stable Genius Leads a Stupid Country," *The Washington Post,* November 19, 2018.

221 "conceal the truth": Anne Gearan and Carol Morello, "Rex Tillerson Says 'Alternative Realities' Are a Threat to Democracy," *The Washington Post,* May 16, 2018.

221 Russell Vought walked into the White House briefing room: Dana Milbank, "Meet the Trump Saboteur in Charge of Undermining Biden—and America," *The Washington Post,* December 31, 2020.

222 "coronavirus will magically, all of a sudden, go away": Tara Law, "Eric Trump Claims Social Distancing Is a Democrat 'Strategy' and COVID-19 Will 'Magically' Disappear After Election," *Time,* May 18, 2020. https://time .com/5838104/eric-trump-coronavirus-disappear/.

222 Reuters-Ipsos: Dana Milbank, "Mr. President, Lock Us Up!," *The Washington Post,* March 10, 2020.

222 *Wall Street Journal*/NBC poll: Mark Murray, "Sixty Percent Believe Worst Is Yet to Come for the U.S. in Coronavirus Pandemic," NBC News, March 15, 2020. https://www.nbcnews.com/politics/meet-the-press/sixty-percent-believe -worst-yet-come-u-s-coronavirus-pandemic-n1159106.

222 "powerful people": Amy Mitchell, Mark Jurkowitz, J. Baxter Oliphant, and Elisa Shearer, "Most Americans Have Heard of the Conspiracy Theory That the COVID-19 Outbreak Was Planned, and About One-Third of Those Aware of It Say It Might Be True," Pew Research Center, June 29, 2020. https://www .pewresearch.org/journalism/2020/06/29/most-americans-have-heard-of-the -conspiracy-theory-that-the-covid-19-outbreak-was-planned-and-about-one -third-of-those-aware-of-it-say-it-might-be-true/?utm_content=buffer1fe05 &utm_medium=social&utm_source=twitter.com&utm_campaign=buffer.

222 virus had been exaggerated: "The Economist/YouGov Poll," March 8–10, 2020. https://docs.cdn.yougov.com/vrbl9mmctz/econTabReport.pdf.

222 "biggest game changers": Colin Dwyer and Joe Neel, "FDA Warns Against Wide Use of the Drugs Trump Hailed as 'Game Changers,'" NPR, April 24, 2020. https://www.npr.org/sections/coronavirus-live-updates/2020/04/24/ 844212806/fda-warns-against-wide-use-of-the-drugs-trump-hailed-as-game -changers.

223 best prepared: Dana Milbank, "Other Countries Are Winning Against the Virus. We Are Quitting," *The Washington Post,* May 8, 2020.

224 "Don't be afraid of Covid": "The Latest: Trump Video Tells Supporters, 'Don't Be Afraid,'" Associated Press, October 5, 2020. https://apnews .com/article/virus-outbreak-donald-trump-health-archive-af2bcc4b75f0a9a0 8355e4e47af77b3d.

224 Among the QAnon beliefs: Kevin Roose, "What Is QAnon, the Viral Pro-Trump Conspiracy Theory," *The New York Times,* September 3, 2021.

224 prophetic insight into the inner workings of the U.S. government: Dana Milbank, "Thanks to the Trump Administration, One QAnon Theory Is Panning Out," *The Washington Post,* September 15, 2020.

224 Whizzinator: Will Sommer, "Man Known as BabyQ Is in Trouble for Using Synthetic Penis," *Daily Beast,* September 11, 2020. https://www.thedailybeast .com/right-richter-austin-steinbart-man-known-as-babyq-is-in-trouble-for -using-synthetic-penis.

225   "they like me very much": Zeke Miller, Jill Colvin, and Amanda Seitz, "Trump Praises QAnon Conspiracists, Appreciates Support," Associated Press, August 19, 2020.

225   May 2021 poll by the Public Religion Research Institute: "Understanding QAnon's Connection to American Politics, Religion, and Media Consumption," Public Religion Research Institute, May 27, 2021. https://www.prri.org/research/qanon-conspiracy-american-politics-report/.

225   "stormtroopers": Caroline Kenny, "Giuliani Defends 'Stormtroopers' Comments About FBI," CNN, May 18, 2018. https://www.cnn.com/2018/05/18/politics/rudy-giuliani-stormtroopers-cnntv/index.html.

226   punctuation error in a tweet: Ben Collins, "Rudy Giuliani Falsely Blames Twitter After Typo Points to Anti-Trump Website," NBC News, December 5, 2018. https://www.nbcnews.com/tech/tech-news/rudy-giuliani-falsely-blames-twitter-after-typo-points-anti-trump-n944136.

226   engaging in screaming matches with TV host: Dana Milbank, "Trump and His Lawyer Can Do Better on Ukraine. I'm Here for Them," The Washington Post, September 20, 2019.

226   Giuliani went to Ukraine: Karen Freifeld, "Giuliani Says Trump Did Not Pay for His Globetrotting Push for Biden Probe," Reuters, September 29, 2019.

226   at least eighty-six judges: Rosalind S. Helderman and Elise Viebeck, "'The Last Wall': How Dozens of Judges Across the Political Spectrum Rejected Trump's Efforts to Overturn the Election," The Washington Post, December 12, 2020.

227   claimed that Pennsylvania: Jude Joffe-Block, "Pennsylvania Did Not Have Hundreds of Thousands of Phantom Absentee Ballots," Associated Press, November 30, 2020.

227   "You couldn't possibly believe": Glenn Kessler, "Fact-Checking the Craziest News Conference of the Trump Presidency," The Washington Post, November 19, 2020.

227   charges against Dominion: Alan Feuer, "Trump Campaign Knew Lawyers' Voting Machine Claims Were Baseless, Memo Shows," The New York Times, September 21, 2021.

228   "there is uncontroverted evidence": Jim Mustian, "New York Court Suspends Rudy Giuliani's Law License," Associated Press, June 24, 2021.

228   seized Giuliani's mobile phones and computers: William K. Rashbaum et al., "F.B.I. Searches Giuliani's Home and Office, Seizing Phones and Computers," The New York Times, April 28, 2021.

228   survey by Yahoo! News: Caitlin Dickson, "Poll: Two-Thirds of Republicans Still Think the 2020 Election Was Rigged," Yahoo! News, August 4, 2021. https://news.yahoo.com/poll-two-thirds-of-republicans-still-think-the-2020-election-was-rigged-165934695.html.

CHAPTER 14: VERY FINE PEOPLE

229   hundreds of neo-Confederates: Joe Heim, "Recounting a Day of Rage, Hate, Violence and Death," The Washington Post, August 14, 2017.

229   "Blood and Soil": Meg Wagner, "'Blood and Soil': Protesters Chant Nazi Slogan in Charlottesville," CNN, August 12, 2017. https://www.cnn.com/2017/08/12/us/charlottesville-unite-the-right-rally/index.html.

230   life in prison: Paul Duggan, "James A. Fields Jr. Sentenced to Life in Prison in Charlottesville Car Attack," The Washington Post, December 11, 2018.

230   "You had a group on one side that was bad": Michael D. Shear and Mag-

gie Haberman, "Trump Defends Initial Remarks on Charlottesville; Again Blames 'Both Sides,'" *The New York Times,* August 15, 2017.

230   "Thank you President Trump": Natasha Bertrand, "David Duke Thanks Trump for 'Condemning the Leftist Terrorists' in Charlottesville," *Business Insider,* August 15, 2017. https://www.businessinsider.com/david-duke -thanks-trump-for-condemning-the-leftist-terrorists-in-charlottesville-2017-8.

230   many of Trump's usual enablers: Dana Milbank, "When Trump Needs a Friend, That's What 'Fox & Friends' Is For," *The Washington Post,* August 16, 2017.

231   "darn near perfection": Felicia Sonmez and Ashley Parker, "As Trump Stands by Charlottesville Remarks, Rise of White-Nationalist Violence Becomes an Issue in 2020 Presidential Race," *The Washington Post,* April 28, 2019.

231   private message: Cameron Joseph, "Trump-Endorsed Candidate JD Vance Once Said Trump Might Be 'America's Hitler,'" *Vice,* April 18, 2022.

232   racist fears of immigrants: Greg Sargent, "As Vile as It Gets: J.D. Vance Goes Full 'Great Replacement Theory,'" *The Washington Post,* April 6, 2022.

232   "affective polarization": Nicholas Valentino and Kirill Zhirkov, "The Images in Our Heads: Race, Partisanship and Affective Polarization," University of Michigan, 2018. https://lsa.umich.edu/polisci/news-events/all-news/awards/ valentino-and-zhirkov-win-best-paper.html.

232   presidential preferences: Sean McElwee and Jason McDaniel, "Fear of Diversity Made People More Likely to Vote Trump," *The Nation,* March 14, 2017. https://www.thenation.com/article/archive/fear-of-diversity-made-people -more-likely-to-vote-trump/.

233   white Republicans: Dana Milbank, "A Massive Repudiation of Trump's Racist Politics Is Building," *The Washington Post,* July 3, 2020.

233   White evangelicals: Elana Schor and David Crary, "Evangelicals Stick with Trump, See Upside Even If He Loses," Associated Press, November 7, 2020. https://apnews.com/article/election-2020-joe-biden-donald-trump-race-and -ethnicity-elections-7433585aae55ea0cadd9ea5f0eb00a62.

233   "morally lost": Jeremy W. Peters and Elisabeth Dias, "Evangelicals Closing Ranks with President," *The New York Times,* December 21, 2019.

233   American Values Survey: "Amid Multiple Crises, Trump and Biden Supporters See Different Realities and Futures for the Nation," Public Religion Research Institute, October 19, 2020. https://www.prri.org/research/amid-multiple -crises-trump-and-biden-supporters-see-different-realities-and-futures-for -the-nation/.

234   perceived threat to male identity: Dan Cassino, "Gender Is Costing Hillary Clinton Big Among Men," Fairleigh Dickinson University, 2016. https://blogs .lse.ac.uk/usappblog/2016/03/24/gender-is-costing-hillary-clinton-big-among -men/.

234   "Let's not mince words": Dana Milbank, "Donald Trump Is a Bigot and a Racist," *The Washington Post,* December 1, 2015.

235   "global power structure": Bess Levin, "Trump Goes Full Anti-Semite, Unloads on American Jews in Wildly Bigoted Rant," *Vantiy Fair,* December 17, 2021. https://www.vanityfair.com/news/2021/12/donald-trump-anti-semitism-jews -israel.

235   impartially judge: Nina Totenberg, "Who Is Judge Gonzalo Curiel, the Man Trump Attacked for His Mexican Ancestry?," NPR, June 7, 2016. https:// www.npr.org/2016/06/07/481140881/who-is-judge-gonzalo-curiel-the-man -trump-attacked-for-his-mexican-ancestry.

235   Trump told Jewish Republicans: Isaac Stanley-Becker, "Trump and the GOP

Are Accused of Anti-Semitism Double Standard After Piling on Rep. Ilhan Omar," *The Washington Post,* February 12, 2019.

236   "cities could be washed away": Dana Milbank, "Donald Trump's New Loose Cannon," *The Washington Post,* August 24, 2016.

236   Hungarian nationalist organization: Alexander Smith and Vladimir Banic, "Sebastian Gorka Made Nazi-Linked Vitezi Rend 'Proud' by Wearing Its Medal," NBC News, April 8, 2017. https://www.nbcnews.com/news/world/sebastian-gorka-made-nazi-linked-vitezi-rend-proud-wearing-its-n742851.

236   doubling of anti-Semitic incidents: "Anti-Semitic Incidents Remained at Near-Historic Levels in 2018; Assaults Against Jews More Than Doubled," Anti-Defamation League, April 30, 2019. https://www.adl.org/news/press-releases/anti-semitic-incidents-remained-at-near-historic-levels-in-2018-assaults.

236   relations between white and Black people: Megan Brenan, "Ratings of Black-White Relations at New Low," Gallup, July 21, 2021. https://news.gallup.com/poll/352457/ratings-black-white-relations-new-low.aspx.

236   "the wife is to voluntarily submit": Aaron Blake, "GOP Congressman's Book: 'The Wife Is to Voluntarily Submit' to Her Husband," *The Washington Post,* January 22, 2014.

237   "Western civilization": Robin Opsahl, "Steve King Says All Cultures Do Not Contribute Equally, to Claim Otherwise Is to Devalue the 'Founding Fathers,'" *Des Moines Register,* May 28, 2019.

237   "doing great work in the House": Kevin Quealy, "The People, Places and Things Trump Has Praised on Twitter: A Complete List," *The New York Times,* February 14, 2018.

237   "language become offensive?": Sarah Muller, "Steve King Defends Past Comments Saying 'Western Civilization Is Under Assault,'" KCCI Des Moines, October 1, 2020. https://www.kcci.com/article/steve-king-defends-past-comments-saying-western-civilization-is-under-assault/34241837#.

237   "not academically competitive": Sue Anne Pressley, "Texas Students, Faculty Protest Racial Remarks," *The Washington Post,* September 17, 1997.

238   "president loves America": Darren Samuelsohn, "Giuliani: Obama Doesn't Love America," *Politico,* February 18, 2015. https://www.politico.com/story/2015/02/rudy-giuliani-president-obama-doesnt-love-america-115309.

238   "apologist for radical Islamic terrorists": Nick Gass, "Cruz: Obama 'an Apologist for Radical Islamic Terrorists,'" *Politico,* February 19, 2015. https://www.politico.com/story/2015/02/ted-cruz-obama-radical-islamic-terrorists-115312.

238   "Watch this vulgar man": Dinesh D'Souza, tweet, February 18, 2015. https://twitter.com/dineshdsouza/status/568074632844017664?lang=en.

238   Frank Gaffney: Peter Beinart, "The Denationalization of American Muslims," *The Atlantic,* March 19, 2017. https://www.theatlantic.com/politics/archive/2017/03/frank-gaffney-donald-trump-and-the-denationalization-of-american-muslims/519954/.

238   "smell the falafel": Ruby Mellen, "Mike Huckabee on Letting in Refugees: 'It's Time to Wake Up and Smell the Falafel,'" *HuffPost,* November 16, 2015. https://www.huffpost.com/entry/mike-huckabee-refugees-falafel_n_564a41b5e4b06037734a5470.

239   "rabid dogs": Alana Wise and Erin McPike, "Republican Ben Carson Compares Syrian Refugees to 'Rabid Dogs,'" Reuters, November 19, 2015. https://www.reuters.com/article/us-usa-election-carson/republican-ben-carson-compares-syrian-refugees-to-rabid-dogs-idUSKCN0T82TJ20151119.

239   "anchor baby": Carrie Dann, "Jeb Bush: 'Anchor Babies' Are 'Frankly,

More Asian People,'" NBC News, August 24, 2015. https://www.nbcnews
.com/politics/2016-election/jeb-bush-chill-out-criticism-anchor-baby-term
-n415051.

239   "New York values": Daniel White, "Ted Cruz Dissed 'New York Values' and
New Yorkers Are Not Happy," *Time,* January 15, 2016. https://time.com/
4182887/ted-cruz-new-york-values-donald-trump-republican-debate/.

239   "racism until Obama got elected": Tom Silverstone et al., "No Racism Until
Obama, Says an Ohio Trump Campaign Chair—Video," *The Guardian,* September 22, 2016.

239   "hate White people": Peter Holley, "Congressman: Charlotte Protesters 'Hate
White People Because White People Are Successful,'" *The Washington Post,*
September 23, 2016.

239   "working nights and weekends": Joseph Dussault, "NH State Rep: Women
Deserve Less Pay Than Men," Boston.com, April 24, 2014. https://www
.boston.com/news/local-news/2014/04/24/nh-state-rep-women-deserve-less
-pay-than-men/.

239   "a net positive for everybody": Brianna Ehley, "RNC Chair Priebus: Trump a
'Net Positive' for GOP," *Politico,* August 24, 2015. https://www.politico.com/
story/2015/08/reince-priebus-donald-trump-net-positive-121669.

239   "ranks pretty low": Sarah Pulliam Bailey, "'Still the Best Candidate': Some
Evangelicals Still Back Trump Despite Lewd Video," *The Washington Post,*
October 8, 2016.

240   "Nevertheless, she persisted": Daniel Victor, "'Nevertheless, She Persisted':
How Senate's Silencing of Warren Became a Meme," *The New York Times,*
February 8, 2017.

240   "groped by Abraham Lincoln": Lindsey McPherson, "GOP Congressman
Jokes Ruth Bader Ginsburg Groped by Abraham Lincoln," *Roll Call,* September 20, 2018. https://www.rollcall.com/2018/09/20/gop-congressman-jokes
-ruth-bader-ginsburg-groped-by-abraham-lincoln/.

240   "Chinaperson": Maegan Vazquez, "GOP Senate Candidate Says 'Wealthy
Chinaperson' Comment Isn't Racist," CNN, May 2, 2018. https://www.cnn
.com/2018/05/02/politics/don-blankenship-defense-west-virginia-debate/
index.html.

241   "BUY this election!": Felicia Sonmez, "Kevin McCarthy on Deleted Tweet
About Bloomberg, Steyer and Soros: 'That Had Nothing to Do About Faith,'"
The Washington Post, February 13, 2019.

241   "advantageous to Republicans": Mike Schneider, "Watchdog: Wilbur Ross
Misled on Reason for 2020 Census Citizenship Question," *USA Today,* July 19,
2021. https://www.usatoday.com/story/news/politics/2021/07/19/wilbur-ross
-misled-congress-census-citizenship-question-watchdog/8017463002/.

241   "terrorist agent": Jenna Johnson and Abigail Hauslohner, "'I Think Islam
Hates Us': A Timeline of Trump's Comments About Islam and Muslims," *The
Washington Post,* May 20, 2017.

241   "renegade Jew": Emily Schultheis and Julia Boccagno, "Quotes from Steve
Bannon, Trump's New White House Chief Strategist," CBS News, November 16, 2016. https://www.cbsnews.com/news/quotes-from-steve-bannon-trumps
-new-white-house-chief-strategist/.

241   "inside job": Dana Milbank, "199 House Republicans Have Embraced Anti-
Semitism and Violence," *The Washington Post,* February 5, 2021.

242   "all about the Benjamins": Mike DeBonis and Rachael Bade, "Rep. Omar
Apologizes After House Democratic Leadership Condemns Her Comments
as 'Anti-Semitic Tropes,'" *The Washington Post,* February 11, 2019.

242   "overwhelmingly Hispanic": Daniel Chang, Ben Conarck, and Steve Contorno, "Ron DeSantis Blames Florida Farmworkers for COVID. Aid Groups Say Testing Help Came Late," *Tampa Bay Times*, June 19, 2020. https://www.tampabay .com/news/health/2020/06/19/ron-desantis-blames-florida-farmworkers -for-covid-aid-groups-say-testing-help-came-late/.

242   "staged event": Patrick Svitek, "Five Texas GOP County Leaders Share Racist Facebook Posts, Including One Juxtaposing an MLK Quote with a Banana," *The Texas Tribune*, June 4, 2020.

242   dinner waiting for him: Eli Rosenberg, "GOP Candidate Says Feminists Have 'Snake-Filled Heads,' Hopes Daughters Don't Become 'She Devils,'" *The Washington Post*, January 26, 2018.

242   "responded the worst off to those drugs": "Anti-Pot Kansas Lawmaker Says Black People 'Responded Worst' to Drugs," NBC News, January 8, 2018. https://www.nbcnews.com/news/us-news/anti-pot-kansas-lawmaker-says -black-people-responded-worst-drugs-n835886.

242   Trump appointee to AmeriCorps: Eli Rosenberg, "'I Just Don't Like Muslim People': Trump Appointee Resigns After Racist, Sexist and Anti-Gay Remarks," *The Washington Post*, January 18, 2018.

242   "laziness" and "promiscuity": Eli Rosenberg, "Homeland Security Official Resigns After Comments Linking Blacks to 'Laziness' and 'Promiscuity' Come to Light," *The Washington Post*, November 17, 2017.

242   "war on whites": Chris Massie, "Rep. Brooks: Dems' 'War on Whites' Behind Some Criticism of Sessions," CNN, January 12, 2017. https://www.cnn.com/ 2017/01/11/politics/kfile-mo-brooks-war-on-whites/index.html.

243   "kind of vagrant": Ben Szobody, "Duncan's 'Vagrant or Animal' Comment Draws Fire," *Greenville News*, November 2, 2011.

243   "out of your cotton-picking mind": Christal Hayes, "Ex-Trump Campaign Staffer Tells Black Democrat 'You're Out of Your Cotton-Picking Mind' on Fox News," *USA Today*, June 24, 2018.

243   "diversity is a bunch of crap": Sophie Tatum, "GOP Congressional Candidate: Diversity Is 'a Bunch of Crap and Un-American,'" CNN, June 12, 2018. https://www.cnn.com/2018/06/11/politics/republican-new-jersey-diversity/ index.html.

243   "inherently racist": Megan Twohey, "Rudolph Giuliani Lashes Out at Black Lives Matter," *The New York Times*, July 10, 2016.

243   "BLM and antifa sprang into action": "Giuliani Rails Against Black Lives Matter, Antifa and De Blasio in RNC Speech," *Axios*, August 28, 2020. https://www.axios.com/rudy-giuliani-rnc-speech-151780bd-6c7d-4947-892a -4b08ecf68778.html.

244   "blood coming out of her eyes": Philip Rucker, "Trump Says Fox's Megyn Kelly Had 'Blood Coming Out of Her Wherever,'" *The Washington Post*, August 8, 2015.

244   "To the African American community": Tom LoBianco and Ashley Killough, "Trump Pitches Black Voters: 'What the Hell Do You Have to Lose?,'" CNN, August 19, 2016. https://www.cnn.com/2016/08/19/politics/donald-trump -african-american-voters/index.html.

245   NFL team owners: Bryan Armen Graham, "Donald Trump Blasts NFL Anthem Protesters: 'Get That Son of a Bitch off the Field,'" *The Guardian*, September 23, 2017.

245   "rat and rodent infested mess": Colby Itkowitz, "Trump Attacks Rep. Cummings's District, Calling It a 'Disgusting, Rat and Rodent Infested Mess,'" *The Washington Post*, July 27, 2019.

245   "horrible shape": Kate Brumback and Russ Bynum, "'Falling Apart?' Trump's Insults Not Forgotten in Atlanta," Associated Press, January 7, 2018. https://apnews.com/article/donald-trump-us-news-ap-top-news-football-college-football-d0465a956d384da69ef11b84d6f97b58.

245   "president is onto something": Dana Milbank, "Republican Lawmakers Are Behaving Worse Than Trump," *The Washington Post,* July 19, 2019.

245   "They're bringing drugs": Amber Phillips, "'They're Rapists.' President Trump's Campaign Launch Speech Two Years Later, Annotated," *The Washington Post,* June 16, 2017.

246   "stone-cold criminals": Bart Jansen and Alan Gomez, "President Trump Calls Caravan Immigrants 'Stone Cold Criminals.' Here's What We Know," *USA Today,* November 26, 2018. https://www.usatoday.com/story/news/2018/11/26/president-trump-migrant-caravan-criminals/2112846002/.

246   "let him stay": Glenn Kessler, "Trump's Four-Pinocchio Claim: 'Democrats Let Him into Our Country,'" *The Washington Post,* November 4, 2018.

246   "a real catastrophe like Katrina": Kaitlan Collins, "Trump Contrasts Puerto Rico Death Toll to 'a Real Catastrophe Like Katrina,'" CNN, October 3, 2017.   https://www.cnn.com/2017/10/03/politics/trump-puerto-rico-katrina-deaths/index.html.

246   "done for them": Lisa Marie Segarra, "Donald Trump: Puerto Rico Wants 'Everything to Be Done for Them,'" *Time,* September 30, 2017. https://time.com/4963903/donald-trump-puerto-rican-leaders-want-everything-to-be-done-for-them/.

246   "they knew exactly what was going on": David Smith, "Trump Fans Flames of Chinese Lab Coronavirus Theory During Daily Briefing," *The Guardian,* April 15, 2020.

246   "efforts and transparency": "Trump: U.S. Appreciates China's 'Efforts and Transparency' On Coronavirus," Reuters, January 24, 2020. https://www.reuters.com/article/us-china-health-usa-trump/trump-u-s-appreciates-chinas-efforts-and-transparency-on-coronavirus-idUSKBN1ZN2IK.

246   "very good job": Myah Ward, "15 Times Trump Praised China as Coronavirus Was Spreading Across the Globe," *Politico,* April 15, 2020. https://www.politico.com/news/2020/04/15/trump-china-coronavirus-188736.

246   "Are you from South Korea?": Asma Khalid, "South Korea? Trump's 'Where Are You From' Moment," NPR, October 15, 2015. https://www.npr.org/sections/itsallpolitics/2015/10/15/448718726/south-korea-trumps-where-are-you-from-moment.

247   "campaign TRAIL": John Bowden, "Trump Makes Native American Joke About Warren Campaign Announcement: 'See You On The Campaign TRAIL,'" The Hill, February 9, 2019. https://thehill.com/homenews/campaign/429289-trump-mocks-warren-campaign-announcement-with-native-american-joke-see-you.

247   "total and complete shutdown": Jenna Johnson, "Trump Calls for 'Total and Complete' Shutdown of Muslims Entering the United States," *The Washington Post,* December 7, 2015.

247   "do it legally": Amy B. Wang, "Trump Asked for a 'Muslim Ban,' Giuliani Says—And Ordered a Commission to Do It 'Legally,'" *The Washington Post,* January 29, 2017.

247   "hate our country": Adam Edelman and Dareh Gregorian, "Trump Steps Up Attacks on Progressive Congresswomen, Says They 'Hate Our Country' and Israel," NBC News, July 15, 2019. https://www.nbcnews.com/politics/

donald-trump/trump-demands-radical-left-congresswomen-apologize-him-u
-s-israel-n1029831.

247   "meets in secret with international banks": Jane C. Timm, "Fact Checking
Donald Trump's Defiant Speech," NBC News, October 13, 2016. https://www
.nbcnews.com/politics/2016-election/fact-checking-donald-trump-s-defiant
-speech-n665951.

248   "have a message": Philip Bump, "A Brief History of Donald Trump Addressing Questions About Racism and Anti-Semitism," The Washington Post, February 21, 2017.

248   "lack of knowledge": Felicia Sonmez and John Wagner, "Trump Says Any
Jewish People Who Vote for Democrats Are Showing 'Great Disloyalty' or
'Lack of Knowledge,'" The Washington Post, August 21, 2019.

248   "we did this": Adam Cancryn, "David Duke: Trump Win a Great Victory for
'Our People,'" Politico, November 9, 2016. https://www.politico.com/story/
2016/11/david-duke-trump-victory-2016-election-231072.

248   "psychic connection": Joseph Goldstein, "Alt-Right Gathering Exults in
Trump Election with Nazi-Era Salute," The New York Times, November 20,
2016.

248   "a head without a body": Katie Glueck, "Alt-Right Celebrates Trump's Election at D.C. Meeting," Politico, November 19, 2016. https://www.politico
.com/story/2016/11/alt-right-washington-dc-meeting-231671.

248   "acting like it": Lisa Mascaro, "White Nationalists Dress Up and Come to
Washington in Hopes of Influencing Trump," Los Angeles Times, November 19, 2016.

248   "White supremacist extremist": Dana Milbank, "Donald Trump, Steve King—
and Some Very Happy White Nationalists," The Washington Post, March 15,
2017.

249   "breeding is a form of government employment": Andrew Kaczynski, "Trump
Appointee Carl Higbie Resigns as Public Face of Agency That Runs Ameri-
Corps After Kfile Review of Racist, Sexist, Anti-Muslim and Anti-LGBT
Comments on the Radio," CNN, January 19, 2018. https://www.cnn.com/
2018/01/18/politics/kfile-carl-higbie-on-the-radio/index.html.

249   "culture of our great country": Meghan Keneally, "Trump Says US Culture Being 'Ripped Apart' by Confederate Memorial Removals," ABC
News, August 17, 2017. https://abcnews.go.com/Politics/trump-calls-removal
-confederate-memorials-sad/story?id=49271200.

249   2018 GOP Senate: Jane Coaston, "How White Supremacist Candidates
Fared in 2018," Vox, November 7, 2018. https://www.vox.com/policy-and
-politics/2018/11/7/18064670/white-supremacist-candidates-2018-midterm
-elections.

250   "littered with the n-word": Jane Coaston, "Self-Described Nazis and White
Supremacists Are Running as Republicans Across the Country. The GOP Is
Terrified," Vox, July 9, 2018. https://www.vox.com/2018/7/9/17525860/nazis
-russell-walker-arthur-jones-republicans-illinois-north-carolina-virginia.

250   America First Caucus: David Morgan, "Conservative U.S. House Republicans
to Form 'America First' Caucus," Reuters, April 16, 2021. https://www.reuters
.com/world/us/us-house-republican-effort-form-america-first-caucus-raises
-hackles-over-race-2021-04-16/.

250   three-fifths compromise: Rick Rojas, "Tennessee Lawmaker Is Criticized
for Remarks on Three-Fifths Compromise," The New York Times, May 4,
2021.

250   "authorized by Gosar for Congress Committee": Erin Doherty, "GOP Rep. Paul Gosar Appears to Defend Fundraiser with White Nationalist," *Axios,* June 29, 2021. https://www.axios.com/gosar-fuentes-white-nationalist-fund raiser-5802b42f-8960-480d-8040-b50f7f6ecb63.html.

251   "rotten to its core": Dana Milbank, "Why Does Biden Hate the Flag, Family, Grace, God and America," *The Washington Post,* June 22, 2021.

CHAPTER 15: SABOTAGE

252   "good to Ukraine": Transcript, "Read Trump's Phone Conversation with Volodymyr Zelensky," CNN, September 26, 2019. https://www.cnn.com/ 2019/09/25/politics/donald-trump-ukraine-transcript-call/index.html.

253   anticorruption ambassador: Sharon LaFraniere, Nicholas Fandos, and Andrew E. Kramer, "Ukraine Envoy Says She Was Told Trump Wanted Her Out over Lack of Trust," *The New York Times,* October 11, 2019.

253   "drug deal": Peter Baker and Nicholas Fandos, "Bolton Objected to Ukraine Pressure Campaign, Calling Giuliani 'a Hand Grenade,'" *The New York Times,* October 14, 2019.

253   "talk to Rudy": Josh Dawsey, "'Talk to Rudy': Testimony from Diplomats Highlights Giuliani's Central Role in Driving Ukraine Policy," *The Washington Post,* November 6, 2019.

254   "whatever I want": Michael Brice-Saddler, "While Bemoaning Mueller Probe, Trump Falsely Says the Constitution Gives Him 'the Right to Do Whatever I Want,'" *The Washington Post,* July 23, 2019.

254   "Truth matters little": Dareh Gregorian, "Schiff's Powerful Closing Speech: 'Is There One Among You Who Will Say, Enough!,'" NBC News, February 3, 2020. https://www.nbcnews.com/politics/trump-impeachment-inquiry/ closing-argument-democrats-say-not-removing-trump-would-render-him -n1128766.

254   "exercise impartial justice": Libby Cathey, "Invoking His Faith, an Emotional Mitt Romney Explains Vote to Convict Trump," ABC News, February 5, 2020. https://abcnews.go.com/Politics/invoking-faith-emotional-mitt -romney-announces-hell-vote/story?id=68779768.

255   "system fail": Transcript, "Marie Yovanovitch's Nov. 15 Testimony in Front of the House Intelligence Committee," *The Washington Post,* November 19, 2019.

256   "ability and virtue": "The Federalist Papers: No. 68," Yale Law School Lillian Goldman Law Library, n.d. https://avalon.law.yale.edu/18th_century/fed68 .asp.

256   "despotic government": "Spirit of the Laws," Teaching American History, n.d. https://teachingamericanhistory.org/document/spirit-of-the-laws/.

257   relocate criminals: Dana Milbank, "On Impeachment, the Worm Has Turned," *The Washington Post,* September 24, 2019.

257   "obsolete": David M. Herszenhorn and Lili Bayer, "Trump's Whiplash NATO Summit," *Politico Europe,* July 12, 2018. https://www.politico.eu/article/ trump-threatens-to-pull-out-of-nato/.

257   visit to Copenhagen: Rick Noack, John Wagner, and Felicia Sonmez, "Trump Attacks Danish Prime Minister for Her 'Nasty' Comments About His Interest in U.S. Purchase of Greenland," *The Washington Post,* August 21, 2019.

257   "large scale killing": Kimon de Greef and Palko Karasz, "Trump Cites False Claims of Widespread Attacks on White Farmers in South Africa," *The New York Times,* August 23, 2018.

257   immigrant violence: Eric Bradner, "Trump's Sweden Comment Raises Ques-

tions," CNN, February 20, 2017. https://www.cnn.com/2017/02/19/politics/trump-rally-sweden/index.html.

257   "accomplished more": Matthew Choi, "Trump Bragged About His Presidency and World Leaders Laughed," *Politico*, September 25, 2018.

258   criticize the deal: Peter Baker, "In Congress, Netanyahu Faults 'Bad Deal' on Iran Nuclear Program," *The New York Times*, March 3, 2015.

258   "extremely busy": Rachel Withers, "Trump Skipped Arlington Cemetery on Veterans Day Because He Was 'Extremely Busy,'" *Vox*, November 17, 2018.

258   "loser": Scott Neuman, "Trump Lashes Out at McCain: 'I Like People Who Weren't Captured,'" NPR, July 18, 2015. https://www.npr.org/sections/the-two-way/2015/07/18/424169549/trump-lashes-out-at-mccain-i-like-people-who-werent-captured.

258   "more about ISIS": Haley Britzky, "Everything Trump Says He Knows 'More About than Anybody,'" *Axios,* January 5, 2019. https://www.axios.com/everything-trump-says-he-knows-more-about-than-anybody-b278b592-cff0-47dc-a75f-5767f42bcf1e.html.

258   "any reason": Rebecca Morin, "Trump: 'I Don't See Any Reason Why' Russia Would Have Interfered with Election," *Politico,* July 16, 2018. https://www.politico.com/story/2018/07/16/trump-putin-meeting-election-meddling-722424.

258   "good order and discipline": Helene Cooper, Maggie Haberman, and Thomas Gibbons-Neff, "Trump Says He Intervened in War Crimes Cases to Protect 'Warriors,'" *The New York Times*, November 25, 2019.

258   "so-called judge": Eric Bradner and Jeff Zeleny, "Trump: 'If Something Happens Blame' the Judge," CNN, February 5, 2017. https://www.cnn.com/2017/02/05/politics/trump-twitter-attacks-judge/index.html.

258   "a disgrace": "In His Own Words: The President's Attacks on the Courts," Brennan Center for Justice, February 14, 2020. https://www.brennancenter.org/our-work/research-reports/his-own-words-presidents-attacks-courts.

258   pardoned Joe Arpaio: Kevin Liptak, Daniella Diaz, and Sophie Tatum, "Trump Pardons Former Sheriff Joe Arpaio," CNN, August 27, 2017. https://www.cnn.com/2017/08/25/politics/sheriff-joe-arpaio-donald-trump-pardon/index.html.

259   James Comey: Michael D. Shear and Matt Apuzzo, "FBI Director James Comey Is Fired by Trump," *The New York Times,* May 9, 2017.

259   "dishonest": Krishnadev Calamur, "Trump Calls Trudeau 'Two-Faced' After Video Shows Leaders Apparently Mocking Him," NPR, December 4, 2019. https://www.npr.org/2019/12/04/784549243/trump-calls-trudeau-two-faced.

259   "witch hunt": Larry Buchanan and Karen Yourish, "Trump Has Publicly Attacked the Russia Investigation More Than 1,100 Times," *The New York Times,* February 19, 2019.

259   "total coordination": Savannah Behrmann, "McConnell: In 'Total Coordination' with White House for Impeachment Trial," *USA Today*, December 12, 2019.

260   fast-tracked trademarks: Tommy Beer, "Ivanka's Trademark Requests Were Fast-Tracked in China After Trump Was Elected," *Forbes*, September 22, 2020. https://www.forbes.com/sites/tommybeer/2020/09/22/ivankas-trademark-requests-were-fast-tracked-in-china-after-trump-was-elected/?sh=717d65261d60.

260   family businesses: Jesse Drucker, Kate Kelly, and Ben Protess, "Kushner's Family Business Received Loans After White House Meetings," *The New York Times,* February 28, 2018.

260   billionaire's yacht: Alan Feuer, William K. Rashbaum, and Maggie Haberman, "Steve Bannon Is Charged with Fraud in We Build the Wall Campaign," *The New York Times,* August 20, 2020.

260   phone booth: Dennis Brady and Juliet Eilperin, "Scott Pruitt's $43,000 Soundproof Phone Booth Violated Spending Laws, Federal Watchdog Finds," *The Washington Post,* April 16, 2018.

260   private flights: "Ryan Zinke: US Interior Secretary 'Spent $12,000 on Flight,'" BBC, September 29, 2017. https://www.bbc.com/news/world-us-canada-414 46590.

260   "within the scope": Matt Zapotsky, Devlin Barrett, and Shayna Jacobs, "Judge Rejects Justice Dept. Bid to Short-Circuit Defamation Case Brought by Woman Who Accused Trump of Rape," *The Washington Post,* October 27, 2020.

260   "pardon them": Diane Rehm, "Ongoing Questions About How Donald Trump Will Deal with Business Conflicts of Interest as President," NPR, December 19, 2016.

261   Hatch Act: "OSC Finds Kellyanne Conway Repeatedly Violated the Hatch Act, Recommends Removal from Federal Service," U.S. Office of Special Counsel, June 13, 2019. https://osc.gov/News/Pages/19-10-Kellyanne-Conway-Hatch -Act.aspx.

261   bankruptcy protection: Danny Hakim, "NRA Declares Bankruptcy and Seeks to Exit New York," *The New York Times,* January 15, 2021.

261   Jerry Falwell Jr.: Sarah Pulliam Bailey, Susa Svrluga, and Michelle Boorstein, "Jerry Falwell Jr. Resigns as Head of Liberty University, Will Get $10.5 Million in Compensation," *The Washington Post,* August 25, 2020.

261   Chris Collins: Kevin Breuninger, Dan Mangan, and Tucker Higgins, "Ex–New York Congressman Chris Collins Sentenced to 26 Months for Insider-Trading Tip to Son," CNBC, January 17, 2020. https://www.cnbc.com/2020/ 01/17/chris-collins-sentenced-to-26-months-for-insider-trading-tip.html.

261   dumped stock: Robert Faturechi and Derek Willis, "Senator Dumped Up to $1.7 Million of Stock After Reassuring Public About Coronavirus Preparedness," ProPublica, March 19, 2020. https://www.propublica.org/article/senator -dumped-up-to-1-7-million-of-stock-after-reassuring-public-about-coronavirus -preparedness.

261   sexual harassment lawsuit: Jessica Taylor, "Under Fire for Alleged Sexual Harassment, Texas Rep. Blake Farenthold Resigns," NPR, April 6, 2018. https://www.npr.org/2018/04/06/600343808/under-fire-for-alleged-sexual -harassment-texas-rep-blake-farenthold-resigns.

262   "soul mate": Elana Schor, "Meehan Called Harassment Accuser His 'Soul Mate,'" *Politico,* January 23, 2018. https://www.politico.com/story/2018/01/ 23/gop-congressman-meehan-harassment-soulmate-362461.

262   seek an abortion: Emily Cochrane, "Conservative Pennsylvania Congressman Resigns Amid Abortion Scandal," *The New York Times,* October 5, 2017.

262   as a surrogate: Katie Rogers, "Trent Franks, Accused of Offering $5 Million to Aide for Surrogacy, Resigns," *The New York Times,* December 8, 2017.

262   sexual misconduct: Corky Siemaszko, "Powerful GOP Rep. Jim Jordan Accused of Turning Blind Eye to Sexual Abuse as Ohio State Wrestling Coach," NBC News, July 3, 2018. https://www.nbcnews.com/news/us-news/ powerful-gop-rep-jim-jordan-accused-turning-blind-eye-sexual-n888386.

262   "Completely unrelated": Natasha Bertrand and Theodoric Meyer, "Ex-McConnell Staffers Lobbied on Russian-Backed Kentucky Project," *Polit-*

ico, August 1, 2019. https://www.politico.com/story/2019/07/31/mcconnell
-staffers-lobbied-russian-backed-kentucky-project-1442550.

262　already departed: "The Nominees Donald Trump Tapped for Key Roles During His Term," *The Washington Post,* January 15, 2021.

263　golf caddie: Chris Moody and Alexander Rosen, "How a Golf Caddie Became
Trump's Campaign Confidant," CNN, July 5, 2016. https://www.cnn.com/
2016/04/29/politics/donald-trump-tweets-daniel-scavino/index.html.

263　"less dysfunctional": Kylie MacLellan, "Trump Administration 'Uniquely
Dysfunctional,' Says UK Ambassador to US: Newspaper," Reuters, July 7,
2019. https://www.reuters.com/article/us-usa-britain/trump-administration
-uniquely-dysfunctional-says-uk-ambassador-to-u-s-newspaper-idUSKCN1
U2081.

263　ten days later: Andrew Prokop, "Anthony Scaramucci Is Out Just 10 Days After
Being Named White House Communications Director," *Vox,* July 31, 2017.
https://www.vox.com/2017/7/31/16071196/anthony-scaramucci-communications
-director-fired-trump.

263　paranoid schizophrenic: Ryan Lizza, "Anthony Scaramucci Called Me to
Unload About White House Leakers, Reince Priebus and Steve Bannon," *The
New Yorker,* July 27, 2017. https://www.newyorker.com/news/ryan-lizza/
anthony-scaramucci-called-me-to-unload-about-white-house-leakers-reince
-priebus-and-steve-bannon.

264　a "moron": Jacqueline Klimas, "Tillerson Won't Deny Calling Trump 'a
Moron,' but Does Deny Being Undercut," *Politico,* October 15, 2017. https://
www.politico.com/story/2017/10/15/tillerson-trump-moron-castration-243785.

264　"multiply it": Chris Whipple, *The Gatekeepers: How the White House Chiefs
of Staff Define Every Presidency* (Crown, 2017).

264　"professional liar": Bob Woodward, *Fear: Trump in the White House* (Simon
& Schuster, 2018).

264　*Citizens United* decision: Tim Lau, "Citizens United Explained," Brennan
Center for Justice, December 12, 2019. https://www.brennancenter.org/our
-work/research-reports/citizens-united-explained.

264　convicted Giuliani associates: Kristine Phillips, "Former Giuliani Associate
Igor Fruman Pleads Guilty in Campaign Finance Case," *USA Today,* September 10, 2021. https://www.usatoday.com/story/news/politics/2021/09/10/igor
-fruman-former-rudy-giuliani-associate-pleads-guilty/5570899001/.

264　new voting restrictions: "New Voting Restrictions in America," Brennan Center for Justice, October 1, 2019. https://www.brennancenter.org/our-work/
research-reports/new-voting-restrictions-america.

265　868 polling places: "Democracy Diverted: Polling Place Closures and the
Right to Vote," Leadership Conference on Civil and Human Rights, n.d.
https://civilrights.org/democracy-diverted/.

265　millions of would-be voters: Zoltan L. Hajnal, *Dangerously Divided: How
Race and Class Shape Winning and Losing in American Politics* (Cambridge
University Press, 2020).

265　surrendered campaign finance: Aaron Blake, "Supreme Court Strikes Down
Overall Campaign Contribution Limits," *The Washington Post,* April 2, 2014.

265　super PACs: Matea Gold and Anu Narayanswamy, "2016 Fundraising Shows
Power Tilting to Groups Backed by Wealthy Elite," *The Washington Post,*
July 15, 2015.

266　"decay rapidly": Steve Benen, "Supreme Court Hears Gerrymandering Case
That May Change Our Politics," MSNBC, October 4, 2017. https://www

.msnbc.com/rachel-maddow-show/supreme-court-hears-gerrymandering
-case-may-change-our-politics-msna1026151.

266   large contributors: "Donor Demographics," Open Secrets, n.d. https://www
.opensecrets.org/elections-overview/donor-demographics?cycle=2018.

266   "may be forgiven": Matthew Rothschild, "Justice Stevens's Dissent in Citizens
United Lives On," Wisconsin Democracy Campaign, July 17, 2019. https://
www.wisdc.org/news/commentary/6381-justice-stevens-s-dissent-in-citizens
-united-lives-on.

266   "democratic legitimacy": Jacob Gershman, "Highlights from Justice Breyer's
McCutcheon Dissent," *The Wall Street Journal,* April 2, 2014.

267   "vacate the chair": Lauren French and Jake Sherman, "House Conservative
Seeks Boehner's Ouster," *Politico,* July 28, 2015. https://www.politico.com/
story/2015/07/house-conservative-john-boehner-ouster-120742.

267   "Zip-A-Dee-Doo-Dah": Video, "Boehner Sings 'Zip-A-Dee-Doo-Dah' Before
Exiting News Conference," *The Washington Post,* September 25, 2015.

268   "same boat": Transcript, "Paul Ryan Elected Speaker," *Politico,* October 29,
2015. https://www.politico.com/story/2015/10/paul-ryan-elected-speaker-tran
script-full-text-215351.

268   DACA: Vanessa Romo, Martina Stewart, and Brian Naylor, "Trump Ends
DACA, Calls on Congress to Act," NPR, September 5, 2017. https://www.npr
.org/2017/09/05/546423550/trump-signals-end-to-daca-calls-on-congress-to
-act.

268   shut down: Jonathan Allen, "Trump Is Relishing the Prospect of Owning
a Government Shutdown. But Republicans Aren't," NBC News, December 11, 2018. https://www.nbcnews.com/politics/politics-news/trump-relishing
-prospect-owning-government-shutdown-republicans-aren-t-n946761.

269   "I am alone": Niv Elis, "Trump: 'I Am All Alone' in the White House Waiting on Dems for Deal," *The Hill,* December 24, 2018. https://thehill.com/
homenews/administration/422759-trump-i-am-all-alone-in-the-white-house
-waiting-on-dems-for-deal.

269   government airplane: Catherine Lucey et al., "Trump Grounds Pelosi After
She Imperils His Big Speech," Associated Press, January 17, 2019. https://
apnews.com/article/north-america-donald-trump-nancy-pelosi-ap-top-news
-politics-fd13507e5acf4babb02320c9499d9412.

269   declared an "emergency": Mark Berman, Fred Barbash, and Maria Sacchetti,
"Trump's Emergency Declaration to Pay for Border Wall Faces a Lengthy
Court Battle," *The Washington Post,* February 19, 2019.

269   middle of the pandemic: Kyle Cheney, "Lindsey Graham Seeks Broad Authority to Subpoena Former Obama Officials," *Politico,* May 18, 2020. https://www
.politico.com/news/2020/05/18/lindsey-graham-obama-subpoena-trump
-266471.

270   "acting immediately": Burgess Everett and Heather Caygle, "McConnell Brushes Off Pelosi as She Finalizes Relief Package," *Politico,* May 11,
2020. https://www.politico.com/news/2020/05/11/senate-relief-coronavirus-2
49428.

270   strike a deal: Jeff Stein and Erica Werner, "McConnell Warns White House
Against Making Stimulus Deal as Pelosi and Mnuchin Inch Closer," *The
Washington Post,* October 20, 2020.

270   "election message": Burgess Everett, "McConnell, the Minority Leader with
'Veto' Power," *Politico,* May 26, 2021. https://www.politico.com/news/2021/
05/26/mitch-mcconnell-veto-power-490815.

270   Ukraine shakedown: Zachary B. Wolf and Sean O'Key, "The Trump-Ukraine

Impeachment Inquiry Report, Annotated," CNN, December 3, 2019. https://www.cnn.com/interactive/2019/12/politics/trump-ukraine-impeachment-inquiry-report-annotated/.

271 "spying did occur": Charlie Savage, Nicholas Fandos, and Katie Benner, "Attorney General William Barr Thinks 'Spying Did Occur' on Trump Campaign," *The New York Times,* April 10, 2019.

271 "inappropriate for the president": Lamar Alexander, tweet, January 30, 2020. https://twitter.com/senalexander/status/1223093589200293888.

271 "hard to believe": Dana Milbank, "Matt Gaetz Proves There Is No Bottom," *The Washington Post,* September 12, 2019.

272 "deliberate conversation": Luke Darby, "Fox News Impeachment Expert Ken Starr Says Trump Is in Deep Trouble," *GQ,* November 20, 2019. https://www.gq.com/story/starr-trump-impeachment-over.

272 "looking up": Caroline Kelly and Allie Malloy, "Trump Implies That the Late Rep. John Dingell Is 'Looking Up' from Hell," CNN, December 19, 2019. https://www.cnn.com/2019/12/18/politics/trump-rally-john-dingell-hell/index.html.

272 "almighty wrath": Dana Milbank, "Trump's Unglued Reaction to Impeachment Portends Peril," *The Washington Post,* December 20, 2019.

272 "corrupt people": Allan Smith, " 'Dishonest and Corrupt': Trump Unloads at National Prayer Breakfast After Acquittal," NBC News, February 6, 2020. https://www.nbcnews.com/politics/trump-impeachment-inquiry/trump-holds-newspaper-front-page-headline-acquitted-national-prayer-breakfast-n1131421.

272 "prays at all": Meg Wagner, Mike Hayes, and Veronica Rocha, "President Trump Speaks After Impeachment Acquittal," CNN, February 6, 2020. https://www.cnn.com/politics/live-news/trump-impeachment-acquitted-02-06-20/h_46d0e0be63b42513f58ac49122275082.

273 "all bullshit": Video, "Trump on Russian Investigation: 'It Was All Bullshit,' " *Politico,* February 6, 2020. https://www.politico.com/video/2020/02/06/trump-on-russian-investigation-it-was-all-bullshit-069591.

CHAPTER 16: TRIAL BY COMBAT

274 "sex slaves": Marc Fisher, John Woodrow Cox, and Peter Herman, "Pizzagate: From Rumor, to Hashtag, to Gunfire in D.C.," *The Washington Post,* December 6, 2016.

274 "MUST READ": Politico Staff, "Incoming National Security Adviser's Son Spreads Fake News About D.C. Pizza Shop," *Politico,* December 4, 2016. https://www.politico.com/story/2016/12/incoming-national-security-advisers-son-spreads-fake-news-about-dc-pizza-shop-232181.

275 Death threats: Cecilia Kang, "Fake News Onslaught Targets Pizzeria as Nest of Child-Trafficking," *The New York Times,* November 21, 2016.

275 "remain a story": Tal Kopan, "Son of Trump Security Adviser Spread Baseless 'Pizza Gate' Conspiracy," CNN, December 5, 2016. https://www.cnn.com/2016/12/05/politics/mike-flynn-jr-son-pizza-gate-conspiracy-theory-donald-trump/index.html.

276 white supremacists: Jessica Taylor, "Energized by Trump's Win, White Nationalists Gather to 'Change' the World," NPR, November 20, 2016. https://www.npr.org/2016/11/20/502719871/energized-by-trumps-win-white-nationalists-gather-to-change-the-world.

276 "lying press": Mahita Gajanan, "Holocaust Museum 'Deeply Alarmed' by Nazi Rhetoric at White Nationalist Conference," *Time,* November 21, 2016. https://time.com/4579373/holocaust-museum-white-nationalist-conference/.

276   Nazi salute: Joseph Goldstein, "Alt-Right Gathering Exults in Trump Election with Nazi-Era Salute," *The New York Times,* November 20, 2016.

277   "very unfavorable": "Partisanship and Political Animosity in 2016," Pew Research Center, June 22, 2016. https://www.pewresearch.org/politics/2016/06/22/1-feelings-about-partisans-and-the-parties/.

278   "disapproval of political opponents": Dana Milbank, "America's New Cycle of Partisan Hatred," *The Washington Post,* April 17, 2015.

278   punch a teachers union: Valerie Strauss, "Chris Christie Wants to Punch the Teachers Union in the Face, but He Isn't the Only Candidate Attacking Educators," *The Washington Post,* August 3, 2015.

278   "leading financier": Dana Milbank, "The GOP Field's Calculated Crazy Talk," *The Washington Post,* August 3, 2015.

279   "bad thing": Daniel White, "Trump Supporter: 'Riots Aren't Necessarily a Bad Thing,'" *Time,* March 16, 2016. https://time.com/4262131/trump-supporter-riots-arent-necessarily-a-bad-thing/.

279   "coming to you": Ben Jacobs, "Trump Campaign Dogged by Violent Incidents at Rallies," *The Guardian,* May 11, 2016.

279   violent incidents: Ben Mathis-Lilley, "A Continually Growing List of Violent Incidents at Trump Events," *Slate,* April 25, 2016. http://www.slate.com/blogs/the_slatest/2016/03/02/a_list_of_violent_incidents_at_donald_trump_rallies_and_events.html.

279   "tried for treason": Jonathan Easley, "Ted Nugent: Hang Obama and Clinton," *The Hill,* January 20, 2016. https://thehill.com/blogs/ballot-box/presidential-races/266444-ted-nugent-hang-obama-and-clinton.

279   "firing line": Kevin Liptak and Naomi Lim, "Secret Service Investigating Trump Adviser After Clinton Remark," CNN, July 20, 2016. https://www.cnn.com/2016/07/20/politics/tom-cotton-al-baldasaro-hillary-clinton-treason/index.html.

279   "be a bloodbath": Meghan Keneally, "Experts Warn Against 'Dangerous' Rhetoric Surrounding Election," ABC News, October 12, 2016. https://abcnews.go.com/Politics/experts-warn-dangerous-rhetoric-surrounding-election/story?id=42748882.

279   "I'm afraid": Jeremy Diamond, "Trump: I'm Afraid the Election's Going to Be Rigged," CNN, August 2, 2016. https://www.cnn.com/2016/08/01/politics/donald-trump-election-2016-rigged/index.html.

279   "right chord": Ward Baker, "Memo: Observations on Donald Trump and 2016," September 22, 2015. https://www.scribd.com/doc/291989296/NRSC-Trump-Memo.

280   "100 percent behind": "Face the Nation transcripts March 6, 2016: Trump, Cruz, Clinton, Priebus," CBS News, March 6, 2016. https://www.cbsnews.com/news/face-the-nation-transcripts-march-6-2016-trump-cruz-clinton-priebus/.

280   "times change": Transcript, "House Republicans Hold Media Availability Following Closed Caucus Meeting," CQ Transcriptions, February 26, 2019.

280   "people would revolt": Willa Frej, "Rudy Giuliani Says Americans Would Revolt If Trump Gets Impeached," *HuffPost,* August 24, 2018. https://www.huffpost.com/entry/giuliani-revolt-trump-impeached_n_5b7fd303e4b0cd327dfbb06a.

280   "not even people": Sophie Tatum, "Eric Trump: Democrats in Washington Are 'Not Even People,'" CNN, June 7, 2017. https://www.cnn.com/2017/06/07/politics/eric-trump-hannity-democrats-obstruction/index.html.

280   "deep state spear": Rebecca Savransky, "Gingrich: Mueller Tip of 'Deep State

Spear,'" *The Hill,* June 15, 2017. https://thehill.com/homenews/house/337912 -gingrich-mueller-tip-of-the-deep-state-spear.

280   "tidal wave": Transcript, "Wayne Lapierre, Executive Vice President, NRA, Delivers Remarks at the 2018 Conservative Political Action Conference," CQ Transcriptions, February 22, 2018.

281   "death of a political opponent": Felicia Sonmez, "McGrath Criticizes McConnell over Photo Depicting Her Name on a Gravestone," *The Washington Post,* August 5, 2019.

281   "I bring rage": Bob Woodward and Robert Costa, "Transcript: Donald Trump Interview with Bob Woodward and Robert Costa," *The Washington Post,* April 2, 2016.

281   pipe bombs: Susan Scutti, "Cesar Sayoc, Who Sent Pipe Bombs to Prominent Democrats, Sentenced to 20 Years," CNN, August 6, 2019. https://www.cnn .com/2019/08/05/us/cesar-sayoc-sentencing-monday/index.html.

281   playing baseball: Luke Mullins, "The Terrifying Story of the Congressional Baseball Shooting," *Washingtonian,* May 28, 2018. https://www.washingtonian .com/2018/05/28/terrifying-story-of-the-congressional-baseball-shooting-steve -scalise/.

281   Pittsburgh synagogue: Campbell Robertson, Christopher Mele, and Sabrina Tavernise, "11 Killed in Synagogue Massacre; Suspect Charged with 29 Counts," *The New York Times,* October 27, 2018.

281   "shooting starts": Grace Panetta, "Trump Claims His 'When the Looting Starts, the Shooting Starts' Remarks Weren't a Call to Violence but Instead a 'Fact,'" *Business Insider,* May 29, 2020. https://www.businessinsider.com/ trump-defends-his-when-the-looting-starts-the-shooting-starts-tweet-2020-5.

281   "good people": Kevin Liptak, "Trump Tweets Support for Michigan Protesters, Some of Whom Were Armed, as 2020 Stress Mounts," CNN, May 1, 2020. https://www.cnn.com/2020/05/01/politics/donald-trump-michigan-gretchen -whitmer-protests/index.html.

281   "LIBERATE MICHIGAN": "Trump Accelerates the Unrest," *Axios,* April 17, 2020. https://www.axios.com/trump-unrest-coronavirus-c3b720e9-fae8-48d 9-9de8-0ba8c61e5c61.html.

282   kidnap Michigan governor: Nicholas Bogel-Burroughs, Shaila Dewan, and Kathleen Gray, "F.B.I. Says Michigan Anti-Government Group Plotted to Kidnap Gov. Gretchen Whitmer," *The New York Times,* October 8, 2020.

282   deadliest year: Masood Farivar, "2019 'Deadliest' Year for Domestic Terrorism, Says FBI Director," Voice of America, February 5, 2020. https:// www.voanews.com/a/usa_2019-deadliest-year-domestic-terrorism-says-fbi -director/6183781.html.

282   2,700 investigations: Christopher Wray, "Threats to the Homeland: Evaluating the Landscape After 9/11," FBI, September 21, 2021. https://www.fbi.gov/ news/testimony/threats-to-the-homeland-evaluating-the-landscape-20-years -after-911-wray-092121.

282   high Twitter usage: Karsten Muller and Carlo Schwarz, "From Hashtag to Hate Crime: Twitter and Anti-Minority Sentiment," University of Warwick, October 31, 2019. https://warwick.ac.uk/fac/soc/economics/staff/crschwarz/ hashtag_to_hatecrime.pdf.

282   "too nice": Meghan Keneally, "Trump to Police: 'Please Don't Be Too Nice' to Suspects," ABC News, July 28, 2017. https://abcnews.go.com/Politics/trump -police-nice-suspects/story?id=48914504.

283   Twitter stream: Kevin Quealy, "The Complete List of Trump's Twitter Insults," *The New York Times,* January 19, 2021.

283   "very happy": Press Release, "Highest Percentage of Americans in Four Decades Say Financial Situation Has Gotten Worse," NORC at the University of Chicago, April 14, 2011. https://www.norc.org/NewsEventsPublications/PressReleases/Pages/highest-percentage-of-americans-in-4-decades-say-financial-situation-worse.aspx.

283   *well-being:* Dan Witters, "Americans' Well-Being Declines in 2017," Gallup, November 8, 2017. https://news.gallup.com/poll/221588/americans-declines-2017.aspx?version=print.

284   "Second Amendment people": Nick Corasaniti and Maggie Haberman, "Donald Trump Suggests 'Second Amendment People' Could Act Against Hillary Clinton," *The New York Times,* August 9, 2016.

284   shoot somebody: Jeremy Diamond, "Trump: I Could 'Shoot Somebody and I Wouldn't Lose Voters,'" CNN, January 24, 2016. https://www.cnn.com/2016/01/23/politics/donald-trump-shoot-somebody-support/index.html.

284   waterboarding: Jenna Johnson, "Trump Says 'Torture Works,' Backs Waterboarding and 'Much Worse,'" *The Washington Post,* February 17, 2016.

284   "fix it": "Full Text: Donald Trump 2016 DNC Draft Speech Transcript," *Politico,* August 21, 2016. https://www.politico.com/story/2016/07/full-transcript-donald-trump-nomination-acceptance-speech-at-rnc-225974.

284   hate-based intimidation: Hatewatch Staff, "Update: More Than 400 Incidents of Hateful Harassment and Intimidation Since the Election," Southern Poverty Law Center, November 15, 2016. https://www.splcenter.org/hatewatch/2016/11/15/update-more-400-incidents-hateful-harassment-and-intimidation-election.

284   "stop it": Video, *Trump Addresses Reports of Violence: "Stop It,"* CBS News, November 13, 2016. https://www.cbsnews.com/video/trump-addresses-reports-of-violence-stop-it/.

284   "I won": Monica Langley and Gerard Baker, "Donald Trump, in Exclusive Interview, Tells WSJ He Is Willing to Keep Parts of Obama Health Law," *The Wall Street Journal,* November 11, 2016.

285   "one day as a lion": Jenna Johnson, "Trump on Retweeting Questionable Quote: 'What Difference Does It Make Whether It's Mussolini?,'" *The Washington Post,* February 28, 2016.

285   "good quote": Donald Trump, *Meet the Press,* NBC News, February 28, 2016. https://www.youtube.com/watch?v=ixIWovwR4iQ.

285   "divisive phrases": Patrick Healy and Maggie Haberman, "95,000 Words, Many of Them Ominous, from Donald Trump's Tongue," *The New York Times,* December 5, 2015.

286   "great relationship": Julie Hirschfield Davis, "Trump Lauds 'Great Relationship' with Duterte in Manila," *The New York Times,* November 13, 2017.

286   "president for life": Kevin Liptak, "Trump on China's Xi Consolidating Power: 'Maybe We'll Give That a Shot Some Day,'" CNN, March 3, 2018. https://www.cnn.com/2018/03/03/politics/trump-maralago-remarks/index.html.

286   "deal with": Matthew Choi, "Trump: China Is Easier to Deal with than Pelosi and Schumer," *Politico,* January 10, 2019. https://www.politico.com/story/2019/01/10/trump-china-more-honorable-than-democrats-1096099.

286   "so innocent?": Brooke Seipel, "Trump Defends Putin: 'You Think Our Country Is So Innocent?,'" *The Hill,* February 4, 2017. https://thehill.com/blogs/ballot-box/317945-trump-defends-putin-you-think-our-country-is-so-innocent.

287   "killing terrorists": Beth Reinhard, "Donald Trump Says Deleting Allegedly Anti-Semitic Tweet Was Mistake; GOP Candidate Also Accuses Media of Distorting His Comments on Saddam Hussein," *The Wall Street Journal*, July 7, 2016.

287   "power of strength": Matthew Nussbaum, "Trump Defends Comments on Tiananmen Square, Putin," *Politico*, March 10, 2016. https://www.politico .com/blogs/2016-gop-primary-live-updates-and-results/2016/03/donald-trump -tianamen-square-putin-220610.

287   "enemy of the people": Philip Bump, "Three-Quarters of Republicans Trust Trump over the Media," *The Washington Post*, July 25, 2018.

287   "vile insults": Dana Milbank, "In Trump's America, 'Pizzagate' Could be the New Normal," *The Washington Post,* December 6, 2016.

287   "enemy of the people": Eli Watkins, "Poll: Majority of GOP Agrees News Media Is 'Enemy of the People,'" CNN, August 15, 2018. https://www.cnn .com/2018/08/14/politics/quinnipiac-media-gop/index.html.

287   "body slam": Seung Min Kim and Felicia Sonmez, "At Montana Rally, Trump Praises Congressman for Assaulting Reporter," *The Washington Post,* October 19, 2018.

287   "across his throat": Dana Milbank, "Stop the Mob, Mr. President," *The Washington Post,* October 25, 2018.

287   *Boston Globe:* Rebecca Morin, "California Man Charged with Threatening Boston Globe Reporters He Called 'Enemy of the People,'" *Politico*, August 30, 2018. https://www.politico.com/story/2018/08/30/boston-globe -threats-enemy-of-the-people-804160.

288   *Capital Gazette:* Sabrina Tavernise, Amy Harmon, and Maya Salam, "5 People Dead in Shooting at Maryland's Capital Gazette Newsroom," *The New York Times,* June 28, 2018.

288   "could end badly": Will Sommer, "Annapolis Shooting Suspect Jarrod Ramos Blamed Capital Gazette for Reporting on his Stalking Conviction," *Daily Beast,* June 28, 2018. https://www.thedailybeast.com/annapolis-shooting -suspect-jarrod-ramos-blamed-capital-gazette-for-reporting-on-his-stalking -conviction.

288   "growing animosity": "RSF Index 2018: Hatred of Journalism Threatens Democracies," Reporters Without Borders, April 25, 2018. https://www .politico.com/f/?id=00000162-f9fd-d5ce-a3e7-fffdf8030001.

288   Jamal Khashoggi: "Jamal Khashoggi Killed," Committee to Protect Journalists, October 2, 2018. https://cpj.org/data/people/jamal-khashoggi/.

288   "equal or worse": Natasha Turak, "Investor Tom Barrack Apologizes After Arguing America Has Committed 'Worse' Atrocities Than Khashoggi Killing," CNBC, February 14, 2019. https://www.cnbc.com/2019/02/14/investor -tom-barrack-apologizes-after-defending-saudi-over-khashoggi-.html.

289   "14 years": Chris Cillizza, "Donald Trump Just Keeps 'Joking' About Serving More Than 2 Terms as President," CNN, June 18, 2019. https://www.cnn .com/2019/06/18/politics/donald-trump-term-limit/index.html.

289   "we have judges": Transcript, "Remarks by President Trump at a Lunch with Members of Congress," White House Press Releases and Documents, June 26, 2018.

289   double the rate: Damian Paletta and Josh Dawsey, "Trump Personally Pushed Postmaster General to Double Rates on Amazon, Other Firms," *The Washington Post,* May 18, 2018.

289   "un-American": Jacob Pramuk, "'Un-American' and 'Treasonous': Trump

Goes After Democrats Who Didn't Clap During State of the Union," CNBC, February 5, 2018. https://www.cnbc.com/2018/02/05/trump-calls-democrats -un-american-and-treasonous.html.

289　"almost treasonous": Steve Benen, "Trump Says Coverage of North Korea Talks Has Been 'Almost Treasonous,'" MSNBC, June 25, 2018. https://www .msnbc.com/rachel-maddow-show/trump-says-coverage-north-korea-talks -has-been-almost-treasonous-msna1116241.

289　"absolute authority": Brian Naylor, "FACT CHECK: Trump Doesn't Have the Authority to Order States to 'Reopen,'" NPR, April 14, 2020. https://www .npr.org/2020/04/14/834040912/fact-check-trump-doesnt-have-the-authority -to-order-states-to-reopen.

290　"absolute right": Caroline Kenny, "Trump: 'I Have the Absolute Right to Par-don Myself,'" CNN, June 4, 2018. https://www.cnn.com/2018/06/04/politics/ donald-trump-pardon-tweet/index.html.

290　"very substantial": Anthony Salvanto and John Dickerson, CBS News, *Face the Nation,* February 12, 2017.

290　"absolute immunity": Aaron Blake, "The Supreme Court's Unanimous—and Biting—Rebuke of one of Trump's Many 'Absolute' Claims," *The Washington Post,* July 9, 2020.

290　"King of Israel": Sarah Pulliam Bailey, "'I Am the Chosen One': Trump Again Plays on Messianic Claims as He Embraces 'King of Israel' Title," *The Washington Post,* August 21, 2019.

290　"appreciative" of him: Christina Wilkie and Kevin Breuninger, "Trump Says He Told Pence Not to Call Governors Who Aren't 'Appreciative' of White House Coronavirus Efforts," CNBC, March 27, 2020. https://www.cnbc.com/ 2020/03/27/coronavirus-trump-told-pence-not-to-call-washington-michigan -governors.html.

291　twenty years: Richard Gonzales, "Florida Man Who Mailed Bombs to Demo-crats, Media Gets 20 Years in Prison," NPR, August 5, 2019. https://www.npr .org/2019/08/05/748420957/cesar-sayoc-florida-man-who-mailed-bombs-to -democrats-and-media-gets-20-years.

291　"kill our people": Dana Milbank, "Trump's America Is Not a Safe Place for Jews," *The Washington Post,* October 28, 2018.

291　"get tougher": Manu Raju and Jeremy Herb, "After Republicans Storm Hear-ing Room, Defense Official Testifies in Impeachment Inquiry," CNN, Octo-ber 23, 2019. https://www.cnn.com/2019/10/23/politics/republicans-storm -impeachment-inquiry-deposition-laura-cooper/index.html.

292　"American Patriot Rally": BBC, "Coronavirus: Armed Protesters Enter Mich-igan Statehouse," BBC News, May 1, 2020. https://www.bbc.com/news/world -us-canada-52496514.

292　"under siege": Colby Itkowitz, "'Liberate': Trump Tweets Support of Protests Against Stay-at-Home Orders," *The Washington Post,* April 17, 2020.

292　received death threats: Brian Naylor, "Dr. Fauci Says GOP Sen. Paul's False Accusations Have Sparked Death Threats," NPR, January 11, 2022. https:// www.npr.org/2022/01/11/1072110378/dr-fauci-says-gop-sen-pauls-false -accusations-have-sparked-death-threats.

292　Secret Service detail: Emma Newburger, "Dr. Fauci Says His Daughters Need Security as Family Continues to Get Death Threats," CNBC, August 5, 2020. https://www.cnbc.com/2020/08/05/dr-fauci-says-his-daughters-need -security-as-family-continues-to-get-death-threats.html.

292　"in the face": Jamie Ehrlich, "Maxine Waters Encourages Supporters to

Harass Trump Administration Officials," CNN, June 25, 2018. https://www
.cnn.com/2018/06/25/politics/maxine-waters-trump-officials/index.html.

293 "encouraging police officers": Mark Berman, "Trump Tells Police Not to
Worry About Injuring Suspects During Arrests," *The Washington Post,*
July 28, 2017.

293 "proactively arrest individuals": Ian Schwartz, "Acting DHS Chief Chad
Wolf: Law Enforcement 'Proactively' Arresting People in Portland," Real-
Clear Politics, July 21, 2020. https://www.realclearpolitics.com/video/2020/
07/21/acting_dhs_chief_chad_wolf_law_enforcement_proactively_arresting
_people_in_portland.html.

293 "anarchist jurisdictions": Press release, "Department of Justice Identifies
New York City, Portland and Seattle as Jurisdictions Permitting Violence
and Destruction of Property," Department of Justice, September 21, 2020.
https://www.justice.gov/opa/pr/department-justice-identifies-new-york-city
-portland-and-seattle-jurisdictions-permitting.

293 "adding gasoline": Matthew S. Schwartz, " 'Like Adding Gasoline': Oregon
Officials Blast Trump Response to Portland Protests," NPR, July 19, 2020.
https://www.wclk.com/2020-07-19/like-adding-gasoline-oregon-officials
-blast-trump-response-to-portland-protests.

294 "cannot be unexpected": Allan Smith, "Trump Praises Right-Wing Supporters, Rails Against Protesters After Unrest in Portland," NBC News,
August 30, 2020. https://www.nbcnews.com/politics/donald-trump/trump
-rails-against-protesters-following-unrest-portland-n1238808.

294 "haven't started shooting": Eliza Relman, "The Leader of a Far-Right Militant Group Says Republican Rep. Paul Gosar Told Him the U.S. Was in a Civil
War: 'We Just Haven't Started Shooting Yet,' " *Business Insider,* January 29,
2021. https://www.businessinsider.com/paul-gosar-told-oath-keepers-militia
-us-in-civil-war-2021-1.

294 "stand by": Kathleen Ronayne and Michael Kunzelman, "Trump to Far-Right
Extremists: 'Stand Back and Stand By,' " Associated Press, September 30,
2020. https://apnews.com/article/election-2020-joe-biden-race-and-ethnicity
-donald-trump-chris-wallace-0b32339da25fbc9e8b7c7c7066a1db0f.

295 polling places: "Georgia County Scraps Plans to Close Most Polling Places,"
Associated Press, August 24, 2018. https://www.nbcnews.com/news/nbcblk/
georgia-county-scraps-plan-close-most-polling-places-n903691.

295 "Republican elected": Philip Bump, "Trump Just Said What Republicans
Have Been Trying Not to Say for Years," *The Washington Post,* May 29, 2020.

295 Trump signs and flags: Nick Corasaniti and Stephanie Saul, "Trump Supporters Disrupt Early Voting in Virginia," *The New York Times,* September 19,
2020.

295 "watch very closely": Grace Panetta, "Trump Urges Supporters to 'Go into the
Polls' and 'Watch Very Closely' While Questioning the Integrity of the 2020
Election," *Business Insider,* September 29, 2020. https://www.businessinsider
.com/trump-urges-supporters-to-go-into-the-polls-and-watch-very-closely
-2020-9.

295 "put down": Quint Forgey, " 'We'll Put Them Down Very Quickly': Trump
Threatens to Quash Election Night Riots," *Politico,* September 11, 2020.
https://www.politico.com/news/2020/09/11/trump-election-night-riots-412323.

295 Germany's Reichstag: Dana Milbank, "This Is Not a Drill. The Reichstag Is
Burning," *The Washington Post,* September 25, 2020.

295 "STEAL the Election": Shirin Ghaffary, "Twitter and Facebook Both Label

Trump's Post Baselessly Asserting That the Election Is Being 'Stolen,'" *Vox,* November 4, 2020. https://www.vox.com/recode/2020/11/4/21548733/trump -stolen-election-twitter-facebook-label.

296   "STOP THE COUNT!": Eliza Relman, "Trump and His Republican Allies Want to Keep Counting Votes in 2 States Where They're Behind and Stop Counting Votes in 3 States Where They're Ahead," *Business Insider,* November 5, 2020. https://www.businessinsider.com/trump-wants-to-keep-counting -votes-in-2-states-but-stop-counting-in-3-2020-11.

296   "not seen fraud": Michael Balsamo, "Disputing Trump, Barr Says No Widespread Election Fraud," Associated Press, December 1, 2020. https://apnews .com/article/barr-no-widespread-election-fraud-b1f1488796c9a98c4b1a9061 a6c7f49d.

296   "most secure": David E. Sanger and Nicole Perlroth, "Trump Fires a Cybersecurity Official Who Called the Election 'The Most Secure in American History,'" *The New York Times,* November 18, 2020.

296   "find 11,780 votes": Amy Gardner, "'I Just Want to Find 11,780 Votes': In Extraordinary Hour-Long Call, Trump Pressures Georgia Secretary of State to Recalculate the Vote in His Favor," *The Washington Post,* January 3, 2021.

296   "undemocratic coup": *Post* Editorial Board, "The Post Says: Give It Up, Mr. President—For Your Sake and the Nation's," *New York Post,* December 27, 2020. https://nypost.com/2020/12/27/give-it-up-mr-president-for-your -sake-and-the-nations/.

297   "people forming": Jason Slotkin, Suzanne Nuyen, and James Doubek, "4 Stabbed, 33 Arrested After Trump Supporters, Counter Protesters Clash in D.C.," NPR, December 12, 2020. https://www.npr.org/2020/12/12/94582 5924/trump-supporters-arrive-in-washington-once-again-for-a-million-maga -march.

297   cast doubt: Tyler Monroe et al., "Fox News Has Cast Doubt on or Pushed Conspiracy Theories About the Election Results Nearly 600 Times," Media Matters, November 18, 2020. https://www.mediamatters.org/fox-news/fox -news-has-cast-doubt-or-pushed-conspiracy-theories-about-election-results -nearly-600.

297   "it's got to stop": Kristine Phillips, "Ex-Election Security Chief Christopher Krebs Calls Out GOP on Threats Against Election Officials: 'It's Got to Stop,'" *USA Today,* December 16, 2020. https://www.usatoday.com/story/ news/politics/2020/12/16/christopher-krebs-tells-gop-move-on-false-election -fraud-claims/3921503001/.

297   "was stolen": Morgan Watkins, "Sen. Rand Paul Falsely Claims Presidential Election Was 'Stolen,' Siding with Donald Trump," *Louisville Courier-Journal,* December 16, 2020.

297   "Maduro is doing": Dana Milbank, "We've Finally Identified the Source of Fraud in the 2020 Election. It's Ron Johnson," *The Washington Post,* December 16, 2020.

297   "disenfranchised": Karoun Demirjian, "Senate GOP has Accepted Biden's Win but Continues to Push Trump's Baseless Fraud Claims," *The Washington Post,* December 17, 2020.

297   "should have integrity": Jim Jordan, "Stop the Steal Rally," PennLive, November 5, 2020. https://www.facebook.com/PennLive/videos/1038071873327720/.

297   "wins the election": U.S. House of Representatives, "House Debate on Arizona Electoral Challenge, Part 1," C-SPAN, January 6, 2021. https://www.c -span.org/video/?507672-101/house-debate-arizona-electoral-challenge-part-1.

298   "collectively been reached": "Chairman Johnson Opening Statement," Con-

gressional Documents and Publications, U.S. Government Publishing Office, December 16, 2020.

298 "president-elect": Alexander Bolton, "McConnell Declines in Floor Speech to Congratulate Biden as President-Elect," *The Hill*, November 9, 2020. https:// thehill.com/homenews/senate/525177-mcconnell-declines-in-floor-speech-to -congratulate-biden-as-president-elect.

298 privately urged Barr: Jonathan Karl, *Betrayal: The Final Act of the Trump Show* (Dutton, 2021).

298 "take it anymore": Brian Naylor, "Read Trump's Jan. 6 Speech, a Key Part of Impeachment Trial," February 10, 2021. https://www.npr.org/2021/02/10/ 966396848/read-trumps-jan-6-speech-a-key-part-of-impeachment-trial.

299 "coming for you": Maggie Haberman, "Trump Told Crowd 'You Will Never Take Back Our Country with Weakness,'" *The New York Times*, January 6, 2021.

299 "trial by combat": "Rudy Giuliani Speech Transcript at Trump's Washington, D.C. Rally: Wants 'Trial by Combat,'" Rev, January 6, 2021. https://www.rev .com/blog/transcripts/rudy-giuliani-speech-transcript-at-trumps-washington -d-c-rally-wants-trial-by-combat.

299 breached the barricades: Hannah Allam et al., "Jan. 6 Insurrection: *The Washington Post*'s Investigation," *The Washington Post*, October 31, 2021.

300 "schemed up": Catie Edmondson and Luke Broadwater, "Before Capitol Riot, Republican Lawmakers Fanned the Flames," *The New York Times*, January 11, 2021.

300 Pelosi's evacuation: Devon Link, "Fact Check: Claim About Rep. Boebert and Jan. 6 Insurrectionists Partly False," *USA Today*, October 12, 2021.

300 "more upset": Amber Phillips, "Everything We Know About Kevin McCarthy's Conversations with Trump Concerning the Jan. 6 Attacks," *The Washington Post*, January 14, 2022.

300 twenty thousand: Brakkton Booker, "About 20,000 National Guard Members to Deploy for Inauguration, Officials Say," NPR, January 13, 2021. https:// www.npr.org/sections/insurrection-at-the-capitol/2021/01/13/956458463/ 20-000-national-guardsmen-will-be-deployed-for-inauguration-d-c-official -says.

CONCLUSION

301 draft executive order: Betsy Woodruff Swan, "Read the Never-Issued Trump Order That Would Have Seized Voting Machines," *Politico*, January 21, 2022. https://www.politico.com/news/2022/01/21/read-the-never-issued-trump -order-that-would-have-seized-voting-machines-527572.

301 fake Trump electors: Marshall Cohen, Zachary Cohen, and Dan Merica, "Trump Campaign Officials, Led by Rudy Giuliani, Oversaw Fake Electors Plot in 7 States," CNN, January 20, 2022. https://www.cnn.com/2022/01/20/ politics/trump-campaign-officials-rudy-giuliani-fake-electors/index.html.

301 texted with White House: Bob Woodward and Robert Costa, "Virginia Thomas Urged White House Chief to Pursue Unrelenting Efforts to Overturn the 2020 Election, Texts Show," *The Washington Post*, March 24, 2022.

301 boycotted Biden's inauguration: Christine Stapleton, "Trump to Arrive in Palm Beach County Wednesday, the Morning of President-Elect Joe Biden's Inauguration," *The Palm Beach Post*, January 14, 2021. https://www.palmbeachpost .com/story/news/2021/01/14/trump-arrive-mar-lago-morning-joe-bidens -inauguration/4169335001/.

302 "bears responsibility": Domenico Montanaro, "GOP Leader McCarthy:

Trump 'Bears Responsibility' for Violence, Won't Vote to Impeach," NPR, January 13, 2021.

302   "stop" it: Chris Cillizza, "McCarthy Is Desperately Trying to Memory Hole January 6," CNN, January 14, 2022.

302   "fed lies": Lisa Mascaro and Mary Clare Jalonick, "McConnell: Trump 'Provoked' Capitol Siege, Mob Was Fed Lies," AP News, January 19, 2021. https://apnews.com/article/mcconnell-trump-fed-lies-to-mob-36871d68df56a 10be1c46ed364ad6de6.

302   "lack jurisdiction": Burgess Everett, "McConnell Reveals He Will Vote to Acquit Trump," *Politico,* February 13, 2021. https://www.politico.com/news/ 2021/02/13/mcconnell-reveals-he-will-vote-to-acquit-trump-468988.

302   Liz Cheney: Katherine Tully-McManus and Chris Marquette, "House Republicans Oust Liz Cheney from No. 3 Leadership Post," *Roll Call,* May 12, 2021. https://rollcall.com/2021/05/12/house-republicans-oust-liz-cheney-from-no -3-leadership-post/.

302   "embrace the Constitution": Press release, "Cheney: We Must Go Forward Based on Truth," Congresswoman Liz Cheney, May 12, 2021. https://cheney .house.gov/2021/05/12/cheney-we-must-go-forward-based-on-truth/.

303   McCarthy also blocked: Nicholas Fandos, "McCarthy Opposes Jan. 6 Commission Because It Would Not Study 'Political Violence' by the Left," *The New York Times,* May 18, 2021.

303   defeat the commission: Marianne Levine and Burgess Everett, "McConnell Turns Senate Republicans Against Jan. 6 Commission," *Politico,* May 19, 2021. https://www.politico.com/news/2021/05/19/mcconnell-opposes-houses -bipartisan-jan-6-commission-bill-489573.

303   appointing Jim Jordan: Jaclyn Peiser, "Jim Jordan Said the Congressional Panel Examining Jan. 6 Is an Attack on Trump. Now He May Join the Committee," *The Washington Post,* July 20, 2021.

303   "blinded by partisanship": Tim Hains, "Liz Cheney: Are We So Blinded by Partisanship That We Will Throw Away the Miracle of America," RealClearPolitics, July 27, 2021. https://www.realclearpolitics.com/video/2021/07/27/ liz_cheney_do_we_hate_our_political_adversaries_more_than_we_revere _the_constitution.html.

303   "reeducation camps": Jake Lahut, "Fox News Pushes Conspiracy Theory About 'Reeducation Camps' on the Eve of Biden's Inauguration," *Business Insider,* January 19, 2021. https://www.businessinsider.com/video-fox-news -reeducation-camps-conspiracy-theory-harris-faulkner-2021-1.

303   false flag operation: David Folkenflik and Tom Dreisbach, " 'Off the Rails': New Tucker Carlson Project for Fox Embraces Conspiracy Theories," NPR, November 3, 2021. https://www.npr.org/2021/11/03/1051607945/tucker-carlson -fox-news-insurrection-conspiracy-new-show.

303   accusing the FBI: Mariana Alfaro, "House Jan. 6 Committee Dismisses 'Unsupported' Claim of FBI Involvement in Riot," *The Washington Post,* January 11, 2022.

304   "lying in wait": Julian Mark, "Paul Gosar Demands Name of Capitol Officer Who Killed Ashli Babbitt, Saying She Was 'Executed,' " *The Washington Post,* June 16, 2021.

304   "normal tourist visit": Brittany Shammas, "A GOP Congressman Compared Capitol Rioters to Tourists. Photos Show Him Barricading a Door," *The Washington Post,* May 18, 2021.

304   "hugging and kissing": Colby Itkowitz, "Trump Falsely Claims Jan. 6 Rioters Were 'Hugging and Kissing' Police," *The Washington Post,* March 26, 2021.

304   "ANTIFA orchestrated Capitol attack": Facts First, "Did Antifa Infiltrate Capitol Rioters?," CNN, n.d. https://www.cnn.com/factsfirst/politics/fact check_2de70522-d574-479b-a101-6948f1d78338.

304   "political prisoners": Cristina Marcos, "Cawthorn Calls Jailed Jan. 6 Rioters 'Political Hostages,'" *The Hill,* August 30, 2021. https://thehill.com/homenews/house/570071-cawthorn-calls-jailed-jan-6-rioters-political-hostages.

304   police officers: Felicia Sonmez, "21 House Republicans Vote Against Awarding Congressional Gold Medal to All Police Officers Who Responded on Jan. 6," *The Washington Post,* June 15, 2021.

304   762 people: George Washington University, "Capitol Hill Siege," GW Program on Extremism, n.d. https://extremism.gwu.edu/Capitol-Hill-Cases.

304   "seditious conspiracy": Michael Balsamo, Colleen Long, and Alanna Durkin Richer, "Seditious Conspiracy: 11 Oath Keepers Charged in Jan. 6 Riot," Associated Press, January 13, 2022. https://apnews.com/article/stewart-rhodes-arrested-oath-keepers-jan-6-insurrection-70019e1007132e8df786aaf77215 a110.

304   pardon them: Kyle Cheney and Maeve Sheehey, "Trump Suggests He Might Pardon Some Jan. 6 Defendants," *Politico,* January 30, 2022. https://www .politico.com/news/2022/01/30/trump-pardon-jan6-defendants-00003450.

304   "bamboo in the paper": Caitlin Huey-Burns and Adam Brewster, "The Arizona GOP's Maricopa County Audit: What to Know About It," CBS News, May 9, 2021. https://www.cbsnews.com/news/arizona-audit-2020-election -recount-gop-maricopa-county/.

304   "We are the Storm": Patrick Svitek, "The Texas GOP's New Slogan Echoes a Conspiracy Group. Its Chair Says There's No Connection," *The Texas Tribune,* August 21, 2020. https://www.texastribune.org/2020/08/21/texas -gop-slogan-storm/.

304   praised QAnon believers: Rachel E. Greenspan and Charles R. Davis, "2 Hawaii GOP Officials Resign After State Party Tweets, Then Deletes, Support for Believers of QAnon," *Business Insider,* February 2, 2021. https://www.insider .com/hawaii-gop-official-resigns-after-party-tweets-support-for-qanon-2021-1.

305   critical race theory: Map, "Where Critical Race Theory Is Under Attack," *EducationWeek,* June 11, 2021. https://www.edweek.org/policy-politics/map -where-critical-race-theory-is-under-attack/2021/06.

305   "prohibited topics": Dana Milbank, "DeSantis Saves Florida Kids from Being Indoctrinated with Math," *The Washington Post,* April 19, 2022.

305   restricting voting: "Voting Laws Roundup: December 2021," Brennan Center for Justice, December 21, 2021. https://www.brennancenter.org/our-work/ research-reports/voting-laws-roundup-december-2021.

305   "African American voters": Linda Qiu, "Fact-Checking McConnell's Comparison of Black Turnout Rates," *The New York Times,* January 20, 2022.

306   Arizona laws: Nina Totenberg, "The Supreme Court Deals a New Blow to Voting Rights, Upholding Arizona Restrictions," NPR, July 1, 2021. https:// www.npr.org/2021/07/01/998758022/the-supreme-court-upheld-upholds -arizona-measures-that-restrict-voting.

306   Texas's new congressional seats: Acacia Coronado and Paul J. Weber, "Texas Lawmakers Pass New Congressional Maps Bolstering GOP," Associated Press, October 19, 2021. https://apnews.com/article/elections-texas-lawsuits -race-and-ethnicity-voting-rights-f123a6f0d75fcf442720185f67e79129.

306   57 percent in Texas: Eric Petry, "How the Efficiency Gap Works," Brennan Center for Justice, n.d. https://www.brennancenter.org/sites/default/files/ legal-work/How_the_Efficiency_Gap_Standard_Works.pdf.

306   ties to white nationalists: Erin Mansfield and Savannah Behrmann, "When Does Speech Become Dangerous? Rep. Gosar's Ties to White Nationalists Added to Concerns About His Video," *USA Today,* November 17, 2021. https://www.usatoday.com/story/news/politics/2021/11/17/paul-gosar-attack-on-titan-censure/8595103002/?gnt-cfr=1.

306   "bullet to the head": Reis Thebault, "Rep. Marjorie Taylor Greene's Endorsement of Conspiracy Theories, Violence Sparks Calls for Her Resignation—Again," *The Washington Post,* January 27, 2021.

306   "that's bloodshed": Mabinty Quarshie, "Rep. Madison Cawthorn Calls Jan. 6 Rioters 'Political Prisoners,' Warns of 'Bloodshed' at GOP Event," *USA Today,* August 31, 2021.

306   "should happen here": Maggie Astor, "Michael Flynn Suggested at a QAnon-Affiliated Event That a Coup Should Happen in the U.S.," *The New York Times,* June 1, 2021.

306   Trump could be "reinstated": Tara Subramaniam, "Fact-Checking Sidney Powell's Claim Trump Could Be Reinstated," CNN, June 1, 2021. https://www.cnn.com/2021/06/01/politics/powell-trump-inauguration-fact-check/index.html.

306   "Election Crimes and Security": Lori Rozsa and Beth Reinhard, "Florida Governor Proposes Special Police Agency to Monitor Elections," *The Washington Post,* January 18, 2022.

306   tip line: Julie Carey, "Youngkin Creates Tip Line to Report Mask Concerns, 'Divisive Practices' in Schools," NBC 4 Washington, January 25, 2022. https://www.nbcwashington.com/news/local/virginia-gov-youngkin-promotes-tip-email-for-parents-to-report-teachers/2948440/.

307   incentivizing residents to sue: Sabrina Tavernise, "Citizens, Not the State, Will Enforce New Abortion Law in Texas," *The New York Times,* July 9, 2021. https://www.nytimes.com/2021/07/09/us/abortion-law-regulations-texas.html.

307   sue anyone: Caroline Kitchener, "Missouri Lawmaker Seeks to Stop Residents from Obtaining Abortions Out of State," *The Washington Post,* March 8, 2022.

307   parroted Kremlin propaganda: Jeffrey Scott Shapiro, "The Right's Russian Temptation," *The Wall Street Journal,* April 10, 2022.

307   consultant to Kevin McCarthy: Jeff Stein and Laura Meckler, "House GOP Plots Policy Agenda for 2022 Midterm Elections—With Help from Architect of 1994 Plan," *The Washington Post,* January 20, 2022. https://www.washingtonpost.com/us-policy/2022/01/20/republican-midterm-plan-education-economy/.

307   "going to jail": Peter Wade, "Newt Gingrich, Who Is Advising GOP Leadership, Floats Jail Time for Jan. 6 Committee Members," *Rolling Stone,* January 23, 2022. https://www.rollingstone.com/politics/politics-news/gingrich-jan-6-committee-jail-1289408/.

307   "rule of law unravels": Tom Porter, " 'What It Looks Like When the Rule of Law Unravels': Liz Cheney Fired Back at Newt Gingrich for Suggesting Jailing Members of the Jan. 6 Panel," *Business Insider,* January 24, 2022. https://www.businessinsider.in/politics/world/news/what-it-looks-like-when-the-rule-of-law-unravels-liz-cheney-fired-back-at-newt-gingrich-for-suggesting-jailing-members-of-the-jan-6-panel/articleshow/89096979.cms.

307   "overturn the 2024 election": J. Michael Luttig, "Opinion: The Republican Blueprint to Steal the 2024 Election," CNN, April 27, 2022.

309   During the 1790s: "U.S. History Primary Source Timeline," Library of Con-

gress, n.d. https://www.loc.gov/classroom-materials/united-states-history-primary-source-timeline/.

309   threat of fascism: Alan Taylor, "American Nazis in the 1930s—The German American Bund," *The Atlantic,* June 5, 2017. https://www.theatlantic.com/photo/2017/06/american-nazis-in-the-1930sthe-german-american-bund/529185/.

309   assassinations and upheaval: James Pasley, "24 Assassinations That Changed the World," *Business Insider,* January 10, 2020. https://www.businessinsider.com/most-important-assassinations-in-history-that-changed-the-world.

309   millennials and Gen Z: Kim Parker, Nikki Graf, and Ruth Igielnik, "Generation Z Looks a Lot Like Millennials on Key Social and Political Issues," Pew Research Center, January 17, 2019. https://www.pewresearch.org/social-trends/2019/01/17/generation-z-looks-a-lot-like-millennials-on-key-social-and-political-issues/.

309   white-minority country: William H. Frey, "The US Will Become 'Minority White' in 2045, Census Projects," Brookings Institution, March 14, 2018. https://www.brookings.edu/blog/the-avenue/2018/03/14/the-us-will-become-minority-white-in-2045-census-projects/.

Index

About the Author

Dana Milbank is a political columnist for *The Washington Post* whose work is syndicated nationally. He has also been a contributor to CNN and MSNBC and is the author of the national bestseller *Homo Politicus,* as well as *Tears of a Clown, O Is for Obama,* and *Smashmouth.* He lives in Washington, D.C.